A Dangerous Stir

CIVIL WAR AMERICA | *Gary W. Gallagher, editor*

MARK WAHLGREN SUMMERS

A Dangerous *Stir*

FEAR, PARANOIA, *and the Making of*
RECONSTRUCTION

The University of North Carolina Press CHAPEL HILL

© 2009
THE UNIVERSITY
OF NORTH CAROLINA
PRESS
All rights reserved

Designed by
Kimberly Bryant
Set in Minion
by Tseng Information
Systems, Inc.
Manufactured in
the United States of
America

The paper in this book meets the guidelines for permanence and durability of the Committee on Production Guidelines for Book Longevity of the Council on Library Resources.

The University of North Carolina Press has been a member of the Green Press Initiative since 2003.

Library of Congress Cataloging-in-Publication Data
Summers, Mark W. (Mark Wahlgren), 1951–
A dangerous stir : fear, paranoia, and the making of
reconstruction / Mark Wahlgren Summers. — 1st ed.
p. cm. — (Civil War America)
Includes bibliographical references and index.
ISBN 978-0-8078-3304-9 (cloth : alk. paper)
1. Reconstruction (U.S. history, 1865–1877) 2. Reconstruction
(U.S. history, 1865–1877)—Psychological aspects. 3. Fear—
United States—History—19th century. 4. Anxiety—United
States—History—19th century. I. Gallagher, Gary W. II. Title.
E668.S93 2009
973.8—dc22

                                                        2009009375

13 12 11 10 09   5 4 3 2 1

THIS BOOK WAS DIGITALLY PRINTED.

Contents

Illustrations

Acknowledgments

Many friends have kept me company on my way over to the
Dark Side. William F. Freehling, supportive and inspirational
as always, provoked the paper by persuading me to talk
about Reconstruction at a historical convention and later by
encouraging me to apply historical methods to other people's
madness. Michael Fitzgerald, Joanne Melish, Tracy Campbell,
David Hamilton, and Shearer Davis Bowman were loaded down
with fears (three hundred pages' worth) and wrestled them into
lucidity and temperate language. The staff at the University of
Kentucky's Interlibrary Loan strove to keep me supplied with
microfilms innumerable of newspapers indispensable, and
of course dozens of archives took the trouble to open their
chambers of secrets. Generously, astutely, Gary Gallagher and
Mitchell Snay corrected every mistake they could find, and the
University of North Carolina Press's third reader provided reams
of advice that I wasted no time in following. My special thanks
to Dorothea Anderson, whose assiduous copyediting must have
seemed daunting, especially figuring out the capping of "radical."
Any errors in that regard are, of course, mine. As always, my
parents, Clyde and Evelyn Summers, were my first and last resort
in trying out ideas and arguments. My excellent eldest daughter,
Ariel, began by expressing fears wilder than any published
here—the prospect of Palestinian terrorists invading and
breaking into our car and poisoning the open bag of gingersnaps
on the front seat being among the most remarkable—and then,
in the face of real misfortune, taught me much about mastering
fears that proved after all to be real. It is because of her reminder
of the power not just of fear but of hope that I dedicate this book
to her.

A Dangerous *Stir*

The poet's eye, in a fine frenzy rolling,
Doth glance from heaven to earth, from earth
   to heaven;
And as imagination bodies forth
The form of things unknown, the poet's pen
Turns them to shapes, and gives to airy nothing
A local habitation and a name.
Such tricks hath strong imagination,
That, if it would but apprehend some joy,
It comprehends some bringer of that joy;
Or, in the night, imagining some fear,
How easy is a bush supposed a bear!
   —Shakespeare, A Midsummer Night's Dream,
   act 5, scene 1, lines 12–22

EMPIRE DAY?

Early in the fall of 1866, an alarming event that would have put the republic itself in deadly peril did not happen. On October 11, a Washington reporter for the *Philadelphia Public Ledger* revealed a series of questions that President Andrew Johnson had posed to his attorney general. In effect, they came down to two: Was a Congress that lacked most of its southern membership legal? And did the president have a duty to seat a Congress that did pass constitutional muster?[1]

The inference, easily drawn, was that the president was readying the legal cover for a coup d'état. Assuming that the Democrats picked up enough seats in the House that November to make a legal majority when combined with the excluded southern lawmakers, they might declare themselves the legal Congress. Republican congressmen would meet separately, claiming themselves as the only legitimate legislative branch. But Johnson would have the last word. Backed by the attorney general's opinion, he would send in the army to disperse the Republicans. Perhaps he would declare the Democratic Congress the one true body. Or perhaps he would declare that neither Congress had a better claim and that, till a new Congress met on March 4, 1867, with all the states represented, he and he alone was the government. Either way, a year's worth of Reconstruction legislation would be torn to tatters—and very likely the republic with it. Southerners, many splashed with treason's taint, would rule or

1

ruin. There might be a new rebellion, or a genuine civil war, but whatever the outcome, free institutions would bear the scars forever. A dictator claiming to be upholding the Constitution would have saved the country to death.[2]

The tale was balderdash, of course. To our own ears, the plot it meant to cover sounds perfectly insane. But if so, quite a number of cool-headed Americans went momentarily mad. Corrections followed, but what should concern us most is how readily the original report found believers.

And how could Americans help believing it? In the vexed state of public opinion that autumn, imagined revolutionary plots had become the stock-in-trade of both political parties. By then, there was more than enough circumstantial evidence to lead the most fretful northerners into suspecting that Andrew Johnson might be readying a coup d'état as soon as the elections were over. Some Americans actually let their wish father the thought. They saw a menace every bit as dire that could be countered no other way: a Congress of bloodthirsty revolutionaries, legislating a republic into an empire.

Something particularly nasty was stirring beneath the usual mix of personalities, policy, and constitutional exegesis on which an election campaign usually ran. Perhaps we should heed it. The *Ledger*'s one-day wonder never would have gotten past the editors without a broader climate of opinion to give it a backdrop. Reconstruction policy—the postwar settlement—was shaped not simply from politics, principles, and prejudices, but also from fears, often unreasonable, phantasms of conspiracy, dreads and hopes of renewed civil war, and a widespread sense that four years of war had thrown the normal constitutional process dangerously out of kilter—indeed, so dangerously that the republic itself lay in peril. At the very moment that historians have seen a new birth in America's highest ideals, the idealists themselves saw too clearly some rough beast, its hour come round at last, slouching toward Washington to be born.

Rough beast there certainly was, though not the one most feared: not tyranny, but a very determined anarchy, the terrorism, violence, arson, and murder that white conservatives used to discredit and overthrow the governments imposed on them in the South and to return black southerners to a status of half slave and half free. Let me stress from the outset: what people did, not what they feared, determined the making and unmaking of Reconstruction. Readers looking in this book for a real conspiracy will clutch only at shadows. North and South, the last thing most responsible people wanted was another war, however strongly they feared that one might be forced on them. No mastermind operating in safety from afar directed the hand that pulled the trigger at Ford's Theater. No president dreamed of playing Cromwell and dismissing Congress at musket point. General Ulysses S. Grant was no would-be emperor, Andrew Johnson no would-be king, the radical Republicans no would-be Jacobins, with a guillotine in reserve. The Constitution's friends might tear it apart, but only by trying too hard to protect it from its other friends. On its surface, this book really is the story of how something terrible *did not* happen—and how it did not happen, again and again. Those who read to the end may feel as if they have traveled through a political gallery of bogeymen and nothings that went bump in the night. But any three-year-old child knows that the wolves in the closet at night, the ones that are not there, can seem the most real wolves of all. Beliefs, misperceptions, even fantasies, can shape actions or lend urgency to the insistence that something must be done. They can justify laws, lynchings, and even wars.

What follows is a story not of Reconstruction so much as of *misconstruction*. Library bookshelves groan with longer, broader accounts of the period. They give the period after 1869 its due, which, for a full understanding of how Reconstruction worked, would take hundreds more pages than I give it. Anyone wanting even a fuller account of Andrew Johnson's administration or the awkward progress of Congressional Reconstruction would find more reward in Eric L. McKitrick's *Andrew Johnson and Reconstruction*, Michael Les Benedict's *Compromise of Principle*, and Hans L. Trefousse's biography of Lincoln's unfortunate successor. A scholar would have to be crazy to redo what they did so well,[3] though, as will become plain, my take on Johnson is, if anything, darker than McKitrick's, shrewd and indispensably thorough as his portrait of presidential ineptitude is. Rather, my tale will take up incidents only as they afford a context for that theme of fear and rumor.

This book proposes two challenges to postwar history as presently understood. The first is the role of often unreasonable, sometimes unreasoning, fear in political discourse. Ideas and policies give parties their credentials in the long run. But far more than scholars have cared to admit, big turnouts at elections and the way voters identify themselves with one side or the other may be based on the nightmare in the closet, the terrible unknown that could emerge the moment the lights go down. Historian Richard Hofstadter, in his essay on the paranoid style in American politics, limned the distorted way that the world appeared to those on the far outskirts of public life. He meant to refer to extremists, by his own reading of them: the crackbrained Anti-Mason movement of the 1820s, the Know-Nothings' obsession with plotting Popes, and the John Birchers seeing Red.[4] Compared to politics as usual, these movements may have looked like public outings for nutcases. Some were. But it may have been the degree of paranoia, and not the conspiracy theories themselves, that set them apart from mainstream politics. What Hofstadter left unexplored was how far Democrat, Whig, and Republican shared in the same assumptions, shared in a general sense that there was a "true inwardness" that explained how things got done in politics and, at their most alarmed, that there were real menaces to the republic lurking, menaces with genuine support within the major parties themselves. Conspiratorial thinking was not an anomaly, much less the proof of political extremism. It ran through the bloodstream of the body politic.

And it had very real effects. As this study of Reconstruction may show, it affected what parties and political leaders did. Desperation and dread could make them more daring, even as, paradoxically, the allegations leveled against them helped push them toward moderation and, in some cases, even toward timidity. The conditions set for the former Confederate states and the North's commitment to Reconstruction were shaped by many things: constitutional doctrine, weariness, wariness about military power, short-term political calculations, compassion, idealism. But in the mix, always, were fears that the war had settled nothing, that the Union still lay in peril, that its enemies and the enemies of republican government were more resilient and cunning than normal mortals. And always there was that sense, stoked by the most fervid voices in both major parties, that the mainstream of public life might be too narrow to have room for more than one party—or, indeed, even for all the members of that party.

Already, wary readers will spot the flaw in the book's design: Did "many" believe? How "many"? How intensely did they believe it? How consistently? What census taker counted the number and categorized the nature of the alarmists? How can we separate fearfulness from fearmongering? Does every politician who pulls the fire bell really think there is a fire? The moment we try to gauge the depth of fears, we go trailing into cloudland, though, admittedly, along a pretty thickly strewn paper trail. Even so, in an age before expert polling, knowing what most people really thought, and how seriously they took these fears, can have only a speculative character. Linking fears to consequences takes a certain leap of faith, too. A dozen statesmen can give two dozen reasons for doing what they did—and none of them might be the real one. Causality is easier to prove at some times than at others: the raids on freedpeople's homes and the disarming of black men late in 1865, for example, can reasonably be connected to the widespread rumors of a bloody uprising among former slaves, even if the raiding parties failed to say so. Still, there are times when we cannot know things even for almost certain. Throughout the text, I will put in caveats and cautions, reminders of other possible motives and of the persistent common sense of some, North and South, Democratic and Republican. At the same time, private letters, diaries, recollections, newspaper reports, and speeches afford more than can mere guesswork. Even if the professionals had self-interested motives for working up a scare, the fear they roused could, indeed certainly was, real. Politicians usually have sense to stow away a made-up bogeyman when their audiences begin to snicker. That time would come, and when it did, the derision helped shake the foundations of Reconstruction. But no such skepticism stilled the doomsayers just after the Civil War.

The second argument of this book is more indirect and may be much more controversial. The best scholarship for a generation has restored the aftermath of slavery and the frustrated quest for equal rights to the center of the Reconstruction story. It was an unfinished revolution and, most would argue, a dramatic achievement eventually undone by bloodletting, bulldozing, and a faltering of the northern will. The facts cannot be gainsaid, any more than can the real and driving commitment of most Republicans, especially radical ones, to bring America closer to its ideals of universal liberty, justice, and equality before the law. What they did they could base on very real conditions and events that, without exaggeration, posed serious constitutional and moral challenges. But there is another story, one that may explain both the swift advance within two years after the war's end to comparatively radical policies and the eventual retreat from federal protection for equal rights.

Much has been written about the "second American revolution," the "unfinished revolution" that followed the Civil War.[5] From our own time's vantage point, it gives Reconstruction meaning and relevance—no issue from then is so pertinent to the twenty-first century as the struggle for equal rights. But I am not at all sure that those names would have given Reconstruction so complete a meaning back then. Indeed, it seems to me possible that a "second revolution" was precisely what most white southerners and many northerners of both parties were anxious to avoid.

By that, I do not mean the transformation from an America that was half slave into one where freedom's full possibilities might be glimpsed, if not fulfilled—though white Americans as a whole felt no such commitment. Even among the Republicans of the North, it is an open question as to how intensely many of them held it. The revolution that Americans anticipated or feared was one overturning republican government and leading, perhaps, to a civil war bloodier than the one through which the states had already passed. To understand Reconstruction itself, we have to see what seems so obvious that scholars hardly dwell on it at all: that the first purpose of the North's war was to save the Union, with its republican institutions intact, and that Americans had less of our later certainty that the settlement that they had made would last. This is why the remaking of the Union was based not just on ideals but on fears—fears that seem in retrospect no more than partisan claptrap. On all sides, Reconstruction was based not just on reasoned argument about the meaning of federalism, freedom, and the Constitution but on unfounded dread and preposterous hope. It was founded on a desire to set terms for the last conflict and also on the hope of forestalling the next.

Taking those fears seriously may change the whole mix of motives that explain not just the advance but also the retreat from a national commitment to that "second American revolution." Dispel the suspicion that white southerners were waiting for a call to arms to rule or wreck the republic, remove the sense of crisis that allowed extraordinary measures just within or without the Constitution, and the traditional faith of most Americans would reassert itself, in a national government of limited powers and of states with wide discretion to handle their own peculiar conditions. Take away the traitor heart, and one of the strongest reasons for giving loyal blacks the vote was gone. Reconstruction, as later historians see it, failed. But one important reason that it failed was that Reconstruction, as much of the postwar North saw it, had succeeded. From that success it would take a century to recover.

*"It looks to me," said Mr. Hinnissy, "as though this
country was goin' to th' divvle."*

*"Put down that magazine," said Mr. Dooley.
"Now d'ye feel betther? I thought so."*

—Finley Peter Dunne, "National Housecleaning"

chapter 1

PARANOID POLITICS, 1789–1861

In 1801, the country went to the devil—as usual. It was always doing that, only perhaps not so literally as in the cartoons about Thomas Jefferson. Few though they were, they all had the same message. Americans had put themselves into the clutches of the political Antichrist. Here he knelt, at the altar of Gallic despotism, preparing to burn the charter of America's liberty. And here he clutched at the carriage of government, doing his best to keep patriots from turning back the invasion of French cannibals. But a third artist caught his truest essence in "Mad Tom in a Rage." Fired up with brandy, the wild-haired Jacobin struggles to pull down the pillar of the republic, with help from his best friend, the Black Man, the Prince of Darkness. "Mad Tom," as it happened, was that old soak and infidel Thomas Paine. It was Jefferson who played Satan.[1]

Learning history from political cartoons is as risky as learning barbering from attending regular performances of "Sweeny Todd." Symbols were crude. Cartoons had to make points so simply that even political illiterates could understand them: Tories marching into the mouth of Hell, Congress about to sail down a waterfall into Satan's claws, His Unholiness with a crown on his head casting a vote for the antiwar Hartford Convention or handing the employer a Democratic ticket to "grind the workies" or, looking suspiciously like Andrew Jackson, pulling the strings with tempting baits for office seekers.[2] True believers have a talent for spying false deceivers everywhere. For that matter, as scholars have pointed out, the further from the political center a group happened to be, the wilder its fantasies about who really tugged the wires and how policy was made.[3] Every society has visionaries, who are as likely to imagine a new heaven on earth as they are a new Hell already under construction.

All the cautions hold true. Yet, in the end, they fail to cover the whole ground. For people in mainstream politics really did believe that Thomas Jefferson was doing the devil's work. Paranoia reached all the way to the center of political discourse. It was there before the two-party system formed, and it remained a distinct flavoring in every group's political concoctions.[4] It did not exist because partisans forced it on their audiences but because it was the easiest way to make sense of the world around them—and it was all the easier to accept because polemicists had been inspiring it for so long. Liberty and Union were not just inseparable; they were in danger—now and forever. All of the machinery of a partisan press, all the whipped-up excitement of participatory politics and stump speaking, made sure that when the war was over the same forces that had operated in the past would operate still, appealing to voters' worst fears and setting the opposition in the worst, the most subversive, light.

None of these forces were at all new. Paranoid politics stretches back as far as people have had a voice in what their rulers do. Fears of secret plots by Catholics or the Crown's servants—to bring an army from Ireland, to reenact the massacre of the innocents, or to blow the parliamentary system higher than Guy Fawkes's barrels of gunpowder would have blown Westminster Hall—sent crowds into the London streets and hurtled England closer to revolution and civil war.[5] What seemed to be conspiracies against liberty or against order hardened Whigs and Tories into treason snuffers and persecutors. "Popish plots" nearly kept the king's brother off the throne and ten years later drove him into exile.[6] Even in piping times of peace, English politics seethed with explanations that fastened on backstairs intrigues, hidden motives, the long-term plan not yet divulged or whispered only to the trusty few, and, on the extremes of both parties, the language of conspiracy.[7]

What made them think this way? Rounding up the usual suspects is almost too easy. Everyone knew that evil results must come from evil intents, that political devils could quote Scripture, that fair appearance often hid vile reality. In a day when everything of moment happened at court, politics necessarily became personal, the working not of forces but of strong-willed men who knew exactly what they wanted. Easy explanations were also comfortably conservative. The system itself needed no tinkering. Remove the man, and

"The Times." 1799, artist unknown. "Triumph Government; perish all its enemies. Traitors be warned: justice though slow, is sure." George Washington and the army ride to repel an invasion of French cannibals. Two traitors try to prevent him: Albert Gallatin of Pennsylvania snarls, "Stop de wheels of de gouvernement," and Thomas Jefferson stands, giving him aid. A patriotic dog expresses his opinion on the leading Republican newspaper.

troubles would end. A conspiratorial mind-set also was fostered by the outlook that scholars have dubbed classical republican thought. As it happens, that one ideology included a whole snarling pack of dogmas, not all of them purebred. Many who shared the assumptions would have shrunk from founding a republic and would have called instead for a patriot king, a protector of precedents and cherished traditions. Self-professed republicans would have come to blows over what government could be trusted to do and how far the people themselves ought to be trusted.[8] But among the most useful essentials of republicanism was an idea tested by history, that liberties were fragile and that a government of mingled, shared authority was unstable. One branch of government or another would encroach on the prerogatives of the other.

Power, by its nature, grew and expanded, seeking new advantages for itself and new increments of power. It also concentrated in fewer and fewer hands. In the process, it corrupted the holders. For those with authority, nothing was so tempting as political intrigue and backstairs plotting, as conspiracies and scheming. Given free rein, power almost assuredly meant corruption and tyranny, for there was no end except total and absolute control that it would accept.

American colonial politics shared in those political paranoias and panics only fitfully. Some colonies never really had the kind of factional fights that England had. But in the diverse Middle Colonies, in New York and Pennsylvania especially, where there were cities and a readier means of broadcasting political information through the weekly press, the fear of tyrants and usurpers at home became a staple of political rhetoric. It became one of the strongest forces pushing on American resistance to the Crown in the 1760s—not just the enormities that imperial authorities had committed but the ones that these were sure to lead to. Fearful colonists looked at the struggles in England and saw "a junto of courtiers and state-jobbers," "instigated by the devil and led by their wicked and corrupt hearts," out to subvert liberty in the freest nation in Europe—and, in every riot suppressed in gunfire, in every arrest for sedition, they saw a broader "passion for arbitrary dominion," lubricated with the spoils, the pickings, the outright graft that a wealthy and powerful government had at its command. It was not just to protect liberty from the present "CUP OF ABOMINATIONS" but to protect from inevitable future encroachment that the colonists took up arms and in the end cut themselves loose from Britain.[9]

But there were endless enemies, and the same terrible way of thinking quickly infected the republic of the patriots. Before George Washington's second term was completed, a party system had come into being of Federalists and Democratic-Republicans. If the Democratic-Republicans, under Thomas Jefferson and James Madison, took on the fears of classical republicanism, which feared any government encroachment and increase in power, and offered as one remedy for it the countervailing power and influence of the states, with their own separate rights, the Federalists took on the fears that Tories ever since Charles II's time had held, that a breakdown in the established order would mean a breakup of all things and a society where all the passions and forces, unleashed, would undermine every institution on which ordered progress depended. If the Jeffersonians could look to England and its new sedition laws for an example of what might happen here—and what, to their eyes, did happen, with the Sedition Act of 1798—the Federalists looked to France, where the recalibration of the powers of king, lords, clergy, and Commons had brought short-lived constitutions, mob violence, terrorism, and, in the end, a directory of tyrants cloaked in the language of republicanism.[10]

No army of Federalists scoured the countryside putting Republicans to the sword, of course. What small rebellion did arise was handled bloodlessly. When Americans had their own "revolution," it was in the 1800 presidential election, in which, by peaceful and customary process, the Jeffersonians came into power and the supposed tyrants accepted defeat without a struggle. No guillotine ever rose in Rittenhouse Square.

Indeed, by the 1840s, the permanency of a party system, if not of the specific parties, had forced those who liked to summon up republican nightmares to rethink some of their basic assumptions. The "baneful effects of the spirit of party" that George Washington's Farewell Address had referred to had been a textbook case of the early distrust of party as a conspiracy against the people's will. Now a fresh generation reversed the argument. Republicanism and party government were not just compatible; they might actually be inseparable. Against the threat of the ambitious man, the Napoleon or Caesar, parties could throw up all the barriers of an institutionalized and widely expressed opposition. Parties would not undermine the republic. They might slow its decline, by scouring out scoundrelry and exposing freedom's secret enemies. What Catiline could escape the argus eyes of professional faultfinders?

Whigs and Democrats expressed it differently, to be sure. Whigs railed at party government as "a moral pestilence." They reminded voters that lockstep loyalty endangered liberty. Many Whigs detested it so deeply that they would never have dreamed of voting anything but a Whig ticket. But, then, they liked to claim that their party was not really a party at all—not in the many deplorable senses that the idea of party had come to have. Members responded to their own consciences, not to party discipline. They were not in it for spoils. Indeed, in many elections they were not in it at all: Whigs, more than Democrats, had to have living issues to motivate them to attend the polls, and in many off-year elections a decisive share of them stayed home. They saw themselves as members of the antiparty party led by the antipolitical politicians. Democrats, for their own part, described parties as the protectors of liberty, against the moneyed men who, otherwise, would have everything their own way. Only political discipline could keep the forces together in defense of republican freedom.[11]

The Whigs' ambivalence, though, should give historians pause. Long after party government became the norm, it still took some explaining away. An antiparty tradition survived. Mainstream politicians needed to absorb it and apply it in new ways, not dismiss it as outmoded. The idea persisted that one party was more legitimate than the other. Whig and Democrat were willing to grant their organization the exclusive role of the people's one true watchman in the night. They lagged badly in extending the same courtesy to the opposition. If "our friend, the enemy" had gone out of existence completely, only the disgruntled on the outskirts of the surviving organization would have called for setting up a new opposition party, just to keep the winners from eating the very paint off the walls of public offices. Parties so ached for the day that their enemy was eliminated, removed forever, that they kept crowing over the dawn that never came.

Given the opportunity, each side made the case that really there was no legitimate opposition party at all. The Whigs were no Whigs. They were Federalists—Tories once removed—who had toasted success to America's enemies in one war and, true to tradition, spoken on behalf of Mexico in another: "Mexican Whigs—British Whigs—aid & comfort to the enemy—Federal Whigs—moral treason party—abolition party—black tariff party—unpatriotic party." The Democrats, for their part, never got the respect that went with their name. Whigs called them "Locofocos," after the brand of matches that one radical sect in the Democratic Party had used to light their convention hall with, after conservatives had departed, shutting off the gas. They were not really democrats with big or small d, and Whigs on many occasions declared themselves the true democrats, and the real republican party.[12]

Alongside the fealty of so many eligible voters to one particular party, too, we must set the wide distrust of "politicians" and the low reputation of politics. Any government was sure to raise "weak men and scamps" to power, an Ohioan wrote sourly. "Go not to the sword of Caesar to find out the cause of the destruction of Roman liberty; seek it not in the camp; but go to the forum thronged with inflammatory orators and aspiring demagogues, with souls dead to their country's honor and spotted with corruption." (Whigs had plenty of ammunition to fire against Caesar, too; their fear of Andrew Jackson's readiness to ignore the law whenever it served his own ends and to stretch those constitutional provisions broadening a president's power was the strongest reason why they called themselves Whigs in the first place.)[13] That distrust, even detestation, helped explain why so few congressmen remained around for more than a single term. Parties played on it, by associating all the evils of the politician's trade with their opponents. Every coalition became a "bargain and sale" and, needless to say, was always the most shameless and corrupt bargain and sale in history, "equal only in enormity to that which attended the treason of Arnold." Every deserter was a disappointed politician, a broken-down hack whose ambition could only be satisfied now by going with whatever party was willing to pluck him off the trash heap to which he had been so properly consigned. These were not exceptions; these were the standard characteristics associated with the "politician": avarice, cupidity, ambition, unscrupulousness. It was for this reason that parties often found it easiest to elect politicians by pretending that they were something else and that their opponents were nothing but.[14] Power corrupted, tainted, distanced the holder from those he was meant to serve. To make sure that power reflected the people's will or the people's best interests, the electorate must change commanders constantly and share authority widely. It was not simply to make politics more effective but to give it the veneer of being the people's will that impelled politicians to take on the trappings of a rank and file duly consulted, by replacing the caucuses that had chosen candidates with conventions, elected by meetings of the party faithful at the local level.

The two-party system therefore had to shape its language to fit those suspicions and, every so often, take advantage of them, and this was easier because Whigs and Democrats saw themselves as members of a special, exclusive kind of party, a party of the people. Always the search for subversive conspiracies, for Catilines and Caesars, went on. Party tub-thumpers really did love to make voters' flesh creep, but they had good practical reasons for doing so. Americans were always on the move. Ten years' time, and every community would be made largely from strangers. Many settlers hardly stayed around in a community long enough to fulfill the residency requirements for voting—which in some places was about as long as the time it took to deposit a ballot in the box. Consequently, party papers had to drill home the issues every day and on every occasion, to whip up the most ardent passions on the least occasion, and to give partisans the most passionate of reasons for supporting the good cause—whatever that happened to be. Fear worked perfectly well, and fears with a pedigree best of all—the dread that the hard-won liberties that America alone enjoyed would be wheedled away.

As before, there still were always conspiratorial forces that explained how things really worked, the "true inwardness" of every event. It might be, as Democrats had it, the moneyed aristocracy, built on paper money. Or it might be, as Whigs saw it, the demagogues stirring up envy, resentment, greed, and other passions far more detestable, to win power and spoils, without the slightest care for the people in whose name they acted. Either way, the fears were there. "It is 'sink or swim' with the Nation," a Whig in North Carolina wrote as the 1840 presidential election neared, and "if we do not succeed in the coming elections, I believe, 'The People' will never elect another President, till we have had another Revolution."[15] Classical republicanism, in other words, was not so much dead as translated. What we call liberalism could exist in the economic sphere—every person out for himself and pursuing individual aims—and yet, in public life, liberal political language had no such vogue. Instead, there the preferred rhetorical devices were of the old Country versus the Court, the idea of conspiracies and designs. The watchword was always the same: "ETERNAL VIGILANCE IS THE PRICE OF LIBERTY."[16]

That vigilance, however, and the willingness to smell conspiracies against liberty, was a force that no party system could contain. In pulpit and pamphlet, Protestants talked of the menace posed to the republic by Catholic agents. Other true believers discovered hellish plots to usurp the republican government and enthrone "a Grand, Sublime, Royal, Ten Times Thrice Illustrious, and Absolutely Sovereign Masonic King," an event so imminent that only "the interposition of . . . Divine Providence" kept Freemasonry from completing its designs.[17] Down south, the old revolutionary brand of republicanism that saw parties themselves as the enemies of free government survived into mid-century. In places like South Carolina, where there was no two-party system and, indeed, very little consent of the governed, it defined politics; among the restless outriders, like John Quincy Adams and Wendell Phillips, the men who held their party ties most lightly, that sense of party as something illegitimate and nefarious persisted. The tighter, the stronger, party ties were, the less the republicanism looked like that of the founders. When the *Cincinnati Gazette* accused southern chivalry of having learned its ideas in "such schools as these of Rome and Greece," where republicanism and caste went together, it was not the compliment that one of the Founders would have taken it for.[18]

By the 1850s, the party system that Whigs and Democrats shared could no longer contain the republican suspicions. There were just too many outsiders, each group holding conspiracy theories of its own about the "true inwardness" of politics. The parties had not created that suspicion of secret agencies that ran through society, though they had put it to use. By midcentury, as the issues that they could offer to the voters became less compelling, they found themselves the victims of it. For those who rose to challenge them played off against the idea of politicians as in some sense illegitimate—go-betweens that no longer served as go-betweens—mediators that mediated things that should not have been mediated, by giving away things that they had no right to concede, to win things that nobody really wanted and nobody could really trust them to keep.

That fear of parties and conspiracies fed the Know-Nothing movement generously. The Know-Nothings were based on a vision of a Catholic conspiracy, which was lavish and outlandish, but also on the very real and plausible idea that the party system had been shifted off balance by the coming in of immigrants, many of whom knew little about what the parties stood for and who voted with clannish and blind loyalty. On them were blamed the drinking and depravity of the age. Parties had become "mere festering excrescences on the science of government," one nativist wrote. Let "the dead carcasses with all their pestilent fragments be entombed"![19] But the Know-Nothings themselves became a menace to be shunned, because in order to operate in a dangerous world they chose to act through secret societies and lockstep loyalty. The longer the Know-Nothings strutted and fretted on the public stage, the more they looked like a vehicle for hack politicians and has-beens to work their way into office. No movement can less afford politicians for their leaders than a movement meant as an attack on politics itself; no party based on a fear of conspiracy can long survive, when it looks like a conspiracy itself.

The Know-Nothings elected governors and senators and ran a presidential candidate, who did better than most third-party nominees do, but their glory days were brief. Much more portentous was the way in which the conspiratorial mind-set attached itself to the slavery issue. That broke the Jacksonian party system for good and the Union with it.

With the collapse of the Whig Party and the rise of the Republican Party, a new interpretation arose for why slavery had expanded so far beyond its original confines. Advocates of the "slave-power conspiracy" spoke of a plan, long since implemented, by which the planter minority among the slaveholding minority in the South had seized control of politics below the Mason-Dixon Line and then, by keeping their own interests foremost, had come to dominate the caucuses and conventions that chose those men occupying the commanding heights of national politics. They had bent the Democratic Party to their will by suborning and buying what northern leaders they could with favors and promises of higher office; those that could not be bent were broken or driven from politics. Step by step, the corruptionists and Calhounites, northern "doughfaces" with no interest higher than their own personal gain and southern slaveocrats with no aim except domination of a nonslaveholding majority, had pressed the country into wars of conquest and smashed the barriers to slavery's spread that past compromises and tacit promises by the Founders had raised.[20]

Abolitionists placed the start of the conspiracy at the founding of the republic; to them, the Constitution itself was part of the fettering of American freedom. Republicans dated the success of the conspirators much later, as within their own generation. The America that the Founders designed could be restored with relative ease. Elect a president, banish the dishonest stewards of freedom's rightful estate, and the plotters could be foiled. But the moment of peril had come, so grave that all other political issues became trivial. A few years more, with the patronage of the presidency and the decisions of a packed

Supreme Court behind it, and the Slave Power would claim the whole West for slavery. Freedom, isolated and sectional, would be hemmed in, whittled away. If slavery triumphed, freedom—white people's freedom—and the essence of the Constitution itself would be lost for good. Only a united effort by the North to keep slavery from the territory could check this "conspiracy against liberty." Conspiracy theory allowed Republicans to bill their program not as a revolution but as a restoration.[21]

Democrats, for their part, never admitted any such conspiracy. But in Republicans they saw a conspiracy of abolitionist fanatics. The word "abolitionist" could mean just about anything, the way conservatives used it. Generally, it meant a degree of antislavery belief greater than whatever the person using the term held. But it also carried with it connotations of treason and of a willingness to "let the Union slide." Stray statements by Republicans were dredged up to show that they were out to wreck the Union, or to rule it utterly. If theirs were treason, Democrats meant to make the most of it. Again and again they brought up the alleged words of Speaker of the House Nathaniel P. Banks that he was prepared to "let the Union slide." The churches themselves paltered with treason. "No Democrat can go into any of the Protestant Churches now-a-days . . . without having his feelings wounded and his self-respect debased," the *Cleveland Plain Dealer* complained. "In fact, the finger of scorn is pointed from the pulpit at Democrats, for the crime of preferring the Constitution and the Union to Seward's Higher Law and disunion."[22]

Democrats needed badly to make this case, for it was among their own supporters and from an entirely different crew of outsiders that the language of real disunion came. From 1850 on, the South was full of conditional Unionists, men who swore by the old flag, as long as their demands were met and as long as the system was frozen in place. One by one, they added to the number of possible actions that would make a severing of the Union necessary, and the actions grew more and more possible, because they were less and less radical.

Most intense in this stance were the southern rights men, some of them Democrats and many of them distrustful of any political party at all and convinced that the very term "national Democrat" was a sign of someone who would sacrifice the South's interests and its honor for pelf and power. Again and again, they drew their own opponents in lurid terms, as "submissionists," and made the issue one of personal humiliation. The North's intentions were put not in terms of competing interests and needs but in terms of a determination to humiliate southern manhood, to put it in the wrong and to make southerners into slaves—not in their tasks, perhaps, but in their status, compared to those who would decide what was truly Christian and what the Constitution meant.[23] Every act by the North was treated as an insult and as part of a pattern.

That conspiratorial mind-set bred an eagerness to look for traitors, and southern whites did so eagerly and energetically. Some of those traitors they hanged. Others they drove out of the South or silenced; but the more the critics of slavery were silenced, the stronger the fear of interlopers and intruders became. By 1860, the white South behaved like a section under siege. Worst of all, southern rights men knew that they could not trust white southerners to stand firm, given the chance. The South, too, had its doughfaces, prepared to palter if bought or bullied to do so, its ambitious placemen eager to sell out for a national office, its farmers and nonslaveholders in the upper South who shrugged off the threat to southern civilization.[24]

They must be awakened by constant agitation, by presenting every incident in public affairs in its most fearsome aspect. Southern rights advocates thrived on crises, in order to keep a drowsy public awake and to reinforce its sense of southerners as a separate people in imminent danger. Southern rights spokesmen served as sentinels, always spotting enemies on the march, always sure that every armistice was a secret surrender of the South's outlying posts. "Ye look the men your fathers were," a South Carolina poet appealed:

Your limbs, they were not made to bend
Methinks ye carry sword and spear—
And see—where smiles the treacherous friend!

His smiles are deadliest signs of strife,
The serpent's venom with his eye:
War, brethren, battle to the knife,
Or lose your ancient liberty![25]

Such a way of looking at the sectional crisis in the 1850s was almost certain to sharpen exactly the wrong kind of skills: the talent for overstating every injury, for rubbing every itch until it became a sore, and for seeing to it that no sleeping dog lay—at least for long. By 1859, South Carolina in particular was in a perpetual state of alarm, and the same could have been said for more and more of the Cotton South with every incident.

That alarm had plenty to do with the sense of peril brought about by the recognition that the slaves themselves were potential enemies in the white South's midst. Black uprisings were few. And those few failed within hours or were betrayed before the first blow fell. But that did not change the larger fear that they might happen.[26] Rumors of arsonists, of hidden saboteurs, of prose-lytizing northern fanatics became incessant, and when a very real attack took place on Harpers Ferry by an abolitionist bent on seizing the guns for purposes that are not entirely clear even now (one biographer speculated improbably that Brown may have meant to flee to the hills and to arm white recruits for raids on the slaveholders, with a few guns left over for any free black who happened to volunteer), white southerners did not need to take much trouble to figure out what caused it.[27]

Issues, real and serious, underlay the secession of the Deep South in the wake of Lincoln's election in 1860. But the action could not have happened without a complete breakdown, North and South, of faith in the other section's intentions, and without a real feeling that any national party had to be a sellout. It could not have happened without a sense of conspiracy, which fed on fears much wider than events in the 1850s justified and a sense of immediate crisis. For secessionists, Lincoln's victory did more than assure a momentary bar to slavery's expansion into the territories or southward along the Gulf. It augured the beginning of the end. Convinced that the abolitionist fanatics gave the real marching orders to Republican leaders, whatever mild statements were uttered in public, the southern rights sentinels warned that all slavery was in immediate danger. With federal patronage to buy friends down south, Republicans would form the nucleus of an antislavery party. Their president would pack the Supreme Court to read the Constitution as an abolitionist document. Free states would be admitted wholesale, the better to get the supermajority needed to ratify an abolitionist amendment and pack the Senate beyond recovery. With a plethoric purse and a vastly expanded army at arm's length, Lincoln could crush any southern state that raised a fuss, or, his agents all in place, he could rouse slaves to do his dirty work for him. "Are we to wait until the knife of the assassin is applied to our throats, or shall we trust to a returning sense of justice, under the scrambles for place produced by elections?" a Maryland congressman demanded. Rightly, the South demanded a "final reckoning and ample settlement" at once.[28]

Paranoia became the order of the day in Deep South politics. Sure that Irish canal workers were helping slaves escape, a North Carolina mob attacked their camp and killed them. On Election Day, rumors spread in Texas that the moment men headed to the polls slaves would butcher the women and children left at home, seize the weapons, and fire the houses, and when their masters came home, they would slaughter them, too; abolitionists, it seemed, had not only persuaded the blacks to act but had invited each man to pick out the white lady he most preferred to spare for other unmentionable purposes.

Editors printed tales that they could not verify, sure that if some of the stories were impossible, at least a few of them had to be true. Besides, as they knew, it would galvanize southern opinion for the southern rights cause. "The excitement growing out of these matters has killed off all conservative feeling in Texas," a northern journalist wrote. It certainly gagged it.[29] One Unionist later commented bitterly that his allies stayed home when the time came to vote on secession, because they preferred reading about martyrs to becoming them.[30]

The depth of southern anxiety, the pervasiveness of conspiratorial thinking, were all in plain view, for those who would look for them. The disunionists had formed a much broader constituency by 1860 than ever before, and Democrats were well aware of it. The people must put down fanaticism north and south, John L. Forsyth of the *Mobile (Ala.) Register* warned Philadelphians, because the "office-holders and politicians" would never do it. "As there is a God in heaven they will pull down the pillars which support the fair fabric of this Union, and involve you inevitably in a civil war." Forsyth should know; he had waged a bitter and losing struggle all that year long against Alabama's fire-eaters. From where he stood, he could hear the pillars tottering.[31]

Republicans were quite willing to quote the disunionists; every such remark only proved that the Democratic Party was the true party of secession. But so did Douglas Democrats, who were trying to win northern votes away from the Breckinridge Southern Democratic candidacy. And in that camp, they could find quotations aplenty. "Break up and dissolve this Yankee government," J. D. F. Williams urged his listeners. Instead of letting it slide, R. D. Gayle prayed, "Let the Union rip." Vice President John Breckinridge may not have been the Benedict Arnold of his day, but to Douglas Democrats he was a latter-day villain every bit as bad, the true heir of Vice President Aaron Burr, who had conspired to set up a southern Confederacy, tearing the Gulf states from the rest of the Union in Thomas Jefferson's day; and was it not also true that Breckinridge was related by blood to Burr? The best the *Cleveland Plain Dealer* could hope for was the same ignominious end. Even more flagrantly, the *Philadelphia Press* compared Breckinridge to John C. Calhoun, the nullifier, and Douglas to the Andrew Jackson who put the Union foremost. The "New Nullifiers" had forced the 1860 campaign to face one overwhelming issue: Union or disunion.[32]

Douglas himself made that very issue his theme, and it was from him more than from any other public figure that the charge came of an extensive conspiracy, "a mature plan . . . to break up the Union." Lincoln's election was not only hoped for as the act that would set it off; it was part of the Breckinridge Democrats' plot to see that the Democratic Party remained divided until Election Day, so that Lincoln could be elected. (He was right about some of them, at least, and Breckinridge voters, whatever they intended before the election, became the southerners likeliest to secede after it.) In that sense, then, every vote for Breckinridge was a vote to make Lincoln president—and the last president the United States would have. Douglas believed it, too. "No time must be lost, and no effort spared," he wrote an editorial ally early that summer. "We must make the war boldly against the *Northern abolitionists* and the *Southern Disunionists*, and give no quarter to either."[33]

And yet, so besotted with the Slave Power conspiracy was the Republican Party that, outside of the cluster of old Democrats in their ranks, all the statements from the South failed to convince many of them at all. They knew perfectly well what the South was about: its plotters intended to take over the nation they were in, not break off and form one of their own. The disunion talk was just a ploy to get what they wanted. If they could not sucker northerners into surrendering their just rights, they would scare them into it. It was an old game. The North was full of Union-savers, always dependent for their persuasiveness on the bluster of that southern corps of professional disunion-shriekers. It looked like a racket, in two senses of the word, an extortionist's threat uttered at full-lung capacity. The best cure for the threats, a New York Whig wrote in 1854, was to invite South Carolina to make them good. "March & stop talking about it. How can they stand alone?"[34] When William Yancey of Alabama threatened that "the people of the Cotton States will cut up very high fandangoes, and go out of the Union in defence of their rights," the *Cincinnati Gazette* set him right. "This is a commercial age, and Mr. Yancey will find that these heroics are entirely lost," it predicted. "Nobody will overturn the Government of Washington, and the Cotton States will submit as quietly to the 'constitutional form of government' as if it were not administered by Republicans." Stories that the "solid men of the South are really contemplating disunion" and were sending agents to France and England to negotiate commercial treaties in case a Confederacy came into being were laughed off as designed for Republican consumption and to "scare timid people out of their senses," until they yielded to every southern demand. Were northern men so unsexed that they would be intimidated by gammon like that? When Wall Street got the willies just before election time, Republicans insisted that this was a fake, too, a put-up job to make the secession bluster seem a bit more real, by suggesting that it was widely believed by men of property.[35]

Even when suddenly disunion became a reality, Republicans were so convinced that they knew the "true inwardness" that many of them failed to take it seriously. Many of them convinced themselves that it was a ploy, taken to a slightly more dramatic plane, but still nothing more than a trick to win new concessions. South Carolina would lead the procession, but those who trooped out would troop in again, soon enough. Later, there were predictions that secession, far from being well thought out, had been an impulsive action that would be rued sooner by the perpetrators than by the Union that had lost their allegiance. Secession would simply "deprive the idiots who are concerned of their mails, their Federal Courts, and all the advantages of the Union, [and would] load them with double taxes, reduce the price of slaves, depreciate their property, and damage nobody outside of their own crazy boundaries," the *Indianapolis Daily Journal* hooted. "We say let them secede if they can't stand it to have a man legally elected who don't choose to regard them as the almighty arbiters of the nation, whose fancies must be conciliated and prejudices satisfied, at the expense of every claim of humanity, and every demand of justice and right." Sadder but wiser prodigal sons would weary of living on husks and would beg for the chance to return.[36]

None of Republican hopes proved true. On the contrary, their worst fears came to pass. As all of their visions melted away, Republicans came to the conviction that secession had been a conspiracy, prepared long in advance by a select few; that it had been forced on the South against the wishes of the vast majority of the white population; that it was a minority movement; that it was proof in itself that the Union's enemies were more wily, more powerful, than anyone had dreamed; and that democracy, at least in the South, was a myth.[37] With such leaders, the people of the South could be pushed, pulled, prodded—even to their deaths.

Republicans overstated conspiracy's role, but they had at least some basis. Rare is the revolution in which the discontent below has no encouragement and definition from those above, if only in the selection of enemies. In a moment of crisis, every meeting not open to the public gets labeled a conspiracy, every strategist and tactician a conspirator. Republicans were right. Small groups of influential men, meeting in private and corresponding with each other, *had* directed the timing and process of secession, as far as they could.[38] By every standard of political measure, there really had been conspirators. Without ground as fallow and ripe as the South in 1860, armed men would not have sprouted where the dragons' teeth of disunion had been sown, but others had readied the soil and done the sowing.

The secession crisis quickened the pulse of political paranoia. Americans no longer had to *imagine* conspiracy after 1861. They had *seen* it right before them, in secession conventions and in armed masses springing up within months—conventions that northerners convinced themselves were put-up jobs, created by the Slave Power, forced through by the silencing of all opposition and the suppression of reasoned debate, and passed against the will of a true majority. But the conspiratorial origins of the Confederacy also may help explain the limits Republicans would find on themselves in trying to put the Union back together again four years later. If the small minority of slave owners could drive the southern majority like sheep, what kind of reconstruction based on consent could possibly work? Could any healthy society have stood much chance of growing in a South where such leaders held sway? And if the South was such a deferential society where a clique of a conspiring few could have their will so easily, might not new conspiracies, new disunions, break out just as easily, if the southern states should be restored to their old place in the Union? Would not the North be outfoxed, cheated, and in the end outgunned, in the same old way, by the bullies who had controlled things as they pleased before?

Citizens, every day shows that you are upon the
threshold of revolution.
—*Colonel Henry B. Carrington*

COPPERHEADS AND CONSOLIDATIONISTS, 1861–1865

Genteel and levelheaded, a proper silk-stocking Manhattan lawyer, George Templeton Strong knew better than to believe party rant. But, even for him, secession winter seemed full of conspiracies, palpable but unprovable. The day after the election, a "silly report" came from Washington that Governor Henry Wise of Virginia was plotting "a raid" on that city at the head of "a ragged regiment of rakehelly, debauched Virginians," and although Strong would not have put it past Wise, the tale sounded too wild for belief. Another day passed, and more convincing reports came of "privy conspiracy and rebellion, treason and secession," in the Cotton South. Most of the treason Strong saw was overt, not secretly planned and fomented, an ebullition of bad temper and spoilsport spleen. But other notes appeared as the crisis moved into December. "Willy Cutting talks mysteriously of an organization to revolutionize the city immediately upon the secession of the South," he wrote on the first of the month. "New York and Brooklyn are to be a free port, and with one or two adjoining counties, . . . to constitute an independent principality[.] Mayor and Common Council to be kicked out, if not hanged, and suffrage to be confined to owners of $5,000 worth of property."

In Washington, just after New Year's, Strong heard rumors that a Virginia mob would attack the city, and this time he did not laugh it off. "People are sending off their families to Philadelphia and New York," he noted. "These incendiary fires are supposed to be part of the revolutionary programme." Only the foresight of General Winfield Scott had persuaded the villains to turn their attentions elsewhere.[1] (Within forty days, Strong noted that Henry Wise and his "foray of Virginia gents" had missed their golden chance to destroy the electoral ballots before Congress could count them, "after they had killed and beaten General Scott and his Flying Artillery, that is." But he really believed that the intention had been there, thwarted only by the old soldier and the unexpected display of Union sentiment in the Border South.)[2] By now, the talk about a conspiracy in New York City had solidified. An armed mob would seize the armories of the militia companies, smash their way into the banks, and plunder the homes of top Republicans. Deeply involved in the plot was "a renegade Englishman," editor of the *Washington Constitution*, and, Strong added, there was "the best moral evidence" that a congressman-elect from New York City backed the plan. Before the end of January, Strong had become convinced that treason had prospered with active aid from the Buchanan administration.[3]

No longer did Strong doubt the rumors he heard. He took it for granted that there was a plot to assassinate Lincoln on his way to the inauguration. The railroad train carrying him was to have been derailed and knocked off an embankment, and, it was said, the president-elect sneaked into the capital in the early hours of the morning dressed in a long military coat and a Scotch cap. Granting that the tale sounded "a little romantic," Strong knew that the "Southern fanatics" were prepared for anything, and he only hoped that the conspiracy could be proven fully. (Strong did not report another widely circulated fable that Senator Louis Wigfall of Texas had plotted to kidnap the president and install a southern successor, but he might well have believed it.)[4]

Thus, when South Carolina's cannons opened up on Fort Sumter and the call went forth for volunteers to suppress the insurrection, it brought a kind of relief. All the Union's enemies had ranged themselves in the open. Indeed, to Strong's surprise, there were nowhere near as many as he had thought there would be. Southern cities counting on help from "a strong revolutionary 'Democratic' party" in New York found that the Democrats ranged under the same banner as did George Templeton Strong.

Compared to the actual events, all of Strong's fears look fantastical. But others supped even more heartily on rumor and fancy than he. And the stories he heard did have a basis in fact. There *were* plots to assassinate Lincoln and to overthrow Virginia's government in order to thrust it out of the Union.[5] Most of all, any well-read northerner could name the conspirators who for donkey's years—at any rate, for Buchanan's term, which was much the same thing—had been working to dissolve the Union and who took the credit for its accomplishment. But northerners who wanted to see plots did not have to hunt far for the evidence. Exciting times and overheated emotions made any terror seem possible.

As the war went on, those suspicions only found more proofs to feed on. By 1863, the most antiwar of Democrats were talking of "the minions of a corrupt and venal administration" bent on "establishing upon the ruins of the Republic, a despotism, more odious than has ever disgraced the civilization of any age of the world." Defeat in the 1864 election, an Indiana Democrat wrote, would fasten on America "the most corrupt and insupportable of all tyrannies—a centralized, sectional military despotism,—and the utter subversion of the noblest structure of free government ever devised or instituted by the wisdom of man."[6] "Conspiracy is afoot!" the Republican *Cincinnati Gazette* warned. A "few treacherous leaders" were sundering a people who should be united. Northern Democrats dared not express openly their intention to overthrow the government in Washington by "a revolution." "They would establish a despotism of terror under republican forms. For this purpose they are laboring that all the patriotic sacrifices of the people in this war . . . shall result in the triumph of the rebellion by our surrender."[7]

Language as red hot as these Democrats and Republicans hurled at each other in wartime invites skepticism. Nonpartisan newspapers treated it as pure display, the rhetorical equivalent of kerosene torches and Roman candles at a party shindig. From a campaign manager's standpoint, extreme talk paid. Democrats had lost the presidential election largely because they were divided. Outside the slave states, Lincoln did have a majority of voters. But Democrats could argue that, in their discouragement, their own organizers had essentially let the campaign go by default. The voters had been misled. Democrats had warned that Republican victory would bring on secession.[8] Events proved them true prophets. To make bad matters worse, Republican stubbornness had thrown away the last chance of a compromise that would have confined the secession contagion to the Gulf states. So, from the moment Lincoln took office, the Democrats could imagine themselves reversing the electoral landslide of 1860.

It could only happen if the conservatives made common cause under the Democratic banner and included some erstwhile Republicans. Swing voters were ripe for the taking in the Border South and in much of the Border North as well, not to mention among the staid, conservative German communities of southeastern Pennsylvania, the farmers of southern New Jersey, and the business district of New York.[9] A party that veered too far from the traditions and precedents of the past republic, with its emphasis on law, public order, and legal process, would send the hosts scattering, looking for shelter. To do that, Democrats had to prove Republicans not simply wrongheaded, but radical — subversive and threatening to the institutions that their party gave lip service to protect. Their every act must be seen as part of a conspiracy by fanatics outside of the party system, as crackbrained abolitionists eager for a general smash-up of property and society. Republicans saw the same logic. If they were to survive, they would need to paint themselves as the true conservatives, fighting to protect the flag, Constitution, and law. Democrats must be treated as so far beyond the pale of traditional politics that no respectable man would dare entrust his conscience to them.

This explanation makes the direction that the rhetoric took sound like a cynic's gambit: manipulative politicians sounding the alarm, perhaps while they exchanged broad winks with each other. But just the opposite was the case; the second big reason why passionate intensity infused party screeds was that both sides believed their very words. Real events fed the more fantastic fancies. Words like "ruin" sprang easily from Democratic pens, because for once the country really was close to ruin.[10]

Defeat breeds a horde of scapegoats, and the Union endured battlefield defeats more bloody than any war in living memory had been. More Americans were killed or wounded at Shiloh than in two years' fighting in Mexico; more men fell at Antietam than in all the battles of the Revolution. As one setback followed another, Republicans and Democrats alike looked for agents of treason close to home. The Joint Committee on the Conduct of the War hunted out slackness and incompetence in the officers' corps, but its investigations were aimed at more: to show that disloyalty to superiors, even a half treason to the North, had made commanders throw away possible victory and fail to exploit military advantages. That search for the "true inwardness" that politics had made so important now became the driving force for senators, sure that with a little more probing, they could unmask traitors on their side of the picket line.

Democrats, too, knew that the negligence or worse of leaders closer to home must be one of the great unrevealed causes of Union defeat, but, for obvious reasons, they found it among civilian leadership. After all, the generals sweltering under the most probing investigation were Democrats, and suspicion had fallen on them in the first place because of their politics. It was no less evident that, for many Republicans, striking a blow at slavery mattered almost as much as saving the Union—perhaps more. When the president issued his Emancipation Proclamation and the War Department began inviting the states to enlist black regiments, the war changed its character dramatically. Now white southerners, their whole way of life threatened, would have fresh reasons to fight to the death. Could that have been the Republican plan all along?

Out of the Democratic imagination came a secret conspiracy by fanatics, the true managers of the party in power, to end slavery or have the old Union perish and two nations arise. One of them would be uncontaminated by "the peculiar institution" and, because it was smaller, more easily dominated by the power-mad extremists and protected manufacturers of Puritan New England, with their crazy, selfish ideas of a political economy where eastern banks and industrialists could grind money out of the toilers everywhere else. All the occasional remarks of Republicans expressing less-than-wholehearted support for the Union were revived, and the radical assertions that they wanted no return to any Union in which slavery stood inviolable were treated as the voice of the whole party. The South was not the only intended victim. Propertied men in the North should feel dread, too. No established institution was safe. "The Abolitionist is a revolutionist," the *Cincinnati Enquirer* reminded readers. "His desire is to have revolution succeed revolution, until his ideal of perfection shall be realized." The cost in human life only made revolution more appealing. "Nations—such is his theory—must be baptized in blood, in order to be regenerated; the deeper and redder the baptism, and the more frequent, the more complete the regeneration." These men, on the distant outskirts of American public opinion, now sat at the center of power. They headed the leading committees in House and Senate. They forced the president to do their bidding. "Of course this same Abolition party are opposed to the South ever being represented in Congress," the *Louisville Democrat* charged. "It would upset all their calculations and disappoint their hopes. They don't want the Union restored; it is not their interest."[11]

What was in their interest was power and a national government with authority wider than any ancestor had dreamed of wielding. They exposed themselves perfectly in the names they offered for two of their most powerful warships: the *Puritan* and the *Dictator*. Every big wartime measure provoked a constitutional debate over the special "war powers" that the administration could draw on in a time of emergency. Republicans drew the constitutional limits in various ways, and some spoke as if there were no limits at all. In crisis, the president was "clothed with power as full as that of the Czar of

Russia," an Illinois politician insisted. To Democrats, such arguments were traitorously wrong. Senators who spoke of the Constitution as suspended in wartime should have been expelled in disgrace and "arrested on the spot." Accept the premise that Congress could usurp powers not constitutionally granted, a conservative Republican cried, and "the days of the Republic are past, and the days of the Empire begun."[12]

Black freedom would come at a high price, in that case, but the down payments were already being made, and not only by the soldiers whose lives were wasted in what the administration would turn into a losing war. Republicans were extracting that price at home, in their subversion of the Constitution and their insistence that anyone who did not share their own views was disloyal. "It is a wonder that this traitor is tolerated on the face of the earth," a Wheeling newspaper stormed of Congressman Clement Vallandigham, one notorious critic of the war, "much more that he is allowed to sit in Congress, like Catiline in the Roman Senate." Brutus "slew a man in the Capitol, whose lowest characteristics would have ennobled Vallandigham."[13]

Closely connected with these measures was the rise of the Union Leagues and the machinery of imposed loyalty. Called "loyalty leagues," the first associations formed as a means of getting out the argument in favor of the war and countering Democratic criticisms of the way the war was being fought. Members worked to inspire audiences to enlist, to contribute to the comfort of soldiers in the field, and to buy war bonds. They issued pamphlets and speeches, provided forums for congressmen and ministers to explain the duties of nationalism and the limits of state sovereignty, and in some places endorsed candidates.[14]

A lobby on behalf of a special understanding of nationhood, one outside the party system, would have been alarming in any case. But the Union Leagues did more than express and give a louder public voice to the Republican versions of nationalism. They also redefined just what loyalty entailed and how far it was consistent with what until then had been seen as appropriate levels of liberty. They defined the nation and the citizens' responsibility to the nation-state in ways that Democrats found alien, even frightening.[15] And, unlike parties, which could be checked or controlled by the people through caucuses, conventions, and their will as expressed at the ballot box, there were no checks at all on the Union Leagues. They meddled in politics without allowing politics to meddle with them.

In all the conspiracy theories the key elements had included the secret society and members whose consciences were made subservient to their oaths. Republicans would call on this imagery in attacking the Democrats and their subversive secret societies, but so, too, did Democrats see the Union Leagues in that way. They had taken on the fearful trappings of a cult. When Pennsylvania Democrats lost a key county in October 1864, they blamed the lockstep discipline of the "secret leagues." Backed with the power and unlimited means that the Lincoln administration provided, the conspirators could promise and suborn without stint. What would they do, with guns in hand? Word had it that Yankee abolitionists had raised a million dollars for arms and spread them among the Union Leagues out west.[16]

Not just in one place but in many it had become unsafe to print a Democratic newspaper, and just about nowhere was it safe to express sympathy with the Confederate South's motives or admiration for its leading men. Democratic presses were made the first victims, and Democratic citizens all over the country were either maltreated or exposed to insult. Inspired by "the teachings of a lying, incendiary press," a mob broke into the office of the *Luzerne Union*, in Pennsylvania. In other cities, editors were tarred and feathered. Presses were smashed. Democratic dissidents were run out of town.[17] Local authorities turned the other way. Democrats suspected that the violence had not just the tolerance of those running government but even their active support and incitement. It was a "well known fact" to their editors that from the very start of the war the opposition had "inaugurated a system of mobs and outlawry by which to overawe and crush out all opinions but their own."

The Lincoln administration did more than abet the mob. It turned the army into a special police. With the writ of habeas corpus suspended, provost marshals ordered the arrest of thousands of Americans without warrant or due process. The closer anyone looked at the cases, admittedly, the more defensible they seemed. The administration used its powers in the Border South, where there was an imminent danger of Confederate armies invading and where an active network of Confederate fifth columnists was at work. But Democrats argued that the emergency could never justify the means. "The Constitution was not constructed upon a sliding scale," an Illinois senator reminded the chamber. The protections that civil law provided, the guarantees of due process available in peacetime, applied always, not just when the administration found them convenient.[18] At the very least, the arrests had a chilling effect on frank debate of the government's handling of the war. At worst, they allowed martinets arrayed in despotic authority to harry anyone out of favor in Washington and swing elections their way.

Maryland Democrats swore that they had been cheated out of victory in the 1863 elections of congressmen, and they found still more compelling evidence of swindling in the vote on a new constitution in 1864. Abolishing slavery, the convention put it before the voters, had left little to chance and not very much to the voters' will. "Look at Maryland, which was supposed to be voted for Lincoln," Senator Willard Saulsbury of Delaware charged. Did anyone dare tell him that the electorate chose freely? Soldiers manned the polls. Republican fuglemen challenged conservative voters, and partisan registrars turned them away. Delaware's electorate had been culled the same way a year before, the senator added. Soldiers' threats and daunting loyalty oaths required of every voter had kept Democrats home. Administration hirelings promised the kind of pettifogging enforcement of the election statutes that for the most trivial infraction would send a conservative from the polls to the penitentiary. On terms like those, even Saulsbury steered clear of the polling place.[19]

But there were too many nonresidents in uniform glad to cast the votes that people like Saulsbury relinquished—or so the Democrats alleged. In loyal states, Republicans were accused of getting the majorities they needed by sending soldiers with just the right politics home on furlough at just the right time. To hear Democrats tell it in 1864, the administration made up shortfalls at home by collecting Lincoln majorities in camp. Democrats lost because they could not get their message to the troops. Abolitionists had free access to the camps to poison soldiers' minds against the whole Democratic Party as an association of Butternuts and Copperhead traitors, an Indiana volunteer complained. Those Democrats who kept the faith had to overcome two great obstacles to voting their conscience. There was no secret ballot and no official one. The two were closely connected. Parties, not the government, issued ballots, with their exclusive slate of candidates for recipients to vote if they chose; the organization with greater means of distributing its tickets could turn out a bigger vote. And since the ballots must be carried to the polls, rather than being marked in seclusion by the bearer, a voter's choice could be spotted by others, in this case by commanding officers, who might respond with all the reprisals that the color of authority could devise. As McClellan tickets went into the mails, winging their way to the army camps, the complaints began flying back. Ohio Democrats sent packages of ballots to the front and received them back by mail, unopened. They heard reports of captains and lieutenants who forbade the men from getting the tickets of their choice.[20]

Indeed, whether the Union was restored or not became almost irrelevant. Either way, liberty might well not survive. The more bitter the war, the more certain that no reunion of hearts, North and South, could come about; and the less the nation could depend on southern consent for a restored Union, the more certain it was that the Union would be restored in name only—one country only until the South had the force at its disposal to take up arms again, or one country forever, held so by the iron hand of the military despot. By degrees, Americans would come to accept as natural and normal the extraordinary measures that in wartime had been resorted to. Military trials and arrests without warrant, martial law, invasion of private homes, state-sponsored terrorism toward dissent would be necessary forever, until they became part of the real, the unwritten constitution of the republic, the framework under which policy was made and government carried on.[21] That was the largest threat, the great peril of letting Republicans make a war on slavery as well as on disunion, and of cutting capers over established constitutional usages, to crown the war with hollow victory. The longer the dying went on, the stronger the northern people's willingness to do anything or everything to bring the agony to an end.

Putting all these parts together into a larger whole hardly even taxed the imagination. Who could miss the intentional strategy, looking far beyond the next election to the long-term destiny of the nation? Was it inconceivable that Republicans were plotting not to save the Republic, not even by misjudgment to destroy it in the process of pursuing other ends beyond preserving the Union, but, in fact, to destroy freedom? Could it be that the administration's aim was not to restore the South but to subjugate it, creating a subject people, the better to dominate the rest of the United States and, in time, to end freedom there as well? "New England Puritanism has nearly accomplished its purposes," a Democratic newspaper contended, and that purpose was to break up a republican form of government for a different, a consolidated one. One day before the president predicted a new birth of freedom, former congressman John G. Davis of Indiana wrote as if he stood at the wake of liberty. Indeed, he and others doubted if the damage ever could be repaired or the republic restored to what it had been. At most, the public mind must be prepared "to save the remnant of popular liberty that may be gathered among the wreck that is surely upon us."[22]

That saving might take ferocious means. As Philadelphia Democrats held their grand torchlight procession just before the 1864 election, they met a rain of mud, missiles, and stones from the rooms of the Lincoln League. Republican rowdies smashed in party banners, and in the melee an aged Democrat was killed. "Democrats are never guilty of such acts of blackguardism and brutality," screamed a partisan paper, "but the time is not far distant, we fear, when the lawless hangers on of this administration will cause the streets of all our towns and cities to be deluged in blood. — Democrats will not much longer see their friends and neighbors murdered in cold blood without retaliating."[23]

The Lincoln League's bombardment was more than rudeness. It expressed the Republican view that Democrats could never acknowledge: that the parade represented not loyal opposition but treason's false front. To them, the managers of the Democratic Party had become the unwitting apologists, even the secret allies of treason. Even though a sea of Union flags waved in northern cities in the spring of 1861, Republicans quickly sensed an army of traitors undiscovered, unwhipped, unhung, ready to welcome quite another banner, if anyone dared raise it. Coming out on behalf of the South was inconvenient for the moment, but those who had apologized for slavery for so long were not about to change their minds, even if they changed their colors. The moment Confederate troops needed their help, their northern sympathizers would be ready to give it. Until then, they would discourage, dismay, and disaffect.

Republicans therefore were quick to believe any rumor of secret societies—always jam-packed with Democrats—out to hamper enlistments and send aid to the Confederacy. Within months of the war's beginning, they centered their attention on the Knights of the Golden Circle. Such an organization did exist before the war. A fabulous schemer, George Bickley, had founded it to promote private invasions of Central America, where filibustering armies could overthrow local dictators and create slaveholding states, ripe to be added to the Union. Bickley's ideas kept shifting: now sponsoring a revolution in Mexico that would drive out the priests and install "superior Anglo-American civilization," now touting his Knights as a private army to defend southern rights from abolitionist conspiracies—anything and everything that would entice suckers into coughing up a five-dollar membership fee. He passed out charters for local chapters in the Ohio River valley and, to hear him tell it, had a dazzling success in recruiting members. In fact, the last one heard of most of those chapters was the announcement of their having been founded. The numbers in the Knights grew as fast as the men in buckram that Sir John Falstaff claimed to fight off—and from the same source, a wild imagination. All the same, Bickley offered his services to Mississippi's governor in secession winter, and with it the fealty of as many as 50,000 Knights (none of them were ever heard from again). The New York Tribune may not have hit near the mark when it suggested that Bickley calculated his talents as worth 35,000 men and his assistant's as worth the other 15,000 when he made the offer—that is, assuming that he had an assistant.[24] It was all theater, as real as the blood-curdling deeds that Bowery actors impersonating Knights of the Golden Circle reenacted on the stage.

When the war began, the laughing ended. Rumors conjured up a plot by the Knights to seize Washington, D.C., and keep Lincoln from being inaugurated, or to stir Kentucky to leave the Union. Eighteen thousand Californians were said to have joined, and with the United States commander on the West Coast, Albert Sidney Johnston, to lead them, they would wrest the Pacific Coast from the Union. Nobody told Johnston about the plan, and the Knights never did brandish their lances in the Bluegrass. But still the beliefs continued to grow. By the end of 1861, Republican newspapers were charging that the filibustering movement had invaded the Democratic Party and in some places had conquered it outright.[25]

The Order of American Knights looked just as puny. Founded in New Orleans before the war to colonize Central America with slaveholders, it had been all Order and no Knights. In wartime, its founder had come north to build an army of civilians. Phineas C. Wright was intensely hostile to the Lincoln administration and proposed reviving his old organization to give the Peace Democracy a military presence. Only by countering force with force could opponents of the war protect their lives and liberties from Republican mobs. If the Union League was a radical army in waiting, conservatives must arm to meet it. Early in 1863, Wright traveled through Illinois, founding local "temples" of the Order. In Indiana and New York, a few sympathizers gave him a friendly hearing. They, too, wanted a mutual-protection society for their cause. Sympathy came cheap, but members hardly came at all. By 1864, the few Knights there were wondered whether it made sense to carry on. When their national convention assembled, a few delegates tried to have the body disband and rename itself the Sons of Liberty.[26]

Republicans did not need to strain the evidence to suspect that a call to resist by force of arms would find takers in the North, but theirs was the faith that could move mountains, after having made them from molehills. They insisted that the Knights of the Golden Circle were enormous, that most of the leading Democrats in the Midwest belonged. In Indiana, a grand jury issued its opinion that 15,000 citizens belonged to the society. Having "secretly renounced" their allegiance to the United States, the traitors worked to stop enlistments, hamper the collection of taxation, and provide intelligence to the Confederate government. Crowds heard how the organization recruited Illinois residents, armed them, and sent them south into Confederate service. A fracas between white and black laborers in Brooklyn could not have been spontaneous. The *Tribune* was sure of that, because if Indiana had 15,000 traitors, so must New York, and Knights members surely instigated the fight. In fact, every incident touched the circumference of the Golden Circle. On his own "personal knowledge," Senator Zachariah Chandler of Michigan declared that the group had infiltrated the army—knowledge that apparently did not include a single name that he could report to the War Department. For those

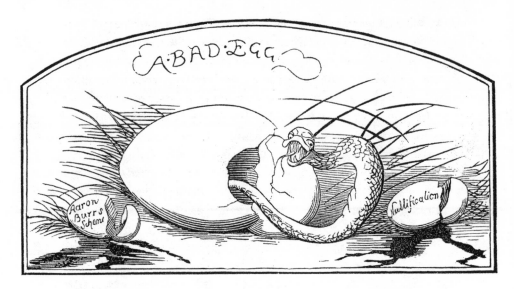

"A Bad Egg." 1863, from *Ye Book of Copperheads*. The Civil War opponent emerges, a snake hatched from one of three "Tory" eggs. The others are nullification and Aaron Burr's plot, reputedly to take the West out of the Union in Jefferson's day.

who wanted to see treason unmasked, let them attend a campaign rally in Indiana, especially for so notorious a critic of the war as Daniel Voorhees, the "tall Sycamore of the Wabash." "Who has not attended a Voorhees meeting and witnessed his conservative constituents on their way home, cheering for their idol Davis' favorite generals, etc.," wrote "Loyal Democrat." (Since he wrote it for a Cincinnati newspaper, the answer among readers was probably, nobody.)[27]

The danger of extreme menaces was that they allowed extreme action. It was time to clean out the secret disunionists, a colonel shouted to a Union audience. "The day had come when, if a traitor opened his black lips, that every Union man should give him a passport to the devil where he belonged. When he found a traitor right here in the North, he would shoot him, like any other dog."

The Northwestern Conspiracy of 1864 must be seen in that context. That there was such a conspiracy sane men could hardly doubt. Mississippi and Virginia newspapers had talked of it. A Rebel senator had offered a resolution to recognize the Northwestern confederacy whenever it broke free. Former Democrats had alleged that their old compatriots favored it; northern newspapers had considered the idea during the secession crisis and may have been considering it still. For some editors, some such drastic step as the Old North-west detaching itself from the war effort offered the greatest prospect of forcing the North's fanatics to offer reasonable terms to the Confederacy. Only when afraid of a new disruption of the Union would they act to restore the old, and in that effort—unquestionably patriotic—Democrats in the Ohio River valley would mediate the differences between the warring sections. No sooner had Republicans lost control of the legislatures of the Midwest than the stories took on new life. "As I went to bank at 10 I met Govr. [Oliver P.] Morton," Indiana lawyer Calvin Fletcher recorded in his diary early in 1863. The governor "seemed much depressed," as well he might: to him had come many affidavits, alleging "a conspiracy around to take the government of the state out of the union & assist in making a new Empire joining with the S. W. slave states & leave the Yanky states." Three days later, an officer in the Indiana state arsenal told Fletcher of fears that "the Secession sympathizers were suspected with intention to take the arsenal," and his own handing out of arms on the quiet to loyal civilians, just in case. The governor expected the attack to take place on January 8, the day on which Democrats gathered for the putatively harmless purpose of honoring Andrew Jackson. Other Republicans spent ten days worrying that the new legislature would wrest "the Government from the constituted authorities & revolutionize. They the secession sympathizers have secret societies all thro' the state (this state perhaps others)," the diarist added. Sergeant William Miller, on the front lines in Tennessee, had "Some pretty Sharp talk" with an old friend from the Midwest, who not only defended the South but claimed that the North was "ready to raise up . . . and help the South." Also stationed in Tennessee, Calvin Fletcher's son wrote home furiously against a body that, to judge from the newspapers, was "*kicking* right against us . . . trying to stur up strife & civil war right at home, who utter their *traitorous secession* sentiments, out in *public*, open *day light*." Send 20,000 Union soldiers home again to Indiana and "we'll make the whole cowardly set tremble in their boots. The whole Set will be *exterminated*. They will not receive the mercy that would be shown to a *Southern* Reble." Reading the lawmakers' sentiments, he felt only disgust. "They ought to be *hung*, shot down like dogs. And every man expressed a wish to *stretch* a *dozen* or so himself."[28]

Democrats knew too well how so many soldiers felt. With Republican encouragement, regiments down south held rallies and signed petitions demanding the suppression of antiwar dissent. Enlisted men spoke freely of marching north and clearing out the traitorous politicians in Springfield, Indianapolis, and Harrisburg. Soldiers returning home to Indianapolis for the local elections beat up alleged secession sympathizers and silenced those who used what Calvin Fletcher called "abusive language to the Government." A month

From *Ye Book of Copperheads*, 1863. The author shared some Union soldiers' wish that the army clean out wartime dissenters, without any of the niceties of constitutional process.

later, troops harassed Indiana Democrats gathering for their state convention. Union soldiers shoved through the crowds, arrested as they pleased, and that night commandeered the excursion trains leaving town, to confiscate any guns they found.[29] If the most militant opponents of the war thought their freedoms so much at risk that they would be justified in arming to protect themselves, or in forming party militia to defend liberty, that willingness reflected more their fear than it did their treason. But it could certainly be seen the other way.

The starring villain of the piece, H. H. Dodd, was a recruiter for the Sons of Liberty with visions of making it a mutual protection society and a political pressure group that might force the Democratic Party closer to the Copperhead point of view. In the summer of 1864, press exposure of the Sons of Liberty and the Order of American Knights, wildly exaggerated and alarmist though it may have been, made very certain that any ambitious partisan with an eye to future advancement would shun either one like typhoid. Looking for help from elsewhere, Dodd turned to Confederate agents in Canada, who promised him $10,000, presumably expecting that he would use it to foment war behind Union lines or arrange for an uprising. Dodd may have meant to do just that. In any case, he let it be known that the Sons of Liberty had become a full-scale movement, a secret army with four "major-generals" handling its different districts. As the chief conspirator, he may only have meant to use the movement to meet force with force, if Lincoln's lackeys used the army to purge the polling places of Democratic voters. A cluster of shabby intriguers, all Democrats on the outskirts of the party, gathered around Dodd, and among them they managed to ply agents and government informants with tales of tremendous secret organizations, all working to murky but monumental ends. In early August 1864, he broached his plan for "an uprising" to an Indianapolis editor. A "council of sixteen," he informed him, had decided on "revolution," and the date was scarcely a week away. The moment of truth would come at a Democratic rally. Properly whipped up, the crowd would be ready for heroic measures. Dodd had worked out a raid to set free Confederate prisoners of war outside of Indianapolis, Chicago, and other places. In Kentucky, his allies would mount a coup, seize government supplies, and ready for war with the Lincoln administration. The editor was horrified. Prominent Indiana Democrats were thunderstruck and forced Dodd to agree to lay his plans aside. By the time government raids netted the chief conspirators and traced their funding to Canada, the danger—if there had ever really been any—was past.[30]

The Northwestern Conspiracy provided the ideal exposure of how far some Democrats had fallen from a "legitimate political opposition." In a presidential campaign, its timing came perfectly. Rebellion and Copperheadism were links of the same sausage, ground from the same dog, as one newspaper put it. "Swallowing either would place the health of this Union beyond the aid of the most skillful and untiring Sanitary Commission." But it was more than a convenient election-year stunt by the Republicans to defame the whole Democratic Party. The assertions of ringleaders in the plot that they commanded thousands of revolutionaries, and the clear evidence of Confederate involvement, were enough to make any suspicion seem credible, however hard they now protested that they had been fooling all the time. "The exposure of the Sons of Liberty has been made, every word is true," Colonel Henry B. Carrington announced to the public. "Harrison H. Dodd, Grand Commander of Indiana, has been on trial. Proof was overwhelming. . . . Citizens, every day shows that you are upon the threshold of revolution. . . . The traitors intended to bring war to your homes."[31]

Very real responses to fears bred counter-responses. Admittedly, all the secret societies together do not seem to have amounted to much. High-ranking Democrats did nothing to keep party members from joining but steered clear of involvement. Not even most Peace Democrats had much to do with either set of Knights—assuming that they could find any of them. But in another sense the organizations were an extreme expression of a very real concern among Democrats, that the Constitution was in such danger that it might take desperate measures to set things right again. When soldiers were sent into some midwestern areas to arrest deserters, they had to fight armed crowds, as many as 2,000 strong in one case. In some counties, resisters shot and killed recruitment officers, and the incidents happened where Dodd's preparations had gone furthest. Certainly in the Midwest there were men who feared that they would need to arm in self-defense. Quite possibly Democrats who believed the republic to be at risk foresaw the day when they would have to pay with their lives for their liberty, and they were storing guns for that purpose. That may have explained the very unusual plank in the national platform in 1864, asserting the constitutional right to bear arms and implying the right of Democrats to muster in their own self-defense. It certainly could be read into the warning that party leaders uttered that if the opposition tried to deny free elections in the Border South the Democrats would resist to the end. For the conspiracy against liberty that Democrats saw made them bold in vowing to use revolutionary methods against any revolution. Let those who urged violence against dissenters beware, the *Cincinnati Daily Enquirer* warned. "Poisoned cups return to the lips of those who mixed them; mischief haunts the violent, and they who take up the sword perish by the sword."[32]

Those warnings included invocations of assassination. Who could blame them, if they were right in reading Lincoln as the man who "spit upon the Constitution" and "strangled the Goddess of Liberty." "Lincoln has been a worse tyrant and more inhuman butcher than has existed since the days of Nero," editor Mark M. "Brick" Pomeroy raged. Whoever voted for Lincoln betrayed the country. "He who, pretending to war for, wars against the constitution of our country is a traitor, and Lincoln is one of these men. . . . And if he is elected to misgovern for another four years, we trust some bold hand will pierce his heart with dagger point for the public good." Optimistically, the *Philadelphia Age* foresaw Lincoln losing his office and mentioned rumors that he would don the old Scotch cap and cloak he was said to have used to escape being killed in 1861 on his way to Washington. He would need them even more, heading home![33]

In retrospect, the 1864 election looks like a vindication of the democratic process. After three bitter years of war, the campaigns went on pretty much as usual. Caucuses, conventions, mass meetings, processions, and wide open debate of the issues proceeded as smoothly as ever before. For all the cries of intimidation and censorship, editors north of the Ohio River spoke with voices as unrestrained, not to say shrill, as in peacetime. But Democrats were too frightened and angry to celebrate the larger survival of American institutions. Far more plainly they saw the incidents, intimidations, and intimations of worse persecution to come.[34] However the conspiracy charges turned out,

Republicans believed that the country had barely escaped disaster. "We have been on the brink of civil war in the North," former secretary of the treasury Salmon Chase wrote just after the election. "Nothing but divided counsels of opposition leaders saved us from it. The strength & ramifications of the conspiracy, now being exposed at Indianapolis, of which the recent attempts at St. Albans, Sandusky, Chicago, & . . . other places were parts, are frightful."[35]

When the 1864 returns were in, then, quite a few Democrats did not share in a sense of relief. They would have lost if every precinct had been polled fair and square, most of them admitted, but that only made it the more insulting that they had been cheated as well. Democrats had not the slightest doubt of how their enemies' command of Congress came in the border states. There, military force and disfranchisements had won the Republicans enough House seats to organize Congress and, in case that was not enough, to appoint Elections Committees prepared to seat whom they pleased. Grimly, Indiana Democrat William P. Davis wrote his defeated kinsman, former congressman John G. Davis, that fraud had decided the state result that October. If so, could November's presidential balloting promise any better outcome? Lincoln's reelection would come, however the opposition turned out. "If by fraud and force they have carried a pretended election," the *Boston Courier* threatened, the minority nonetheless was "powerful in numbers, strong in resolution, organized to meet the exigencies which may be before them."[36]

The Democratic mood, then, as the war came to an end, was a sour, dispirited one. Nearly all Democrats were glad to see the Union restored, and without exception they greeted peace as a relief. The great driving forces that had been impelling the country toward corruption, ruin, and arbitrary rule would be removed. Restoring the republic to its ancient balance could begin. But some feared that it was already too late for salvation. The experience of war may have fatally marred the character of Americans. "Is not our country in the last agonies of decay and dissolution?" former Indiana congressman John G. Davis wrote as the Confederate armies surrendered. His correspondent could give him no reassurances. "The seeds of sin, crime, wrong, injustice & demoralization, are sown so deeply that my hopes of the future are dark & dim," an Illinois Democrat wrote in May 1865. "I cannot see any light ahead to give me hopes of the continuance of Republican institutions, such as we once enjoyed." America would end the war with "an Oligarchy of wealth, and a nation of *paupers*—the sequence to the combination must be serfdom & Slavery sooner or later," "and [in] the end *Monarchy*."[37]

Or, perhaps, anarchy. There was one last proof that political nightmares could come true. On April 14, 1865, just days after the Palm Sunday surrender of Robert E. Lee's Army of Northern Virginia and the flight of the Confederate government, "Brick" Pomeroy's appeal for an American Brutus was answered. Shot from behind by John Wilkes Booth, the president died early the following morning. In the midst of northern celebrations that the worst was over, the news came as doubly shocking. Conspiracy lived. Within hours, proofs emerged that the act was not the work of some lone madman, as the attempt on President Andrew Jackson's life thirty years before had been. A gathering of Confederate sympathizers had worked out a much farther-reaching plan to wipe out the effective leadership of the government. An impetuous young fool had been sent to cut the secretary of state's throat but had only managed to slash him from chin to ear before escaping. Killers had been assigned for the vice president and the secretary of war, though neither had the nerve (or the malice) to follow through. Unsubstantiated reports spread that the conspiracy also meant to do in the Speaker of the House, the chief justice, former vice president Hannibal Hamlin, and other cabinet officers.[38]

"Sic semper tyrannis is the motto on the shield of Virginia," cool-headed former attorney general Edward Bates wrote in his diary, "and this may give a clue to the unraveling of a great conspiracy, for this assassination is not the act of one man, but only one scene of a great drama."[39] The North had been beset for years with rumors that the president was going to be killed or kidnapped. What could be more natural than that one of those reports proved to be well founded? The Confederate press for four years had printed threats to Lincoln's life and wishful dreams of what would happen if he were removed through violence. The *Selma Dispatch* had posted a million-dollar reward for the murder of Seward and Lincoln before the second inaugural. A clerk in the Interior Department told how on April 14 he had talked with eight Confederate generals at the depot on their way home. "I tell you, sir, there are agencies at work which you Northern people know not of," one of them insisted, "and at the proper time they will strike, and the Confederacy will yet raise its head to some work and win for itself a name among the nations." Within a day, the hints took on a fuller meaning.

Indeed, it was not the southern will to do the deed that surprised Lincoln's friends, only the timing. So much of the advantage of killing the president was gone, now that the Confederacy was hopelessly gone too. What they had overlooked until now was the motivation of blind revenge, the desire to bring their enemies as low as they had been brought themselves. To those who wanted to see conspiracy, the danger was laid bare—and too late.[40] "Damn the rebels," Secretary of the Navy Gideon Welles raged; "this is their work." From the War

Department, a dispatch pinpointed the plot's origin in Canada and suggested that it had been given the go-ahead in Richmond.

On May 2, President Andrew Johnson issued a reward for Confederate leaders. In his proclamation, he charged openly that the assassinations had been "incited, concerted, and procured by and between Jefferson Davis, Clement C. Clay, Beverley Tucker, George Sanders, W. C. Cleary, and other rebels and traitors." The belief took a lasting hold on northern imaginations, though not all, and on almost no southern ones. "I cannot believe that he had anything to do with that vile affair," a Georgian had written in his diary days after Davis's arrest. "I cannot believe that this new and horrible phase of treason was planned by any government leader at the South," a Democratic financier wrote his friend, Lincoln's former postmaster general Montgomery Blair. But even he connected the plot to "treason," and others had less doubt.[41] French newspapers speculated that Secretary of War Stanton might have been behind the plot for his own advantage; but Stanton, as alarmed as anyone else, had fantasies that *New York Tribune* editor Horace Greeley was involved. The new president did not waste his time on imaginings like those. He laid the blame on Davis and his cabinet. "They shall suffer for this," he muttered, clasping one hand in the other, "they shall suffer for this."[42] The military commission trying Booth's associates did its best to be fair, but the judges never had any doubt that they were trying small fry. The real perpetrators lay beyond the seas, all but the arch-conspirator, Davis himself, by now lodged in Fortress Monroe and awaiting trial for treason. Tainted evidence linking Booth to the Rebel authorities was believed precisely because the examiners took Confederate involvement for granted.[43]

Those suspicions died slowly. Almost a year later, the House passed a resolution instructing its Judiciary Committee to look into the guilt of the men accused in the proclamation; another year on, and the president and the secretary of state were still directing the interviewing of witnesses, hoping to find the authoritative proof that would tie Davis to Booth's schemes. None surfaced. The further the investigation proceeded, the clearer it became that the most expansive witnesses were the most crooked, their memories capacious enough to "remember" anything that would help themselves. Twenty years later, Senator John A. Logan of Illinois wrote his own take on the war, subscribing to the conspiracy theory as far as evidence allowed him. By that time, even Logan had to admit that Booth initiated the plot, though only after Rebel propaganda poisoned his mind and cankered his heart. Logan admitted that Confederate authorities' awareness of what Booth was up to could not be "distinctly proven." But they would have disavowed knowledge of it in any case and have destroyed all the possible evidence that showed guilty knowledge; and that, Logan argued, at least offered a strong suspicion that they were "not innocent."[44]

Links to the Peace Democrats of the North, who had called for Lincoln's assassination, were too shaky to bring any indictments, but these, too, seemed plausible enough to alarmed Republicans. "Behave yourself in future, boss," the New York Copperhead organ had taunted the president midway through the war, "or we shall be obliged to make an island of your head and stick it on the end of a pole. Then, for the first time, Lincoln's cocoanut will be well posted."[45] Readers pondered over the curious editorial on that same Friday in a Democratic newspaper in Ashland, Pennsylvania, which proposed the decorations for Lincoln's funeral procession—hours before Booth committed his act.[46] Once more the Knights of the Golden Circle earned the credit for deeds that their founder had never imagined.

But were these suspicions so groundless after all? In recent years, some of the hysterics of 1865 have been revived—with endnotes. Able to plumb archives closed to Lincoln's contemporaries, a few scholars have suggested that the conspiracy theorists glimpsed real monsters stirring. A long string of circumstances and possible events has been woven together to show that the conspiracy to kidnap the president and then to assassinate him had backing from the very highest ranks of the Confederate government. Frothier imaginations have found a link to cotton smuggling and the disappointment of the smugglers in their gains being lost. Popular accounts even have fingered radical Republicans, as being fearful that Lincoln would defy their dictates and confident that his successor would not. These studies are marvelous to behold, each apparently proven from firsthand sources, each impossible in view of the other theories' evidence.[47] It is only a wonder that the second gunman on the grassy knoll did not make his appearance, perhaps from the back of Ford's Theater.

Certainly the Confederacy relied on spies and carried on a secret war, hunting for friends and looking at ways of hurting enemies in the civilian North. Jacob Thompson, of the Confederate State Department, had been a master of ingenious schemes and an abettor of troublemakers who could harass the North from the rear. There were plans to break open the prisoner of war camp on Johnson's Island, in Lake Erie, and set Confederate inmates free. Dr. Luke Blackburn of Kentucky had ideas of spreading yellow fever in the North through infected clothing—which might have been effective, if yellow fever actually spread that way.[48] People who would introduce disease into the

North with infected rags might be ready to do anything. Still, the plan's complete failure and the paltry results from the Northwestern Conspiracy and the prison camp liberation scheme show how poor the odds were of keeping any plan secret or making it work.

Kidnapping Lincoln was fantasized about, at least by some white southerners. One Alabaman, who signed his name "George Washington," had written Confederate president Jefferson Davis that the only way to end the war would be to abduct Lincoln, after which Davis could "make him sign any agreement you wish that is right in the sight of God."[49] In the summer of 1864, indeed, a Confederate colonel, Bradley Johnson, thought up a plan to capture the president during General Jubal Early's raid on Washington and bring him back to Richmond. Altogether, the idea seemed brilliant, but Early reassigned Johnson. Nothing came of Johnson's plan. He was deflected into a planned raid on a prisoner of war camp that was so badly gummed up and so widely known on the Union side that it was called off. Super-secret plans always worked as long as they never got close to real people or were applied under actual conditions.[50]

The truth probably is what most of the reliable evidence suggests. Far from being well laid, the actual plot against Lincoln was full of improvisation. Like most conspiracies in the real world, it had to keep adjusting as events outdated it. At one point, John Wilkes Booth had plans to kidnap the president and use him as a hostage to force the release of Confederate prisoners of war. The exchange of prisoners began again, but the kidnapping conspiracy continued, until the hopelessness of the Confederate cause was so clear that no sudden blow could have revived it. Only then did Booth reveal his real aim to kill the president, the vice president, the secretary of state, the secretary of war, and General Grant. Some parts of the plan were vaguer than others. The attempt on the life of Grant and the secretary of war never got beyond theorizing. But the intent to kill Lincoln and Seward was very real, and, as far as the assassins could manage it, it was carried out.

All the same, there is no evidence at all that Booth acted on orders from Richmond — or, after April 2, from wherever the Confederate government happened to be that day. The summer before, he had traveled to Montreal, where Jacob Thompson had been orchestrating his secret war. Perhaps they met — but possibly not. It is improbable that Thompson gave the go-ahead to an assassination that Booth had not yet decided on himself, and it is not absolutely certain that he endorsed a kidnapping attempt. The Confederacy was counting on a Democratic victory to arrange an armistice and perhaps accept Confederate independence. Why abduct a president who was likely to lose within the next few months? A failed attempt would almost certainly stir such a storm up north that Republicans would win in a walk. Secretary of State William Seward had been very nearly right, at least in reference to the public men he knew best, when he dismissed murder threats. "Assassination is not an American practice or habit," he wrote the consul in Paris early in the war, "and one so vicious and so desperate cannot be engrafted into our political system." Perhaps not in ordinary times, but then, as Seward's own scar from ear to chin would show, war provides an excuse for extraordinary methods. The most one can say for sure is that no Confederate leader espoused assassination in principle, and, after the deed was done, some of them at least rushed to express their abhorrence of it.

Booth, on the other hand, was more than willing to allot whatever discredit was due to Confederate authorities—the more so to persuade others to join his conspiracy and convince them that they were part of a very high and noble bit of business serving the Confederate cause. The more they thought that they had backing, the more likely they would be to act with him. Booth, indeed, went out of his way to bring them into the plot by implicating them so deeply, if with circumstantial evidence only, that his capture would certainly mean their own ruin and probable execution as participants in an assassination plot. Several of them were trapped, and in the last days before the fatal act would have withdrawn if they had had the chance.

What, then, motivated Booth? His own diary would answer that question best, along with his own publicly held views. A frank southern sympathizer, the assassin stood with the most extreme Copperheads, imbued with the conviction that the republic itself was in mortal danger, that those in power who had taken freedom away had no intention of handing it back. Lincoln was "Bonaparte in one great move," he raged to his sister, just after the 1864 election, "that is, by overturning this blind Republic and making himself a king. This man's re-election which will follow his success, I tell you—will be a reign! . . . You'll see—you'll see—that re-*election* means *succession*." As a good Shakespearian actor, he knew well the story of Julius Caesar—he had played the role, with his brothers. Now he saw himself as performing the deed that Democratic editors and speakers had all but called for, to perform as an American Brutus. He was not saving the Confederacy; he was saving the republic. If he had had his way, it would have happened on April 13, the Ides of the month, reminding the country of that other assassination, 1,900 years before (as it happened, Booth failed to carry out his plan on the Ides, and sacrificing Lincoln's life on Good Friday offered quite a different analogy for ministers working up their Easter sermons). It made perfect theater: a derringer from the town of Northern Liberties, a dagger with "America, Land of the Free" cut into its blade, and a Latin motto, "Thus ever with tyrants," to drive the historical reference home. Because, like so many Democrats, he saw William Seward as the arch-conspirator, the power behind the throne, the enemy of freedom, Seward, too, must die.[51]

"Until today nothing was ever *thought* of sacrificing to our country's wrongs," the fugitive assassin wrote furiously. "For six months we had worked to capture. But our cause being almost lost, something decisive & great must be done. But its failure was owing to others, who did not strike for their country with a heart. I struck boldly and not as the papers say. . . . I can never repent it, though we hated to kill; Our country owed all her troubles to him, and God simply made me the instrument of his punishment. The country is not what it *was*. This forced union is not what *I* have loved. I care not what becomes of me. I have no desire to out-live my country." A few days later, pursued and finding doors that should have been open closed to him, he wrote, even more wretchedly, "With every man's hand against me, I am here in despair. And why; For doing what Brutus was honored for, what made Tell a hero. And yet I for striking down a greater tyrant than they ever knew am looked upon as a common cutthroat. My action was purer than either of theirs. . . . I struck for my country and that alone. A country groaned beneath this tyranny and prayed for this end. Yet now behold the cold hand they extend to me."[52]

There are two points worth noticing about Booth's plot. First, from the circumstantial evidence and the wider context of what people of Booth's way of thinking were saying, level-headed northerners had reason to suspect a wider political conspiracy. There was no bevy of Brutuses waiting to finish off the president, but there were quite a lot of Booths who talked about drastic means for saving the republic and took their precedents from the ancient Rome where tyrants were put to the knife. Northerners suspected, as it turned out, correctly, that at least some Confederate civilians had assassins' souls, if not assassins' will or opportunity. "Hurrah! Old Abe Lincoln has been assassinated," a diarist rejoiced. "The man we hate has met his proper fate." A cavalryman lauded the conspirators as "heroes of the Confederate revolution" and talked of naming his son Booth. Other southerners certainly did. One of them became doorkeeper in the first Democratic House after the war. Indeed, an occasional onlooker only regretted that the killings had not spread wider. "Assassination is by no means a favorite amusement of mine," a North Carolina woman wrote, "but I think sometimes that it is a pity that Boothe's crazy fit did not last a little longer."[53]

The enthusiasts may have been in a minority down south and positively scarce up north, but threatening language had been easy to find all along.[54] For years, northern Democratic newspapers had uttered veiled invitations to would-be assassins, and often not particularly veiled ones at that. Booth's fury at finding (nearly) every door closed in his face was not so absurd after all. He had made a mistake quite peculiar for an actor: he had taken the words of editors and politicians as sincere and not just as exercises in chewing the scenery. And, presumably, he had taken their insistence that the republic really was in mortal danger from a Caesar seriously enough to feel that something had to be done about it. Nor did that kind of talk end after Lincoln's death. Apologists for the assassination continued to thrill select Democratic listeners for years to come, and their audiences never called them to account. A few stray editors honored John Wilkes Booth: "A young man of generous impulses, fine attainments, manly sentiments, and noble aspirations," who smote "the foul usurper" to free his country from "iron rule." They printed with perfect seriousness a medium's discovery that in the next world Lincoln was a humble shoemaker, with Booth as his foreman. When generals gathered to confer at the health resort in White Sulphur Springs, Virginia, a Democratic newspaper noted that Lincoln had gone to the *red* Sulphur Springs. An Ohio newspaper rejoiced that Lincoln's body had been embalmed. Ten years hence, when politics had returned to normal, it would be in fitter shape to hang "on the gallows tree, as has happened to dead tyrants heretofore." The past only illuminated the future, and some of the noisiest voices said so plainly. Nominate another Lincoln, the *La Crosse (Wis.) Democrat* cried in early 1868, "and the country will produce another John Wilkes Booth, with his sic simper tyrannis, . . . and the man is now even ready for the work!" By no means were the Pomeroys and the Henry Clay Deans with their vaunting language of Lincoln as a tyrant the true voices of Democracy. Even some Democratic newspapers begged the rank and file to shut Dean up or at least stay away. But Dean could always get an audience, and Republicans had some excuse for the *Philadelphia Press*'s gibe that Democrats disapproved of impeaching presidents only because they preferred their own method: assassinating them.[55]

Second, it is striking how easily Booth was able to convince his accomplices that they were part of a much larger design than they could possibly see, with wires running to Richmond and Montreal, and with co-conspirators, invisible for the moment but well-posted on the larger plan. To convince his confidants that there was a "true inwardness" and that the managers at the top were cold-eyed, skilled professionals who knew exactly what they were doing was necessary for the whole conspiracy to be taken seriously; but what Booth told them they had no trouble believing. They, too, had absorbed the American idea that something larger and darker lay behind what the public saw on the surface—its "true inwardness," as the catchphrase went.

The assassination, then, stood by itself as an event, but it had very significant props in what had occurred over the four years before. Years of conspiratorial thinking made it a natural consequence. At the same time, it afforded potent proof that the thinkers' darkest fears had been right all along.

Disbanding the armies took place surprisingly quickly. Dismantling the systematic way that each party read the others' intentions, and that North and South read each others' wartime deeds, would take much longer. Republicans may have been wrong to believe that leading Democrats were in cahoots with treason. They certainly let the wish father the thought, and where they could change ambiguities into certainties, they bent every effort to bend every fact. But believe it they did, and the belief long outlasted the war. There were, former Democratic general John Logan wrote years after that, "elements of proof" that leading congressional Democrats "were trusted Lieutenants of the Supreme Commander of over half a million of Northern Rebel-sympathizers bound together, and to secrecy, by oaths, which were declared to be paramount to all other oaths, the violation of which subjected the offender to a shameful death somewhat like that of being 'hung, drawn, and quartered.'" Logan could not point to a single such offender killed; and the fact that among the number, which was incredible on the face of it, not one admitted to taking such an oath never seems to have deterred him at all. Democratic actions, insisted Logan, were done at the diktat of "their Rebel masters at Richmond." On that plan, to agitate the North, day after day, Democrats rose in House and Senate to air "disloyal opinions" and denounce the government.[56]

The war, then, had not cleared the miasma in the political air. It had intensified it, and with good reason: for four years, proofs of conspiracy had cropped up everywhere. Reconstruction policies might develop through policymakers' calculations of self-interest or by the clash of conflicting ideals and the mingling of separate, insistent issues, but through all the debates would run something else: that profound suspicion of the other side's commitment to preserve liberty and Union. Those who started the war might be preparing for another. Those who menaced American liberty lived on, to finish the fell work left to do. The new iron dome on the Capitol seemed a fitting symbol for an age where peace presaged those two terrible possibilities, iron rule or a new recourse to cold steel.

The prejudices and shams and delusions of
half a century have melted away in the fiery
crucible of war like wax in a flame.
— "Y. S.," Cincinnati Gazette, *June 6, 1865*

The posts coming tiring on,
And not a man of them brings other news
Than they have learn'd of me: from Rumour's
tongues
They bring smooth comforts false, worse than
true wrongs.
—*Rumour, in Shakespeare,* Henry IV, Part 2,
Introduction, lines 37–40

chapter 3

BLACK SCARE

The South after Slavery

The good news came just in time for Emma LeConte of Charleston. By April 1865, not even the most cheerful southern newspaper could deny that Yankee troops had pushed deep into the Cotton South and that Robert E. Lee's army was penned up in Virginia. The Confederacy would need a miracle. But the Confederacy had an ally at last. Determined to protect its new empire in Mexico, France had declared war on the United States. LeConte believed the stories. What troubled her over the next few days was how the particulars kept changing. "A thousand rumors filled the air," she wrote, disenchanted, in early May. "Now the French fleet was at New Orleans—now at Beaufort, now at Georgetown, and finally it was confidently stated that this ubiquitous fleet had defeated the Yankees at Hampton Roads."

Confident statements were a wartime press's stock in trade. Not just in South Carolina, but all the way to Texas, newspapers and rumors gave the fall of the Confederacy an unreal aspect. Northern newspapers muddled their facts, too, of course, and in the confusion of battle, no reporter could be expected to know more than the soldiers thought they did. Generals died on the front page much more often than in real life, and battle casualties were as flexible as gutta-percha—as inflatable as balloons. Northern newspapers might as well have had a lying editor, just to coordinate the flocks of canards sent flying, of defeats turned into victories. But southern newspapers were measurably worse at sifting out the truth from wishful thinking. Some of them discovered in Sherman's march to the sea the retreat of a desperate man, trying to escape his army's destruction, and rejoiced in his taking Savannah: everyone knew that he had intended to seize Augusta and free the prisoners at Andersonville. In Virginia, Grant's army had "melted away," and he could find no replacements. In Georgia, the Confederacy would end the year just as well off as it had begun. And west of the Mississippi River, all the Union forces had been completely destroyed. Much of Virginia, Georgia, and Tennessee had actually been cleared of enemy forces—Atlanta included![1] Such delusions only made the outcome more traumatic. "What is the cause of this sudden crushing collapse," Emma LeConte wrote from Columbia. "I *cannot* understand it."[2]

If anything, the war's conclusion only intensified the tendency to accept misinformation. Desperation breeds the most outlandish hopes, and for Confederates who, until the very end, could not imagine ultimate defeat, the wildest rumors were welcome, when they promised a revolution in events. Word spread that in the last throes of the Confederacy its greatest moment had come. At the end of March, reports reached Pooshee plantation that fifty French ships were blockading Charleston and that the Union forces were about to evacuate the place; a man who had boarded the gunboat to take the oath of allegiance brought the word.[3] Later, the news spread that the French fleet was sailing toward Washington to blockade the city until the United States came to terms and recognized Confederate independence; and foreign navies were even then bombarding New York City. Three weeks after Robert E. Lee's surrender, Henry William Ravenel wrote in his private journal the wonderful news that the French had recognized the Confederacy and had gone to war with the United States; better still, they had just captured New Orleans. Reportedly, General Sherman had proposed an armistice, one of the terms of which was recognition of Confederate independence. "Almost too good to be true," Ravenel wrote. It was, in fact, almost too silly to be believed. But a week later the same tale reached another planter's wife, who had also heard that the French had sunk three gunboats on the Mississippi River. Two weeks after General Joseph Johnston actually had surrendered his forces, Kate Stone, in Tyler, Texas, got word that Johnston had marched on Augusta, Georgia, with 125,000 men and would make a gallant fight. As late as May 13, the rumors about European recognition were still circulating in South Carolina.[4]

Misinformation certainly was not an exclusively southern product. But between northern and southern misapprehension, there was a world of difference, and war's end may have made the gap worse. Northern newspapers could pay an army of reporters to spread across the South to gauge how far the defeated states were reconstructing. They could station reporters at the constitutional conventions and send regular letters from the capitals, but they also collected information from farms and villages. Southern newspapers were lucky to have their own reporter in New York. More coverage than that they could not afford. Confederates were not, as northerners were, inveterate readers of news. Their best papers were nowhere near as fit to give full reportage of events as northern journals had been. New Orleans had the closest equivalents to the newspaper offerings of New York City, but the *New Orleans Times* and the *New Orleans Picayune* served up pale imitations of Manhattan's rich foreign and domestic reporting. Journalism lacked the means, the resources, or the will to do much, and it is significant that the most important southern newspapermen were not associated with the breaking of news but instead with the crafting of clever sayings and cutting epigrams from such people as George Prentice and Henry Watterson—both, significantly, from the northernmost edge of the Border South. The great newsgathering papers of the South were the *Louisville Courier-Journal* and the *Baltimore Sun*. Significantly, too, there were no great southern reporters in Washington that had the national fame that Sidney Andrews ("Dixon") of the *Boston Daily Advertiser* or Henry V. Boynton ("H. V. B.") and Whitelaw Reid ("Agate") of the *Cincinnati Gazette* had. Indeed, for broader coverage of what was happening in the South in 1865, the best investigative journalists came, one and all, from northern cities: Cincinnati, New York, Chicago, and Boston. There were no resources, and no real interest, on the part of southern papers to describe what the South was like and no equivalent for the South of roving reporters catching the spirit of the section—not even of the North.[5]

So, to a large extent, in the months just after the war, the white South went at it blind. Or, rather, it saw with dreadful clarity things that did not exist. But what it thought it saw defined how it would react to events and kept it from taking advantage of the political situation to craft a postwar settlement acceptable to Congress.

Where newspapers did not go and could not give full information, southerners had to rely on report and rumor. Anticipations of the French fleet had no lasting consequences, but impressions about the way slaves took to their new freedom did. These may have been the most important news stories of that first postwar summer, of greater moment than any action out of Washington, the unavoidable topic in every diary and private letter. Especially in the countryside, stories about the freedpeople's stupidity, dishonesty, incapacity, and malice ran full and free: of slave conspiracies that may or may not have happened, of attacks that had not occurred, of atrocities just a neighborhood or two away, of arsonists without number—or corroboration.

Blacks coming into the cities alarmed white residents, who begged local Union garrisons to "secure the remnants of our property still left us" and guard "our wives and daughters" from the "uncurbed animosity and evil passions of a class of people who have never yet known how to govern themselves." As long as too many black people congregated without work or hope of feeding themselves, close by towns where black Union soldiers were stationed, worse than petty crime seemed in the offing. The former slaves were "in reality a volcano—yes, a volcano of insatiable and demonic hatred," a Georgian warned.[6]

Every act of black insolence had a meaning of its own. Jostling between white and black soldiers at an Independence Day celebration in Mobile brought some bruises and bloodied heads, with blacks on the receiving end and with the police using the disturbance as an excuse to collar "colored girls" and force them to choose between "outrage" or arrest. But to one white Mobilian, the brawl foretold "the scenes of San Domingo." Whites must expect to "strike for liberty or death, justice or blood." The "conduct of the negroes" in this neighborhood or that "looks suspicious if not threatening," the *Albany (Ga.) Patriot* warned in September 1865. Former slaves "hold nightly meetings on various plantations, the real object of which their owners have been thus far baffled in all attempts to fathom." The reporter was not so baffled: "By sly hints and murmurs, the white people are given to understand that Christmas will be the time when all differences will be squared and past wrongs righted."[7]

If there had not been rumors, that would have been far more surprising. The South was trying to return to a Union and a Constitution as they had understood it before the war, and it was also returning to the pattern of thought about uprisings that had existed before the war. Slavery had never been able to get by without feeding on fears of abolitionists stirring up their human property. They were always catching suspects. "The murderous designs of these fiend-like fanatics would not only place the firebrand in our dwellings, but prepare their knives for the cutting of our throats," a Louisianan wrote in 1835. Mobs seized, whipped, and killed, and almost always, after the act, newspapers asserted that the proofs of conspiracy were beyond dispute. Every few years, the South would panic over supposed plots by slaves. In thirty years, well over four hundred people were killed, nearly all of them slaves.

Rumor connected Nat Turner's uprising with "500 Yankees," none of which could be identified or were ever caught. A panic the year before began when there were reports that an antislavery pamphlet had fallen into slaves' hands. No proof of any uprising ever surfaced, but North Carolina vigilantes beat hundreds of slaves and killed several dozen more. Slaves were put under the lash until they confessed whatever was demanded of them, and their words were used as proof that "nearly all negroes" in this county or that had taken part in the plot. Fears were intensified by the general practice of silencing any doubters. Those who protested mob action became victims of mobs themselves or were accused of being thieves, abolitionists, and agitators. "The school boys have become so excited by the sport of hanging Abolitionists, that the schools are completely deserted," a Texan boasted.[8] Now that blacks were freer to move and commune with each other and Yankees were in plentiful supply down south and with federal troops present to afford at least the appearance of acting as a deterrence against vigilante justice, white southerners must have felt that the slave time terrors were worse than ever.

Two assumptions fed off each other. Among blacks, the feeling grew stronger that there would be a redistribution of land down south at the end of the planting season and again around the usual end-of-the-year holiday that slavery had permitted, at and after Christmastime. Federal officers marveled at how quickly the rumors spread.

The rumors were based on very real facts. There had been promises of re-distribution, and there were laws on the books—notably the Confiscation Act of 1862—that might have made a wider distribution quite possible and quite legal. In the Sea Islands, the redistribution checkered a thirty-mile swath, spreading from Charleston to Florida, under General William T. Sherman's field order. Abandoned property, plantations innumerable, were being worked by black labor and being treated almost as if the freedpeople, and not the old owners, held title.[9]

Nor, freedmen protested, did freedom really mean much without real economic independence. Gang labor could not give it; wage labor and coerced contracts gave them nothing. But with land, they could be their own masters, indeed. A few of them staked off parts of their old masters' plantations. Others, unable to accept that ground tilled by them for years could be alienated completely, planted even after they were told that the titleholders would claim it, crop and all. No lasting redistribution happened, or very nearly none. Already by the fall of 1865, the abandoned properties were being reclaimed and, with federal help, restored. Johnson's amnesty proclamations had that effect, at least. The Freedmen's Bureau made very clear that its first purpose was to "regulate labor" and not to make a new deal in the allotment of land.[10]

Yet the rumors continued and strengthened. Word spread that a "head man" would make freedpeople "more free" come Christmas.[11] But the rumors of land redistribution meant that blacks held off on signing new contracts until the start of the year. "There seems to be a general agreement & concert of action among them throughout the South to refuse contracting for next year," Henry William Ravenel confided to his diary in early December.[12] Or could that concert of action have larger ends? Their reluctance only increased white fears that this refusal to sign was based on a determination to open the year in quite a new way—by taking their lands by force or by other acts of violence, a Christmas uprising. That was how a planter near the Great Pedee River understood the facts. "The Negroes have made up their minds that land is to be given them at New Year's," he told a traveler, "and of course it will be a great disappointment to them when they find out that time has gone by and nothing has been done for them." Families near the coast would be murdered and some property destroyed. That would start "the work of extermination." All of this had what passed for confirmation. The planter's nephew had been told by somebody that a black person had blurted out "that there hadn't been any war to what there would be." "You mark me," a white farmer near Lynchburg warned a reporter, "thar'll be a heap of trouble when Christmas comes, when the end o' the year comes, and the niggers' time is out that they's hired for."[13]

From Noxubee County, grim news came to Mississippi's governor. With 16,000 blacks and only 5,000 whites at most, the county was at the mercy of the former slaves. The white company of U.S. troops had withdrawn and incidents had broken out, of unmistakable import:

> Mr. Bird Joy, a man well known for his prudence and humanity, was driven from his plantation by the Freedmen for attempting to institute a search upon his own plantation for meat which had been feloniously killed the night before. . . . In the eastern portion of this county the Freedmen have been holding large meetings at night in which they gravely discuss the ways and means by which they could acquire & hold possession of the states of Alabama, Mississippi, Louisiana and Texas. These meetings are largely attended and the negroes are well armed. Well authenticated reports reach us almost every day and from every portion of this Prairie Country, that the negros are preparing for a collision with the white races, determined in no wise to be subject to the owners of the plantations upon which they have heretofore resided. An idea prevails among them that the lands of the country are to be equally distributed and all who now hires himself for another year are to be in some way branded or returned to bondage. . . . Threats of violence and rapine are made constantly upon our

streets by both citizen negros and the colored soldiers and no disposition is manifested to conceal their disgust for the white population.[14]

Citizens in Panola County were just as alarmed. There, the withdrawal of black soldiers had alarmed freedpeople into expecting that it was the prelude to a white move to reenslave them. Agitators were urging them "to begin at an early day, perhaps about Christmas, a massacre of the whites, in order to ensure their freedom," and assuring them "that if the whites are got out of the way here, that then they will have no further apprehension—& that this Country will then be given to them by the northern people forever as an inheritance." Thousands of Colt revolvers had come south since the war's end. Whites had not bought them, but somebody had, the *Memphis Appeal* told readers. "This is known."[15]

Elsewhere, too, it seemed, blacks were meeting by night and drilling. Some of their gatherings were fraternal assemblies, and others were held to talk politics. They met by night because it would not have been safe to gather by day, and because, working in the fields as most of the men were, they could not spare the time. But the very fact that the coming together was after dark brought up all the most sinister possibilities. Everywhere there were reports that the meetings were military conspiracies. The blacks had muskets and shotguns. They were drilling for future action. Some workers carried their guns to the fields daily. To anxious whites, a Negro insurrection would make the Civil War look like a schoolyard scuffle. As one North Carolina merchant worried, "Total annihilation would be the war cry on both sides." A war of the races must mean the extermination of one race or the other; it could end nowhere else. In such a war, there were no bystanders and there would be no rules.[16] "We speak advisedly," an editor informed readers; "we have authentic information of the speeches and conversations of the blacks, sufficient to convince us of their purpose. *They make no secret of their movement.* Tell us not that we are alarmists." In the Carolina upcountry, residents grew panicky as autumn advanced. "Some think already of removing to the cities about Christmas holiday times and thus be more protected of the most feared period, the first of January," A. Beaufort Simms wrote from Columbia.[17]

White southerners expected the worst, even without evidence. It had been an article of their faith that slavery was necessary, because two races could not possibly coexist on terms of equality. Only by the severest of subordination could one race keep the other from striving to dominate. Only by slavery could natural savages be bred into Christian behavior—whatever civilization they had, slavery's coercion had imposed upon them. Freedom would remove all restraint from a race that knew no restraints from within. It would begin the fight for mastery, and this could mean only violence. That violence, once begun, had no known stopping place, no assured end. Freedom "will begin the work of extermination," a South Carolina planter wrote.[18]

Anything seemed possible, because in the summer of 1865 many masters discovered that slaves whose gratitude and docility they had counted on had been concealing their real feelings all the time. Letters and diaries express the shock of white southerners at finding out that people they had grown up with were strangers—people whose character and intentions had remained wholly beyond their ken. This provoked cries about Negro ingratitude for all the kindnesses of slavery and almost no reflection that masters might have blinded themselves in their own perceptions of how benevolent the institution of slavery was.[19] But if whites could have understood blacks so little, then one of the bulwarks of their security was gone. To understand the black mind was to hold the outposts for white self-protection. Those who knew their freedmen's hearts would have advance warning before a blow fell. Now they had no guideposts to rely upon. An unknown world made for a frightening one. The whole race had become "worse than Devels," a South Carolinian wrote the president. "If they don't massacre the white Race, it is not because the desire don't exist."[20] Troops must be sent, before the inevitable outbreak.

Every small action of the freedpeople came freighted with meaning. Blacks speaking together in whispers boded no good. Daring to speak up loudly with each other boded still worse. "Uncivil words" hinted at uncivilized minds, and a South Carolina landowner was positively alarmed when his people did their assigned work of slaughtering the hogs. They did it with such "fiendish eagerness!" Their "delight in the suffering of others" might extend further than the assigned task, and, given the chance, they might "stab & kill" others besides four-legged victims. There were ill omens when former slaves refused to abide by curfew hours on the old plantation and "cut up sometimes until ten or eleven," a doctor warned the local military commander. They would even sing and dance. A black girl told the doctor's mother that she would resist, if she were given a whipping. Put together, signs like that promised "an outbreak at any moment," and without troops to protect him, this doctor would have to flee his plantation for the safety of the nearby town. A Georgia planter sensed "conspiracies." What could it mean when former slaves sang together in their quarters? To a Columbia woman, it conjured up images of that "horde pouring into our houses to cut our throats and dance like fiends over our remains."[21]

Small incidents became signs of larger purposes, and isolated events linked into patterns. An old musket in a freedman's house became a great cache of arms for secret black armies. A hunter in the woods looking for squirrels became an army gunning for masters. In the Louisiana low country, whites trembled at authoritative reports of regiments of black cavalry organizing and drilling. Federal officials scoured the landscape and caught up with the culprits, "some negro boys . . . playing soldier, with wooden swords."[22]

Fear spread further because of the news from Jamaica. A riot in a provincial capital that left a few dozen dead was followed by a military crackdown with hundreds of executions. The first dispatches came on authority, with Governor Eyre reporting "a most serious and alarming insurrection." Used selectively, the news from the Caribbean fit very well with Democratic warnings that blacks, if set free, would begin a war of races, menacing women and children, and confirmed that the former slaves were unfit for any more than a tightly controlled and truncated liberty. Newspapers like the *New York World* had a strong political interest in finding and spreading exactly that kind of story, not only to keep the white South fearful of Republican intentions but also to stir up the white vote in the North against a growing movement for Negro suffrage.

So the news out of Jamaica was an all-too-expected horror—10,000 whites were at the mercy of 315,000 blacks and 75,000 mulattoes, the *New York World* cried. The outbreak "evidently has been long contemplated, and is intended to be a war of extermination."[23] Nor were these newly freed slaves who were repaying old scores. They were blacks given all the rights and powers that wild-eyed northerners wanted to give to American freedmen. No concession had tamped down their "fiendish passions and barbarian ferocity." Black men insisted that the island should be all their own—that no white should live there, even on terms of equality. The scenes that resulted were "worthy the original negrodom of Ashantee or Dahomey." Heads were cut off, bellies were ripped open, and women shrieked for violence as implacably as did the men.[24] Clearly, no help, no education, no missions for moral improvement could change a Negro. Let the South be warned! "A people steeped in beastly immorality, and on the declivity towards heathenism, ought not to be made voters." Indeed, laws must keep them from owning land, or the cotton kingdom would fall into the ruin that Jamaica's sugar plantations had come to.[25] Not that white southerners needed the warning. They had read the accounts, too. "Any wrong, real or imaginary, even a blunder or erroneous suggestion of over-zealous friends in Northern States may cause scenes of bloodshed such as have lately been exhibited in Jamaica," former Confederate official Clement C. Clay wrote the president from his prison cell in Fortress Monroe. "To borrow Mr. Jefferson's figure, the South no longer holds the wolf by the ears—he is loose & she must keep ever on the watch." Never had white southerners needed the national government as its "guardian" so much, "especially where there is a large negro population."[26]

But both the premises and the background for the Jamaica disturbances were wrong. Out of 441,264 people, only 2,000 were permitted to vote, and then only for assemblymen. The school system provided for freedmen was pitifully small; the government spent thirty times as much on salaries for its local officers. Denied a right to the land, former slaves had been forced to work in a degrading serfdom disguised under the slightly more appealing title, "tenancy at will." This was not equality, nor anything like it. Far from being a terrible insurrection with "fiends thirsting for human blood," the government had found a local outbreak that turned bloody only after soldiers fired on a crowd of demonstrators. The riot was quelled before the day's end. There were no battles, not so much as a skirmish, against Her Majesty's soldiery or the colonial militia. The reign of terror on the island was committed by the white authorities against the black population, and black atrocities were exaggerated or concocted to justify the stern measures that the colonial governor used against his subjects. As later evidence showed, the turbulence on the first day had been used by the planters and the governor to commit

> the most shameful murders and floggings and indiscriminate destruction of negro villages, all of which was done upon a people who made no sort of resistance. After these English gentlemen had "catted" hundreds of women as well as men, and had hanged or otherwise killed over two thousand people, after reporting themselves surrounded by "thousands" of armed and desperate rebels, and in the most imminent peril, after describing great bands of insurgents traversing different districts, pillaging and murdering the defenceless planter's families, their Governor and leader shamelessly confesses that "not a lady or child has been hurt," and "not a single casualty has befallen any of our soldiers or sailors, and they are all in good health."[27]

The truth never caught up with the stories that sped south. White masters needed no reminder from the *New York Herald* that Jamaica stood as "a terrible warning of what may occur here, and what bloody scenes may be enacted" if radicals even dared discuss the issue of Negro suffrage in the future. A year after the initial tales had been refuted, the *Charleston Mercury* was still warning that without stern white control black barbarism would realize in America "the condition of Jamaica and Hayti."[28]

Even some defenders of the freedpeople expected terrible events. The *Christian Recorder*, the voice for the African Methodist Church, worried at the danger in army recommendations that former slaves stay and work for their old masters: The government had taught blacks to fight and if need be to kill their masters; it had armed them. They could never live close by and in harmony ever again. Violence was sure to happen. A Union officer told one northern traveler that if occupation troops were taken out of Virginia, either blacks would be reduced to worse than slavery or there would be a Negro insurrection, and a Mississippi agent for the American Missionary Association thought the same.[29]

How much truth was there in the rumormongering? In regard to political mobilization, there was a great deal; concerning preparations for race war, there was little or none. From Georgetown, South Carolina, the military commander reported that most of the fears of an insurrectionary spirit being roused in the freedmen by black troops amounted to nothing. He admitted that blacks had larger expectations "than it will be possible to gratify," but, he added, that was not an "unusual state of things in political bodies," and they meant to reach their ends by petitioning and memorializing the government into action.[30]

A Freedmen's Bureau officer checked out reports of one supposed militia company on a plantation in upstate South Carolina. He saw some forty men, women, and children lined up near a cabin, some shouldering sticks, others with gun stocks or gun barrels, and others with nothing at all. The few complete firearms could do everything but fire—the case with every other story, upon his investigation.[31] An alleged black secret society in Atlanta, supposedly formed to foment trouble with the white people, was in reality an association to care for the sick, to raise money for a colored hospital, and to find homes for the homeless. A northern businessman in Louisiana met rumor with common sense. If blacks meant to rise, they would have risen already, "so great are the injuries inflicted upon them in one or another manner." With word of "numberless atrocities" against the freedmen coming to him in Mississippi, he found it far likelier that whites were deliberately goading blacks into desperate acts, the better to find an excuse "to turn upon them and annihilate them."[32]

No insurrection happened, and Christmas came quietly. A "negro riot" in Alexandria proved, upon examination, to be former Confederate soldiers, stoked with bad whiskey and firing off their guns at any dark-skinned person who happened to be on the streets.[33] White observers who never expected trouble reminded their friends of their own level-headedness, and others denied that they had really believed the wild talk after all. The meetings for New Year's Day at which the final details of the uprising would be fixed proved to be rallies for celebrating Lincoln's Emancipation Proclamation, issued three years before to the day. Speakers exhorted blacks to use their freedom responsibly and well. Ministers offered prayers. Freedmen's Bureau officers told those gathered to work hard and save their money to buy land. In Charleston, the meeting closed not in cries for the master's blood but in a crowd of 10,000 joining to sing,

> The year of jubilee has come,
> Return, ye ransomed sinners home.[34]

"It appears that there has been a great alarm without any cause," the Reverend Samuel A. Agnew wrote from Mississippi. If anything, the Christmas panic may have stripped some of the respect away from whites that blacks had been inclined to give them. "As affairs have turned out the negro must think that the white people are afraid of them."[35] Army commanders hoped that lessons were learned the other way. "Christmas week has passed, and the dreaded and much-talked-of insurrection of which you never dreamed has not come," General Davis Tillson told a convention of Georgia's freedpeople:

> You have given still another proof that you can not, as a race, be even goaded to acts of violence and murder, that as in the days of the rebellion, . . . you are the same, kind, gentle, trusting people, putting far from you all the suggestions of hatred and revenge, patiently waiting for the hand of the Lord to bring your deliverance, and looking to him to avenge your wrongs. In this respect you have a history, and a record, unsurpassed in the annals of the human race.[36]

Whites were writing a very different history, and their fears of a Christmas uprising encouraged them to shoot, rob, and ransack freedpeople's houses. "The Rebbles are going a bout in many places through the State and robbing the colered peple of arms money and all they have and in many cases killing," Calvin Holley wrote the commissioner of the Freedmen's Bureau:

> They talk of taking the armes a way from [black] people and arresting them and put them on farmes next month and if they go at that I think there will be trouble and in all probability a great many lives lost. They have been accusing the colered peple of an insorection which is a lie, in order that they might get arms to carrie out their wicked designs—For to my own knowledge I have seen them buying arms and munitions ever since the lines have been opened and carrying them to the country.[37]

It was not just in fear that white vigilante gangs during the Christmas season disarmed every black they could find, broke into their houses, and confiscated guns. Blacks without the means to defend themselves would have no protection against intimidation and might come more readily to terms in making contracts. But the fear was present. White governors mustered the militia into force again, but local, unofficial militia were already appearing everywhere. Often they were no more than vigilante gangs, often modeled on the old slave patrols, and with much the same function—to keep blacks in line and to crush out their assertion of rights as freemen. But of course they were also meant for protection and as scouts for the first signs of an uprising. In South Carolina, Governor Benjamin F. Perry asked the General Assembly to reorganize the state militia, to forestall "insurrection and domestic violence," and by early November the appropriate legislative committee had prepared its recommendations, quite explicitly with the former slaves in mind: Armed might was needed, because blacks had "become so thoroughly contaminated with false notions as to their rights." Just after New Year's, lawmakers put the militia under the command of former major general Martin W. Gary of Edgefield. There and elsewhere, patrol laws were strengthened and adjusted. Towns expanded the number of police. Counties mustered makeshift, unofficial militia companies on their own, usually made of ex-Confederates and directed by "gentlemen."[38] The federal army received a barrage of requests for guns and applications to form white military units for self-protection. Under pressure from alarmed white landowners, commanders were instructed to make it emphatically clear to the freedmen that they must expect no land. Rather, the army would use its influence to see that they signed labor contracts and would enforce them. The sped-up pace at which black soldiers were mustered out sent its own message, that in any clash, white soldiers would stand behind the masters' titles, not with the freedmen's aspirations. Union soldiers, in some places, joined the patrols or carried out the sweeps for arms, and in Wilmington, the local commander urged the citizenry to form voluntary military companies for their own protection. The "entire power of his command" was at their disposal, guns and ammunition included.[39]

Fear alone did not inspire southern legislatures to pass the Black Codes, which defined ex-slaves' freedom within narrow limits. These laws were aimed at forcing blacks to labor, if possible for their old masters, and forbade them from acting as witnesses against whites. Black children could be "apprenticed" into forced labor without compensation, and black adults could be classified as vagrants and set to work, under laws so vaguely phrased that they would allow regular roundups of freedpeople at harvest season. These laws were not the immediate results of fear, any more than were the penalties of the whipping post and sale at public auction meted out exclusively to black defendants. Hatred, resentment, contempt, and the conviction that free black labor could not continue without the most rigid controls all explain the Black Codes. But behind them also lay the fear that any step toward equality would make other steps easier. The closer the races came to equality, the greater seemed the likelihood of violence, and not just with blacks as victims and corpses. Unsurprisingly, then, the Black Codes took away the right to bear arms among the freedpeople, and local law enforcement looked for excuses to take their guns away. White southerners were alarmed especially at the prospect that they would no longer be able to disarm blacks, under the federal civil rights law. This ability they saw as essential.[40]

There was a war of races, to be sure. In that, white southerners were correct. But the victims were black and the perpetrators were white. For any harsh comments that former slaves made about white people, and northern correspondents who had come south found few, there were plenty of bloodthirsty and brutal comments about blacks. John Richard Dennett, traveling to Charleston, heard a planter family regaling themselves with reports that Yankee officers were making "short work" of uppity black soldiers. "I wish they'd shoot 'em all," the lady of the house exclaimed. "If I could get up tomorrow morning, and hear that every nigger in the country was dead, I'd just jump up and down." Her husband was less certain. "They'll go fast enough for me if they last a few years longer," he remarked.[41]

Deeds matched words. By the winter of 1866, a spate of reports had come north that showed a real reign of terror against black freedpeople, unnoted in the press and unpunished in the courts. From Texas, Assistant Commissioner E. M. Gregory of the Freedmen's Bureau counted cases "by hundreds, ranging from downright murder, savage beatings, merciless whippings, hunting men with trained bloodhounds, through all the lesser degrees of cruelty and crime." Matters were worst in the interior, wrote the bureau's inspector general. There, fearing no arrest or punishment, whites shot blacks "like wild beasts, without any provocation." A few sportsmen killed just "to see a d——d nigger kick" or because they wanted to prove their good aim. Three blacks died because, their killers explained, they needed to "thin the niggers out and drive them to their holes." The upper South may have been less violent, but even there army officers counted hundreds of cases of injustice.[42]

The black scare did not end in 1865 or 1866, any more than did the butchery. Because contracts gave out at year's end and blacks became footloose with their future intentions unpredictable, planters always dreaded the Christmas season. So many people set at liberty without contract or commitment for the year ahead were tinder, just waiting for a spark. They could meet together more easily, and always the doubt was revived of whether they would contract at all when the time came—though they always did. James Sparkman, managing a South Carolina plantation, went to town at season's end in 1866 and took part in secret talks with a few "respectable citizens" who had uncovered "an insurrectionary movement, wide spread and terrible in its plot." Every man and child would be put to death on one unknown night in the next two months. Women would be spared "for servile and licentious purposes." As summer came to an end, South Carolina planter John D. Palmer had his ears filled with a dire tale from a former slave "in whose truthfulness he ha[d] reasons for confidence." One Johnson had been said to be visiting black dwellings all around the neighborhood and advising the men to make "military companies" just like those being set up along the Santee River. He had found takers, too. Three of Palmer's own employees became officers. The more Palmer looked, the worse things seemed. Sworn sources that did not want to be identified by name told him that those companies from the Santee meant to march to Barnwell courthouse, growing in numbers of local recruits as they traveled. Their object was "to kill every white man they could find, and take what they wanted."[43]

All through 1867 there were reports that the newly formed Union Leagues were more than recruiting agencies for a biracial Republican Party. They were paramilitary groups, out to prepare the blacks for warfare. "I beg to represent to your Excellency our unsafe situation, from threats made by freedmen, who say they have been promised land and if it is not given to them they will have it by fighting, and such bloody times were never before seen in this country," an alarmed Virginia farmer wrote the president in November. "They are well armed and are buying largely of the country stores the heaviest shot & musket caps & also say it will take place soon."[44] As the Union Leagues spread, so did the reports of freedmen mustering and drilling. Armed Union Leaguers had been seen going to meetings and later going armed and in groups to the polls. In Alabama, local citizens panicked when Union Leaguers brought a fire engine to their parade. Some onlookers thought it was an artillery piece, and others thought that it was hollow and "at a signal would disgorge ferocious blood thirsty niggers to cry havoc and at once to proceed to steal, pillage, rob, burn, revenge, & kill everything before them."[45]

Militia companies there certainly were. Field gangs had tried out precision marches in upstate South Carolina at the time of the 1865 harvest, apparently imitating the colored infantry stationed nearby. The trappings and ceremonies of military companies certainly seemed to be a plausible indication that if freedmen could form armed bands they would do so. By late 1866, blacks in

Charleston were parading "in full Zouave uniform" and, following the ritual so common with regiments at the start of the Civil War, accepted a "beautiful banner" from the women of the community, with becoming ceremony. The one thing they lacked, it seemed, was weapons. There was no reason for white onlookers to doubt that those would come out into the open when needed. Marching companies trooped back from work in the fields to the beat of a tin pan, for lack of a drum, and army officers in the countryside reported troops of blacks, well drilled and armed with fowling pieces, clubs, and cornstalks. These were hardly armaments to strike fear into the hearts of the far more heavily armed white population, but they were not all that reassuring either. Federal authorities had documented cases of the military societies imposing discipline on wrongdoers in the black community, bringing thieves to justice and in one Carolina county catching three hoodlums who had beaten up a black minister for belonging to "the d——d Abolition church." It seemed like the beginning, though only a bare beginning, of a separate system of force, defense, and law.[46]

In fact, the number of incidents in which freedmen used their arms at all, much less on whites, proved to be very few. It was quite true that blacks often went armed in public, but so, far more often, did whites. It was, as some northern observers noted, a southern phenomenon, and one that neither side could abandon, because of fear of the other. A local Freedmen's Bureau agent tried to determine the truth about one marching company along South Carolina's Santee River. Members admitted belonging to "armed organizations" but made clear that their purposes were purely defensive. "They avow their purpose to be the protection of their rights," he reported.[47] When blacks carried their guns to the polls it was not to intimidate whites so much as to prevent whites from intimidating them or, as one white historian admitted, to array themselves in so solid a body "that no white influence could reach them."

The Union League's white organizers did not encourage blacks to arm, and many of them tried to prevent it, fearful that it would do much more harm than good. In a crisis, whites always could outgun them and would welcome the excuse to do so. Secrecy was one way of preventing violence—unfriendly whites could not break up meetings that they had not heard about until afterward.[48] If they came to Union League meetings, let it be without arms, John Keffer begged freedmen. Some meetings opened with a stacking of arms near the podium or on it, and Keffer refused to speak to one gathering until this had been done. In some places, activists persuaded blacks to drop their plans for forming a military company. It was the blacks themselves who led the way in

"The Civil Rights Scare Is Nearly Over." Thomas Nast, *Harper's Weekly*, May 22, 1875. Drawing on a well-known hoax, Nast shows the blacks as wild beasts let loose from the zoo, to the terror of white geese. His point was that fears of the blacks as savages were the result of rascals playing on the gullibility of fools. The specific occasion was a civil rights bill that was all but dead, eight years before the Supreme Court knocked it down entirely, but the image fitted a long-standing situation. Ten years before, there had been geese aplenty.

seeking a chance to arm and drill, not their white leaders. Some local chapters of the league would march in military fashion with or without guns.

And arming, they believed, was necessary, because neither the authorities of the law nor the white communities would do anything to protect them. With the rise of the Ku Klux Klan, it became clear that most sheriffs were afraid to act, and most federal troops—what few there were—would most likely arrive too late to do more than make a belated response to terrorism. State after state drew up plans for creating a militia and then put the plans away lest white Democrats be further enraged at the sight of blacks in uniform. Thus, if blacks did not arm themselves, they stood little chance of any real protection.[49]

There were no black insurrections, there were few riots in which blacks were the sole instigators, and there were fewer still in which blacks did not do most of the dying. But that was not the Reconstruction that whites read of in the conservative press and probably believed. Every white murder was denied or justified with the present threat of black violence. "With Loyal Leagues in every precinct, whose sentinels stand armed with government muskets," the *Montgomery Mail* screamed in late 1867, with an actual negro insurrection at Perote; with a recent negro mob at Union Springs, where a Northern adventurer pretended to have been shot; with an actual mob and threats to burn the town of Greensboro, when a negro was recently killed; with an army of negroes marching upon Columbus, Miss., to sack the stores; with another battalion of negroes organized to sack and burn the towns of Marion and Meridian; with a negro loyal league firing upon a company of young men in South Carolina; with negro mobs driving whites from the street cars in New Orleans; with a negro mob applauding Hunnicutt when he declared that the streets would run with blood; with a league at Richmond and Charleston which orders whites from those cities; with a negro mob . . . in Montgomery dispersed by Federal sabers; with a negro mob at Hayneville calling out . . . that "the thing has commenced"; with another mob at Tuskegee assailing the jail and threatening to rescue criminals; with another mob at Kingston threatening the lives of officers who attempted to make arrests — with a radical party which attempts to clothe these with supreme power . . . with all these facts before them, we consider the remarks of . . . the other assassins of our liberty, as the very inspiration of insanity or desperation.[50]

A war of the races was seen as always imminent, which certainly impaired white judgment. And that fear remained a persistent part of the white psyche for long after Reconstruction was under way. Every race riot attested to its power and impact. Every uprising was based on excuses and explanations of black military operations — intended, planned, prepared, and, somehow, never actually implemented. But the fears gave a license for white responses and to overt violence. Every race riot seemed to begin with stories about black conspiracies. A riot in Falmouth, Virginia, created what one conservative newspaper called "the most intense excitement and dread. The people [white people] are dreadfully alarmed." The unspoken assumption was that blacks had started it or planned reprisals. The casualty figures — fifteen blacks killed outright and one white slightly wounded — told the real story of who the aggressors were. "'Order has been partially restored,' we are told," a skeptical newspaper commented. "Probably when the rest of the colored people have been murdered, it will be entirely restored." But that, as other editors pointed out, was always the way. Before any massacre of blacks, the southern wire service hummed with news of black armies, mustering in secret to fall upon the white communities, or of a "war of races" begun by the Negroes. Only later, after the notion of black aggressors had been fully planted, did the numbers come out, with the supposed aggressors making up most of the victims.[51]

The siege mentality gave the white conservative South an instinctive distrust of change, for fear of where it would lead. That sense of danger was heightened by the other aspect of proslavery thinking—uprisings usually happened when outsiders, white agitators, brought on trouble. Fanatics and mushy philanthropists inspired the blacks in Jamaica. Who could doubt that countless agents were working for the same ends among the freedmen? For never had so many northerners come barging into the South: schoolteachers, Freedmen's Bureau officers, soldiers, Yankee would-be planters, and black soldiers. Never had so many brought egalitarian notions with them. "There are many John Browns yet in this South land of ours," a Memphis newspaper warned. "They are prowling about the country, on their hellish missions; bent on mischief, and ready at all times to stir up that strife in which alone they can live."[52]

But these emissaries were seen as only the advance troops for the real enemy of the white South, the one that lay to the north. Former Confederates had only surrendered their armies, not their assumptions about just what motivated northern politicians. They returned to the Union as convinced as ever that the force driving the antislavery agitators had been sinister—not so much a crusade to expand human liberty as to constrict white freedoms, a view that the conservative Unionists among them shared. In the meetings and speeches for Negro suffrage, they saw a threat to freedom itself. The "tide of fanaticism is pressing you heavily in the North and there is danger if yielded to that this nation will go down in blood," a Louisville attorney warned the president. The very people whose grandparents had nosed out witchcraft were behind it all, but that was to be expected: all history showed that American liberty was never safe under northerners. Always the "active & ingenious mind of the North" threatened the liberty of the citizen and the government's very existence, unless controlled. As one right was impinged upon, it opened the way to violate another. No northerner had been reelected president except Lincoln, "and he did not survive it 60 days after his inauguration, showing in the judgment of this nation . . . that Northern men & Northern minds won't do to administer this government."[53]

The war had proven the North's unfitness, and southern editors now accepted those assumptions when reading the intentions of those northerners setting the terms of peace. They spoke of military tyranny, of conspirators—Radicals—in the Congress, subversive of all the rights and freedoms of the old Union. That much, at least, the war had taught them, and there had been evidence enough. Creative uses of the loyalty oath had put the border slave states under tighter Unionist control. Military satraps had decreed elections and supervised constitutional conventions, and executive fiat had recognized bogus state governments in the formerly occupied Confederate South. Coming out of the war, it was only natural, on seeing the perpetrators of these outrages in power, to presume that they were still the same conspirators as ever, bent on achieving their ends, even among the ruins of a republic that they had plundered and defiled.

The menace was no more real than the Christmas uprising or the French invasion, but that made it no less potent a force. By December 1865, whites in the former Confederate South saw themselves under a double siege, conspired against from below and from above. The fog of war had given way to the mist of peace.

> *What is the "life of the nation,"—of the*
> *United States? Plainly nothing else but the*
> *Constitution.*
> —New York World, *March 14, 1864*

chapter 4

HAVE WE A CONSTITUTION?

As the news of Lee's surrender came south, white southerners puzzled about what it all meant for them. Many assumed that there would be negotiations between the Confederate government and that of the United States to work out a reunion, unaware that the Confederate government had dissolved and that the whole point of the war for the North had been that there could not *be* any lawful Confederate authority. No doubt the talks were going on between authorities on either side, Henry Ravenel wrote hopefully; there was no report, but necessarily they would be kept secret until an agreement had been worked out. Probably "our institution of slavery as it existed before the war with some modifications, may be retained," Ravenel surmised, "& amendments to the Constitution defining the Rights of the States." Or, conceivably, the southern states would call conventions "with a view of returning." Better still, all the states could call a convention to work out the terms of reunion. Georgian exile Kate Stone, in Texas, had darker delusions. "Another month and our Confederacy will be a Nation no longer," she wrote in mid-May, "but we will be slaves, yes slaves of the Yankee Government." In fact, the Confederate nation had been nonexistent for a month, but news traveled slowly to Texas.[1]

The war may have brought a new birth of freedom, but the old dreads, very much alive, attended the christening. From our long view, that wariness seems dafter than it did at the time. Things had turned out much better than the fearmongers had foreseen. The disunionist conspiracy had been foiled. Those ringleaders not locked up, dead, or discredited had skipped the country. Jefferson Davis himself had been captured. Press canards described the former Confederate president "running through bush and through briar, in the cumbrous disguise of hooped skirts" and complaining to his captors that "he had thought the government too magnanimous to chase women." Arch-conspirators who go in for cross-dressing rarely pose much of a threat thereafter. Human ogres ended up in Madame Tussaud's, but the petticoats that Davis supposedly wore became a must-have curiosity for P. T. Barnum's circus.[2] With an excuse to shut down the political process, the North had held a presidential election, right on schedule. The mammoth army that might have snuffed out freedom held a grand march in May 1865—and went home. The republic stood and had withstood.

Over several generations, Americans understood the war's meaning in just that way, but it did not come so naturally in 1865, for the very good reason that the war had exposed how right the warnings had been. The republic *had* been in danger; secret assassins *had* been plotting; dissidents *had* been jailed. Free government had not been killed, but it had been wounded, and nobody could be sure how deep the wounds went. Four years of dark, bloody deeds could only intensify the search for subversives: the ghosts of Caesars in Washington, of white Catilines and black Spartacuses in the South.

The first place to look, needless to say, would be at the scene of the crime, around the Constitution itself. To understand the fears for the republic at the end of the war, it is essential to understand the abstract arguments about constitutionalism that went along with the very real problem of reunion. The Constitution did matter. It was a living document to those who fought over the meaning of the Union, reinforced in sermons, tracts, and speeches on all sides. Never had Democrats invoked the Constitution so regularly or with such fervor as at the end of this war. "What is the 'life of the nation,'—of the United States?" the *New York World* demanded. "Plainly nothing else but the Constitution." Making a perfectly consistent case for any constitutional remedy was no easy task, but Americans could not leave the theoretical alone. As in the war, they wanted any settlement to be able to use true constitutional doctrine as a touchstone.[3]

Orestes Brownson, with his tidy legal mind, allowed that the complexities of constitutional theory after the war were baffling to the public mind:

Are the States that seceded States in the Union, with no other disability than that of having no legal governments? or are they Territories subject to the Union? Is their reconstruction their erection into new States, or their restoration as States previously in the Union? Is the power to reconstruct in the States themselves? or is it in the General Government? If partly in the people and partly in the General government, is the part in the General government in Congress or in the Executive? If in Congress, can the Executive, without the authority of Congress, proceed to reconstruct, simply leaving it for Congress to accept or reject the reconstructed State? If the power is partly in the people of the disorganized States, who or what defines that people, decides who may or may not vote in the reorganization?

No wonder, as he complained, that thinkers and policymakers indulged in "much crude, if not erroneous thinking, and much inconsistent and contradictory action."[4]

If the states were sovereign, as John C. Calhoun had insisted, and had made the Union, rather than the Union giving them being, then secession simply dissolved the ties that they had made with the national government. States they remained, in or out of the Union. With the defeat of Confederate armies, they were still contracting parties, with the power to govern themselves. Thus, states need only take up the rights and duties as members of the Union that they had voluntarily relinquished. No outside power needed to set the states in motion. Governors, legislatures, and special state conventions must restore their ties to the Union. And that, after the fall of Richmond, is what some southern leaders tried to do.[5]

Such a constitutional theory, for all its clear logic, led where just about no northerner any longer was prepared to go. If a state could voluntarily resume its place in the Union, it could sever it again in the future, whenever it chose. If it simply repealed the ordinance of secession rather than admitting that it was null and void, the war might as well not have been won. For that matter, if the secessionist theory had been right, the war should not have been fought. The national government would have had no business making war on states for exercising their right, and all the war would have settled was which side was stronger.

Northern Democrats took a different line—that of the states' rights ideas of Andrew Jackson and not those of John C. Calhoun. States had rights and spheres of action that were primarily, even exclusively, theirs and not the federal government's—the right to decide who could vote, for example. But secession was not a legitimate states' right. When states had come together under the Constitution, they had surrendered it. The states could not secede. People within those states, claiming to represent the state, had passed illegal ordinances declaring the states out of the Union. It was not on the states but on the traitors within them that the nation had waged war. The states had not been brought back into the Union; they had never been out. National authority had not been overthrown, as Johnson told Philadelphia politician A. K. McClure. It was "simply in abeyance," and when the Rebellion ceased, the states resumed "their proper place in the Union."[6]

If that were so, the states kept all their rights and powers. Their laws, except for those directly challenging the authority of the national government, still held. All that needed to be done was to set legal governments in motion. Illegal southern authorities could not do that, but the national government could, interfering as little as possible. It might, say, invite the South to call elections and permit southern whites to assemble constitutional conventions. With that, Reconstruction would be complete, with the southern states restored to their places in Congress on the same terms as they had enjoyed before the war.[7] But the federal government could not impose conditions, any more than it could on New York or Illinois.

At least the way Democrats explained it, their constitutional rendering of Reconstruction had a pristine logical clarity, undistorted by trying to allow for messy facts or explain away inconsistencies. The very word "Reconstruction" showed fuzzy thinking, if not unconstitutional intent, the *New York World* insisted. Nothing could be reconstructed unless it had broken down or had to be built anew. But the Union had not broken down. The proper word, therefore, should be "restoration." Such a reading left only two coherent positions on Reconstruction—theirs and the radical Republicans'. The radical Republicans wanted to make the South into conquered provinces, and from no misguided motives. They saw quite clearly that their own ascendancy depended on keeping the southern states unrepresented in Congress or, failing that, represented only by representatives that danced to the North's tune. Any third option would be intellectual nonsense. Americans must resolve "either to rule these states by military power, and suppress the legislative authority of the states over the subject of labor, forcing the adoption of our plans, or restore the federal Constitution to its ordinary working." In taking certain indisputable rights away from a state, such as the right to hold slaves, the government stripped the state of any inalienable right. "Either the ultimate sovereignty must be in the aggregate or not," the *New York World* lectured the conservative Republican editors of the *New York Times*. "The moment you deprive any state right of sanctity you necessarily deprive all of sanctity."[8]

Democrats were not inventing a constitutional bogeyman. A "conquered provinces" theory did exist, and it had its champions, notably Thaddeus

Stevens. In its own way, too, it was unclouded and logical. The law forbade murder, but murders happened. A true reading of the Constitution made secession unlawful, but secession had happened. Nobody could doubt that the Confederates had created a working government. They had raised armies and navies, taxed, recruited, and spent. The Confederacy was not the work of a few malcontents, forcing the mass of white southerners into a new nation to which they were forced to hold allegiance. It had had broad popular support. It had spoken for the southern public. If that were true, hanging a few "traitors," like Jefferson Davis, made no sense at all. They had been citizens of another country, newly made, making war on the United States, and as such, were entitled to all the rights of enemy combatants under the rules of war. For all its potential uses, Stevens's theory fit pretty well with what many white southerners knew was the case. Denying that the government had any right to try anyone for treason, South Carolina's provisional governor, Benjamin F. Perry, only confirmed the basis of the conquered provinces theory. "It was a legitimate war between two sections," he told a Fourth of July crowd. Calling "such a war a rebellion simply is a misapplication of terms."[9]

But if Stevens was right, the Union had not been restored. It had been newly forged. It held domain by right of conquest. That gave the government the right to do as it pleased, applying the provisions of the Constitution only as far as it willed. State lines could be erased, voting requirements changed, the lands of enemy aliens parceled out. Civil governments could be created or military ones left in place until Washington decided how to make the South a reliable part of the new nation.

For all its hard-eyed logic, any theory that allowed arbitrary power such full discretion had no chance even of carrying most radicals. A people who had fought the war not only for the Union but for the Constitution were not about to propose that the Constitution could be dispensed with entirely in eleven southern states.[10] Stevens's radical colleague, Senator Charles Sumner of Massachusetts, offered a much more palatable theory, allowing broad national supervision of the Reconstruction process, but within the Constitution. The states owed their legal existence to the making of the Union. The ordinances of secession that southern conventions passed had been illegal, null and void, in claiming that they alienated even a single square inch of national domain or the people in it from the national government. Severing their relations with the national government, they did not become part of a new, independent sovereignty; nor did they dissolve their boundaries. What they could do and did do, legally, was to surrender their statehood.

Unlike Stevens's theory, the so-called state-suicide idea denied that any legal entity known as the Confederacy existed; and also unlike it, Sumner's concept left the people in the former states under the Constitution, with all the rights guaranteed to citizens anywhere in the republic. They had only lost the power to govern themselves, until the United States government set the terms for doing so, just as it could with any unorganized part of the national domain. Authority for deciding such matters rested with Congress. Under the Constitution, it could make all the rules necessary for governing the territories; but even more important was the authority it possessed to ensure that every state had a republican form of government. The Constitution reined in Congress but left it plenty of latitude to establish public school systems, to decide who should vote and when elections should be held, and to confirm or reject anyone that the president nominated as territorial governor. Then Congress could oversee the process by which those territories wrote constitutions and prepared for statehood, exacting conditions as its members saw fit.[11]

Sumner's theory came closer to the constitutional center of Republican thought than did Stevens's, but it still remained at some distance. More moderate colleagues were uneasy with any scheme that gave Congress the power, even potential, to mandate Negro voting or, indeed, to merge and divide onetime states as Congress saw fit. They insisted on basing their policy not simply on the power to guarantee a republican form of government but on the special authority that wartime emergency gave them. Most Republicans therefore leaned to a more conservative theory than Sumner's—in one respect, indeed, more conservative than the president's. The states remained as they had been before the war: the same in shape, scope, and authority. But by announcing their divorce from the United States, they had done lasting and serious damage. The states still existed as political entities: with their legislatures, apportioned as before, their voting regulations, the form of their executive officers, the structure of their court systems. But in their relationship to the Union, the states had so put themselves out of kilter that they lacked the power to set themselves right. That far, at least, the congressional theory fit perfectly the presidential practice. The *Charleston Daily Courier* expressed the first perfectly in explaining the second:

> The body politic of the State, it is true, remained, but it possessed neither life or spirit. It presented the appearance and figure of a State without the capacity to perform any of its appropriate functions. The soulless corpse has become a living being. The re-establishment of a provisional civil Government and of the tribunals of justice and the re-installment of the vari-

ous public officers, will impart vigor to the system and invest it with the attributes of life and progress.[12]

Where the *Courier* fell short was in assuming that President Andrew Johnson did that and no more. Hailing the president as the protector of states' rights doctrine, pretending that his conditions set upon the South were merely requests, to which the states reciprocated out of good will, the writers ignored how far the Reconstruction that went into operation in the eight months after the end of the war had been mandated by national power. "His measures of reconstruction do not allow that the State Governments have any existence, and . . . utterly sets aside their Constitutions, and treats the States as domain of the United States, without government, and to be provided with government under regulations by the United States," a Republican newspaper pointed out in June 1865:

> With a stroke of the pen, preceded by a stroke of military power, he strikes out of existence every State, county, and township officer, from Governor and Legislature down to Constable; he appoints a Provisional Governor; he orders elections, prescribes who shall vote, disfranchising many who are voters under the State constitutions; he prescribes qualifications for voters, and test oaths, and after all he holds the results of the elections subject to revision, as has been done in Louisiana.
>
> Each and all of these measures assume that the State Governments have ceased to exist, and that these districts are United States domain or territory without local government, and that it is the right and duty of the United States to supervise the formation of local government, and to govern them until they have shown themselves qualified to form and carry on a loyal government.[13]

The real dispute, then, did not come over whether the national government should set terms and put state authority into motion. It came in a basic constitutional particular: which branch should define the terms on which the states must be restored, and, in this matter, Republicans thought theirs the more conservative position of the two. As they had been arguing for years, governments must be based on law and not on fiat. However far the Constitution could be stretched into a new reading of the law in wartime, the end of the emergency required the national authority to move back to its peacetime confines as quickly as practicable. Nowhere did that apply with more force than to the discretion claimed by a commander in chief over civil government.

"The Little Boy Would Persist in Handling Books above His Capacity. And This Was the Disastrous Result." Possibly Thomas Nast, *Harper's Weekly*, March 21, 1868. No one could miss Andrew Johnson's passion for the Constitution. But, as the cartoonist suggests, the president's application of its principles may have shown that he honored it more than he understood it.

Johnson might argue in favor of a weak central government and robust states with a wide array of exclusive rights, but when it came to power within the national government, he followed the examples of Andrew Jackson and the wartime course of Abraham Lincoln. In his constitutional interpretation of his own powers, he was downright radical, investing himself with the most generous possible interpretation of what presidents were allowed to do as military commanders. Even during the war, that had been one of the worries of Congress concerning Lincoln. Far from wanting to make Congress superior and turn the president into a nullity, as Democrats later would charge in Johnson's administration, Republicans wanted to return to the traditional role of presidents from before the war, where policymaking had been the prerogative of the people's representatives, with advice and input from the executive branch.[14]

Any Reconstruction policy based on military force and decree rather than on statutes and resolutions carried the nation further from the consent of the governed. Presidents were to execute the law, not make it. Yet, in wartime, they did more than make law. They made ersatz governments. Lincoln had revitalized states by military appointment and proclamation, called elections out of their designated time and without state legislative sanction, and set the conditions for recognizing new governments. Such a use of presidential power stretched the office beyond anything attempted before, and it opened two dangerous possibilities.

First, despotism gave a dubious parentage to any supposedly republican form of government. "Elections supervised by military power are worse than no elections," the *Cincinnati Gazette* argued. "Elections whose result has to be revised are not elections. It would be arbitrary power in its most dangerous form, for between it and the simulation of elections there would be no responsibility for anything." To such an authority, no people eventually free to govern themselves would feel any loyalty. In the case of the southern governments that Johnson helped devise, the risk of overthrow became a certainty. Modest turnouts of voters elected constitutional conventions. New fundamental laws were written up. But in not one state did the reconstructors submit their work to the voters for approval. Why, Republicans asked, had the state builders not dared put their handiwork before the people—unless they knew that it would be turned down?[15] How long would a people not consulted about the terms of Reconstruction feel any obligation to abide by them?

Second, government by fiat threw the whole reconstruction process into peril. A decree freeing the slaves might strike a blow against slavery, but could it stand legal challenge? That reason, among others, impelled Lincoln himself to seek a final constitutional settlement, a Thirteenth Amendment abolishing slavery. But the same grounds for concern lay in Johnson's policy, creating provisional governors and pardoning men not yet convicted of crime in the courts. Even as it defended him in late 1865, the radical Republican *Cincinnati Gazette* reminded readers that without national law, every act reconstructing since the Rebellion was over, by the states and by Johnson himself, failed the constitutional test. Johnson's provisional governor was "an unconstitutional officer. His proclamation to elect members of Congress is unconstitutional. These things were done from an apparent necessity. But it does not follow that Congress, the constitutional representation of the people, is obliged to accept these unconstitutional acts. They may repudiate the whole of them."[16]

Even radicals agreed that the president had a part to play, including some say in the conditions imposed on the southern states. Presidents might even appoint provisional governors to keep order until the Congress could come into session. But decrees were no way to make a lasting lawful authority. A state derived its legitimacy from the people and from its providing a republican form of government. Only states that fit that qualification had a right to representation in Congress, and the Constitution gave Congress the power to decide what constituted republicanism. Empowered to keep out or admit southerners claiming the right to seats in that body, it could set the conditions for a reconstructed South.[17]

The remedies of Congress and the president differed in the substantial particulars of what conditions should be imposed on southern states and the murkier generality of how far they should at least appear to be tenders made on the states' own volition. For Johnson, annulment of the secession ordinances, repudiation of the Confederate war debt, ratification of the Thirteenth Amendment abolishing slavery, and steps guaranteeing the former slaves the wider scope of rights given to free blacks were enough. But Congress wanted considerably more substantive protection for black rights and demanded a greater token of loyalty than the election of reluctant disunionists and wartime bystanders. The president set conditions on the southern states and then, to make his demands fit better with the much more restrictive constitutional theory of the Democrats, portrayed them as no more than suggestions for what they might do—suggestions that were repeated much more menacingly when not obeyed and that most white southerners saw as required of them. Congress insisted on explicit demands, coupled with explicit acceptance of those demands by the southern states. These were not minor divergences, though all through 1865 Johnson's purposes were so murky that it was hard for Republicans to be sure just how dramatic the differences were.

Whatever else the moderates' Reconstruction theory allowed, it looked to a restoration of the states. National power might make the postwar settlement fairer, wiping out slavery and keeping a white South from hollowing out freedom until for blacks it barely deserved the name. Using the powers under the Thirteenth Amendment, Congress might enact a law protecting the essential civil rights of all Americans and creating a definition of national citizenship that made no distinctions on the basis of color. The power to aid the transition to peace would permit Congress to continue the Freedmen's Bureau that already was in operation feeding and caring for those most in need, white and black, encouraging the development of a school system for the former slaves, and easing the transition from slave to free labor. But, in the end, most Republicans were not looking to a new, centralized Union in which the national government interfered and intervened without end. They wanted to be rid of the high taxes and large armies that wartime demanded, and the sooner the southern states returned to normal, the better. Not even among most of the radicals was there any idea that when the southern states were returned to their full rights in Congress they would be any less states than the northern ones, or with more limited rights. States' rights, they would have agreed, were not so much a threat to the national authority as a necessary supplement and counterweight to it. The nation was, rightly governed, a synthesis, not an amalgamation, "a chemical compound and not a mechanical weld." Republicans, almost as much as Democrats, were federalists to the bone, wary about centralized power, distrustful of rule by martial law and military decree, and convinced that the first resort for the making of public policy must remain in the states and localities, not in Washington.[18]

Seeing this latent conservatism is vital: it will explain why mainstream Republicans, from the first, were vulnerable to the Democratic cries that they were tyrants and why they acted so hesitantly in remaking the South. Far from being fanatics, they hoped to make as few permanent changes as the public safety and their reading of the Founders' true intentions would allow. Rather than welcoming the Reconstruction question as an excuse to enhance national authority, moderates dreaded it and before long were heartily sick of it. That resistance was present from the first, and it grew ever stronger as the war receded into the past. It certainly helped dampen their enthusiasm for action that those most in need of help were black southerners. Even many Republicans who came to give them the vote held doubts about their fitness for the franchise, or at least their readiness. Future events strengthened all those doubts, with the earnest aid of news reports coming from a South where the telegraphic press coverage lay almost entirely with the white conservatives. But the unease about using national power would have been there in any case—and strengthened, regardless of the color of those seeking redress from Washington.[19]

The conservative strains to Republicanism also explain why Johnson's policies, no matter what they had been, would have excited alarm in Congress. Everything he did between his coming to office in April 1865 and the assembling of Congress the following December showed a man at best ready to stretch his constitutional authority to the utmost and at worst a usurper. Laws that inconvenienced him, like the requirement that executive appointees be able to take the "ironclad oath" of loyalty, were ignored or explained away. Lincoln had assumed emergency powers after the firing on Fort Sumter but had summoned Congress into extra session soon after to give his actions a legal basis. Johnson let eight months elapse. Only the assurances, explicitly given, that his actions were only an "experiment," with the implication that Congress would be able to judge whether the experiment had succeeded and make the final adjustment, tempered the worry that Republicans felt.[20]

They had more to worry about than they knew. In practice, the president's use of national power to make over the South put him nearer the Republican understanding of Reconstruction than the Democratic one. But he was using them to set up a political order sure to bring in fifty to eighty more Democratic congressmen and twenty Democratic senators, if not more. It meant a speedier return to "the Union as it was," with power left in the hands of white conservatives. Fudging the facts was a cheap price to pay for a friend like Andrew Johnson, and Democrats started fudging almost at once. Claiming that Johnson's theory of Reconstruction was their own, they tried to make it seem as if he had simply restored the states, or done as little reconstructing as he could, to set them on their feet again.[21] Now Congress had nothing left to do; and, more important, Congress had no power to do it. The war was over. Emergency powers no longer applied. As soon as a state had renewed its fealty to the Union and created governments that in the views of its electorate were republican in form, the states could take their old places in the nation's councils.

Democrats had excellent reasons to make this position the absolute touchstone between lawfulness and usurpation. Four years of being accused of being traitors put the strongest kind of pressure on northern members of the party to show that they were the true Unionists and that their antagonists were the real disunionists. That same need was even stronger among white southerners, who were trying to sell an unconvinced North on the idea that they had become the truest, if the newest, defenders of the Union and the Constitution.

By itself, that explanation of real partisan advantage makes the Democratic Party and the South sound much more cynical than they actually were. In fact, the war had trained them to suspect the worst from the majority party and to expect the worst treatment at its hands. Eight months into the peace, Clement Vallandigham found how well remembered his wartime opposition remained. A mob roughed him up as he boarded a train, and the more violent ruffians had to be restrained from hauling him out of the cars and "fixing him" with a hemp necktie. Shootings, jailings, military courts, and accusations of treason against mere dissenters were not the kind of incidents likely to motivate the victims to give their oppressors the benefit of the doubt. The war's end brought no end to their innermost thoughts about "the party of despotism," any more than it turned Confederate patriots into lusty Unionists overnight.[22] They looked for plots against liberty and, naturally, found them.

Even if the white South had understood the North's intentions perfectly, to be sure, it would have resisted. The least change that most northerners expected down south — an end to slavery, a lessened inequality of rights between free blacks and whites, the swearing off of secession not just in present practice but as a legitimate right, and an end to the skewed representation system that let white southerners count some or all of four million voteless blacks in apportioning their share of House seats — was far more than any responsible official in the South would have given willingly. But the readiness of those who controlled politics postwar to give ground was lessened by the fact that their constituents, and they themselves, were left in the dark. Worse, with northern Democratic newspapers to guide them, they saw terrible things stirring in that dark — phantasms and demons.

The poverty of southern newspapers meant that most of them had to be guided, far more than northern ones. As has been noted already, they lacked the funds to create a strong cadre of reporters. Most of them could afford no more than a slimmed-down distillation of the Associated Press dispatches lavished on northern cities. What news they received, however, they interpreted on the basis of what they had always thought they knew about national politics, and that, for the most part, was in the way that Democrats had explained it to them. And why not? As enemies went, Democrats ranked among the best. On constitutional issues in wartime, they had spoken well, even if they lacked the will or the numbers to turn their good intentions into actions. This had not been their war, after all. "Through all the reign of blood they have stood upon the Constitution and the Union under it," one Peace Democrat boasted.[23]

By no means did white southerners think that all northerners were the "whining zealots, fanatical experimentalists, [and] mischief-making busy-bodies" that Republicanism, at its worst, sometimes appeared to be. There were even some good Republicans, whose natural moderation would show itself when peace became a fixed fact. And, of course, the great mass of northerners could be brought to see that their own self-interest lay in giving the former Confederacy generous treatment.[24] Under the circumstances, former Confederates were willing to admit that with time and good behavior by the North, they could be brought to forgive it. But for the moment, there was not the faintest doubt that all the political momentum lay with the unfathomable, fanatical minority of northerners, the so-called Radical Republicans.

With them, there could be no peace, because the radicals were at war with the basic principles of the republic itself. Hatred and fanaticism were their chief traits. Charles Sumner had no interest in hangings and only a passing interest in disfranchising white southerners. Consistently, the Massachusetts senator raised his voice for equal rights for all and a ballot box free from the color line. It made no difference. To southern editors, his was "the statesmanship of Robespierre and of Danton, of the guillotine; banishment and confiscation; for no law but that of might, and no Constitution but the decrees and advancement of fanaticism"—it was revenge, pure and simple, for the caning that a South Carolina congressman had given him, just as Thaddeus Stevens's passion for equality was malice because Confederate armies had burned his ironworks—in both cases a thirst for vengeance blessed with foresight, since the beliefs showed up years before the injuries were done to either man.[25] Radicals' insistence on Negro suffrage could not be based on its merits. It must arise from some designs to degrade white southerners by making them the slaves of those who so recently had been slaves themselves. Its aims, in other words, were not just to eradicate the southern identity but to strip southerners of their sense of manhood. Indeed, one editor argued that the real aim of Negro suffrage was to do away with suffrage completely, by so defiling the very idea that the electorate would in the end be glad to surrender any say in how the country was governed.[26]

Radicals were not a normal political faction. They were revolutionaries, and their every act was scrutinized, to discern exactly how it furthered the hidden design. Every so often, observers actually spotted it. "The policy of the Radicals is revolutionary throughout," a political scientist charged. "The Reconstruction act is revolutionary, in reducing the states to territories—in subjecting them to military domination—in enfranchising the negro population in opposition to the will of the people of the states—in forcing the states to ratify constitutional amendments against their will, thus changing the Constitution by revolutionary violence." "Revolutionary violence" had carried the law itself, the "revolutionary exclusion of Southern representatives" and "the revolutionary intimidation of the co-ordinate branches of the government."[27]

Nourished by "a knot of transcendental infidel philosophers" like Ralph Waldo Emerson, who wanted to kill all the whites in the South and replace Christianity with a gospel of lust, Radicalism, according to the Democratic reading, had no respect for law or tradition. At best, they had contempt, at worst, they openly detested the American system of government. They claimed to have preserved the Constitution, and so they had, after a fashion, the *Cincinnati Enquirer* sneered: As soon as they came to power, "they folded it up carefully and put it away in one of the pigeon-holes of the War Department, and from that day to this they have never looked at it or in any way considered it in existence." There was no patriotism in them. "The Union as it *was*—never!" one Connecticut orator was said to have cried, meaning, as any Democrat could show, a Union where state and national authority shared the governing. Radicals were centralizers, despising any and all states' rights. In General Daniel Sickles's boast of northern leniency, Democrats found proof of the notion of absolute national authority that Radicals reputedly held. "The north had given [southerners] their lands, their houses, their railroads, and all they have, for they were ours by the laws of war," Sickles shouted, "and it would have been no injustice for us to have kept them." When northerners used the word "nation" or referred to a "national" Union rather than a "federal" one, they exposed themselves as political aliens.[28]

Aided by Democratic polemicists up north, southerners fashioned an argument to show that they were, as they always had been, the true Unionists. Long ago, the *Raleigh Sentinel* reminded readers, the "radical party" had declared the Declaration of Independence a lie and a cheat and the Constitution "a league with hell." They started the war, really, but not to restore the Union, only to destroy slavery. To the "leaders of the Republican party," it was "a hated and hateful government." Now that the war was over, they were on the high road to attaining just what they wanted. "They virtually assert that the war, instead of saving the Union destroyed it," Governor James E. English of Connecticut charged; "instead of defeating secession, [they] made it an accomplished fact." "I arraign the Republican party as the party of Disunion," Daniel W. Voorhees of Indiana cried. "I arraign it . . . for being the only party which recognizes disunion."[29]

What, then, was the end purpose of radical policy? Southern whites insisted that it was the upraising of "Negro commonwealths" and, in the process, the ruin of the South, utter and complete. Their chief desire was "a war upon our own countrymen after they have submitted to the laws." One constitutional theorist predicted a double-headed policy—first to ruin the whites and then to ruin the blacks. Radicals would confiscate the lands to hand over to the freedpeople, even as they flooded the land with German immigrants, thrifty and politically reliable. Blacks were so penny-foolish that they would not be able to keep their lands long and, against "Dutch industry, and Dutch thrift," would lose out quickly and be "thrust into extinction."[30]

What the radicals wanted, white conservatives were sure, was not a settlement but permanent control for the North, even if that meant erecting a tyranny or spurring on a revolution. By degrees, liberty would be lost and "the dread serpent of despotism will be found ere long dragging its loathsome form over the ruins." No Democratic speech or editorial fulmination seemed quite complete without bringing in the French Revolution, the Reign of Terror, Marat, Robespierre, or blood.[31] An Alexandria woman wrote fearfully of insurrections that would come into their midst among the "negroes," chivvied into it by those who "*profess* to be their *best* friends." Northerners "will secretly lead them on to destroy the Southern people, and then openly turn and exterminate them (for in their hearts they hate the race)—and take full possession of the coveted Southland." If blacks were allowed guns, "another and worse war, we believe to be inevitable." Those abused as Rebels would be vindicated by posterity, a South Carolinian wrote, but only after "the chains of despotism now being forged by the rabid Republicans of the North are firmly fastened on the limbs of the whole people North and South. Then and not till then will the world discover, who it was that warned their countrymen of the near approach of the robber band and periled all to save the Constitution and the rights of man."[32]

To hold the black vote, Republicans would have to confiscate southern whites' property and would be forced to make blacks voters in northern states, too. A bill would be revived and passed, creating a standing army of half a million men, strong enough "to crush out all opposition to its power, by force of arms." "Military force is the essential support of all centralizations. Let the Radical scheme of power once be fairly established, and the country will be placed under the rule of the sword." Then westerners would feel the same yoke that they had helped place on the southern neck. Armies alone could never sustain centralized power. So the Radicals would create a privileged aristocracy, the way the monarchies of Europe had done. New England capitalists would be the next lords. The "old government—the government of their fathers"—would perish in fratricidal war, and "a limited or absolute monarchy" would emerge, after "seas of blood" were spilt.[33]

Radicalism had all the exaggerated powers expected of all conspiracies. Through cunning, bullying, and well-applied grass roots pressure, the "ultras" had far more weight than their numbers deserved. The peace terms the Republicans spoke of were theirs. Charles Sumner, being groomed for president—and sure to be nominated, one Washington correspondent declared—controlled the Senate, forcing the moderate leaders to "hide their diminished heads." (Sumner's real influence on other senators was, in fact, feeble, and the chances of him running for president were minuscule.)[34]

Southern readers never came close to understanding the real dividing lines within the Republican Party. To imagine that there could be any position between that of the president and the most wild of radicals became unthinkable; to assume a moderate northern opinion separate from the president's and capable of fending off the doctrines of Thaddeus Stevens became unimaginable. Johnson's version of Reconstruction afforded the only alternative to Stevens's "reign of terror . . . more bitter and unrelenting than that of the Jacobins of France." That southerner, then, seeking middle ground with the North, was a traitor to be driven from the company of honest men. It was useless making concessions to northern moderates who, for all southerners knew, could not help themselves; the radicals in charge would accept nothing less than everything. Each demand would be followed by another, any guarantee given would be succeeded by new requirements. "If we should tomorrow 'eat the leek' of the proposed Constitutional amendment, with its debasing conditions, crushing out our very life and subverting the character of the government as well," the *Raleigh Sentinel* averred, the "cowardly and hyena-like instincts" of the Radicals would inspire them to "fresh schemes of ruin and degradation." Having killed constitutional liberty, they would proceed to mutilate the corpse.[35]

The assumptions that the northern Republicans calling the tune were "radicals," that all Radicals were fanatics, "tract distributors, mesmeric lecturers, colporteurs and spiritual mediums," with "no public record known among gentlemen,"[36] that most northerners, not being fanatics, therefore could not be radicals, and must be at heart with the Democrats, allowed the white South to imagine itself on the verge of constant rescue by the forces of good, the forces that were sure to triumph the moment an election set them right. Confident from the first that there would be no harsh policy, convinced quickly that Johnson was with them rather than against them, they told themselves that the president spoke for northern opinion. The mass of northerners were conservative. Between Democratic and Republican moderates, all of whom backed the president wholly, there was the kind of majority that in the next set of elections would drive out the South's bitterest enemies quickly.

That misinformation and disinformation had a serious consequence for the South's view of its own options. It let southerners imagine that they could get away with rejecting the terms of the Congress—that the purpose of the North was not of guarantees but instead the age-old determination to humiliate the South. For that reason, the southern legislatures need not go beyond the bare minimum of conditions set by Andrew Johnson to meet any of the Republican demands.[37]

Unable to see real differences of view within the Republican Party or the relative strength of the different factions—if, in the end, it branded every bit of legislation a radical triumph—then the South surrendered all its power to maneuver between the factions and get the best possible deal for itself. Delusion and illusion made the extremely small chance of a sectional understanding next to impossible.

That built-in suspicion of Republicans' purposes and constitutional absolutism turned the messy business of interpreting the implied powers of the Constitution into an apocalyptic conflict, one in which no middle ground could exist. Key to the Democratic argument was to make Thaddeus Stevens into a serious menace; and that could only be done by showing that Congress did his bidding. Editors and orators thundered that, however prettied up with constitution-parsing, all Republican theories of Reconstruction were the same as Stevens's. All of them believed that the South was a conquered province, because, outside of Democratic doctrine, there was nowhere else to go. To treat the states as less than completely valid was as good as treating them like territories, and running them like territories only admitted that they were "not of the Union," Secretary of the Navy Gideon Welles complained. It granted that they had indeed seceded. "It promotes disunion, dismemberment, alienation, and is extreme partyism rather than patriotism." Any attempt to find a middle ground simply had no logical defense. Again and again, they cited Stevens's supposed confession that everything Congress had done was outside the Constitution as merely his brutal honesty in confessing what every other Republican knew to be true.[38]

Welles was referring to one specific act. At the very start of the 39th Congress, Republicans had refused to admit the delegations from the seceded states until a joint committee of fifteen had investigated whether they had the "republican form of government" that the Constitution insisted upon. In the Democrats' easy slide of language, denying the southern states representation in Congress was to keep them out of the Union. Anything less than full resto-ration of the political relations that the states had once enjoyed was in effect to deny the existence of those states as states. Every moderate voting against admission was a practical disunionist, a devotee of the "conquered provinces" doctrine.[39]

The rhetoric of constitutional fundamentalism made choices seem stark. They were anything but. If Republicans read implied powers into the Constitu-tion, Democrats read implied constraints, and just as creatively. Some of them found built-in limitations to the process of amendment not stated in the docu-ment itself. To be legitimate, an amendment had to fit the larger intentions of the Founders. Opponents of the Thirteenth Amendment argued that slavery was among those rights too embedded in the Founders' original purpose to be removed. Not three-quarters of all the states nor even all of them but one had any right to tell the remaining state what domestic institutions it could permit, Democrats cried. The same logic applied even more forcibly to the Howard Amendment, the proposed fourteenth amendment. In its transfer of such broad powers to the national courts and Congress, it changed the essen-tial nature of the document that Madison, Hamilton, and Washington had created. It broke the principles upon which the republic was made by chang-ing the balance of power between nation and states. Only traitors, enemies of republican principles, would propose a change like that. Worse steps must fol-low. The "Moloch will be satisfied with nothing short of our utter prostration. ... No friend of Constitutional Union can embrace it, without being privy to his own and his people's ruin." But even such an amendment could not be valid without the president's approval and, one congressman asserted, without a popular referendum. The Founders may not have thought to mention it, but legislative ratification was insufficient.[40]

Constitutional caprice was, in fact, the monopoly of neither party. When a New Jersey congressman announced that nobody could be prosecuted for treason because the right of revolution was among the "inherent" powers, it gibed with a Johnson Republican's insistence that the constitutional definition of treason did not apply to most Confederate volunteers, because, under the Constitution, their allegiance was made conditional on the national govern-ment protecting them.[41] By not stopping the erection of disloyal state authori-ties, Senator Edgar Cowan of Pennsylvania argued, the nation had failed to "guarantee a republican form of government." Treason was Congress's fault, not those who took up arms against the government. One southern news-paper explained why impeachment was impossible. Under the Constitution, it declared, the moment Johnson was removed, the secretary of state would be required to call a new presidential election, and all the southern states would be entitled to a vote. They would be sure to elect a conservative, the last thing radicals could afford to let happen. (Others speculated that Johnson could resign and call a new presidential election himself.) Two years after the war ended, the *New York World* discovered that right of rebellion that Confederates had claimed to be exercising. It had been hidden in the Second Amendment. The right to keep and bear arms must imply "their right to use arms," said the *World*, "otherwise the guarantee would be as idle as a right to keep guns without triggers." Therefore the Founders had designed the Constitution to assure people of the weaponry they needed to cast off oppression.[42]

All such readings took imaginative delvings into the supposed spirit of the Founders, just as Republicans were doing in defining the guarantee of a republican form of government as involving greater assurances of equality than Jefferson's generation had provided. But Democrats refused to admit that they were doing any such thing. Having distorted the Republican position into something far more absolutist and centralizing than it was, they squeezed and shaped their reading of what Andrew Johnson had been doing, until it seemed to fit their own take on the Constitution snugly. He became the defender of "the Constitution as it was," against "the Party of Revolution."[43]

The closest possible exegesis of the Constitution could only polarize the two sides and only add to that sense of urgency where extreme action became acceptable to ward off a genuine, subversive threat. One of the most dangerous flash points was over the admission to Congress of the congressmen elected from the governments formed in Johnson's Reconstruction. If the Democratic assumption was right, members could be excluded from Congress on the grounds of personal unfitness, but entire states could not be. When Congress did so, then, it perverted the power to judge the qualifications of its own members into the power to define which states constituted a Congress and which did not. That, Democrats declared, was revolutionary and illegal. "Have we a constitution?" a Georgia editor demanded. If so, "is it not about time that its provisions were respected and carried out by those who make so great pretentions of being its defenders?"[44]

The clamor was more than constitutional one-upmanship. It opened up grave, even revolutionary, implications. Former cabinet member Thomas Ewing voiced one of the most extreme, proving to ultra Democrats' satisfaction that there had not been a legal Congress since 1861.[45] The argument based itself on the Constitution's requirement that Congress contain two senators from each state. Eleven southern states went unrepresented in both houses. Instead of seventy-two senators, that body had only fifty. The Constitution declared that it took a majority of senators to make a quorum and to pass a bill, which meant, said Democrats, a majority not just of those present but of the whole body. In wartime, the requirement might not hinder legislation; the Constitution could not require that senators be counted who chose not to attend. The southern states refused to send delegations to Congress, and these absentees could be deducted from the total. But, by 1866, peace reigned. The southern states chose to send representatives and senators to Washington. Barring individual disqualifications for personal disloyalty in wartime, those members had a right to their seats. Admitted or not, they must be counted in calculating the total number of senators and in deciding how many members it took to make a majority. Under those circumstances, the Senate had fallen some fifteen votes short of what it needed for the two-thirds required to override a presidential veto. The civil rights bill, among others, had therefore not been overridden at all and was not the law of the land—Judge Edmund Abell of the first district court of Louisiana overturned it on those very grounds. Indeed, without eleven states in attendance, the entire Congress itself might be illegal, a gang of "pretenders to the functions of national legislators." The president, the *New York Daily News* concluded, had no obligation to execute the will of "an assemblage of usurpers, or to carry out the unconstitutional measures of an unconstitutional legislative body." On the contrary, permitting radicals to put laws so passed into operation would be fatal. "The very soul of our republicanism will have passed away."[46]

But if it was illegal, then the actions of such a Congress were thrown into question, by whatever margin it passed its measures. Had it a right to make regulations for the unrepresented states? Or to legislate at all? Before long, Democratic newspapers began to dub the assemblage on Capitol Hill a "rump Congress" and made allusions to the "rump Parliament" of England in the wake of its own civil war.[47] It did not escape Democrats' notice that Puritan fanatics had been responsible for each, or that the effect had been arbitrary government from the first, culminating in the complete loss of the public's faith in representative institutions, and, in the end, military rule.

Rhetorical devices come freighted with larger meanings. Democrats' larger meaning, not at all difficult to discern, was that they would feel free to challenge any action that the so-called Congress attempted in the courts as null and void. They would deny legitimacy to any political settlement that the Republicans established and work to overturn it. What, for instance, should Maryland's former Confederates do about the loyalty oath required of them before voting? The oaths, the *New York World* insisted, were unconstitutional. They had no moral force. Those who had joined the Rebellion should feel no qualms about perjuring themselves in order to regain the franchise and win the state back. "Take the oath as you would give a promise to a highwayman pistol in hand, and then treat it as you would that highwayman after you had got out of his hands."[48]

The most extreme critics of Congressional Reconstruction would look for a Cromwell of their own. They found him, or hoped they had, in Andrew Johnson. "You are Commander-in-chief of the army and navy," wrote one correspondent. "This power was given to the president to enable him to 'repel invasion and suppress domestic revolution,'" and the writer made it clear that those powers included the "*revolution* and *rebellion*" Congress made. Johnson was "as much bound to put it down as was Abraham Lincoln bound to wage the war to suppress the late rebellion."[49]

Beyond a few Copperhead editors, the implications of a coup on the republic's behalf remained unspoken when Congress met in December. But already, across the North, there was a growing feeling that, amid all of the things that had gone very much right since General Lee's surrender, something else may have been going very wrong. The language of a stigmatized and astigmatic southern press and the actions of white lawmakers mixing defiance, resentment, and dread had unsettled the conquerors. Northward, among Republicans, the relief over the war's end turned into perplexity, then doubt, and, as the months passed and the self-reconstruction of the South proceeded apace, a mounting suspicion. Never had victors been so generous, never had the defeated responded so truculently. Northern Republicans were irritated at the limits placed on black people's freedom, but they were far more concerned by the signs that the Rebellion's old masters were being escorted back into power. Increasingly, it became clear that the majority of white southerners had not been bullied into secession. They had gone willingly. They were rebels still. To elect the vice president of the Confederacy to Congress was a sign that repentance had not gone all that far. For those unaware of how reluctantly Alexander Stephens had followed Georgia out of the Union and how earnestly he had worked to cripple the Confederate president, it seemed a sign that "the reptile spirit of secession" lived on, "ready to display its fangs at any moment." Disunionists, "dagger in hand [and] ready to strike down the Goddess of Liberty," stood at the portals of the Capitol.[50] Perhaps, given the slightest chance, white southerners would go to war again. Were they preparing for that chance? Was it possible that this time the Rebels could win it?

The people must, ere long, perceive,
What should not be denied,
That when of Congress I took leave,
That worthless body died.
Its acts are null, and have been nil,
From that day e'en to this;
And must be, till the House I fill
With such men as Davis!
—Zedekiah Comitatus,
"Reconstruction on My Policy."

chapter 5

DO THEY WANT STILL MORE BLOOD?

Andrew Johnson's Reconstruction

A visitor meeting Andrew Johnson at the White House would hardly have noticed that he was no gentleman. Stoutly built, thickset, muscular, his black hair tinged with gray—he had deep, dark, piercing eyes and a firm mouth. In all, one reporter thought, the face bespoke indomitable will and courage, a warm spirit, and a generous heart.[1]

Andrew Johnson *was* no gentleman. Popular politics winnowed them out, and few places hosted a more rough-and-tumble people's politics than eastern Tennessee. Charles Nordhoff, a Washington correspondent who struggled to like Johnson, came to pronounce him "an unmitigated curse to the country," "really vile, vulgar, coarse, mean, bad in every way, & not least in a kind of low cunning, wh. always defeats himself." Ohio governor Jacob Cox, who tried to follow Johnson's political course and balked when he found that it led out of the Republican Party, sighed that the president was "always *worse* than you expect, and the lowest impulses and most foolish thoughts he has, are the very ones that come uppermost & control him in the moment of action."[2]

Cox and Nordhoff were too disillusioned with Johnson to note his good qualities—his diligence, patriotism, personal loyalty, and, when dealing with callers, his courtesy—but they did notice the same fundamental flaw, those impulsive ways in which his mind worked. Those ways led down dark corridors, into suspicion and self-delusion about the nature of national politics. The president had reason enough, for he had been trained in a harsh political school. Born without influential patrons or family wealth to ease his rise, Johnson had worked his way up: alderman, state legislator, congressman, and governor. It was a fight every step of the way. The candidate needed to look out for himself, well aware that he faced not only the most searing personal attacks but now and then the possibility of being beaten or killed. More than once, Johnson had spoken to the click of pistols being put on the ready in the audience.[3]

In such a world, the talents it took to rise were not those of accommodation or wider alliance but of combat and defiance, the little man standing against his supposed betters. "Was there ever a compromise made in which some one was not wronged, in which some one of the parties did not lose?" Johnson demanded of the Senate. "There is a great principle of right somewhere; let us ascertain where the right is and let the North and South maintain it, neither making concessions."[4] For East Tennesseans, willing to believe that the ruffled-shirt aristocracy of Nashville offered them nothing but contempt, convinced of their own status as outsiders, the more as their nationalism became an anomaly in a state where even most Unionists put conditions on their loyalty, Johnson's aggressiveness and his identification of himself with the outcast yeoman farmers could only do him good in politics, and, of course, his belief was entirely sincere. His career was more than the "series of mob-ridings" that one journalist described it as being, but his capacity for invective and discovering enemies certainly showed up in his rise to power. It really did seem, as the reporter put it, that he "always hated somebody." To those who thought themselves his betters, the emotion read as an inferior man's seething envy.[5]

Defiance and courage served Johnson well in the spring of 1861, when Unionism melted away across the state. Stumping against secession, he braved bullies and threats. Three years as military governor of an occupied Tennessee surrounded by enemies could not have made him feel any less the loner. His move to the vice presidency may have added to his feeling of isolation. For all his efforts, he impressed Congressman Henry L. Dawes as helpless "to make himself an agreeable, entertaining or instructive man in company." Take away the devotion to the Union, and he and his Republican allies had little to say to each other. Some had accepted him on the ticket with misgiving. Their doubts deepened when he made a drunken spectacle of himself at Lincoln's inaugural and had to be pulled down by the coattails. If he felt that much of official Washington held him in no love, a lifetime of experience can hardly have tended his mind in any other direction. "Nine parts of a man astraddle a hyperbole, he swung from poverty to power with all his ill-breeding," a usually sage reporter wrote. Such surroundings only strengthened Johnson's inclination to shield his soul from exposure and his opinions from challenge.[6]

Many reasons, then, made Johnson distrustful, insecure, and jealous for his own reputation. But these qualities were crippling. They meant that, listen to advice from all sides though he might, Johnson would not be very good at heeding it. He would not take counsel and would be slow to ask it from those whose views did not resemble his own. They also meant that, vigilant as he was to the plottings of enemies, he would particularly favor explanations of events in which sinister forces worked against him from the shadows.

In this, the president was ill served, especially by the advisers around him. Too much could be made of this. There were more moderate men in his cabinet at the beginning, Republicans in good standing with their party, many of them nearly as hostile to radical demands as he was. But one by one, they found themselves shunted aside and found that if their political careers were to continue anywhere within the Republican Party—and there was nowhere else that they could go—they must resign their offices and give up the thankless task of deflecting the president from his course. The president was not shaped by bad advisors' bad advice. He chose them himself and listened to them because their take on the world fit his own.

Among them, two had an especially pernicious influence. The first came from the irrepressible Blair family. The Blairs had Democratic pedigrees that Johnson could hardly help honoring. The patriarch of the clan, old Francis P. Blair, had been the great Andrew Jackson's newspaper voice. Through the *Washington Globe*, he had preached the true doctrine for years against Hunker Democrats, the very kind that Johnson himself had fought: the men who chartered swindling banks and lobbied through subsidies for themselves and awarded themselves with mail contracts, the cormorants of privilege. One son, Frank Jr., had been a bold Union general, as bold against radical supporters of emancipation as against the Confederates. The other, Montgomery Blair, had become Lincoln's postmaster general. Frank Blair's influence in Missouri was considerable; Montgomery's in Maryland was the greater for the patronage thrown his way. Credentials like these gave what the Blairs said particular credibility, and they had passed the test of friendship to a suspicious, beleaguered man: it had been to the Blairs' home in Silver Spring, Maryland, that Johnson had retreated when the press was abusing his performance at Lincoln's inaugural.[7]

With their influence gone among Republicans and a very doubtful future in the border states that "unconditional Unionists" ran, the Blairs needed a new political deal badly, one that would refurbish and even restock the Democratic Party—with the Blairs vaulted into leading positions. Bringing the Democrats and the new president together would do both. It would give the party an extremely influential friend and would cut Johnson loose from the mass of his supporters who, as far as the Blairs were concerned, should have been his enemies. Even without their role as go-betweens to shape their advice, the Blairs' take on politics would have been a toxic one. It always had been the language of goodness surrounded by the conspiracies of enemies. Once, it had been the followers of John C. Calhoun, nullifiers, who, to hear the Blairs tell it, had hijacked the true Democratic Party and carried it far from what Jackson would have allowed. Then it had been the base intrigues of Montgomery Blair's cabinet colleagues, Secretary of State William Seward and Secretary of the Treasury Salmon P. Chase, both supposedly unscrupulous and shamelessly corrupt. Frank Blair Jr.'s first oratorical fireworks on his return to the House in 1864 had been an exposure of Chase's plots to usurp the place belonging to his chief. His brother spent his energies trying to convince the public that Seward had been cozy with the secessionists before the war and had invited them to take Fort Sumter, all the while trying to persuade the administration to sell out gallant Major Robert Anderson and his garrison.[8]

Now the Blairs worked their hardest to make Johnson see how ill the world worked, and who was most responsible. The Thirteenth Amendment had passed, thanks to "the progressive & honest War Democracy," acting out of patriotic motives only, Montgomery Blair wrote him, "& yet I know that Mr. Seward made Lincoln believe that he had carried that Amendment by Corruption." He had no fears "that either Seward or Stanton or any body else would rule you," which, of course, implied that this was exactly what those two cabinet officers had in mind.[9]

The father was even more disturbing. At the beginning of August, he wrote a long letter, full of advice for the president as to what should be done and filled with strikingly misguided assumptions. "The rebellion is crushed," Blair acknowledged, but the same evil had returned in a new form. "It sprouts out with the bold front of negro equality." Those favoring it wanted "amalgamation," adulterating "our Anglo-Saxon race" and its government with "Africanization." The supporters of black suffrage aimed at "revolution, a breach of the Union by a vote of Congress." The whole movement was just putting into policy the wish of Salmon Chase, who (according to Blair) had said, "Let the

Seceding States go, they are not worth fighting for." Instead, they would set off a civil war, white against black, faction against faction.

Johnson must be on his guard, Blair went on. Secret disunionists were conspiring with "the highest cabinet officers," who used their patronage and personal influence "to thwart the President's great scheme of adjusting the Union." With encouragement, they might get so strong that they would run the government "independently of the Executive." Johnson ought to dismiss them. Let him not dally with conciliation. "You can do nothing to appease the ambition of these aspiring men. They look beyond you & rely on their measures to defeat you as the means of compassing their own ends. You must appeal to the people and rely upon the power of your principles to accomplish the general work you & they have at heart to make you victorious."[10]

The second baleful influence was even more dangerous, because as cabinet officer he saw the president more regularly and because his close contacts on Capitol Hill gave him credibility as an observer of Republican alignments. Gideon Welles, the prickly secretary of the navy, was an old states' rights Democrat who turned away from the party when it seemed to fall under the control of the Slave Power. Taking a narrow view of what the Constitution permitted and, like most old Jacksonians, naturally wary of any effort by Congress to expand its role at the expense of the executive, the secretary of the navy was out of sympathy with Reconstruction from the first, especially on a Negro suffrage basis. His diary would become an indispensable source on the inner workings of the Johnson administration, but it revealed a take on politics that came close to delusional. As dogmatic as the most headstrong radical, utterly unable to rethink basic premises as the southern situation changed, he quickly assumed that whoever disagreed with him must be fool, knave, fanatic, or traitor.[11]

Nobody measured up to Welles's standards of statesmanship outside the cabinet and barely anyone within it. He suspected all of his colleagues of working to curry favor with the president's enemies or of preparing to desert the administration for their own advantage. Secretary of War Edwin M. Stanton was a blustering coward, a fawning hypocrite, a spy working for the Republicans in Congress. Secretary of State William Seward was a meddling, gossiping wireworker, too friendly with the president's enemies. His cunning had driven Montgomery Blair from the cabinet in 1864 (it had not); Stanton was his tool, nothing else. No wonder they worked so well together! When both of them strove to keep Congress and the executive on speaking terms, Welles knew how to read that, too. Both of them were radical accomplices, out to wreck

Johnson and undo his program. And why not? Both men, Welles was sure, were ravened with presidential fever.[12]

Congress was worse. Welles knew radicals when he saw them. Increasingly, they became anybody out of agreement with him. Moderate senator William Pitt Fessenden of Maine was one and James Grimes was another. As far as Welles was concerned, all that separated them from the Sumners was bad digestion, ego, and ill temper. When they came out against the president, injured vanity explained it—that or their having once been Whigs, who no doubt resented seeing so lowly a Democratic plebeian as Andrew Johnson rise so high.[13] Policy was made, to Welles's thinking, by "the master spirits," cunning and radical men, "arrogant, presuming, and dictatorial." That was only natural; Welles knew how events came about. Small, crafty minorities of intriguers led the masses wherever they pleased. Secession was just one case. Now the same was true about the radical minority and the Republican Party as a whole. Congressmen could not be voting as they believed. They acted under the whip of party, "which is cunningly kept up with almost despotic power." By August 1865 the secretary was suspecting that all the criticisms of Johnson's Reconstruction came from those out to foist Negro suffrage on the South and that necessarily those who favored impartial suffrage must intend that sex-drenched horror, "social equality."[14]

Laden with misconceptions, Welles eagerly passed them on to the president and, incidentally, every proof he could find that cabinet officers were working against him. In the end, the secretary of the navy's impact can only be guessed. Certainly he complained that Johnson kept his own counsel and did not take others into his confidence; he chafed at the president's restraint as hesitancy, even timidity, and was sure that Seward had poisoned his chief's mind—just the kind of behavior Welles expected from such a confirmed old Whig. Whatever effect Welles did have, however, could only have reinforced the president's own suspicion that enemies were lurking in his own official family, that his opponents were driven by selfish, crazed, or treasonable purposes, and that the smartest politics would be those that rallied the people against the policy-makers on Capitol Hill.

But Johnson did not really need advice on which to base his view of northern politics. All he had to do was revert to the southern preconceptions of the 1850s, a task made all the easier after three years' absence from Washington. Quick to see in antislavery men a fanaticism that Tennessee politics had always insisted was their chief characteristic, he readily returned to the views he had had before the war, that they were disunionists as bad as the secessionists and every bit as much traitors. Seeing them as Democrats had cast them before the war, as men "ready to go to war" to destroy slavery just as white southerners were to protect it, Johnson assured a correspondent of the *Times* of London that treason and a thirst for war remained among those who had won. "Each side was willing to sacrifice the government in order to gain its object." The South had simply "struck first" — which implied, of course, that the North would have struck eventually. Now "rebellion" was "swinging round to the other end" of the Union, with radicals ready to sunder the country "rather [than] have their supremacy destroyed by the re-introduction of the South."[15]

Johnson was not talking about extremists outside the party system. He was accusing the most respected Republican officeholders. Nor was he claiming merely that there had been fanatics north and south. He was insisting that the Republican Party itself had, before the war, been a party prepared to make war on "the Government" and that it was preparing to do that again. This was more than a semantical description of Congress's refusal to admit southern states to representation. It was an assertion of armed treason being plotted or hatched.

It could be nothing less, because Johnson could never understand how level-headed men could really believe in equal rights for blacks. Detest the planters though he might, he had never seen slavery as a wrong done to its immediate victims. The injury, he insisted, was more to the poorer whites who had been forced to compete with the labor that their rich neighbor owned. Johnson's cure would be to spread slave owning more widely, not to raise "every splay-footed, bandy-shanked, hump-backed, thick-lipped, flat-nosed, woolly-headed, ebon-colored negro in the country upon equality with the poor white man."[16] Taking this view, he could explain away the antislavery activists as either crazed idealists or conspirators with some unspoken and darker end in view. As soon became clear, that darker end to Andrew Johnson was power itself, the power to dominate the Union, even at a cost to its original institutions. Such men could not be reconciled with halfway measures, negotiated with, persuaded out of their positions. Confidential friends heard him compare the radicals to Robespierre and the Jacobins in the French Reign of Terror, and he offered unanswerable proof: Robespierre, too, had favored giving blacks the vote. America's radicals were as "bloody-minded as the cowardly Robespierre had become when his power departed and dangers environed him."[17] They must be beaten, and, fortunately, Andrew Johnson knew that he had the people on his side.

The people — the mystic people who could do no wrong — had always been with Johnson. That faith had carried him through hard times and seething recrimination. Now the president grew convinced that the people of the country were with him and against the radicals. Many of those who wrote him letters that fall did their best to help him see the world that way. A friend from Tennessee approvingly quoted a former Confederate general who declared that Johnson had "saved Republican government, and kept the Radicals from establishing a monarchy or despotism." For himself, he was confident that the conservatives of all parties and a "United South will enable you by the blessing of God to put down the *Radical Distructionists*—and preserve law, order and constitutional liberty."[18]

Johnson's failure to distinguish between moderates and radicals and his conviction that the people stood with him against radicalism made the president ready to assume that when Congress opened the majority would accept his Reconstruction governments and admit their representatives to Congress. Only radicals could reject the credentials of loyal men from a reconstructed Tennessee. But House and Senate insisted on investigating whether any valid, republican governments existed in the South, fit to elect congressmen, and referred the whole question to a newly designed joint committee of fifteen. That may have been the moment in which Johnson decided that the radicals ran Congress and, having seen the radical Thaddeus Stevens offering the resolution creating that committee, rated Stevens as the unofficial dictator of the House.[19]

A defter politician would have read the cues from Capitol Hill differently. Republicans did not just proclaim, ever more loudly, their faith in Andrew Johnson. They sent their most influential leaders to the White House to explain every step they took and to provide reassurances. Even the joint committee offered conciliatory possibilities: if a Reconstruction program could be delayed for several months until the committee reported its findings, the Johnson governments down south would be given a chance to prove their worth and radicals would be effectively muzzled. They could offer Reconstruction plans, but these would be referred to the committee without debate and buried there. Tennessee as a state could not participate in the Congress, but Thaddeus Stevens himself offered the resolution inviting the members-elect from Andrew Johnson's own state to take seats on the floor.

But the most important thing that the president should have been listening to was the silence, interrupted by spatters of rhetorical applause. Republicans went out of their way to show how consistent their ideas were with what Andrew Johnson said and did. The radicals were scathing in private, but in public they tried to claim the president for their side. When Thaddeus Stevens rose to speak in December, he offered his own Reconstruction proposals with all the grumbling admission that his views expressed no mind but his own and that his only words about Johnson were those of praise. Ben Wade of Ohio couched his criticisms in words that spoke of a president whose policy had improved greatly on Lincoln's, was "right as far as he has gone," and only needed his work secured by several steps on the part of Congress.[20] Johnson's conservative apologists, and only they, spotted the unbridgeable abyss between Congress and president and scrutinized every stray phrase to prove that an implacable enmity existed—an enmity that no radical publicly admitted to having. What clamor radicals made came from editors and agitators. Even they, for the most part, saw the president as mistaken, not menacing.

Charles Sumner's alienation from the administration was no secret, but what a keener observer might have noticed was how sedulously he left the president alone. Blurting out the word "whitewash" about a presidential message insisting that order and law prevailed down south, Sumner backed off at once, protesting that he had not meant any criticism of Johnson's patriotism or intentions. For the next four months, he spoke not a single word against the administration or its Reconstruction policy; indeed, his greatest speech was against the constitutional amendment that the president had declared himself against. Even after the president had singled him out for personal attack, Sumner made no reply. He worked up some remarks about Johnson's veto of the civil rights bill but never delivered them. Sure that Johnson had gone badly wrong, the radical senator had spent months persuading himself that when the president saw the effects of his policy, he would let Congress change it. By New Year's, Sumner held onto only the faintest of hopes—but it was a discernible hope, all the same.[21]

Sumner's restraint went for nothing. From Welles, the president received a full account of what the senator was saying in private and the secretary's version of what other people had told him about Sumner. And he embellished it, placing Sumner within "a deep and extensive intrigue" against Johnson. The president was even given a clipping that Sumner had sent Welles to show the effects of Johnson's policies down south but which could also be read as a threat to impeach him.[22]

By that time, Welles's suspicion of "radicals" had grown into the conviction that a conspiracy was under way to destroy the executive branch and overthrow free government. At the heart of the plot was the joint committee of fifteen. "Congress in both branches . . . are but puppets in the hands of the Directory and do little but sanction and obey the orders of that committee," he wrote. The Republican Party had become "a mere machine of Thad Stevens." The plotters were planning to "divide the Union" and would plunge America "into a more wicked rebellion . . . than that from which we have emerged."[23]

Welles did not understand Republicans or the dynamics of policymaking in Congress at all. Stevens did not chair the "Directory," as the newly created Joint Committee on Reconstruction came to be labeled. The resolutions he reported from it had passed against his desires. The two great pieces of legislation that were to provoke the president's wrath came out of the Judiciary Committee; the joint committee had had nothing to do with them. The Directory's one foray into legislation that winter was a proposed constitutional amendment that radicals hated and, defying Stevens, managed to recommit in the House and then kill outright in the Senate. The only victory that House radicals could claim had been a bill giving all black adult males in the District of Columbia the vote, a bill smothered in Senate committee.

Whatever Johnson believed precisely, it came pretty close to what Welles was telling him. Disturbing hints of his thinking appeared every so often. Early in February 1866, a delegation of blacks, led by Frederick Douglass, called at the White House to pay their respects and to express a hope that the president could see his way clear to favor Negro suffrage in the District of Columbia. Scarcely had the formal courtesies been exchanged before Johnson burst out with his own thoughts. Black people had always hated poor whites like himself, he asserted, waving away Douglass's denial. Slaves preferred the large planters for their masters because they considered it more "respectable." To give blacks the vote would bring on race war. If freedmen did not like the laws they suffered, let them emigrate! Then, at length, the president defended himself against charges that none of his callers had made and, indeed, that the two leaders of the delegation had firmly denied, that he was not the blacks' true friend. It was a bewildering performance, except to insiders. As one secretary confided, Johnson "no more expected that darkey delegation . . . than he did the cholera. He saw their little game." They were "but tools of Sumner, Old Thad & Company duly instructed, who came here to trap him, if they could." As soon as they filed out, the president exploded. "Those d——d sons of b——s thought they had me in a trap!" he raged. "I know that d——d Douglass, he's just like any nigger & he would sooner cut a white man's throat than not!"[24]

Before the end of January, Republicans were more uneasy than they admitted publicly. The president was beginning a deliberate press campaign of leaked and vetted statements, setting himself against Negro suffrage in the District and against the proposed constitutional amendment. The provisional governors had been withdrawn from the South, and the new, conservative civil governments had been given discretionary authority. Republicans would need a huge capacity for denial to still think that the president meant his Reconstruction program as an experiment. They could still tell themselves that he would permit changes: a continuation of the Freedmen's Bureau with its aid to former slaves making labor contracts and its military courts open to black testimony where white courts were not. He had listened and made suggestions before Senate judiciary committee chairman Lyman Trumbull of Illinois introduced a civil rights bill, protecting equal justice and equal penalties under law, and had made no objection to one provision, affirming that black people had the right of citizenship. Still, things seemed to be going wrong down south, and the president's inaction in redressing them raised concern.

Others claimed to know Johnson's mind as well as Republicans did. The most frightening of them were the southerners, now appealing to him as their true friend against the radicals—by which they meant all but a half-dozen congressmen in the majority party—and hailing him as the strong hand who would remedy years of unconstitutional actions in one swift blow. In late January, disturbing word came from New Orleans to Congressman James A. Garfield. One of the wealthiest bankers, Jacob Barker, had just returned from a trip to Washington. There, he had urged the president to set up a Congress made up of southerners and, presumably, their northern Democratic sympathizers, and, as soon as it organized, to declare it equally legitimate with the sitting body. And, Barker was telling friends, the president liked the idea "but had not back bone enough to recognize it." Of course, the Unionist passing on the story assured Garfield, "nobody here believes the President held any such view." Loyal men knew that the moment southerners tried any such trick, "they would very soon have been in session at Fortress Monroe by virtue of compulsory process."[25] But why was Johnson bending an ear to such talk at all? Why did he not make his real feelings better understood?

Republicans would not have felt better if they had known. From the start, the president suspected plots against him. When, before the session began, the former and future Speaker of the House, Schuyler Colfax, gave a speech announcing the party position, he only expressed what most moderates intended: harmony with the administration but legislative guarantees for loyalty and equality before the law down south. Just about no Republican saw any conflict between the two—but Johnson did. The very idea that "this little fellow" dared make a speech before the presidential message (two weeks before) proved his villainy. Colfax's address must be a plot to coerce the administration and define its policy.[26] Congress's doings had become, in his mind, the "preconcerted measures of the Radicals." The appointment of the Joint

Committee on Reconstruction struck him as a plot to set up "an irresponsible Directory," in the style of the French Revolution, that would dictate to Congress. As for the refusal to readmit Tennessee's representatives, Johnson knew exactly how to read that. The radicals meant "nothing short of a subversion or change in the structure of government," he told his cabinet. "The unmistakable design of Thad Stevens and his associates was to take the government into their own hands . . . and to get rid of him by declaring Tennessee out of the Union."[27] (No Republican, not even Thaddeus Stevens, had brought up any such idea, and when Democrats raised it as a mere academic debating point, they had been given a crushing reply.)

What made that misreading so serious was not simply that it was untrue or that it ascribed to the radicals intentions that none of them had. It also assumed that over the large body of lawmakers the radical minority had cast a spell. Their legislative skills, their talent for eloquence or parliamentary procedure, had given them influence far beyond their real authority. That made them dangerous, and that made an appeal to the moderate men in Congress chimerical. Moderates, even if well meaning, could not escape the webs that radicalism had spun for them. Johnson's recourse from the first, therefore, must lie beyond Congress, with the people, and with an appeal to the people.

This assumption was as dangerous to Johnson as it was to harmony in policymaking. Increasingly, it confined him, shutting him off from the voices, one by one, first of radicals and then of moderates, as they became persuaded that his ears were closed to them. The letters coming to the White House came from an ever more limited share of the political spectrum, particularly from the Democratic end of it. In time, the president would receive only the advice he wanted, reinforcing his own fears and prejudices and making reconciliation with the Republican leadership all the more difficult.

In view of Johnson's record of loyalty to the Union, suspicions might seem unimaginable. Yet the stretch was not as far as it seemed. By mid-February 1866, a very good case could be made that the more the public knew about Andrew Johnson, the less he resembled the man they thought they had known. Having sworn that traitors must be punished, he had spent the summer and autumn raining pardons down on landowners and Confederate generals. The only political prisoner in any peril of standing trial was former Confederate president Jefferson Davis, and the government was lagging in acting on his case. By the end of 1865, thoughtful observers believed that the chance for any other criminal prosecutions had passed. Not even many of the radicals wanted bloody punishments any more; many never had. Still, the change in the president seemed significant. Having spoken of being a Moses to the black people a year before, Johnson had been half-hearted in pressuring his newly made governments in the South into guaranteeing essential civil rights, much less opening the right to vote to all men, regardless of color.[28]

Conditions change and judgments with them, but to Republicans that was not the point. If Johnson's views had shifted, he concealed them. Later defenders would maintain that the president was misinterpreted because he made such a good listener. Visitors read support in his silence and agreement in his failure to gainsay them. That was true enough. Johnson limited his pugnacity to stump speaking and was shy about being disagreeable, even in conversations with white people that he disliked. But it was not as simple as that. Johnson knew perfectly well how his silence would be read. He went out of his way to mislead callers. Even when he spoke up, he was less than candid. In the political campaigns in the fall of 1865, Johnson had remained entirely ambiguous, not correcting the impression, which Democrats had spread far and wide, that, in all respects, he stood with them and against the "Radicals," by which they meant not just one strand of the Republican Party but the great majority of its members.

His message to Congress had been equally ambiguous, more so than an inability to express himself could explain. It had been couched in terms that would deceive moderate Republicans into thinking that he was still with them, while signaling to Democrats that he was something else entirely. As bad news came from the reconstructed South, the White House left a clear impression that the president felt dissatisfied with the situation and would not object to Congress sharing in the work. At no time had he insisted that Reconstruction was exclusively an executive prerogative, and his words were so carefully chosen as to lead prominent senators to believe that civil rights legislation would be quite acceptable, providing that it was properly drawn up.[29] When the veto messages came, moderate Republicans felt deceived. The vagueness looked like the double game that it probably had been all along.

Even more than just holding back his fullest feelings or failing to share his purposes with callers, he had shown an almost uncanny ability to plant misimpressions. Not even most radicals could have asked for more than Johnson's announcement that the "life breath" of southern states had been "suspended" and his insistence that the nation had a duty to secure "a republican form of government" there. To a delegation from Indiana, he promised not just punishment for traitors but what sounded like confiscation.[30] Ben Wade of Ohio was even a little alarmed at how wholesale the president's ideas of punishment seemed to go. When Charles Sumner called to urge that the new governments down south be elected by loyal men white and black, the president told him,

"On this question, Mr. Sumner, there is no difference between us. You and I are alike." Heading homeward that evening, the senator imagined that "the battle of my life seemed to be ended," and the republic "rose before me, refulgent in the blaze of assured freedom, an example to nations." He never knew that at the very time the president had given him reassurances, he had been telling another caller that Sumner's policy "was simply secession in another form" and that Sumner "and his friends would produce results that we had made a war to prevent."[31]

At the president's behest, Chief Justice Salmon P. Chase toured the South advocating Negro suffrage as a representative of the administration's intentions. While he was gone, presidential proclamations reorganized the southern states on a white-voter basis. Chase was not simply undercut. He was discredited. Not surprisingly, he felt as if he had been set up.[32] Other leading radicals, among them Senator Henry Wilson of Massachusetts, Congressmen James Ashley of Ohio, and William D. Kelley of Pennsylvania, had the same experience as Sumner.[33] The president's declaration that letting Negroes vote assured a war of the races fit poorly with the man who, months before, had praised Kelley's speech in favor of universal male suffrage and had explained to callers that if he had a vote in Tennessee he would open up the ballot to both races.

Radical Republicans had been led to understand from their interviews with the president that he favored impartial suffrage, but they and moderates alike, even after the proclamations created southern governments on a white-voter basis, were misled even further by the assurance that nothing, in the end, had been settled. The new governments were only provisional, until Congress could come into session and arrange a permanent settlement in the South. Radical congressman George S. Boutwell had taken alarm at the terms in the first proclamation, that of May 29, 1865, which created a government in North Carolina. Hastening to Washington, he went with Vermont congressman Justin S. Morrill to the White House to protest. The president assured him that "the measure was tentative." Johnson meant to see how the experiment worked and would issue no proclamations for other states until he had had time to judge the results. Great was Boutwell's chagrin when within the fortnight he read a similar proclamation issued for Mississippi and, within a month, proclamations for Georgia, Texas, Alabama, South Carolina, and Florida. Boutwell never called at the White House again; Sumner did, in one last testy conversation, and went away not just empty-handed but also bareheaded: the president had mistaken the senator's silk hat for a cuspidor.[34]

Comforted with private assurances that Johnson expected Congress to adjust Reconstruction, moderates overlooked the conspicuous absence of any

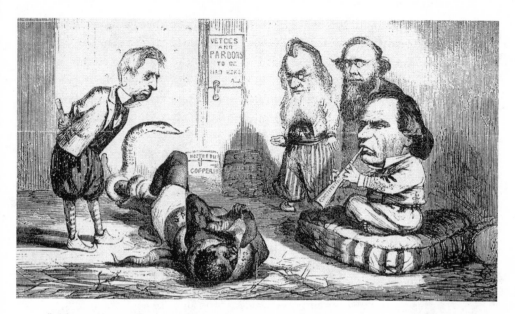

"Andrew Johnson's Reconstruction; and How it Works" (detail). Thomas Nast, *Harper's Weekly*, September 1, 1866. The president plays the pipe of the Constitution, charming two snakes—southern Rebels and northern Copperheads—who are strangling the former slave. Secretary of State William Seward looks on with interest; Secretary of the Navy Gideon Welles and Secretary of War Edwin M. Stanton actually seem to be enjoying the spectacle. This may have misread Seward's position—given the chance, he would have moved much closer to the moderate Republican majority in Congress. Stanton was even more distressed at what he saw as an abandonment of loyal men down south.

such reminder that Congress had the last word in his letters and orders to southern provisional governors. By the start of 1866, almost nobody thought that new governments could replace the ones Johnson had set in motion; every day they took deeper root. It became more certain that whatever change the president would allow, he would not let Congress simply begin the reconstructing process all over again. But even then, Republicans thought that their direction could be shifted and their worst impulses restrained, and in this, at least, the president would agree with them.

It was with a feeling of betrayal, not simply surprise, that Congress met the insulting, implacable tone in the Freedmen's Bureau bill veto. Moderate Republicans could accept some of the arguments against the specific provisions of the measure. The bureau did involve a lot of expense at a time when the government should have been cutting back on its spending; it did create a potentially dangerous source of federal patronage; it did continue the military courts to which former slaves appealed, instead of leaving justice to civil authorities.

But all of Johnson's protests, so blind to any recognition that black southerners needed protection, only spoke to a larger point. For the first time, the president was making quite clear that Reconstruction was at an end, that there was just about nothing left for Congress to do. More than that, Johnson indicated not just that Republicans had made bad law but that they might lack the authority to make any law at all, until the South had returned to its place in Congress. He implied strongly that the House and Senate had been abusing their right to judge the qualifications of their own members. They could not "shut out, in time of peace, any State from the representation to which it is entitled by the Constitution."[35] That might mean that no law touching the South, whatever its provisions, would receive presidential approval. It might also mean that Congress itself was of only questionable legality. At the very least, the moderates had found out what Boutwell, Chase, and Sumner knew already. The president's word could not be trusted; his silence had to be positively distrusted. If he was reliable in nothing, could he be capable of anything?

Finally, for those fearful of a President Johnson prepared to use military force to overthrow the republic, there was his wartime record and his Reconstruction. Defend it as Democrats might, Johnson had been a forceful military governor in Tennessee, reading the Constitution to mean whatever served his purposes best and dispensing with any part of it that kept him from doing what he wanted to do. He had arrested and suppressed avidly.[36] Republicans, for their part, did not have to wonder whether Johnson would prove to be a usurper. By their reading of his actions since the war's end, he was usurping already. Did it seem so far-fetched to think that he might try even bolder usurpations, all the while telling himself that he was doing it as the shortest, most efficient way to save the Constitution?

Washington's Birthday made the ideal moment for mass meetings of conservatives, upholding the president's Reconstruction policy. Unfortunately, it also was the ideal moment for the president himself to break loose. Promising his advisers that he would give a few perfunctory remarks to a crowd of serenaders, he launched into a full-scale speech, much of it written out and read by candlelight. Later, Secretary of the Treasury Hugh McCulloch insisted that the president surprised himself. Under "the influence of the excitement produced by the immense crowd that surrounded him he was betrayed into utterances that he would not have made under other circumstances." But a hostile reporter saw no excitement in the speaker's face. "Every word was measured," he wrote. "He means mischief. His face incarnated it. His every word intended it."[37]

Mischief the president made, but mostly for himself. The speech did two things dramatically. First, it removed quite a few illusions about who Andrew Johnson was and where he stood. In one of his first appearances since taking the oath, he showed not the dignity that the press had vested him with and that all presidents were expected to show but the aggressive and personal temper of a stump speaker. The appeals for vindication, the associating of himself not just with Christian charity but with Christ himself, the use of the personal pronoun three times per minute in a speech slightly longer than an hour—all might have thrilled listeners. In cold print, the effect was much less attractive. Preaching conciliation, Johnson declared implacable war on those who disagreed with his policy.

Second, it became starkly clear that to the president what separated him from his opponents was not a disagreement on basic principles but a traitorous conspiracy. He had restored the Union. Congress, by its lawless refusal to admit southern representatives, barred the way to peace. Indeed, "we find ourselves almost in the midst of another rebellion." The framers of a new constitutional amendment were not simply misguided; they were "engaged in the work of breaking up the government." Conspirators thirsted for revenge. Eight million southerners "were to be annihilated and destroyed." But the real culprit was the Joint Committee on Reconstruction, "an irresponsible central directory," which had seized "nearly all the powers of government" without consulting Congress or the president. Traitors as bad as Jefferson Davis led the fight on the president. As the crowd called for names, Johnson could not resist. "I say Thaddeus Stevens of Pennsylvania, is one; I say Mr. Sumner of the Senate, is another, and Wendell Phillips is another." Seizing on a grumble by Stevens that for less presumptuousness than the president had shown King Charles had lost his head, Johnson took that remark as an announced intention by the majority party to slay him. "I make use of a very strong expression when I say that I have no doubt the intention was to incite assassination and so get out of the way the obstacle from place and power," he cried. Were "they" not satisfied "with the blood which has been shed? Does not the murder of Lincoln appease the vengeance and wrath of the opponents of this government? . . . Do they still want more blood?" Let it be shed! If need be, let him be sacrificed on an altar to the Union![38]

The implication that Johnson's enemies had killed Lincoln and were out to kill him (and eight million more besides) and the suggestion that the moderates' purpose in framing an amendment was to destroy the Union were astonishing charges. Accusing leaders in Congress of treason could hardly clear the air. Even some of the president's closest allies in the cabinet were dismayed, and Republicans still seeking some middle way between president and Congress were appalled. "Johnson could not walk our streets today & live, if curses and maledictions could have buried him out of sight," a Rhode Islander commented.[39]

The general feeling among Republicans was one of shame, not of fury. The prestige of Johnson's office and, worse still, the presumption of statesmanship that most presidents counted on as their political capital had been stripped from it. Ten months before, "the president was assassinated & the people mourned," a minister told his congregation. Now "the President assassinated himself & the people blushed." Desperately, Republicans sought reassurance from representatives in Washington that there had been some good excuse. "Was he drunk?" one wrote hopefully.[40] But there was plenty of anger, too, and, for the first time among the most alienated radicals, the stirrings of fear. "It is not, as you will see by reading the 'veto Message,' simply a question as to whether this particular bill shall become a law," Congressman John Lynch of Maine wrote the governor, "but whether Congress is a part of the Govt." Johnson really thought himself in danger "of being thrown out of the Presidency, if not being assassinated," editor John Wien Forney wrote. "God knows what we may expect at his hands."[41]

Republicans began to wonder whether they had seriously misread Johnson's character and not just his principles. With the Washington's Birthday speech, they discovered how little they had known him. The pugnacity, the extremity of language, all opened fearful possibilities. Against what he thought was treason, would Johnson do as he had done in Tennessee, playing the tyrant for the sake of the republic? Now the fears of a new war created by newly inflamed language came into the open. "In this crisis the man who tries to calm the temper of political parties is I think in the path of duty," an Ohioan wrote his senator. "The danger of more strife and bloodshed may be and I devoutly hope is passed, but such language as Mr. Forney [publisher of the *Washington Chronicle*] is using and many others is producing great bitterness . . ." A few saw it as a summons. "The blood and treasure of the country are as ready as when we had to cut our way to Washington through Baltimore," a Maine resident assured the chairman of the Joint Committee on Reconstruction.[42]

Extremists in the South gave an even more alarming response to Johnson's speech. "If the wretches who now constitute a packed majority of the Rump Congress have to be driven from the Legislative halls they disgraced at the point of a bayonet before peace can be restored, we say let them be driven out," the *Mobile (Ala.) Tribune* announced. A tiny cadre of hotheads expected a military action against the traitors of the North. They welcomed it. "I wish to Heaven Andy Johnson was a soldier and would call for volunteers," one supporter exclaimed as the speech ended. "I guess he would get enough to drive those congressmen off Capitol Hill." Others around him agreed. They swore that they would be the first to sign up; it would give them pleasure to hang senators. If Johnson really meant what he had said about the traitors up north, the *Chicago Times* asserted, he should make his words good by ordering Stevens, Sumner, Phillips, "and their confederates in Congress and all over the country" arrested for treason. "In no other way can this Northern rebellion be promptly quelled, and the public quiet restored." That was for starters. If "the rump Congress" did not give up its "revolutionary and lawless practices" and admit southern lawmakers at once, the president must do his duty, "constitute himself the Cromwell of the time, and dissolve the rump by military power."[43]

Rodomontade was cheap. No Democratic armies mustered; no senators echoed the call. For that matter, even most Republicans, after the first shock, reasoned that Johnson had misspoken. Sobered up, he no more wanted to break the republic than he wanted to break his party. Moderates seized on a few halfhearted phrases to show that he would sign a Freedmen's Bureau bill nearly as good as the one just vetoed. They predicted that he would accept the civil rights bill working its way through the House or, if he could not agree to it, would favor another quite like it. (Johnson intended no such thing. His second veto was even more implacable and even more defiant of Congress's authority than his first.) But the monthlong truce between veto messages had a more nervous air. The talk that there might well be a coup d'état in the works never quite stilled. Even men who did not consider themselves alarmists looked at the intemperance of Johnson's language and the recklessness of his defiance and wondered how far he would go in resisting congressional policy.[44]

As the civil rights bill neared final passage, Democratic newspapers predicted that Johnson would refuse to enforce it. He might not interfere in its operations—the burden of responsibility for making the law operative would rest with the courts. Nor could he declare the law unconstitutional on his own independent judgment after it had gone through both houses. But he could use the pardoning power to set free every person sentenced for violating its provisions, the *New York World* remarked—the pardoning power was unlimited and an indisputable constitutional prerogative. A few Republicans expected still worse. Under the influence of Copperheads, one Illinoisan wrote, Johnson "may become an imitation of Louis Napoleon and attempt to do what the friends of Genl. McClellan wanted him to do [that is, turn out the Congress at bayonet point]. The Genl. was restrained by cowardice. He was afraid he would get hurt, but Andy is a more dangerous and desperate man." After the civil rights bill veto, rumors spread that Democrats had felt out General Grant's willingness to let a putsch go forward. The *Chicago Tribune*'s correspondent dismissed the fears, but on rather worrisome grounds: whatever Johnson's intentions, he knew that the odds against a successful coup were too great to overcome, as long as the War Department and the army were in loyal hands. And it would be hard to find military officers who would support the president if he tried drastic remedies.[45]

Any renewal of good feeling after the overriding of the civil rights bill veto would be optimism trumping experience. The language on both sides sharpened considerably. For the first time, a very few Republican newspapers began to discuss the possibilities of impeachment. Democrats rushed to make it seem like the party's general will and to frame it as part of an overarching conspiracy to depose the president and negate the executive branch for good. Conservative journals explained that the admission of Colorado, with its two senators, would give them the acquittal-proof margin they needed. Discovering "crimes" enough would be a mere formality. Without so much as a trial, the Senate would convict instantly. All of these events would transpire within the month. "Of course, an attempt to impeach the President would mark the beginning of revolution and civil war, that would end no one knows where."[46] For Johnson's removal would not happen without a struggle. Congress would order the president's arrest. The president would follow his friends' advice and resist by every appropriate means. No impeachment by a "rump assemblage" was binding. Already the president knew about the designs, a reporter close to him declared, and he had readied himself for action. So conservatives accompanied the prediction that Congress would use technically legal means to further an unconstitutional design with the vow that they would use openly illegal means to protect the true meaning of the Constitution. Impeachment "means the inauguration of a civil war . . . in every city and village of the North," the *Cincinnati Commercial*'s reporter declared in early April.[47]

Over the next eight months, the president and his defenders would spy conspiracies to unseat or kill him and discover preparations for a civil war being devised up north. They ascribed the riots in Norfolk and Memphis, where whites did most of the killing and blacks most of the dying, to radical conspiracies. "The Black Republicans plunged the country into one civil war," an editor warned. "Is it unreasonable to suppose that they would not stop at plunging it into another?" Johnson's supporters wrote him about dark designs to which they had somehow become privy: a plot, for example, based on trumped-up letters proving the president's collusion with Confederate leaders, that would allow the Congress to seize and jail him. While lawmakers debated a bill ordering his arrest, the ringleaders had arranged to surround the White House with guards to keep the president from delivering orders for the representatives' arrest and to station a squadron of soldiers east of the Capitol to fend off armed attack.[48]

Along with that sense of a republic under siege came scattered Democratic calls for the president to restore the republic of the fathers by extraordinary means. Democrats grew more open in their insistence that a Congress excluding the mass of southern representatives violated the spirit if not the letter of the Constitution. It became "the Rump Congress," its very legality thrown into question. Increasingly, the president's own language had grown more menacing. In his speeches, he referred to the Republican lawmakers as a body hanging on the verge of government or as a pretended Congress. Having begun by questioning the right of Congress to legislate for states not yet permitted representation in the Capitol, he became increasingly bold about questioning the right of Congress to claim itself a lawful assemblage.

And the natural question was, what would he do about Congress, if he could? And what could he do, if he would? From northern Democrats the appeals came in the spring of 1866. John Campbell, of Philadelphia, praising the president's work to "save the Union," urged him to keep his courage and challenge any "revolutionary proceeding" that would shear the executive of the power to remove obstructive officeholders. In addition, he must call on the southern representatives to come to Washington in December next, when the lame-duck session of the 39th Congress met. They should take their seats. "Should any Revolutionary and bloody faction attempt by violence to oust them you have the power to see that the law shall be vindicated and the Constitution obeyed." But, of course, that implied that the southerners would take their seats without the recognition or acceptance of the Republican majority— and that the "power" the president had would not be to "vindicate" the law so much as to use force to keep southerners in the places they had chosen to take. It meant, in effect, the use of bayonets against the Congress.[49] The president's oath obligated him to uphold the Constitution, and the only way was to use his powers as commander in chief to restore a Congress in which all states were represented. "If he can do it by moral influences," the New York Daily News granted, "so much the better. If he cannot do it without calling upon the bayonets at his command, let him do it nevertheless. He has force enough to insure the victory of republicanism over faction."[50]

Even as the civil rights bill lay awaiting Senate action, the moment of truth seemed to have arrived—at least to a few fevered editors. A presidential proclamation announced the war's official end. Johnson expressed nothing more than fact, though the document threw into question what little military supervision remained down south and put the use of military courts permitting black testimony in jeopardy. But some Democrats found the implications much farther reaching. By declaring the war over, Johnson had taken away the best excuse Congress had for not recognizing the southern governments' senators and congressmen, they argued. The president was laying the groundwork for a refusal to recognize any act of the congressional fragment until they did so. He had prepared the legal basis for military action to bring House and Senate into line. Fearmongers may have taken a hint from the president's own organ, the *Washington National Intelligencer*, that the proclamation would be "immediately followed by other action on his part." The *Louisville (Ky.) Courier* issued what sounded like a summons to arms. A "revolutionary junta" of "traitors—who are recognized as traitors by the people . . . a mad and reckless faction leading a minority of the people to establish a central despotism"— impersonated Congress. Every day it met was "a triumph of treason." Neither the courts nor the president must recognize it as a lawful body from that moment on.[51]

Convinced by Democratic rhetoric, some southern editors really believed that differences over the Constitution had brought the North to the flash point. When the fracas began, they predicted, the South would stand by the president, but he would find supporters aplenty north of the Mason-Dixon Line. This time the army would crush the rebels of the North. Only radicals opposed Johnson, and they would find themselves outgunned. "The President has power, and they know it, to plunge the country into another revolution, in which all the power and help of the North will be swamped," a Washington correspondent wrote gleefully. ". . . The revolution has reached the North, and may be felt there with more severity than it has ever been felt anywhere in its progress."[52]

Some southerners dreaded the set-to. Others hoped that the South could stand aside and profit by the outcome. But others only wanted a rallying cry. A Mississippian wrote in April 1866:

> Judging from public State papers & debates in Congress, Your Excellency may shortly find it needful to sustain the authority of The United States Govt & the Constitution thereof by, & with such armies as by the said immortal instrument are legitimate. In the event of such necessity, I tender my services & can raise in thirty days 1000 trained men, of the late Confederate army, as artillerists, who will bear the banner of the union, to sustain the constitution, wherever you will direct.

Furthermore, the correspondent promised the services of Governor Benjamin G. Humphreys, who would "cheerfully" help in any way that the president asked. And in what may have been a veiled reference to the idea that "submissionists" were as lacking in masculine resolve as they had been before the war, in their readiness to abide by the law set down from Washington, he closed, "I do confidently assert that all the *men* of Miss. will sustain the Govt. & Constitution under your authority."[53]

War was not coming. But it was not a healthy sign in politics when level-headed people thought war a real possibility. Nobody was less susceptible to hysteria than the very unradical senior senator from Maine. But after the civil rights veto, William Pitt Fessenden felt that he could not rule out "another fight," though when it came, "that will be the final one." Such fears were a distorted reflection of real concerns, more widely felt, resulting from a Constitution being applied to a situation that the Founders had never anticipated.

By history's standards, the white South groaned under no tyranny; by the twentieth century's standards, the United States was nowhere close to "consolidation" and complete centralization. But the presence of soldiers in the southern streets, of provisional governors and General Orders from army headquarters, and the proposed revision of the Constitution to add to national oversight were like nothing that Americans in peacetime had known before. Considering how far war had brought them from "the Union as it was" and the Constitution of their parents' day, none of the fantasies one year after Appomattox seemed so far-fetched. "Who can doubt in view of the terrible determination displayed by Andrew Johnson on the one side, and the headlong ferocity evinced by the Radicals . . . on the other, that we are on the eve of great events, perhaps of bloody ones?" a South Carolina correspondent wrote.[54]

That Congress has, with malice, sought
To raise a new rebellion.
Both Seward, Weed and I have thought
Too true to need repellion,
That the massacre, at New Orleans,
By Congress was concocted,
To me is clear, as pork and beans,
Or a strong brandy cock-tail!
I'll bet a keg of rum or two,
As fine as e'er was bottl'd,
That Sumner, Wade and Stevens knew
The negroes would be throttl'd!
—Zedekiah Comitatus,
"Reconstruction on 'My Policy'"

chapter 6

HORRORS ON HORRORS ACCUMULATE

July 1866

Creeping fear never quite turned into galloping panic, but by summertime alarm was palpable in reasonable men. Fear did not so possess the minds of lawmakers that they quit debating the constitutional and practical aspects of a lasting Reconstruction. It certainly did not throw the party into the hands of its ultras. The Freedmen's Bureau bill that ended up passing was more modest than its vetoed predecessor. The constitutional amendment that emerged from the joint committee, far from being dictated by Thaddeus Stevens, tore out the very provisions he thought essential.

As a peace settlement, the not-yet-Fourteenth Amendment was revolutionary more in its potential uses than in its actual wording. Guaranteeing the national debt against repudiation and annulling forever the obligations incurred for the Confederacy, it proclaimed a national standard for citizenship that could not be denied on the grounds of race or color. It granted the essential civil rights and left the political ones—the right to vote, hold office, and sit on juries—to the states. States could give or deny black citizens the vote, but those unable to vote could not be counted in apportioning the state's share of House seats. Not a single Confederate was disfranchised, but those who had broken their official oaths to uphold the Constitution had to await congressional dispensation before holding office.[1] Congress made no explicit promise to readmit representatives from any state that ratified, but it left the strongest possible hint by readmitting Tennessee as soon as ratification was announced. Congress stood as safe from military overthrow as ever. No ready-made armies mustered in the South. The *Chicago Times* and *New York Daily News* sounded the trumpets for legions of Copperheads that never massed. And time was on the side of peace. The further in the past the war receded, the more impractical it became for yesterday's soldiers to heed the call to arms.

Putting the fears in perspective is essential. But doing so does not mean that they amounted to nothing. If anything, the disquiet had spread wider by summertime. Nobody was more levelheaded, less radical, than "the Ohio icicle," Senator John Sherman. But the president worried him. "I almost fear he contemplates civil war," he wrote his brother, General William Tecumseh Sherman.[2] Within that fortnight, the secretary of the navy glimpsed plots on the other side. There was a "revolutionary feeling of the leading Radicals, who are, in fact, conspirators," Gideon Welles jotted in his diary. Former postmaster general Montgomery Blair assured him that a new civil war was brewing and that Radical leaders were planning it out. Not by chance a Wisconsin congressman offered a resolution to distribute thousands of guns from the federal arsenal to northern state governors. Was it to keep the president from using the army against Congress, by effectively disarming the national authority? Or could it be part of a deeply laid plot to build up state militia that, when needed, would back a power grab by Congress?[3]

In that context, a trivial, even silly, controversy took on graver meanings. Republicans (at least those with a Whig background) long had found it more than odd that no president they elected left the office alive: William Henry Harrison, Zachary Taylor, Abraham Lincoln. In the fever of early summer, a curious book sharpened old suspicions. John S. Dye's *History of the Plots and Crimes of the Great Conspiracy to Overthrow Liberty in America* traced all three deaths back to the Slave Power. Harrison and Taylor were as much victims of foul play as Lincoln had been. Southern secessionists had been set on bringing the Texas Republic into the Union as fresh slave territory in 1841. Whigs would never accept so revolutionary a step, but Harrison's vice president was Virginia Democrat (and later Confederate officer) John Tyler. Harrison's removal assured annexation and gave an excuse for a land-grabbing war with Mexico. Taylor had stood in the way of the giveaway to southern interests, misnamed the Compromise of 1850. Perfectly well on the Fourth of July, he had suddenly and unaccountably sickened and died. Doctors, no doubt well paid, pretended that "cholera morbus" felled him. They knew better. Timid and weak, James

Buchanan seemed too conservative for southerners to rely on. Having made a firm old Unionist his secretary of state and having replaced Jefferson Davis as secretary of war, he must be eliminated to make way for one of the inner group of revolutionary plotters. The day after his cabinet was announced, Buchanan fell dangerously ill at the National Hotel. Sheer luck spared his life. Abraham Lincoln, then, was not the first victim of conspiracy but the fourth. The only difference in crimes was the method. Thus, according to Dye's *Plots*, all the victims before Lincoln had been poisoned.

History has justly forgotten this book. Dye's had been a dubious, even scurrilous, career, and his "proofs" took great leaps of faith. His supposed evidence only worked if one ruled out natural causes, ignored Harrison's actual symptoms, found a motive in beliefs that the president never expressed but might have been "understood" to have held, and, naturally, had nothing so inconvenient as an exhumed body and an autopsy to show it to be the fantasy that it was. But Dye's book seemed less outlandish then than later, because, for some Americans, it confirmed what they already suspected and at the time of Lincoln's assassination declared publicly. For those hungry to explain American politics with long-nurtured conspiracies, here was a natural.

Instead of being laughed away, *Plots* won public attention, and a few editors recommended it, although, if they had any criticism, it was that Dye was telling a twice-told tale.[4] It already was well known that there was "a fatality attending Northern men in the Presidency, when the Vice President is a person of southern sympathies," the *Cincinnati Gazette* reminded readers; "that firmness in a national position is fatal to the president when the Vice President is more subject to Southern influences." Who had forgotten the southern threats in 1856 that if a Republican won the presidency he would never live to enjoy the office? Or Mark M. "Brick" Pomeroy's death wish for Lincoln? Or the attempt that winter on Senator Benjamin Wade's life, or the threats against Sumner's, or the little box he had received with the severed finger of a black man inside? Folklore insisted that any president not affiliated with southern interests was "sure to die" and that the office had an unofficial life insurance policy attached when a Democrat held it. Democratic politico "Prince John," John Van Buren, reveled in it, having told one audience that spring that among the good qualities of electing Democrats was that they never died in office and that he had good grounds for predicting that none ever would. Lincoln's assassination needed no explanation, nor did Andrew Johnson's sudden conversion from threatening the southern masters to appeasing them. Understanding his peril, the *Indianapolis Journal* argued, he took "an early insurance on his life by joining the party that assassinated Abraham Lincoln."[5]

Or was there something even worse? Jane Swisshelm's *Reconstructionist* stood on the feminist fringes of Radical Republicanism, but as early as April it had traced the conspiracy further back. "The business was to get the President, and they got him," the journal charged. "That it was the South which nominated Mr. Johnson, through indirect influence . . . there is no longer any doubt." Nor was there any doubt that "he was prepared beforehand to serve the purposes of treason" and that his elevation and Reconstruction policy "were part and parcel of the assassination plot." Swisshelm drew back from claiming that Johnson had actually shared in, or even known of, Booth's conspiracy ahead of time. That mattered not at all; the important thing was that the conspirators knew Johnson for what he really was. By fall, partisans closer to the Republican center were dropping hints that the president had arranged for Lincoln's murder.[6]

Democrats were outraged at the insinuations. The *Cincinnati Enquirer* pointed out that not one scrap of proof showed that Harrison and Taylor had died anything but a natural death; in any case, it asserted, the Democratic Party could not be blamed for the three presidents who died in office. It was perfectly evident, for example, that John Wilkes Booth had been framed, the editor protested. Who actually killed Lincoln? The *Cincinnati Enquirer* knew it for a fact: the Radical Republicans. Why should they stick at killing one of their own? They were fanatics, assassins by training and nature. There had been plenty of Radical death threats (none of which the *Enquirer* thought fit to detail), and knowledgeable people understood that the only reason the president issued the Emancipation Proclamation was that Radicals extorted it from him "by personal fear."[7]

Such an interest in the past was more than a ravening after historical truth. It pointed the way for events yet to come. As the *Enquirer* warned, what Radicals had done before they certainly would do again. When they chose so militant a man as Ohio's Ben Wade for president pro tempore, in the line of succession, it showed "a thrifty preparation for fatal accidents." If impeachment failed, Radicals were doubtless whispering to each other that the knife or the pistol could do the job, and thousands would rejoice when the deed was done. Philadelphia's foremost Republican editor, John W. Forney, was quoted as having suggested to a crowd that measures might render "impeachment unnecessary." Did these include assassination? Democrats ached to think so. If Johnson was killed, the *Philadelphia Age* predicted, "then the nation has no future. The government is gone . . . and even the name of the United States will become a synonym of reproach in all parts of the world." Yet it had no doubt that Forney had not only urged assassination but he had perfected the arrangements at the recent convention of southern loyalists in Philadelphia. Contrariwise, for the *Gazette*, the president's coming to power by murder explained why all his violent threats against Congress had to be taken seriously. His language against Congress was "the talk of an assassin at heart; of a man who will stop at no murder that will advance his own ends." The *Gazette* would not need to look far for willing murderers. Republicans claimed to have heard private vows from the South to blow Congress up and kill leading Radicals. When Democrats carried a transparency in one Baltimore parade, which depicted a coffin with the label "Thad Stevens's overcoat," it could be read not just as a wish but as a threat, as much one in its own way as that of the Democratic campaigner in Pennsylvania who informed listeners that John Wilkes Booth was America's Robert the Bruce, and that "the time will come when a monument will be erected to Booth higher than that erected to Lincoln."[8]

"I shall be heartily glad when Congress adjourns," banker Henry Cooke wrote his brother and partner, Jay Cooke, in late June. "It has 'worn out its welcome.'" Reporters and many congressmen felt so, too. They sweltered. Many lawmakers fell sick and went home the moment the important work seemed done.[9] But the alarm over Andrew Johnson had gotten so high that when the chance to adjourn for the summer came radicals tried to prevent it. On the evening of July 11, the Republicans gathered to set a departure date. "We are in a very exciting caucus," Congressman Rutherford B. Hayes of Ohio wrote his wife. "Hot as blazes." He was not thinking of the climate. John Farnsworth of Illinois wanted a resolution to keep Congress in session until the December term began. During the interim, he warned, there might be schemes to restore the Rebels to power. The president, Eben Ingersoll of Illinois shouted, was both a traitor and a madman. His conspiracies must be protected against. From George Boutwell of Massachusetts and William D. Kelley of Pennsylvania came like expressions of fear. A "conspiracy was on foot to put the Government into the hands of rebels," Boutwell told the gathering, "and the president was a party to it." Unless resistance was prepared, the president would seize the Capitol. Kelley reminded his colleagues that the president was pronouncing every bill that they passed null and void, for lack of southern representation. Senator Henry S. Lane of Indiana, in most matters a conservative Republican, had worked himself up into a fury, too. He also was ready to remain all summer, he cried, if need be "at the point of a bayonet; . . . if a victim was wanted, he was ready." A million soldiers would rush to Washington to uphold Congress against the president's designs! "Our friends in Congress are getting the most absurd idea into their heads . . . that was ever cherished outside of a Lunatic Asylum," Massachusetts congressman Henry L. Dawes wrote his wife. "We had a caucus last night, and nothing short of the wild ravings of the Girondists before the French Revolution would parallel our proceedings."[10]

Cooler tempers if not cooler temperatures prevailed in the end. At the next caucus, "the bedlamites," as Dawes called them, were outvoted, if narrowly. Republicans set a tentative day for adjournment a week hence. The decision was battled against and adjusted. Still another caucus prolonged the session an extra week. Well aware that congressmen had sweated too long to remain in town any longer than they had to, Thaddeus Stevens tried to compromise. The members would go home on the thirtieth, but both houses' presiding officers could call Congress together whenever necessity required, possibly in October. Even this plan lost badly. There was something to be said for scorching temperatures after all, Dawes admitted, in spurring adjournment. "If the republic doesn't die of the combined effect of Johnson's treachery and our madness then it is immortal."[11]

Congress still had work to do, but in July's broiling emotional atmosphere, how it went about its tasks only fired the suspicions on both sides of usurpation and conspiracy. Seven months before, the restoration of Tennessee might have served as a peace offering between president and Congress. But not now—not when the state's readmission hung on its willingness to ratify the constitutional amendment. Governor Brownlow summoned a special session to ratify the amendment. Democrats knew that they lacked the votes to prevent it. Their one hope was to make sure that nobody had the votes, by keeping a quorum out of reach. Two dozen refused to heed the governor's call, and five more, reaching the assembly, realized that, with their departure, the rest of the legislators would find themselves powerless. Some Democrats left town, and others hid. Two roamed Nashville's streets, flaunting their absence from the chamber. "I came here to break up this d—d legislature," one representative well into his cups confided, "and by G—d I am getting along very well with my work. I sent home three last week, this week I have sent home several others, and to-morrow, I am going home myself." He kept his word.[12]

Unionists raged at this "vile, illegal and revolutionary plot to disorganize the House of Representatives," and they were sure the real blame lay with the administration. Allegedly, the Conservatives had received messages from the White House itself. A Tennessean (never identified) had seen a letter to some member (also never identified) directing the program and detailing which lawmakers should absent themselves. "Renewed threats against the lives of the Gov. & other prominent men are out," the correspondent (also unidentified) wrote Congressman Elihu Washburne of Illinois, "& all this is the effect backed by the Prs't [president]. A very trustworthy man the other day was telling some of the R. R.[railroad] men they were disobeying the law & they, prominent men, at once said there would be no Brownlow & his government before sixty days have passed." Vague reports spread of money and promises of federal office from Washington. A federal officer boasted that within two months' time—as soon as Congress had adjourned homeward, probably—the president would overturn the state government and put it under military rule. The story was fabulous, but Johnson's course had been so capricious that listeners could not rule it out.[13]

"The Johnson faction . . . is bolting, on advice from the White House, to prevent the ratification of the Amendment," Governor Brownlow grimly wrote his friends in Washington, "but it will ratify nevertheless." Eventually, the House ordered the absentees arrested. Several of them were hauled back to Tennessee and imprisoned in the cloakroom. "I see the shadows of '61 flitting once more through these halls," a state senator announced. "I can almost hear the step of the assassin. The shadow of treason may darken, but the substance shall not occupy again! This is a lawful government—a government of the majority; it has a right to live and it *will* live!" Conservatives went to the local circuit court for a writ of habeas corpus, which the House of Representatives refused to acknowledge. A judge charged the head of the arresting party with contempt. After a three-day trial, he was found guilty and his prisoners were ordered released. A posse armed with pistols was collected, but the sheriff found himself unable to push into the capitol—a counter force blocked the way. By the time the corridors were clear, the legislature had voted through the amendment. The two Conservatives were set down as "present but not voting," and the Speaker of the House, who protested that no quorum was present, was later deposed.[14]

The reading of General George Thomas's dispatch in the cabinet meeting excited consternation. He wanted to know whether he should arrest the dodging lawmakers. Excitedly, the president snapped that if Thomas "had nothing else to do but to intermeddle in local controversies, he had better be detached and ordered elsewhere." Secretary of War Stanton had been of the president's mind and wondered whether he should send that rebuke, word for word. "My wish is that the answer should be emphatic and decisive, not to meddle with local parties and politics," said Johnson. "The military are not superior masters." It was an answer that took on particular irony a week later when a crisis blew up in New Orleans. So eager was the administration to make its refusal known that the newspapers had hold of Stanton's telegram refusing Thomas's request before Thomas himself received it.[15]

Tennessee's irregularities paled beside the catastrophe in Louisiana. The first news out of New Orleans came from the Associated Press, and, sensational as it was, it fit the pattern of every riot that the Associated Press's notoriously conservative dispatchers sent north.[16] On July 30, 1866, there had been some serious killing done. A body of radical troublemakers, pretending to call back into session Louisiana's 1864 constitutional convention, had brought on a civil outbreak. Riotous blacks—some 30,000, one source claimed—had swaggered in the streets. Naturally, they picked a fight with the police, who had been sent after violence erupted. Any bystander watching the attack "of armed and infuriated negroes" would have rushed "to the rescue of the assailed guardians of the peace," the *New Orleans Times* announced. "Well and bravely did [the police] respond," a correspondent wrote the *New York World*. But for them, "not one member of the so-called convention would have been saved." Hundreds of blacks owed their lives to the policemen's intervention, and forty policemen suffered wounds trying to protect their prisoners from whites.[17] An illegal convention, called in defiance of the courts and aimed at enfranchising blacks, had, it would seem, met a harsh but not wholly unjustified fate.

Facts were inconvenient things. Even as the dispatches winged north, other, official reports came from federal military authorities on the spot. If the attackers were friends of the convention, what, exactly, had the police saved them from? The police had not been ordered out to suppress disorder. They had been on hand before the fighting began, and, more curiously, the "armed and infuriated negroes" did most of the dying. Three hundred of them were wounded—and only seven policemen. Further corrections revealed that no court order, no decree, no legal process, had forbidden the convention's meeting. The black mob actually had been a procession. Most of its members had come unarmed. Among the crowd in Mechanic's Institute there were no more than a dozen revolvers, and when police broke into the hall to protect them, their own guns blazing, delegates had fended off their rescuers with tables and chairs, for lack of any other means.[18] But the police, who, as the mayor admitted, usually did not carry sidearms, had somehow forgotten to leave them home that day.

As the evidence mounted, the story from the South changed. Whoever had suffered, witnesses came forward to prove that the radicals had planned it all. They had been asking for it, quite literally. They wanted a bloody set-to and thought that they could win it. One of the few white leaders killed, Dr. A. P. Dostie, a former state official, had addressed a great crowd of blacks at a mass meeting the Friday night before the convention met, inviting them to come armed on the opening day and promising that if a hand were laid on them, the streets would run with blood. So they did—Dostie's own. He deserved that and more, to southern editors' way of thinking, as he became an arch-conspirator in the plan to force race mixing on the South. But behind Dostie lurked a larger power, that all-pervasive, cunning force that southern news-paper readers already understood to be grasping for national power. Louisi-ana's radicals would never have dared act without the encouragement, even the instruction of, leading Republicans on Capitol Hill. A judge later testified that Dr. Dostie, "the head and tail of the whole concern," had told him that "he was awaiting news from Washington, and then he would let me know, be-cause he intended to call the convention." Dostie was too dead to deny it, but he hardly needed to. Only the convention president could have summoned the delegates. Dostie was not even a member of the convention.[19]

By the time the truth of the New Orleans affair became known, the allega-tion that Republican leaders had approved of the convention in advance, or even ordered that it be summoned, had become a staple of Democratic report-ing. In its most improbable form, congressional Radicals had insisted on the meeting being called as a way of provoking violence that might be turned into an inspiring campaign issue. Wild-eyed "Radicals"—who, in fact, included leading moderates within the party and even conservative men—were quoted as uttering hair-raising language. General Nathaniel P. Banks, so cool to radi-calism that within the year he would be suspected of acting as stool pigeon for Andrew Johnson, was "said to have stated that the Radicals wished anarchy and bloodshed in the south. It would be convincing proof that the Southern people were not fit to be in the Union. He said it would be a great card for his party." Senator William Pitt Fessenden, whose detestation of his radical colleagues occasionally verged on the pathological, was quoted as exclaim-ing, "What if people do kick up a row, all the better for the North." And the undeniably radical Thaddeus Stevens of Pennsylvania, who just a week before had been quoted as saying that the 1864 convention was "that d——d bogus concern of Banks," a body that, now "that it is dead . . . may stay in ——, where it belongs," now was alleged to have insisted, "Of course it's revolutionary; ain't these revolutionary times?"[20]

The proposition that delegates would show up unarmed to be slaughtered for the sake of a good Republican sensation was, to say the least, implau-sible. The popular version then became a Radical plot to disfranchise white ex-Confederates, enfranchise blacks, and, without taking a vote of the people in Louisiana, bring the state into the Union under its new, bogus constitution. With that purpose in mind, the convention's newly chosen president, Rufus K. Howell, came to Washington and won the blessing of Radical leaders.

But that story had very serious problems, as well. For one thing, if congressional leaders had inspired the calling of the convention in the first place, Howell had no reason to go to Washington for an approval that he could take for granted—and private letters show that when he set out, he went hoping, not expecting. For another thing, as Howell himself admitted and as Washington correspondents for the New Orleans newspapers made clear, Republican congressmen were downright tepid about a scheme reconvening a constitutional convention two years after it closed up shop. The would-be presiding officer was not asking their approval for issuing the call; that call was already issued. What the judge had hoped for was encouragement and assurances of protection. Instead, most representatives that he met with ducked commitment. They had no opinion or advice and could offer no substantial help. In caucus, Boutwell tried to keep his colleagues in session by pointing out that the Louisiana convention might need their support. Indeed, the *New Orleans Times*'s Washington correspondent heard that Stevens and Nathaniel P. Banks had been warning members in private "*that the Louisiana Convention could not meet unless Congress was ready to back it*." The caucus was unimpressed. Congress adjourned on July 28. Convinced from the first that the scheme "would result in riot and bloodshed," Edward Durell, the original president of the convention, had refused to issue the call for reconvening, after seeking backing from Washington and getting only silence in return.[21]

Howell returned with chicken feed. A few Republican congressmen had allowed that if the convention reconstituted itself to cover all the parishes in the state, and if it wrote a document that Louisiana's electorate then ratified, they *as individuals* would not *rule out* accepting it and readmitting Louisiana on that basis. This was reassurance of a sort, of course. Howell was quite aware that Republicans might not accept any revised form of the constitution under any circumstance. They had failed to admit loyal representatives elected under the 1864 constitution. Radicals who insisted that the whole process had been illegal from the beginning were not about to stultify themselves by accepting a document with such an origin, no matter how improved. "Sir, it never was legally born," Thaddeus Stevens is said to have snarled, "—it was a bastard."[22]

The real supporters of a new convention were not the leaders of Louisiana's Republican Party at all. Having fought Nathaniel P. Banks's bayonet-built state from the start, they had watched with a certain grim relish as the beneficiaries, one by one, had been mauled by their erstwhile allies. They may have wanted congressional action, declaring Louisiana a territory, perhaps, but in any case they wanted a completely new political deal based on universal suffrage. Rightly, they may have suspected that the most such a convention would attempt would be to disfranchise the mass of white voters and throw out the sitting officeholders. (Significantly, at the "incendiary" meeting on the Friday before the convention, the one speaker who talked about Negro voting promised it only to those meeting a property qualification, which in most parishes were numbered slim to none.) Howell's trustiest sponsor came from the conservative end of the Republican Party in the House, Nathaniel P. Banks himself. Howell may have gone looking for help, but at least he wanted an assurance that the delegates would not be taking risks for no good purposes and for certain repudiation in Washington. He came back with nothing more than a grudging permission to go ahead, at his own risk. After consultations, he testified later, "I did not *find such legal difficulties in the way as to prevent our making an effort* to amend the Constitution in that mode" (italics added).

Just the promise to keep an open mind signaled some progress. But the progress was very small, for it was certain that when the elections were held to fill vacancies to the convention, the Unionists could not possibly win without heavy military support, and that support simply was not to be found. In other words, any reasonable delegate would have seen that the convention was doomed and any election in which blacks tried to vote was sure to be bloody. Small wonder, then, that New Orleans reporters described Howell's homecoming as "tinged with the somber feelings of the expectant martyr, rather than with the radiant hues of the returning and exultant victor."[23]

Which brings up the puzzle: what were the delegates after? Why did they come unarmed to the opening day of the convention? Perhaps they were madmen and fools, who had not predicted the consequences. More likely, they knew the consequences very well and guessed wrong. For one thing, the first assembling of the convention would be the safest. There were too many vacant seats of delegates from 1864 who refused to attend to transact business; everyone was agreed on that. The convention could not fill the vacancies. New elections would have to be called, and only the governor could issue the necessary writs. J. Madison Wells, while friendly to the idea, wanted the job done right. He insisted on delegates from the whole state, not just from the few parishes in Union hands in 1864. The governor's proclamation must cover seats vacated by death, resignation, or a failure to appear. The "express understanding" the leaders had with Wells was that they would hold a perfunctory meeting, make a list of remaining vacancies, and adjourn until the governor had called elections and the seats had been filled.[24]

It also would be the only one that Unionists could count on controlling. They may have hoped that the governor's writs would permit only old Union men to vote, though they saw the governor as a political eel as shifty as any state could produce. For elections open to blacks as well as whites there was no realistic chance. Only overwhelming force could keep Rebels off the poll books. The governor could not be trusted to take such risks as those, even if he had had the means, and the prospects were that in the parishes that the Confederacy had controlled till the war's end the Confederates' friends would be returned as delegates. If the convention intended on revolutionizing Louisiana's politics by a new document, it had not the faintest hope of succeeding.

Undoubtedly, the members expected a confrontation with the state authorities. Of that they had received warnings enough. They knew that a grand jury was sure to indict them within days and that the president had indicated a willingness to put the army at the service of the mayor in suppressing the convention. What they were anticipating was arrest and an appeal to the federal courts, and they had already arranged for immediate bail, once the convention met. At best, they could challenge the indictments — the grand jury had no power to indict when the court was in recess and could win a ruling that the convention was, indeed, lawful. At least one judge on the state supreme court would give them a friendly hearing: Rufus K. Howell himself. At worst, they could be denied release on the writ of habeas corpus and would cool their tempers in jail until the next session of the court in November. Either way, they risked a much less dangerous form of martyrdom than the kind that some of them, in fact, met with, and one sure to spotlight how poor a chance free speech and free discussion had in the former Confederate South. It was precisely because they expected arrest that some of them left their sidearms at home.[25]

They were wrong — and quite right. Within days of the massacre, in which loyal blacks and whites were butchered, a New Orleans grand jury handed down indictments — but of the delegates. Not one policeman, fireman, or other member of the mob that did the killing was ever accused of any crime. On the contrary, Judge Edmund Abell, in his charge to the grand jury, informed them that every citizen had a duty to help law officers. If it became "necessary" to kill rioters, "it is not murder, but justifiable homicide."[26]

On the day that the delegates assembled, a parade of Unionists, white and black, marched toward the convention hall at Mechanic's Institute to tender their support. Witnesses disagreed about what happened next, but one old soldier on hand saw a policeman step in front of the procession. "This was a pretty set of damn negroes to be invested with political rights," he shouted. "They all ought to be on there masters plantation put in stocks and whipped to death." As the black marchers ordered him away so that they could pass, he drew

"To Union Men. The New Orleans Convention or Massacre, Which Is the More Illegal."
Thomas Nast, *Harper's Weekly*, September 8, 1866. Nast drew even more prophetically than
he knew. Within weeks, a Louisiana judge would hand down indictments of the delegates.
Not one assailant in the riot was charged.

his revolver and fired into the crowd. One participant was wounded. With drums beating, the procession pressed ahead, but more police were closing in. At the fire stations, the bells rang, a summons for action already agreed upon. Whites, heavily armed, many of them with white cloths tied around their arms so that police and firemen could recognize them in the fighting to come, rushed toward the parade. As it reached the Mechanic's Institute, the shooting began again. There were plenty of policemen now, split into two squadrons and commanded by former Confederate officers.[27]

This time the disturbance did not end. Unionists were shot down. "It was a butchery not a combat!" a New Orleanian wrote.

> The police and city officials composed of the scum of confederate armies and southern desperadoes have been at the bottom of this conspiracy. . . . *One hundred* corpses in the lapse of one single hour, men, struck by two or more shots, unable to fly, beaten to death with clubs like mad dogs! . . . When a miscreant, a beast in human form[,] put a cigar into the mouth of a dead human being, when badly wounded men were dragged by the feet, their heads beating lustily against the pavement to be thrown into a flayers cart[,] then I could not think but shuddering of the fate of any unfortunate Union man falling into the hands of these infuriated *beasts*.

Black bystanders died just for being in the area. "I saw 13 dead in a space no longer than from our house to Cor[ner] of Jay and Frank St.," a northerner wrote home. Dostie was badly beaten and taken prisoner by the police. While in their custody, he was shot five times, "left for dead, tramped on, thrown into a filthy cart & taken off." "Oh, General, horrors on horrors accumulate," an old friend of General Benjamin Butler's wrote him.

> . . . the Rebel Mayor John T. Monroe armed his Rebel Police with Revolvers and Bowie knives and privately ordered them to go and massacre not only the members of the convention but all the loyal men that could be seen within and around the Mechanics Institute[. T]he plot was laid or planned by the Rebels John T. Monroe[,] Lieut Gov Voorhies and Maj. Genl. Herron[. B]etween the Rebel police and Rebel Citizens they butchered fifty of our loyal men and wounded about two hundred[. T]the mob was led on by Tom Adams the chief of Police and . . . Adams could be seen shooting down loyal men in the crowd whilst the cowardly murderer John T. Monroe was hid during the execution of blood *conspiracy*.[28]

To northerners, the riot was not simply a shock but a surprise. Not one northern newspaper had connected the convention's summoning to Congress.

Keen in reporting every detail of supposedly secret caucuses and generous in reporting remarks never made, the Democratic press had not so much as breathed a word about a Radical plot to help their Louisiana cohorts march to their deaths. Only after the convention met and the fury in the streets needed explaining away did a partisan press discover the horrid secret of its real workings. Complete proof soon would show that plans "for inciting the riot were concocted in this city," wrote William H. C. King to the *New Orleans Times*. No such proofs were furnished, but quite a lot of evidence showed that whites had been readying for trouble for days. The *Times* itself mentioned a "preparatory meeting" on the Saturday evening before. When a Radical newspaper pointedly asked what it had been preparatory for, the language was quickly dropped. In the end, the closest conservatives came to documentary proof for their case was a witness's revelation that he knew of a letter written from a member of the Joint Committee on Reconstruction to Republican leader Benjamin Flanders, urging that the convention meet "at all hazards . . . and trust the consequences." Inflammatory words, indeed, except that when next the witness quoted the same passage, both the language and its meaning had shifted into something far more cautious. Cross-examination explained the discrepancy. The witness had never seen the letter, much less read it. He was not sure to whom it was sent, after all (and Flanders denied ever receiving it), and had no idea who had signed it (every committee member denied having written such a letter), and two of the three people purported to have claimed to have seen it were unavailable, having been killed in the riot. Neither the letter nor the third corroborator ever made an appearance, though Democratic newspapers quoted the committee minority report as authority that the letter had been proven to exist—and was signed by none other than Banks (or Stevens or Samuel Shellabarger, depending on the account). Of course the minority report made no such claims.[29]

The response from the White House was more disturbing still. From the first, the president and those around him took the side of the police. "Violent and revolutionary proceedings have taken place in New Orleans," Secretary of the Navy Gideon Welles wrote in his diary. He meant the convention. "Riot and bloodshed were the unavoidable consequences." The word "rioter" occurred again and again around the cabinet table, and always it applied to the victims, not their murderers. As official military reports came in from General Philip Sheridan, declaring the incident an outright massacre, premeditated by the police, the Johnson circle's views changed markedly—about Sheridan. He lacked judgment, Welles decided. Honest in intentions, his first wire, much more critical of the Radicals, could be trusted—but not the later corrections, which held the police to a sterner account. He must have been "tutored . . . either from Washington or by some one at New Orleans duly advised."

Those secret advisers loomed large even before all the facts emerged. In his very first notice of the tragedy, Welles reported "indications that the conspirators were instigated by Radicals from Washington and the North to these disturbances." A day later, "indications" had hardened into indisputable fact. "Radical Members of Congress" caused the riots, in "a deliberate conspiracy" to start the first in "a series of bloody affrays through the States lately in rebellion. [George S.] Boutwell and others have stated sufficient to show their participation in this matter," Welles wrote. "There is a determination to involve the country in civil war, if necessary, to secure negro suffrage in the States and Radical ascendancy in the General Government." Nor did Welles keep his views secret from Johnson. Within days, they had found another coconspirator, the hapless General Absalom Baird, who had been responsible for keeping order in New Orleans but who had arrived with his forces six hours after the trouble began. It was his fault, after all, and, Welles reminded the president, sending Baird to New Orleans doubtless had been one component in the Radical plot. Now that the president thought about it, it occurred to him that Baird had worked for the Freedmen's Bureau—no mere coincidence.[30]

Without a doubt, the president believed in the congressional conspiracy every bit as much as Welles. He saw to it that portions of Sheridan's telegram about the massacre were removed before it was released for publication, portions that cast blame on the police or civil authorities in New Orleans. His wires to Sheridan were even more revealing. In a series of loaded questions, he all but insisted on answers throwing the blame on the convention delegates and justifying their suppression. That much the country could read plainly. Only a month later, on his campaign swing, did Johnson reveal the scenario of conspiracy behind his attitude. "If you will take up the riot in New Orleans, and trace it back to its source, or its immediate cause, you will find out who was responsible for the blood that was shed there," he told a St. Louis crowd a month later. "If you will take up the riot at New Orleans and trace it back to the radical Congress, you will find that the riot at New Orleans was substantially planned. . . . Yes, you will find that another rebellion was commenced, having its origin in the radical Congress."[31]

For Republicans, the Louisiana affair showed again the readiness of Johnson to trample on the Constitution when it suited his purposes. By his own argument, Louisiana was wholly restored to the Union. The national government could not interfere with conditions there. Yet he had interfered. A week before he had bridled at the involvement of the military in Tennessee's political struggles on Unionists' behalf. No such restraint and no such constitutional scruples guided him now. For months, the *New York Evening Post* had tried to find ways of defending Johnson. Chief spokesman for the radical Democratic tradition within the Republican Party, it had juggled its conflicting commitments to human equality and states' rights. New Orleans resolved its doubts for good. "Are we to understand that a state in the Union cannot hold a convention without the permission of the United States?" it demanded. "The President . . . has done an act contrary to all his written and spoken policy." If the state that even Lincoln had treated as restored to the Union still had to remain under Johnson's approval or face the consequences, Republicans were only too right to charge the president with usurpations.[32]

Might it be a precedent for a much larger interference? Unionists feared, and the *Richmond Whig* could only hope. If the president meant it when he said that the body on Capitol Hill simply "assumed" itself to be a Congress, when it was merely "a Congress of part of the States," he could give his words practical application as soon as members trooped back for their next session, by preventing their assembly. In Louisiana, he "expressed his opinion very decidedly in regard to irregular bodies claiming legislative powers." What was Congress, the *Whig* asked, if not such an assembly? More reasonably, Republicans wondered where Johnson thought his power to meddle in other states ended. Unionists held Tennessee, Missouri, Maryland, and West Virginia by denying Confederate sympathizers the vote. If Johnson could forbid conventions, could he call them to revolutionize? Might he use military forces to deliver the Border South to the enemy?[33]

Tennessee and Missouri conservatives hoped so. Some counted on it. In the summer of 1865, rumors had spread through Tennessee that "the Blood Faction," a secret cabal, was planning to call its own set of elections in August, not just for the legislature but for governor. The plotters would take the state's 1834 constitution as their authority, on the grounds that the latest fundamental law had no legal basis. In such an election, none of the disfranchising amendments that "Parson" Brownlow had enacted would apply. Former Confederates could vote and would sweep the state. What made the report more worrisome was the news of an "authority from Washington." The president, it seemed, was working out plans to topple Brownlow and install General Gordon Granger as military governor. Concerned more by the first possibility than the second, Brownlow appealed for federal troops to make sure that the election ran the way loyalists intended it.[34]

All the reports proved false, but by the spring of 1866 a movement was stirring to call a new constitutional convention outside of the requirements of the state's constitution and form a new government. "There has been much talk of calling a new convention," old Cave Johnson wrote in April. Only the worry that "it might be seized hold of & used to the injury of the policy of the administration" held promoters back. "Give us a Military Governor or any thing else, [which] would be better than what we now have." James B. Bingham, editor of the *Memphis Bulletin* and one of the owners of the *Nashville Union*, arrived in the capital in May just in time to discover the movement under way. Democratic legislators had gathered to make a plan for the future. "At that meeting, they resolved to send you a delegation from their own body to ask you to permit them to get up meetings and send delegates to Nashville to form another State government, and upturn or overthrow the present State government," Bingham warned. Bingham told them plainly that the plan would be "revolutionary and disorganizing." The caucus dropped the idea, but a number of "malcontents" continued to agitate for the scheme.[35]

In July, when Congress readmitted Tennessee to representation, the movement reawakened. The *Memphis Argus* invited the president to wipe out the current authorities and hurry up with "civil reorganization." Ambitious men circulated in Nashville rounding up signatures on petitions recommending themselves for positions under the anticipated military governor. "Now my dear friend if there is any chance in the world supercede Brownlow with a military govern," a Tennessee legislator wrote the president. "My daily prayr. is give us a good Military govern. and let him regulate tennesse and then we can get along." In the longer run, the insurgents were seeking a new constitutional convention, chosen by unauthorized elections. It sounded very much like the mirror image of the New Orleans gathering, as the *Memphis Avalanche* admitted gladly. But, it pointed out, two big differences made Tennessee's gambit legitimate: this convention expressed the people's will, and Andrew Johnson would back it. The *Avalanche* was wrong, at least on the second point. By fall, the new-convention movement had dwindled away, but not before giving the alarmists two months of fretful speculation.[36]

Similar fears stirred editors as they looked at the parlous situation in Missouri. To bolster their majorities, the Radical state legislature there had passed a registry act that required a loyalty oath of all prospective voters. Conservatives seized on one provision that allowed anyone accused of disloyalty to put his name on the poll books. The exercise was not as empty as it sounded: rejected ballots would be kept and, on court appeal, might be counted. Given a full conservative turnout, local results, and even state results, might be reversed. So the opposition mobilized and mounted an aggressive campaign to bring out every potential voter it had. Mass meetings turned rowdy. Two rallies scheduled for the same night in the same town left nine people dead. Bushwhackers barged into registration offices to disrupt proceedings. Radicals volunteered their services, and their shotguns, to guard the officers and, conservatives cried, to scare the opposition. The cries grew even louder as the governor mustered a volunteer militia to help keep order. He had a case. Under the best of conditions, Missouri would have needed armed forces. Four years of marauding and bushwhacking had turned great swaths of the state into chaos. But in a rough election year, non-Radicals saw any move to arm Radicals and turn them into the state's gunslingers as outrageous. Their real purpose, conservatives charged, was to strong-arm the governor's allies back into office.

Federal troops afforded an alternative to Radical cadres. In mid-August, the president arranged to have General Winfield Scott Hancock pressure the governor into accepting the change. The governor accepted willingly and promised to disband the volunteers. Hancock grumbled that promises outran performance. He suspected that Radical forces had simply gone underground, turning into secret armies that would come out if needed. Eventually, both sides became convinced that the federal army would be the force of first and last resort, and only to be called out when the governor asked for help. By then, there had been more than a month of speculation about what the president *might* do. Rumors spread that he would use presidential fiats and force to wipe out the restrictions that kept former Confederates from voting. Then General Hancock's forces would impose the executive will on the state. Conceivably, there might be open war between Fletcher's militia and the army and the start of a civil war, which would quickly spread, as Unionists from other states flocked to help out the governor.[37]

Those Unionists were already armed and organized, or so conservatives thought. With both parties brooding on the prospect of civil war, a new society of Union veterans, the Grand Army of the Republic (GAR), became one of the uncertainties. Founded the winter before, it spread out of Illinois throughout the Midwest and by summer had gained a national presence. Plenty of reasons beyond politics made soldiers set up a fraternal society to share their memories, and organizers claimed that they were not a party machine. Still, the GAR's leanings were strongly Republican and fiercely against the "rash admission to place and power" of any ex-Confederate. When the radical Soldiers' and Sailors' National Union League called a national convention at Pittsburgh, most western delegations were GAR members. By late fall, the movement had reached the east, rivaling and sometimes taking over the Boys in Blue clubs.[38]

Every mass meeting showed the GAR's public purposes—bounty equalization and support for Congress's side in the dispute over Reconstruction. But worried conservatives glimpsed something more dangerous behind, a real army, muskets and all, prepared to march on Washington and overthrow any but the radical authorities. Rumors were most circumstantial in Illinois, Ohio, and Indiana, where informed fantasists had details of secret meetings among GAR leaders to map out how to take war to the president himself. The White House commissioned Charles O'Beirne to look into the reports. He sent back frightening information in the Midwest. Talking to army officers who claimed to have seen the GAR lodges at work, he learned of arms shipments in transit and guns handed out to members. In St. Louis, an alleged witness described one meeting where the Republican governors from the West had met with General Logan and talked about choosing a dictator to reign, once Johnson was eliminated. General James Steedman, a strong Democratic supporter of the president, assured O'Beirne that the Radicals meant to impeach the president as soon as Congress came back into session. The Grand Army would be ready down to the last haversack to march on Washington and give the Congress the backing it needed, in case Johnson tried to resist. All of this had been done without most GAR members knowing a thing about it, according to O'Beirne. But let the president not doubt for a minute. "The G. A. R. are drilled to the sound of the bugle and summoned by the call." Johnson must act. He must remove the arms stored at Springfield and stock "at least 50,000 stand of arms at Washington."[39]

Others raised the same alarm. In Ohio, the GAR terrified General George McCook, a sometime Democratic candidate for Congress. "Our Governor or some one else has been distributing guns to the 'Army of the Republic[,]' a secrete [sic] political organization," he wrote the president. General Sol Meredith had a similar tale to tell from Indiana. There were stories of arms stockpiled in St. Louis "for the use of the revolutionists, white and black," in "open insurrection and rebellion against the national authorities." The "most satisfactory evidence" showed that Governors Richard Oglesby and John Fletcher of Missouri were part of a wider plot for a coup, right after the midterm elections. So said a recruit "initiated into their schemes," who had fled anything so "highly treasonable" at once. Their only concern came over who should take charge of the country. Grant and Sherman were too unreliable, Indiana governor Oliver P. Morton was too ambitious, and fuddled Senator Richard Yates of Illinois was too incompetent.[40]

Military preparations there may well have been, though O'Beirne seems to have misread the motivations. Governors and officials in the Midwest felt a particular anxiety that it would be Johnson who used troops first, and they were scrambling to find ways to match gun for gun and force for force, not to overthrow the republic but to preserve it. Nominally, Americans were at peace, a leader in the Illinois GAR wrote to Trumbull, "but does it ever occur to you that we may again be driven to arms? The persistent and unyielding course of the Administration . . . will in the absence of the proper checks imposed by a loyal and fearless Congress lead to a rupture that will sink into insignificance the impoverishing war that has just ended." Indiana's Morton was ready for trouble. If "internecine strife" came, he would "rush it with the same spirit, and the same men who had crushed the rebellion." Saying so was easy enough, but the state military forces, like the national ones, had scaled down drastically, and relying only on them might not meet the need. "I feel that we ought to have more arms in our possession, but the state has drawn all its quota," Wisconsin governor Lucius Fairchild wrote Senator Timothy Howe. Another 5,000 to 10,000 would be good to start with, though Fairchild was afraid even to let the administration know what he was planning. "I have been very careful as yet not to show publicly that I have even a shadow of fear for the future," he concluded. For worried executives, the private armies, the new minutemen, made up of experienced veterans, able to leap to arms the moment they were needed, made a useful, even an essential supplement to their own power.[41]

All in all, the heated term seemed to have thrown some ominous shadows across the future. Most of them were shadows only. The only senator to die violently, James Lane of Kansas, died at his own hand. But the blood in New Orleans was real. After that, to both sides, anything seemed possible. From one midwestern governor to another came the proposal that the heads of state confer on a military response to Johnson's next, gravest move. Let southerners draw their swords and throw the scabbards aside, a Confederate general told a Memphis audience. "Soon I expect to hear the straggling shots of the skirmishers breaking into the roar of musketry; and finally, the deafening boom of the cannon. Then where shall Tennessee be?"[42]

Congress is a conspiracy
Of wicked usurpation;
And means, I think, to ruin me,
And make laws for the nation!
'Tis an excrescence, or pretence,
Upon my outskirts hanging,
For I'm the Government, and hence,
Will stand no Congress banging.
—Zedekiah Comitatus,
"Reconstruction on 'My Policy'"

 *chapter* 7

DO YOU WANT ANDREW JOHNSON
FOR PRESIDENT OR KING?

Republicans took a calculated risk in going home when they did. By that time, they had good reason to think that any coup was months away. In fact, they could pinpoint it to the very day. The president's close friend, former postmaster general Montgomery Blair, deserved the thanks for that. There would be no onslaught against the present Congress; conservatives would count on seizing the next one, where they could make a semblance of doing the fair thing. Even with every southern lawmaker admitted, the Thirty-ninth Congress would have working Republican majorities. The midterm elections were sure to lessen the ruling party's margins. Without a supermajority up north, the southern delegations could tip the balance toward Johnson and the Democracy. Defections from the Republican Party into a new National Union organization committed to upholding the president's policies would ensure the counterrevolution. "The radicals now have 120 members in the House and complete control of both branches," Blair assured listeners:

> But they will not have 120 members in the 40th Congress. Not a man among
> them expects it. The Democrats and national Republicans North and south
> will affiliate and elect a majority. . . . The radicals will continue the policy of

exclusion; the president will recognize the majority as the legal Congress; the radicals will organize themselves in another Congress and will impeach the president. We shall have thus two Congresses and the contest will result in a war here at the North—neighbor against neighbor, street against street, here in your own city.[1]

Blair's speech set off wilder speculation than ever. A "great crisis" approached, one Alabaman wrote the governor. It would "speedily restore our political rights, or inaugurate a bloody revolution, as the Radicals in Congress appear determined upon rule or ruin." One Vermont editor, however, may have caught Blair's secondary purpose, which was not simply to show what the National Union movement could do but to build up panic among northerners about what would happen if they did not all rally behind a new Johnson party to keep the peace. If so, the two purposes worked directly against each other: the bigger the National Union movement became, the more power it would have to make control of the next Congress up for grabs. From Rome, Georgia, an old Unionist wrote in dismay that loyal men like himself had no chance of being sent to the Philadelphia convention as delegates. Secessionists alone would go, prating about the Union but as eager as ever to begin a new war, if they thought they could get away with it, and as ready, in that circumstance, to denounce the president as a Tory and traitor "or to hang you to the first limb." At least some of those around him had a persistent wish "that civil war should Spring up in the North, so as thereby to paralize the old government and pave the way for the easy achievement of Southern Independence. To foment discord and precipitate this terrible evil upon us, will be the chief purpose of some, whose names are now mentioned as probable delegates to Said convention."[2]

Meeting in a hall bedecked in flags, bunting, and patriotic symbolism, the National Union convention was well orchestrated and firmly controlled, and that was just what was wrong with it. If it avoided revolutionary, dangerous sentiments and emphasized moderation, Republicans could dismiss it as a false show, by pointing to the energetic suppression of any real expression of the delegates' opinions. What were the managers so afraid of, that they must orchestrate every entry and make the most offensive delegates quit the convention? Even so, the declaration of principles that delegates rubber-stamped from committee had some disturbing hints. It suggested that Congress might not have had the right to legislate for a South that was not represented and that no amendment that passed without all the states on hand was acceptable. By one reading, at least, that would not just deny the legality of the recently proposed Fourteenth Amendment but also of the already-ratified Thirteenth Amendment. It was not inconsistent with the Democratic claim that there was no legal Congress at all and that therefore all its actions were invalid.[3]

Johnson's response to the delegation sent from the convention to give him formal notice of its doings parted no clouds. He had sharp words for "a body *calling itself* the Congress of the United States, hanging on the verge of the Government." If that meant anything, surely it meant that the president considered the body less than legal. If so, he would see it as his place to decide when to disregard its laws as null and void or when to refuse to recognize its authority. He had done no such thing so far. He had signed bills that it had passed and sent veto messages to it. But he was opening up the possibility that, given the right measure of support from the people, he might stop doing so. If Johnson lost the midterm elections, Texas Unionists worried, he would impose his policy "by force of arms. The probability of such an event is . . . an alarming thing to the real Union men of Texas. . . . If he tries something so atrocious, we will be caught in a far worse trap than we were before."[4] That was a much less worrisome prospect than the one northern Republicans saw—Johnson's friends winning the elections or even gaining seats. If this happened, the president would feel emboldened to do what the fear of impeachment had kept him from daring to do so far.

Against potential revolution, the last thing Republicans needed was to give Andrew Johnson the excuse of a radical extremism so dangerous that he would have to be extreme himself; and Republicans knew that, in order to check Johnson, they needed to do more than hold the House and Senate. They needed to keep their overwhelming majorities, which meant holding losses to a number much smaller than any dominant party had been able to do before. They could not afford to lose even one man to the National Union movement. At all cost, the party could not afford to look revolutionary itself. It must put its most conservative face on display. In that context, the counterconvention of Southern Loyalists that met in Philadelphia early in September deserves to be understood. With so few Republicans from the unreconstructed South attending, the managers counted on a great turnout from the border states and a supportive presence from the luminaries of northern politics. Governors and senators from Indiana, Illinois, Ohio, Pennsylvania, and Massachusetts were on hand. Every evening, the Philadelphia Union League held a procession and announced speakers. Many of them gave bone-chilling descriptions of the persecution of loyal men in the South. A few, among them Governor William G. Brownlow of Tennessee, issued threats of a renewed civil war. But the convention's real significance lay in what the delegates themselves did.

There the language was more tempered, even though, as Republicans pointed out with wry pride, the delegates had proven themselves all too unmuzzled and uninhibited on the floor—so unlike that convention a month earlier! Proposals beforehand to endorse Negro suffrage, to challenge Johnson's right to issue pardons, to deny the legal authority of his conservative southern governments, to disfranchise Rebels wholesale, or even to honor the Freedmen's Bureau never made it into the platform. Instead, the declaration of principles took much of the same ground that the National Union convention's had covered. It emphasized Republicans' commitment to the speediest and most complete restoration of southern states to their places in Congress that the nation's safety would permit.

The only remedy that the whole body could agree on was the proposed Fourteenth Amendment, with its provisions leaving the states with the power to decide voting requirements. Confiscation, impeachment, a national aid program for Negro education—ideas like these not only went unsupported, but they were not even mentioned in the assemblage. Only after the northern and border states had gone home did a remnant of the convention issue its own declaration of principles endorsing impartial—not universal—suffrage; even then, half the delegates from the Deep South either were not on hand or chose to absent themselves.[5] At the behest of the so-called loyal states from Tennessee on northward, the party had placed itself on the most conservative platform it could, the better to counter any National Union Party movement.

Johnson could have used a more fanatical gathering. Even as delegates assembled, he had embarked on a speaking tour to Chicago and back. The Swing around the Circle took as its cover the need for the president's presence at the dedication of a monument to the late senator Stephen A. Douglas. But, feeling that the voters outside Washington were on his side, or could be brought to see things his way, if they could but hear his case, Johnson decided to do what no president and, except for Douglas, no presidential candidate up to this time had done: he took to the hustings on his own behalf.

For the first few days, the tour went well. The president caused no real stir on his way through the Middle States or at the banquet in Delmonico's, in New York City. The Swing around the Circle was indeed unusual but not a first-time event. Johnson had done one three years before, as governor of Tennessee, and other presidents had gone on speaking tours. The deviltry lay in the details. In Johnson's case, the damage was compounded by his subject matter. No matter how much he would try to appeal to listeners' love of the Union, the speech almost always came back to himself, the wrongs done him, the enemies he had, the purity of his own motives, and the loneliness of his struggle against traitors north and south. As Johnson's set speech became all-too-familiar to his audiences' ears and as it began to mutate from one stop to the next into a more unrestrained indictment of the very Republicans hosting his receptions, the audiences grew restive. In Cleveland, the hecklers started raising their voices, and from then on, throughout the Midwest and back again, Johnson met with constant interruptions.[6]

The rudeness in the audiences would not have been so bad in itself, though the fact that crowds let the disrupters get away with it should have betokened how far the president was imposing on listeners' patience. Indeed, Democrats seized on the ill manners as proof of a larger conspiracy to mob the president, or worse. With no actual proof, the *Indianapolis Daily Herald* charged that the riot that followed Johnson's remarks in the capital city had been arranged by the Grand Army of the Republic. The rioters' real purpose had been to kidnap Grant, Seward, and Farragut. Governor Morton himself had arranged it! From Philadelphia, he had wired some unnamed party to disrupt Johnson's reception.[7] In fact, hecklers sprinkled most campaign rallies, and many of the interruptions came from Johnson's supporters, not his critics, Still, the indignities heaped on the president might have actually provoked public sympathy, if Johnson had left matters alone—that is, if he had not been Andrew Johnson. Johnson was Johnson, always ready to defend himself with the crudest weapons available. He had faced down hecklers in Tennessee on the stump and carried the crowd with him. He may have thought that he could do it again. But what a candidate for governor could do, Americans abhorred in presidents. Statesmanship required a dignity too lofty for back talk. The ripostes only goaded on the rowdies, until every major city became an opportunity to goad the president into saying something better left unsaid.

The angrier Johnson became, the less he guarded his tongue. By the time the tour had reached St. Louis, he had exposed the very man that radicals had been describing—dishonest, petty, paranoid, and menacing. Describing himself as having labored "for years to emancipate" the slaves—indeed, as much "as any other mortal man living," he declared, his policy had been aimed to save them from "task-masters, to be worked with more rigor than they had been worked heretofore," apparently meaning the Freedmen's Bureau agents who helped the freedpeople negotiate contracts with white landowners. All his offending was a refusal to do what Radicals wanted and "hang eight millions of people." His enemies were the "same persecuting, diabolical, and persecuting class" that shed Christ's blood and now were out to spill the blood of "innocent men" in America. The congressional majority was made of "dissolutionists," who were bent on breaking up the Union. "Are you prepared to see our fields laid waste again, our business and commerce suspended, and all trade stopped? Are you prepared to see this land again drenched in our brothers' blood?" Thaddeus Stevens and his friends were traitors as bad as the Confederate leaders. The hecklers were sent there by "their superiors" and given scripted remarks of what to say. His enemies were howling only because they were "the most perfect and complete bread and butter party that has ever appeared in this Government," clamoring to protect their places, but he, Andrew Johnson, would "kick them out just as fast as I can." "Yes, yes, they are ready to impeach—[Voice: "Let them try it"]—and if they were satisfied they had the next Congress by as a decided majority as this, upon some pretext or other they would vacate the Executive department of the United States. [Voice: "Too bad they don't impeach him."]"[8]

The president returned to Washington looking markedly smaller than he left. Distrusted before, he had given his enemies grounds to despise him and, worse, laugh at him. "If all of Mr. Johnson's I's were suffused with tears," the *Sandusky (Ohio) Register* wondered, "what would be the depth of salt water in the streets of Washington?" The belligerence and vulgarity overshadowed all Johnson's high sentiments and appeals for reunion. "Congress is an incendiary," one doggerelist jeered:

I do not doubt a spec;
And burnt, in league with the Old Harry,
Both Portland and Quebec!
. . .

The murders, robbery, and theft,
That scourge the country through,
Are just what Congress might be left,
Or expected to do![9]

No conservative poet offered the same mockery of the deriders, but someone should have. The smaller Johnson looked, the vaster Republicans made his ambitions seem. From the mouths of the traveling party they plucked new proofs of conspiracy. "Do you want a tyrant to rule over you, or your legally elected Governor?" Seward had demanded of Michigan audiences. "Do you want Andrew Johnson to be President or King?" Words that were clearly meant to praise the president's restraint out of context could be used to show that Johnson thought the choice up to him, and that he *might* well choose to be king. Nor was there anything all that comforting in Johnson's boast, "I might have made myself Dictator any day by the aid of the army, if I chose."

Republicans took it to mean that the thought of overthrowing the government had passed through the president's mind, that he had made an account of the forces at his disposal, and that he was warning that only his forbearance stood in the way of the republic's demise. Every time Johnson promised to fight "traitors" in the North, he allowed Republicans to infer that the same means would be justified as had suppressed treason in the South. His words, the *Cincinnati Gazette* asserted, implied "a determination to make himself dictator, as he has already declared himself to be the only constitutional authority; to use the restored rebel power and the regular army to imprison Congress as an illegal body, as he everywhere proclaims it to be; to treat it as a usurpation, according to his method at New Orleans, and to use the restored Confederate power to make the war which he everywhere declares against the loyal people."[10]

The president's enemies were not the only ones to misconstrue Seward's question. The *Augusta (Ga.) Press* countered that "a Dictatorship is feasible and possible." Other countries had had one, and America would submit with as little fuss as they had. "President Johnson as a Dictator, with a view to crush out Radicalism and to restore the Union to its former unity, power, and greatness, would have little difficulty in carrying out his proclamation and his programme. It might be said that he would have no army to sustain him. Ah! least of difficulties is it to manage an army. There would be no lack of bayonets and swords to sustain the Dictator, and under his power, thus concentrated and made effective, opposing forces would melt like snow beneath the rays of a noonday sun." The repudiation of the president's policies in the October elections only made more pressing the need for him to use his powers to "defend the Constitution at any and all hazards." Really, the solution was so simple: using no more powers than Lincoln had exercised, Johnson could crush the radical conspirators, the *Richmond (Va.) Dispatch* pleaded. If the federal government had power to put down disunion before, it had the same power now to arrest the president's critics. "Where is the army? Where is the speaking bayonet? . . . Where the military commissions that condemned loud-mouthed orators to a residence upon the sunny island of the Dry Tortugas? Surely the president still commands all these means." If so, silencing Radical orators and editors would come easily. "The suppression of the Washington *Chronicle*, the New York *Tribune*, the St. Louis *Democrat*, and one or two other papers, would result in the destruction of the Radical party. All the other Radical journals would hold their peace or else come out in favor of 'sustaining the government.'" He must refuse to recognize "the present piece of Congress" and feel no remorse in anything he did to men "who have no more conception of the

KING ANDY I.

HOW HE WILL LOOK
WHAT HE WILL DO.

IMPERO

IMPERO

LIBERTY

LONG LIVE ... KING ANDY I.

DO YOU WANT ANDREW JOHN... ...SON PRESIDENT OR KING

YOU PAYS YOUR TAXES AND YOU TAKES YOUR CHOICE.

Th. Nast.

binding force of constitutional obligations than a blind man has of colors." Johnson could do anything. He knew what every "observing man" must admit, that "the Constitution has been a dead letter for the last five years."[11]

Republicans therefore were all the more ready to believe the story in mid-October that Johnson had asked his attorney general for a legal basis on which to declare the Republican Congress illegal and to come out in favor of a Congress run by southerners and northern Democrats. The very fact that the story appeared first in the *Philadelphia Public Ledger*, one of the stodgiest papers anywhere, gave it ballast, and down on Newspaper Row the banker Henry Cooke found the same report everywhere. "THE EMPIRE TO BE THROTTLED!" an Elmira newspaper trumpeted. The "people's Congress" was about to be dissolved and a new one devised, and the people were to be enslaved. "In other words, we are in the midst of a Revolution. . . . The Republic is in danger. Let the people awake!" In New York, financiers got the speculative heebie-jeebies. Bond selling virtually stopped; gold prices soared.[12]

How much worse the panic would have been had the story been true! But it was not true. When Cooke rushed to the secretary of the treasury for verification, he got drop-jawed bewilderment. In all of Johnson's cabinet consultations, there had "never been a word . . . even squinting in that direction." The attorney general denied every word of the report. The leading Democratic newspaper in the east, the *New York World*, rushed to reassure investors that neither the administration nor the Democrats had plans to cherry-pick a Congress to their liking. If the president really thought the Congress illegal, why did he enforce the laws it passed over his veto? Why did he send it veto

"King Andy I. How He Will Look and What He Will Do." Thomas Nast, *Harper's Weekly*, November 3, 1866. Johnson sits on the throne, flanked by Secretary of the Navy Gideon Welles and Secretary of State Seward (who also appears in the inset below) as the widely presumed prime minister and evil genius behind the president. Liberty kneels in chains, and a long line of Radical Republicans march to the block, beginning with the four singled out in Johnson's Washington's Birthday outburst. Thaddeus Stevens awaits the blow; antislavery orator Wendell Phillips waits his turn, with publisher John Wien Forney behind him and Charles Sumner the fourth in line. Benjamin Butler, *New York Independent* editor Theodore Tilton, *Tribune* editor Horace Greeley, and General John A. Logan wait their turns, and at the back of the line stands Nast himself. The question, "Do you want Andrew Johnson president or king?," was one that Seward asked audiences along the Swing around the Circle, perhaps inadvisably. But there may be a more subtle gibe in Nast's rejoinder: it is the punch line of a joke about a child asking a circus barker which animal one of the attractions is. "Either way," was the answer. "You pays your money and you takes your choice." The cartoonist may be hinting that between Johnson using his powers as president and using them as king would not be any real difference.

messages or sign its bills at all? As it turned out, a Washington correspondent with a gamey reputation had read various bits of information wrong, made up the questions, and fed his surmises to others in the press gang—and then, apparently, used the excitement to make a killing in the gold markets.[13]

The markets stayed jittery through the November elections, and a few Republicans saw the administration's denials as nothing more than a tactical retreat. The Associated Press issued a retraction of the story, "which we *know to be true*," Washington banker Henry Cooke wrote his brother Jay. Given the choice of two bodies purporting to be the one true Congress, the president would recognize the one dominated by "Northern flunkeys and Southern traitors," Republicans asserted. Bayonets would drive the Republican body out-of-doors. That was the plan, with or without a legal opinion for its foundation. From the *Chicago Times*, a vehement Democratic organ, came the insistence that even if the dispatch was a hoax the issue of an illegal Congress was real, and that Johnson must take decisive action to disperse it. The emergency broadened presidential powers, the *Philadelphia Daily News* asserted, to permit Johnson to forbid Congress to meet any longer—all the more when, as in this case, it was not really a Congress at all. For all its protest that no coup was in the works, the *New York World* argued that many people doubted the competence of Congress to legislate, and if the president shared those doubts, "it would be perfectly regular for him to seek the advice of the law-officer of the government."[14]

These fears were possible because Democrats still contended that a Congress without its southern members was a usurping Congress. Their arguments came in different shades of meaning, from the contention that a legitimate authority had overstepped its bounds to a denial that there was any legitimate authority. Some newspapers, like the *World*, contended that, even if the Congress at present was irregularly constituted, its laws had force until courts ruled otherwise, and most would have agreed that Congress only became illegal when it refused representation to states sworn to their old allegiance—if then. But opinions ranged widely. Declaring that no Congress in the constitutional sense existed, the *Cincinnati Enquirer* pronounced its every law "no more binding . . . than the blank paper which is spoiled by printing them on it." Other newspapers took up the southern claim that the legislative branch ceased to exist "because the rebel Jeff. Davis and his followers stepped out of doors and never returned."[15]

The bigger question, though, was whether Democratic members would join southern members-elect in a new, self-proclaimed Congress, if they won enough seats up north. In joint appearances on the stump, Republicans put their opponents on the spot: If southerners organized their own body, what would the Democratic candidate do? Usually, the Democrat dodged. "If I believed I could depend on those southern members to support the Constitution," one Ohio nominee responded, *I would present my credentials to and join the majority*." Some editors all but admitted such an intention, and down south the assumption was general that this was what would happen. It would not be this lawful Congress, but the Radicals who tried to suppress it, who would be making war; the president would not use troops to oust the pretended legislative body but to protect the legal one from revolutionaries. Indeed, he had a duty to "disperse the usurping, revolutionary body, if necessary by force," the *Chicago Times* announced. "If, with the Southern members, we can elect a majority to Congress, that majority shall be recognized," an Ohio candidate for Congress promised his followers. Whether admitted to Congress or not, southern states would vote in the presidential election, and if they gave a Democrat an electoral majority, he would be inaugurated.[16]

Northerners might expect a Congress controlled by Johnsonites and southerners to do away with loyalty oaths, repudiate the national debt, repeal all pensions to Union soldiers, and impose compensation on the North for their slaves, Missouri radical Carl Schurz told a Philadelphia audience. The government's protecting arm over the freedmen would be removed. The country should feel lucky if the reaction went no further. "It is not only possible, but probable, that with one gigantic sweep they will attempt to brush away all the legislation passed by Congress during the absence of the eleven rebel States" and even all the good done by the provisional legislatures and conventions that Johnson had brought into being. The premonitions gathered already! The president himself had questioned whether Congress could act legally with the South barred from its chambers; a North Carolina supreme court judge had pronounced the very convention that the president had ordered to be revolutionary and its constitution null and void. "Is it possible not to perceive where such arguments must lead us? And is there a single result of the war, except the slaughtering of half a million of men and rivers of blood and tears, which they do not involve?"[17]

Except that it might involve that, too. With two Congresses and, after the 1868 election, the possibility of two presidents, a new civil war would be inescapable. "I am exceedingly anxious," former attorney general James Speed wrote a senator. "I really believe that if the Democrats come into power just now that our institutions will be lost. The undisguised purpose of the rebels [is] to get a divided north & renew the fight. This time they say that the fight will be in the North, not in the south. In Ky we have the same issues and the same men to fight that we had in 1860 & 61. God grant that the same arbitriment may not be appealed to." Republicans felt even more sure of winning this time than the last. An impoverished, beaten South, depending on the same northern Democratic allies who had made such big promises in 1861 before scuttling to safety, had to lose in the end. If such a war came, Parson Brownlow promised a northern audience, Unionists would do the job right. They should visit the plantations with "torch and turpentine." Next time, Colonel William B. Stokes told a Tennessee crowd, Reconstruction would be easy. All it would need was a surveyor general to lay off the rebels' land into homesteads. "If you wish, voter, for anarchy and bloodshed, vote with and for the Democrats," the *Auburn (N.Y.) Daily Advertiser* invited readers, "—such a vote is equivalent to voting for another civil war. And if the Democrats bring on another such war, the Lord have mercy on them, for the people couldn't."[18]

The only sure protection lay in such a heavy Republican majority that even the secret conspirators would draw back. Democrats had forty-five members of the House. They would need twenty-six more to make a majority of the whole, even with the fifty excluded southerners. To defeat the conspiracy, voters must keep the minority harmlessly small. Then "the reaction which now surges against you like a sea of angry waves will play around your feet like the harmless rivulet set running by an April shower," Carl Schurz told a northern audience. Even the "damaged intellect" of Andrew Johnson would see at once the futility of any attempt to debauch the people's hearts. "He will learn in season that it would indeed be highly imprudent for him to think of dictatorship." If he went too far, the people would find a fresh application for the president's own aphorism that traitors must be punished.[19]

Democrats played the same game of talking up pending revolution. Charging that "the Radical conspirators" were plotting "nothing less than civil war," the *New York World* invited them to try it. "The bullets and gibbets, however costly, which in that case would assuredly rid us of the inflamers of our first and the plotters of our second civil war, may, after all, be the only way to a calm world and a long peace." In the South, the predictions increased that the president would be forced to take some drastic action, justified by the extremism of his enemies. "The fact is, that extreme radicalism is rapidly gaining ground, and the Republicans are becoming fearful of its effects," the Washington correspondent for the *Charleston Daily Courier* advised home readers. "It will, in its progress, divide Northern communities into two hostile camps, and a social war may be the result." "That this revolution, or attempted revolution of our Government, will produce a counter revolution is inevitable," former governor Benjamin F. Perry assured northerners. "We shall have two presidents, two congresses, and two armies in the field deluging the country in blood and devastation."[20]

A more plausible scenario emerged in the growing murmur of threats to impeach the president. No Republican state platform endorsed impeachment. Most orators left it alone. But some, especially among the radical fringe of the party, suggested that such a remedy might be necessary. To Democrats, well skilled at conflating extremism with mainstream Republicanism, the stray vaporings of a General Benjamin Butler revealed the secret at the heart of the Republican majority. Impeachment, they warned, would be a near certainty when Congress reconvened. A Texas judge was reported as telling one audience that "the usurping President" would be put out after the elections, "and if we leave him his life, we will leave him nothing else." A few also foresaw an even bolder Radical ploy: they would pass a bill suspending Johnson from office until the trial was over and then not bother to hold a trial at all. That would get rid of him every bit as effectively as conviction, and, without any real president, even one of their own party, they could make Congress supreme. Any move to topple the president guaranteed "anarchy and the destruction of the government." The president would resist this revolution, even if it held to the forms of constitutional law. Only "such a body as the Constitution contemplates" could try an impeachment—a Senate with two members *from each State.* Ten southern states could bear witness to how far the present Senate fell from that standard. Both sides would arm, and there would be no child's play about what followed. "It would be the commencement of a bloody civil war in which the credit of the government would be swept away!" the *Cadiz Sentinel* warned Ohioans. Former senator James Wall of New Jersey knew what the president must do, the moment the House offered an impeachment resolution. He should "lay the ringleaders by the heels in Capitol prison: and call upon the North & South to sustain him in his struggle to preserve the Union and the Constitution."[21] Republicans were not surprised at the threats. Impeachment would come if Johnson tried any usurpations, a Maine editor assured readers. If Copperheads unsheathed the sword, they would find instantly on which side the people really mustered.[22]

All the rhetoric sounds hollow in retrospect. Nobody was ready for civil war, and most orators left the subject largely alone. Real issues, argued plausibly, and serious constitutional interpretations made more of a show in the campaign than fears and jealousies did. Even the fears reflected more highly colored versions of real and credible concerns: about how far the Constitution could be stretched to cover national action, once the war was over. Democrats had a case, at least, when they wondered how a federal republic could be brought back to its normal form by admittedly abnormal means. Had Johnson and Seward held their tongues, Republicans still would have seen a serious issue in the president's claiming of executive powers far beyond those of his predecessors. As the humorist Petroleum V. Nasby explained it, Johnson was "agin concentrating power inter the hands of some three hundred members of Congress, and in favor of diffusin it in the hands of one President." The practice of stirring up memories of injuries done by the South and of disloyalty rewarded had not yet been given the label "waving the bloody shirt," but it was pervasive and engaged in with lavish detail. That, and the positive case for the Fourteenth Amendment, played a much bigger part in the campaign than paranoia did.

From first to last, many Republicans were too coolheaded to take the fears seriously. They could tell "the blare of the trumpets" from "the trumpet of the Blairs" and admitted that it was hard to tell "whether War, or the Blairs, is the greater calamity."[23] The would-be impeachers were few, and the whole point of most of the Democratic alarmists was to show that their party was the opposite of anything so un-American as a coup or a revolution. Read differently, just about every allegation of war to come was an assurance of peaceful intentions: *the other side* would strike the first blow, and, Republican editors in particular were quick to remind readers, the second blow would be so swift, so universally supported, that it would be the last. A wild agitator like Wendell Phillips could prophesy a new war, but, the *Kennebec Journal* reminded him, he seemed to have forgotten that America was not another Mexico. The United States "more than any other in the world dislikes anarchy and civil war." Moderates even paused before mentioning impeachment in public. Just discussing the prospect of another rebellion was "positively mischievous."[24]

But denying any desire for a clash is a different thing from doubting that one will occur, or that the other side shares that wish for peace. Reasonable men on both sides could panic, however briefly, and even they could not rule out the possibility that a situation would begin that might get out of their control. Southern planter Thomas Affleck found that lenders in England were so afraid of a new conflict that they closed their purse-strings tight. "This is the day of violence and outrage," the *Richmond (Va.) Daily Dispatch* announced on Election Day. "The spirit of violence is everywhere and in everything at the North. Maryland is the frontier, and while we write may be rapidly becoming the scene of the first collision." Bitterness between the parties up north was too strong to last "without revolution," and then would come "that conflagration which must reduce to ruin our present institutions."[25] (There was no collision — and no editorial retraction later.) So sure were many onlookers that a clash was coming, that the president found himself the recipient of offers of military support. "In the troubles which Seem inevitable in this Country," wrote a Baltimorean who had formerly been a lieutenant in the Army of Northern Virginia, "it may appear to you desirable to have some men under Your Control, who would know no law but your will." As a onetime artillery officer, he could do good service and raise "a regiment of good fighters."[26] The only way to forestall impeachment, a Washingtonian wrote, would be to suspend the writ of habeas corpus in the District. That would intimidate the Radicals, perhaps; but even if it did not, the moment they started impeachment proceedings, the president could "easily have the Conspirators convicted of High Treason & suspend them between Heaven & Earth upon the Haman-like gallows they contemplate erecting for you."[27]

So the political campaign that followed was a referendum on Reconstruction policy, and the fears, hopes, and illusions on both sides helped set the terms of debate. It allowed Democrats to evade discussion of the particulars of the proposed Fourteenth Amendment by insisting that it was a gilded lure: Republicans wrote it, never expecting it to be ratified and always bent on schemes more nefarious and open to Democrats' lurid imagination: Negro voting up north, assassination, armed revolution, "despotic centralization and an overthrow of a republican form of government." Vote, the editors urged their followers, vote as if this election were the last Americans would ever see, for it might well be just that![28]

More important, it let Republicans pitch the 1866 campaign in terms acceptable both to radicals uneasy that the Fourteenth Amendment demanded too little and to conservatives fearful that the radical end of the party was asking too much. Instead of promising actions yet to come, should the amendment fail of ratification, Republicans could stress the great unknown, of a South of dubious loyalty, a white people numerous and armed, and a president who seemed capable of anything. Every seat the Republicans lost put northern Democrats and white southerners one vote closer to a potential majority in the House. Every governorship passed over to the Democrats meant one more state militia that the president could call on for help when he made his move to disperse the lawful Congress and set up a Congress of his own. What were the modest risks that radicals might make blacks into voters, compared to the risk of a second civil war? Republicans were the real conservatives, and their election must come, not so much to assure equal justice as to assure a lasting peace. The very renomination of incumbent congressmen sent a message to the president that no new nominee could send—however more radical he might be: that the people stood by this Congress and proclaimed it legitimate.

In wartime, the sense of crisis—that the war could not be won on the field alone and by traditional methods—had strengthened the influence of the radicals and allowed them to press their other aim, to dismantle slavery. Now the prospect of a republic under threat allowed the radicals a more convincing case that Congressional Reconstruction must advance, rather than give ground to the president and the white conservative South. Indeed, the sense of crisis may have kept the life in a radicalism finding tremendous obstacles in its way. As long as Americans thought about the question of giving blacks the right to vote and hold office simply as a matter of justice, a majority would leave matters as they were. To save the Union, a northern electorate would give blood and treasure—and the benefit of the doubt—to the idealists.

By posing the issues as the need to restrain a clear threat to a postwar settlement already nearly completed and to forestall a renewal of civil war, the Republicans were able to hold their majorities in the Fortieth Congress—there would not be Democratic material enough to make a rival Congress[29]—but those majorities found themselves constrained thereafter in how far they could go. They could not afford to seem revolutionary themselves. Any new governments established in the South must come about by popular consent; any military rule must be only light supervision, with as full a respect for civil liberties as was consistent with the public safety. There could be no sweeping purges of white conservative officeholders across the South, no confiscation of planters' property, no federally funded school system created, even if Republican lawmakers had been inclined that way.

Nor did the alarm end when the returns were in, because it became clear soon enough that Johnson had not learned anything. The very suggestion of flexibility turned him "ugly as the devil" at a caller, and he raved so badly that his Democratic guest threatened to walk out and never come back. He found reasons still to argue that the elections were no mandate against himself or his policy, and that, taking the white southern vote into the calculus, the American people were with him, if they could but express themselves fully. Every unreconstructed southern state rejected the Fourteenth Amendment, and their language was much more truculent, much more reminiscent of the defiance of 1861, than it had been a year earlier. When the Soldiers and Sailors Union called for a convention of veterans to assemble on December 1 in Washington, Democrats sounded a momentary alarm over a possible army of radicals set to march on the capital and the beginning of a congressional army to counter the national one. It proved no more than a rally of unarmed veterans sent to tender their support to the Republican majority in Congress, but, briefly, it allowed conservatives to foresee a military organization that, having feted Congress, would unseat the president.[30]

Plenty of reasons motivated southern opposition to the amendment, but one, less often spoken of but widely present, was that the whole process of submitting the amendment was itself unconstitutional. No change to the Constitution had any validity, the *Charleston (S.C.) Mercury* insisted, unless all the states sat in Congress and unless the president had given the resolution his approval. Two-thirds of Congress had not approved the amendment, former governor William Sharkey of Mississippi argued. No lawful Congress existed. "Any body of usurpers may as well claim to be the Congress of the United States, and New York and Pennsylvania, for instance, may so manage to exclude first one small State and [then] another until they control the legislative power of the nation, with equally as much propriety as the majority now excludes States from representation." With this logic, one Washington correspondent wrote, the president agreed firmly. North Carolina governor Jonathan Worth coolly rejected not just that settlement but any amendment passed "by a fraction of a Constitutional Congress."[31]

Nor could it have made northerners rest easier that among the reasons for southern rejection of the amendment was the conviction that the North teemed with friends prepared, when the inevitable clash came, to take up arms on behalf of the president, the Constitution, and, incidentally, the South. There would be war if Congress got much more radical, and it would be sure to do that. If Johnson resisted passage of the Fourteenth Amendment, southern editors explained, the Republican Party was stymied. Either it must give in and take up the Johnson program, or it must move ahead, into extreme actions sure to rouse northerners against it. The more radical the Congress became, the more likely that it would open impeachment efforts. If that happened, of course, Johnson would resist. No impeachment from a partial Congress would be legal. War in Washington could only work to the South's advantage. From New Orleans, Congressman Samuel Shellabarger of Ohio wrote editor James M. Comly that an uprising was not imminent. Louisiana whites would renew a rebellion only after assessing "the chances of success." They did "not *now* see that chance, and hence have no *present* purpose of renewing the war," he added. "It is this idea of a war inaugurated by the president, to be supported by the copperheads of the North and secessionists of the South, which has prevented the adoption of the Constitutional amendment," a Texas Unionist wrote. "The delusive hope will be clung to till the last moment."[32]

Southern hotheads welcomed the coming set-to. "We have very little left to lose in the South," the *Mobile Register* contended, "and a civil war in the North could hardly make our condition much worse. But the North has splendid property and fabulous luxury and wealth at stake. Let it beware that its unjust use of power does not recoil upon it in the thunders and flame of the most deadly and destructive of wars—civil war. . . . When you threaten us, look to yourself." All Johnson would have had to do when Congress came back into session was to arrest the members and their leading friends across the North, take over the telegraph offices, and order a new election nationwide for the Fortieth Congress, "disfranchising such of the Southern people as in his judgment he might have thought proper," a South Carolinian grumbled. Even now, if he did so, "300,000 muskets would like magic flash to the tap of the drum" to help him "usurp the Government, in order to save the Government."[33]

Fear, suspicion, and delusive expectation brought a high price. As news of the total rejection of the amendment sank in, the Republican majority had three choices. Either it must abandon its program and accept Johnson's as a final settlement of the issues of the war—a total surrender after the voters had expressed their support for Congress's position. Or it could declare the amendment a part of the Constitution on the grounds that only three-fourths of the non-Confederate states were needed for adoption—a risky proposition, certain to lead to defiance, litigation, and a ruling from a very unreliable Supreme Court. Or it could remake the southern state polities to put men in charge who had no dreams of new civil wars and slavery restored. Republicans ended up choosing that last alternative. Days before the Thirty-ninth Congress closed, they had passed the first in a series of Military Reconstruction Acts, setting ten states under military oversight and mandating new constitutions, created by an electorate that was black as well as white and purged of those men disqualified by the amendment from office. They did not forget the armies-in-waiting down south, either. As amended, the army appropriation bill disbanded militia in the former Confederate states, an extraordinary limitation, as one senator protested, on the constitutional right to bear arms. Lawmakers had grounds enough: the harassment and disarming of black communities and the intimidating of free laborers were notorious. Still, members hinted at dangers to come, not just outrages at present. Given presidential sanction, "the arming of rebels" "hostile to . . . the country" would be the "most fatal thing that could be done," radical senator Henry Wilson of Massachusetts explained, in offering the provision. The far more conservative Indiana senator Henry S. Lane agreed. Before any such force could be raised, Republicans must know that it would "fight for instead of against the Government."[34]

This was no general disarming, of course, and Congress meant no interference with Union Leagues armed for self-protection. Even at their most revolutionary, the devisers of the Military Reconstruction Acts held close to the principle that Andrew Johnson had failed to uphold: the constitutional conventions could only come into being if a majority of registered voters showed up on Election Day, and only if a majority of those voting supported the convention. The same rules applied for ratification. And only after new legislatures had been elected and had freely accepted the amendment could southern lawmakers be restored to Congress. Radicals then and later would complain that moderate colleagues had failed to sweep away the illegal Conservative governments or take the bold steps that so great a crisis demanded. If so, theirs was the boldest timidity in the world. Even Republicans who defended the Military Reconstruction Acts did so by pleading dire necessity. Conservatives were aghast to discover the enemy nearly as bad as they had claimed all along. "We are stunned & rubbing our eyes to find if we are awake in America & the 19th century," a Mobile editor wrote.[35]

Now, at last, the Democratic cries of usurpation seemed fulfilled. From the Rio Grande to the Potomac, the congressional majority had established "a military despotism more absolute than any other in any civilized country within the last two hundred years," Senator James R. Doolittle told a Washington crowd. In the shadow of General Washington's grave, a visitor sat in the shade of "a military government more despotic and absolute than any in Poland or Hungary or Ireland." Not since the barbarities that the Duke of Alva's "Council of Blood" meted to the Dutch in the 1500s had Europe seen such oppression. "Never was such a usurpation before attempted as this," Dan Voorhees of Indiana cried. "No act of Napoleon's ever equaled it. At one blow liberty was struck dead throughout one-fourth of the boundaries of this republic, and one-third of the territory is as dead to freedom as the Siberia of Russia."[36]

Carl Schurz, the Missouri radical, could have told them all about real tyranny. He had seen it in the Germany he had fled after the collapse of the Revolution of 1848. As he reminded audiences, the southern version hardly reached amateur status. The Hungarian uprising of the 1840s ended with long rows of gallows rising, all liberally used. When Russia broke the Polish uprising of 1863, the czar's soldiers were let loose to kill civilians without mercy and punish "every whisper against the victorious government . . . with death." Had the North done like the czars, Confederate generals would have become carrion long ago, rather than teaching school and promoting railroad enterprises—and helping write the Democratic platform in New York. When

Governor James English of Connecticut contended that in ten states "every bulwark of personal freedom has been stricken down; freedom of speech, freedom of the press, habeas corpus, trial by jury, the right of suffrage, the right of representation in Congress, every guarantee, in fact, under the Federal Constitution, has been swept away by the remorseless legislation of Congress in these ten States," he could have found ready correction from hundreds of southern editors—if, that is, they had found space amid their free and abusive denunciations of the tyranny under which they suffered.[37]

But Democrats were not comparing the South to a Europe they did not know so much as to a federal system in which they had been raised, in which the states had wide discretion over who should vote and how justice should be administered. "Where is the robe of their sovereignty," an orator cried in 1868, "a white and ghastly shroud covering the forms of dead Commonwealths. . . . Press them to your heart—there is no pulsation, life is extinct. Whisper to them of liberty and equal rights in the Union, and their lips are sealed in death." A Congress that could subjugate the South knew no confines of law. It had adopted the "conquered provinces" theory in toto. "The truth is (and we may as well recognize it) that the Constitution is abolished," the *New York World* announced, "—abolished as a pretended consequence of a war undertaken to uphold its authority." The old Union, an Ohio editor agreed, had been "completely dissolved."[38]

I . . . have been personally the means of
preventing a subsequent civil war, menacing
and dangerous, yet of which little is known.
—General Ulysses S. Grant, on his deathbed

chapter 8

A DANGEROUS STIR IN MARYLAND

When Chauncey Depew made the pilgrimage to the summer resort at Mount McGregor in 1885, he intended no more than to pay his respects to the dying general. Ulysses S. Grant, stricken with cancer, was working hard to complete his memoirs, but he knew there could never be a companion volume on the years after the war. Perhaps that was why, when the New York Central Railroad executive and Republican politico came calling, he felt compelled to tell the unknown story that he would never write. "I have been called as commander of the army to conclude the suppression of one rebellion," he told Depew, "and have been personally the means of preventing a subsequent civil war, menacing and dangerous, yet of which little is known."[1] There had been a moment when President Johnson had made plans for a coup, throwing what force he could raise behind an improvised Congress of southern sympathizers. He needed the army's help, but Grant had barred the way.

An incredible tale! And there was every reason to not believe it. Often the anecdotal diamonds that fell from Depew's lips were only the very brightest paste. This story was news to former congressman Benjamin Butler (not on speaking terms with Grant at the time) and William Tecumseh Sherman (among his closest friends in army life). Old ex-congressman Elihu Washburne, who claimed to know Grant's mind at the time of the supposed coup, denied having heard anything about it. Even if Depew remembered perfectly,

Grant certainly misremembered. He had come to hate Andrew Johnson; the president had used, slurred, and humiliated him. In retrospect, slights turned into enormities, and every little movement took on sinister meanings.

All the same, others—General Daniel Sickles, Horace Porter, and Grant's son Frederick—sustained Depew's recollection. Washington correspondents for one Democratic newspaper confided that the story the general now told was one that they had known at the time and suppressed, presumably because their paper was upholding the president as a protector of the Constitution. And there was one other source of a deep unease that no memory could gainsay: the general himself in the fall of 1866.[2]

The general had been living in an atmosphere of anxiety for months, and it was not surprising that he should have come down with a touch of it himself. As press speculations increased about a potential coup, pressure on Grant as general of the army and on Secretary of War Edwin Stanton had intensified. Republicans urged them not to resign, and, as early as March, Washington correspondents were reassuring readers that neither man would do so. But correspondents were the most prolific unpatented inventors in America, and other ways could be found to get Grant out of the way. When a Washington dispatch reported that Grant meant to go touring to Europe, the *Chicago Tribune*'s editor wrote Congressman Elihu Washburne of Illinois in concern. The general must postpone the trip for a year, at least, a Philadelphian begged. Twelve months, and "our crazy, passionate President will have fully disclosed his hand and we will know whether he is dangerous or not." The appeals grew more emphatic as the crisis seemed clearer. "Things are apparently becoming serious in our National affairs," a Pennsylvania editor wrote, "and if Johnson should thrust a Rebellion upon us, it would be an appalling calamity not to have Gen Grant with us."[3]

Grant could choose his own time of departure. His popularity and his well-known determination to keep the army out of politics made it impossible for the president to fire him. Stanton's situation was much more awkward. As a cabinet officer, he could be dismissed at any time. As other Republicans resigned their posts and conservatives replaced them, the secretary found himself ever more isolated in the president's councils. He was well aware how welcome his retirement would have been. Aspirants for the cabinet seat buzzed like flies around carrion. By summertime, it was common talk that when the War Department secretary vacated, the position would go to General Frank Blair Jr. of Missouri. After the National Union Convention, the Missouri delegation visited the White House to propose his name. But the convention did not ask for Stanton's dismissal. Nobody did but Democrats; and that was one reason why the president was not about to force Stanton out, however much he hoped that the secretary would resign. The other was a well-known fact that Stanton's closest ally in the cabinet was Secretary of State William Seward. The two men were personally friendly, and Seward was absolutely essential, if the president was going to have any credibility with the Republicans.[4]

That left the possibility that Stanton would resign, but that, too, was less likely than it seemed. He longed for rest and wanted to get into private practice; four years in Washington had left him poor in health and in bank account. But like many men assuming great power, Stanton had convinced himself that the army could not do without his abilities. Besides, if "Mars" resigned the War Office to other hands, which hands? To those of a Democrat, some Hotspur ready to do Johnson's bidding, as Frank Blair certainly would? When Governor Oliver Morton of Indiana came calling, the secretary blurted out his fears that a coup was in the works. Morton, who had heard the same concerns from Generals Grant and Pope, replied at once that Stanton must stay in office, personal inclinations be what they might, to protect the army from presidential meddling. Do that, Morton promised, and the party would work "unceasingly to throw the shield of national protection around you."[5]

Stanton's mention of Grant must have carried special weight with Morton. Grant was not an alarmist, by nature. His outer calm reflected an inner equipoise. He was no radical, though by no means the defender of Johnson's policies that the administration made out. His report on the condition of the South in the fall of 1865 had been cautious, to say the least, and in some respects complacent. It saw no immediate threat of a new rebellion—and, indeed, emphasized the loyalty of the former Confederacy.[6]

So matters seemed for the next year. Grant's support for presidential policies was taken for granted by many people, and Republicans had struggled to find grounds for proving otherwise. They were particularly disturbed and had to work their hardest when the president embarked on his trek to Chicago, Grant in tow. The president had hitched his wagon to a star—or, rather, to the three stars on the general's shoulder. Grant was window dressing, proof of the respectable and loyal support that the president claimed as his own and, indirectly, a warning that, in the event of a crisis, the army could be counted on to stand behind the executive.

Some radicals believed it. "Is Gen. Grant in sympathy now with the nefarious policy of the president?" an anxious correspondent wrote Grant's sponsor, Congressman Elihu Washburne of Illinois. "Our Republican friends have relied upon Grant in case of a collision with the president that he should disobey the orders of the President," General Benjamin Butler wrote to Horace

Greeley, editor of the *New York Tribune*. Was that faith really justified? "Can Grant be trusted to disobey positive orders of his Chief when the hour of Peril comes[?] Shall we not be leaning on a broken reed?"[7]

A few years later, when the president and Grant had broken beyond reconciliation, a Union officer, claiming to speak on authority, announced that Grant had tried to beg off the trip to Chicago with all sorts of reasons, and then, when Johnson would not take no for an answer, Grant cut the best deal he could: the president's advance approval of a whole list of field officers, lieutenants, and captains. Putting trusty subordinates in key positions counted for more than two weeks' embarrassment. "If we had not had such men ... in high position, who stand by Grant, Congress would not be safe in Washington for a single hour," J. Warren Keifer told the Ohio Republican state convention. "It is these very men that General Grant secured ... at that time, that now hold the President off from his attacks upon your Congress. There is no doubt of it."[8]

Grant's reservations about the president's southern policy had been there since New Year's and were growing. By the fall of 1866, his optimism about a new, well-adjusted South had vanished; his conviction that Congress must take action had hardened. His own soldiers down south were in danger; his own commanders were being overruled, undercut, and, he worried, outgunned. Presidential directives and decrees had done much to make the situation untenable for occupying forces. Presidential babble had done even more to create a petulant, restless, irritated spirit among the occupied masses. It was because the crowds thought that Grant was with them, at heart, and not with the president, that they cheered him so loudly.[9] They were right, and the president knew it.

This fear of southern disturbances renewed, and just possibly something more serious still, was one of the forces motivating General Grant by the fall of 1866. And to it he added a fear that the president might be tempted to help just such a movement. On October 12, 1866, Grant wrote to his friend General Philip Sheridan: "I regret to say that ... [the president] becomes more violent with the opposition he meets until now[;] but few people who were loyal to the Government during the Rebellion seem to have any influence with him ... unless they join in a crusade against Congress & declare their ... acts illegal[;] & indeed I much fear that we are fast approaching the point where he will want to declare the body itself unconstitutional & revolutionary." Grant added his hope that "commanders in Southern States will have to take good care to see, if a crisis does come, that no armed headway can be made against the *Union*." There was only a distant chance of that happening, and yet it could not be dismissed, because of another incident that Grant had not passed on to Sheridan: Johnson had brought up the question in talking with the general. In fact, the president posed something disturbingly like the questions to the attorney general that the *Public Ledger* reporter had concocted: What would happen if two Congresses assembled, claiming to be legitimate, and if one had a majority of members, made from southerners and northern Democrats? Grant answered at once. "The army will support the Congress as it is now and disperse the other," he said. Was the question merely hypothetical? Could the president have been feeling out where Grant would stand in the crisis? If the pinch came, too, Grant suspected on what troops the president might call — the scattered legions of the former Confederacy. Determined to forestall an outbreak, the general moved to keep the southern arsenals empty of federal arms and munitions that might be seized or turned over to once-and-future Rebels. He sent Cyrus B. Comstock to Tennessee to see what truth there was in the talk of "secret Military organizations." In Texas, Sheridan was instructed to see that the legislature did not muster the state's militia for potential action.[10]

Just at this moment, apparently unrelated events sharpened Grant's suspicions. Mexico's affairs were embroiled in a revolution. For years, forces under Benito Juarez had been striving to overthrow the puppet regime imposed on them by the French emperor, and these republicans were within sight of victory. Emperor Napoleon III had given in to American demands that he disown his New World adventuring. As minister to Mexico, the president had chosen former congressman Lewis Campbell, but he came up with another idea that would give the mission a more formidable aspect. Campbell was a washed-up conservative hack, but, given a military escort at least as far as the Rio Grande, he would carry all the authority of the administration at the highest levels. Send the general who had beaten Robert E. Lee, and the message would be unmistakable: America would fight, if need be, to restore the republic. All of that was plausible, reasonable realpolitik.[11]

But it was at least plausible that another motive also shaped Johnson's decision: This would be the ideal time to get rid of Grant, to send him as far away from Washington as possible. A military crisis was in the making much closer to home than the outskirts of Texas.

Maryland was a Unionist state in spite of itself, and the two-thirds margin that Republicans needed in the House for overriding vetoes depended on its delegation's vote. A full white vote was sure to bring in Johnson supporters, but that was the last thing the unconditional Unionists would have permitted. Under the 1864 constitution, wholesale disfranchisements pared the electorate drastically. Every voter had to take a stringent loyalty oath. Traitors might perjure themselves, but election officers could deny them the right to vote regardless, if they had reason to think the oath had been sworn falsely.[12]

Maryland governor Thomas Swann had been put into power by the Unionists, but, well aware that he could not govern long with them alone, Swann had swung over to the Democrats, ex-Confederates and all. A new voter registration law would put power on the governor's side, and on that of Johnson's friends, by cracking the polling place wide open. Swann could now appoint registrars, with absolute power to decide who was entitled to the franchise and who not, and, for his purposes, "liberal" officers with no concern over wartime loyalties would suit best.

So, throughout the summer, Swann sacked and substituted. As the registrations proceeded, it became clear that former Confederates by the thousands were ready to take any oath that restored their political rights—and that the new officers would accept their word, every time. The president of the Confederate legislature that met in Frederick in 1861 had been arrested by military authorities and lodged in Fort McHenry, but he took the ironclad oath. Another applicant stated to the registrars that he had fired on the Sixth Massachusetts; they admitted him to the suffrage.[13] Swann was on his way to redeeming one of the first self-reconstructed states and ruling out any chance that the state might make a firmer loyal majority by giving blacks the vote.

Baltimore Republicans fought back. The last bulwark against perjured thousands would be the judges of election at the polling places, who could challenge these would-be voters. The governor could not appoint the judges; in Baltimore city and county that job was left to the Board of Police Commissioners, which had chosen judges that it knew favored a strict reading of the Registry Law. The police commissioners had proven it at the municipal elections in October, where Republicanism won easily. With the November elections looming, Swann had to move quickly to ensure a better result. Since the police commissioners were the ones appointing those judges, the only way that this could be done was by replacing these commissioners.[14]

Swann quickly got the cover he needed. Democrats fanned out and collected signatures for the commissioners' removal. By October 18, the Democratic committee with the petition for removing the police commissioners arrived in Annapolis and had an interview with the governor. Late that afternoon, a summons was served on the Board of Police Commissioners, ordering them to appear in Annapolis on Monday, October 22, to answer the charges against them—the specifics of which the governor failed to give.

Unionists quickly implored the commissioners not to obey the summons.

Rumors were flying that the president meant to send in the army to oust the police commissioners and ease Confederate voters' way to the polls. In the face of such a threat, wartime veterans offered their services. An address was prepared to members of the "Boys in Blue" order throughout the city, summoning them "for duty" and admonishing them to "hold yourselves ready at a moment's notice to defend our cherished rights, now being menaced and endangered by the same despicable traitors, whose ready sympathy was always and ever for Rebels in arms." Some 6,000 names were reported back as ready to uphold the commissioners, if needed. But that, Republicans knew, might actually trigger violence. The resistance that Unionists mounted would "in accordance with an understanding between Gov. Swann and Andrew Johnson" cause the president to send in the army.[15]

By October 19, the rumors had become strong enough to burst onto the front pages of newspapers outside of Maryland. As the scenario went, if Swann insisted on their resignation, the police commissioners would refuse to surrender their trusts. "At this juncture the Rebels claim to have the promise of Andrew Johnson to employ force to put down the Union men and to give the State to the traitors," the *Washington Chronicle* announced. If Johnson dared attempt it, Maryland patriots must "appeal to the people of the North to keep open the gateway to the Capital of the Republic." Wherever the news traveled, Republicans saw a clash of arms in the works. Let the administration beware, one Michigander wrote Seward. In Baltimore, "the scenes of new Orleans *cannot be reenacted* without the authors of the iniquity meeting speedy and condign punishment."[16]

It should not be surprising, then, that on the following day, Saturday, the governor hastened to the president's office, to see what support he could be given, and apparently held consultations with General Grant and Secretary of War Stanton. Newspaper reports indicated that the president had declined to interfere. "This is not certain, however," the *New York Tribune*'s correspondent admitted, "and nothing can be known until the time arrives." There was also the troubling information that Johnson made a quick trip to Baltimore the following morning, where, quite possibly, others might have helped inform him on Swann's need.[17]

The police commissioners, on advice of counsel, determined not to go to Annapolis. What they were afraid of was that once they arrived the governor would have the sheriff of the county arrest and jail them and then fill their places in Baltimore. Instead, the commissioners sent counsel to dispute the governor's jurisdiction and to assure him that the commissioners would appear before any proper tribunal to answer charges. This, it was assumed, would be enough to make the governor back down, especially since military force seemed at present to be so available. But in case he was not willing, the news reports declared on October 22, the commissioners and the mayor were prepared "for any emergency that may arise." By this time, Baltimore was in turmoil with meetings called nightly by each side. The Boys in Blue were assembling at their headquarters and gathering information from each ward of the number that could be relied on to help in a resistance. The results, kept secret, supposedly were "known to have been highly satisfactory." If need be, they would "appeal to the loyal citizens of the North for aid." By October 21, the Conservatives were promising to bring the power of the federal government against them and seemed confident that the army itself would be used to help carry out their will. The Washington correspondent for the *New York Times* assured its readers "with entire confidence" that if matters came to the worst and the governor asked military assistance, Johnson would respond promptly. Indeed, the *New York Tribune* remarked, "he appears to promise an army before the Governor has asked it."[18]

Swann responded instantly with a proclamation that sounded like a war cry. "Military and other combinations" were forming in Baltimore to resist the execution of the law, he announced, and he hinted that other states were creating invading armies to move into Maryland just before the election "to deprive her citizens of their just rights under the laws, and to control the people of the State by violence and intimidation." Leaders of "such illegal and revolutionary combinations" had better remember that if blood was shed from "these revolutionary proceedings they will be held to the strictest accountability and the power of the State will be exhausted to bring them to prompt and merited punishment." Unionists were mystified. They knew nothing of armed combinations, and presumably Swann was taking seriously rumors of secret armies of the Grand Army of the Republic drilling in Ohio and Pennsylvania. What Swann's proclamation did was make an unpleasant situation much more volatile, with all the makings of a repeat of New Orleans.[19]

The president was only too willing to intervene. He believed Swann's allegations immediately, but he knew what those "armed bodies from other states" were really after. Given the excuse to march on Maryland, they would turn it into an uprising that might spread to Washington and "thus get him out of the way by a shorter cut than impeachment."[20] He could have sent federal soldiery to Baltimore to keep order for the coming elections. That was the advice of the elder Blair. But the real question was what Grant would do. He might obey orders or he might not. Or he might do the president's bidding but only under protest and thus provide the kind of publicity that the administration certainly did not need—of a clash between the general and his commander in chief and confirmation of suspicions that the president was trying to get hold of the army to use it to overthrow loyal men.

All this in retrospect seems clearer than it was at the time. Divining what may have been the president's thought now comes easily: a more amenable officer must be put in command, someone like the general's friend William Tecumseh Sherman. Finding some excuse to send Grant far away was essential, however. Sherman certainly would not agree to be part of an end run around his old wartime comrade. Send Grant to Mexico, and Sherman would then command the troops and send them where the president directed. "It would indeed have been a Machiavellian triumph to have got rid of Grant at that juncture in affairs at home and at the same time forced him to carry out Seward's policy in Mexico," the general's aide, Adam Badeau, wrote later in his memoirs.[21]

This certainly is the way it could have been seen, and, as a long-term strategy for putting the army in hands friendlier than Stanton's, probably was. The problem with applying the theory to the Baltimore troubles specifically is that Johnson's inspiration came days before the crisis began in Maryland, four days before Governor Swann came to Washington to see what help he could get, and a fortnight before he actually did dismiss the Board of Police Commissioners. Another possibility may work better, though it too rests on conjecture. Rumors were circulating that Stanton, who could not help knowing how unwelcome he was, would retire that fall. Indeed, Stanton kept intimating as much. In view of his sympathy for Johnson's course, Sherman seemed ready-made for the position; the offer would be the sweeter because he still nursed humiliations that Stanton had heaped on him. The one problem was that Sherman would have hesitated to take an office in which he would have to give Grant orders. Always Grant had been his superior in rank, and in the war Sherman had always acted as the junior partner in their relationship. If Grant could be given a prestigious appointment out of the country, one that would mean reassignment of his military duties to some other officer, and, particularly, if he could be sent off on a duty in which he felt a keen interest, nobody would be hurt and Sherman's acceptance of the War Office position would be that much easier.[22]

On October 17, the president summoned Grant to the White House to propose the Mexican assignment. The general did not reject it out of hand. He had taken an interest in Mexico's struggles himself. It seemed perfectly natural, too, that Grant's friend, Sherman, should be called to Washington for a few days. What was not natural was when the conversation turned to a letter that Sherman had written the previous February, supporting the administration's southern policy. Would Sherman have any objection to its being published, Grant was asked. Immediately reminded of the larger political struggle at home, Grant quickly told him that officers did not like going on record as aligned with "one or the other side of antagonistic political parties to be brought before the public." Johnson decided not to leak the letter to the press, but his action had kindled suspicions, or, rather, rekindled them.[23]

A day later, Grant read newspaper reports that the secretary of war was about to resign.[24] That was nothing new. Newspapers reported Stanton's retirement all the time. What was most alarming this time, however, was the conjecture that Sherman would take the War Office "as he harmonizes with President Johnson in his policy of restoring the Southern States to their practical relations to the Union." Could this be a statement on higher authority? It may well have looked to Grant like a veiled use of the information in that as-yet-unleaked letter. At once, Grant sent Sherman a warning of designs unknown involving them both and his guess that the administration meant to have him in Washington "either as Act. Sec. of War or in some other way. I will not venture in a letter to say all I think about the matter," he wrote, perhaps fearful of spies around him ready to inform the president. And Grant threw out an invitation to Sherman that may well have suggested his own distrust of his friend's reliability under pressure: let him stay with Grant when he came to Washington.[25]

Events only reinforced Grant's suspicions. On October 20, the president called in the general and asked him to send an officer to Baltimore to look into the political situation. Johnson made clear that he was looking for an excuse to send federal troops there. Making a show of military force just before an election in anticipation of, not in response to, an outbreak of trouble was unusual, to say the least. Sending them without the governor's declaring an outbreak of violence that he could not suppress and a request for help was unusual in peacetime, and there was no question that Republicans would read it as a deliberate use of force to overawe them. Although Grant did send an emissary, General E. R. S. Canby, to report, he was clearly disturbed. On October 21, he withdrew his offer to go with Campbell. That was "a diplomatic service for which I am not fitted either by education or taste," he wrote the president. There the matter should have rested. But Johnson persisted. On the October 23, Grant came to the White House for the usual cabinet meeting and found Governor Swann in conference with the president. The governor was on hand to ask for federal soldiers, and the president was ready to oblige him. Considering how reluctantly Johnson had sent soldiers to protect loyal men in the former Confederate South, this activism made quite a contrast.[26] When Swann departed and the cabinet convened, it became equally clear that Johnson had no intention of heeding Grant's desires, or of even admitting that he had expressed any. The Mexican mission was brought up almost at once, and the president had the secretary of state read the instructions for Grant's trip to Mexico. Astonished, Grant set the president right at once: he did not want to go. The president grew excited. If Grant would not go willingly, he could be made to go. Was there any reason, he asked the attorney general, why Grant should disobey a presidential order? Before Henry Stanbery could give his views, the general cut him short: this was no military mission, in which Grant's presence was required. He was being sent as a diplomatic emissary. That made his presence a matter of discretion. Grant had every right to refuse the president's request—and refuse it he would. "No power on earth can compel me to it," he insisted.[27]

By now, Grant's suspicions were fully roused. Reasonably, he may have made the link between getting him out of the way and giving Swann a free hand. The more Grant thought about it, though, the worse it looked. The president was bent on mischief much bigger than Maryland could contain. Stanton feared it too. The Mexico mission was "a scheme to get him out of the way in case of trouble here between Congress & the Presdt," he told his staff. Why bring Sherman to Washington at all? Army headquarters did not need to be in the city, and under General Winfield Scott they had been located elsewhere. What was Johnson's purpose in insisting that the commander of the army be Sherman, and that he be so close at hand to the Capitol? The commander who must remain on the ground, Grant concluded, must be himself, and nothing must take him more than a few hours' journey away, not even the marriage of his friend and aide, Orville Babcock, in Galena, Illinois. "I cannot fully explain to you the reason," he wrote Congressman Elihu Washburne, in begging off attendance, "but it will not do for me to leave Washington before the elections."[28]

Maryland was at the top of his fears. On the following day, he responded to Swann's moves to sack the old police commissioners of Baltimore. If the governor was really afraid that the commissioners would violate the election laws, he could remove them for their infractions under procedures already existing. There was no need for outside military force. General Canby's report from Baltimore made that clear and voiced the suspicion that Swann's real purpose was "an effort to secure political power" by nullifying the laws then on the books and opening the vote to former Confederates. Grant sent Canby's report to the president, adding that he saw no reason for sending troops until violence actually occurred. Federal intervention would not calm matters. It would "produce the very result intended to be averted." The army's intervention would be seen "as giving aid to one of the factions no matter how pure the intentions or how guarded and just the instructions." Indeed, Grant added, in a sharp reminder of what a stretch in executive authority Johnson was proposing, he hoped that the president would never compel him "to send troops into a state in full relations with the General Government, on the eve of an election, to preserve the peace."[29]

By the time Sherman reached Washington on October 25, Grant's mind was made up. Over dinner, Sherman was told that the president had every intention of using him as a cat's-paw, "on the supposition that I would be more friendly to him than Grant." If the president ordered Grant to go with Campbell to Mexico, Grant declared, he would refuse to obey "and stand the consequences." And two days later, he did just that, though carefully phrasing Johnson's demand as a "request" that he could turn down as he pleased.[30]

Sherman would not be won over. If the War Department position was offered, he had decided even before arriving at the city, it would be turned down. He had a positive dread of getting further into active politics. But he also had suspected that Stanton was not the real target. This was "some plan to get Grant out of the way," he wrote his wife before he left Washington. If so, he wanted no part in it. Johnson never actually gave him the chance to refuse the War Department position or to take up command of the army while Grant was away. By now, newspaper correspondents who claimed to know were denying that Stanton so much as dreamed of resigning in any case, and dismissing him the week before the election would only have made the Republican turnout surge. It was pretty clear that there was no chance that Grant would go to Mexico on any conditions; but if the president wanted a prestigious military presence to accompany Campbell, was that not just as easily arranged by sending Sherman? Sherman was perfectly prepared to go. That, indeed, was what the president's conversation seemed to be trying to find out. After one last refusal from Grant, the president had orders made out for Sherman's departure.[31]

Now Grant could intervene in Maryland affairs on quite a different basis, as that of a fair broker—and he had very little choice but to do so. The removal of the police commissioners seemed only a matter of time. The governor's remarks confirmed what Unionists had suspected; having just returned from seeing the president again on the evening of October 25, bustling back into Baltimore on the following morning, he seemed to have the support he needed. Indeed, it was even said that a cabinet member had declared that the commissioners must be removed before Election Day. The prospects remained of a wrangle that would last until past the election. The moment the order came for removal, the commissioners would challenge the governor's authority and appeal to the courts, which would postpone final removals until after the elections. This Swann knew perfectly well. Conceivably, he would insist on maintaining his appointments by force. If Unionists resisted, he would call on the president to send in U.S. troops.[32]

The hearings against the commissioners closed on November 1. The prosecution's witnesses, sixty-six in all, testified that in some city wards only Radicals were appointed judges, and that in some wards there were no boxes provided for placing the rejected votes so that they could be considered later on appeal and perhaps counted. They alleged that the judges refused to accept legal votes and that the police threatened the voters with violence. They swore that one commissioner had been seen drunk in the streets and that the whole recent municipal election had been a farce, illegal and unjust. The defense called witnesses to show that whatever abuses there had been the commissioners had had no hand in any of them but had worked from the first to make sure that, as far as possible, there would be a full and fair vote by loyal men, Democratic and Republican. The ballot boxes were shown to be the ones that had always been in use—ones that Governor Swann's election in 1864 had used. Some of the witnesses who had sworn that they saw no boxes for rejected ballots were confronted with proofs that the boxes had indeed been there. There were character witnesses for the special police commissioners, and the charge of drunkenness fell apart as well. Swann did not care. For not having appeared in person before him, the governor announced, the commissioners had given cause enough for their removal, and he did so at once. "The State of Maryland is at this very moment threatened with invasion by armed hordes from other States. Military organizations have been formed in the City of Baltimore for the open and avowed purpose of resisting the authority of the laws. No single step, so far as I am informed up to this time, has been taken by the Police Board to suppress this tendency to anarchy and rebellion, now so threatening, and to excite riot and bloodshed among our people."[33]

On November 1, Swann chose two Democrats to take the commissioners' place. With tensions having risen to a new level in Baltimore and with the president still talking of sending some troops to the city to counter the prospective invasion by Boys in Blue from Pennsylvania, and asking Grant and the secretary of war about the availability of men for that purpose, Grant had to act on his own. That same afternoon he went to Baltimore to work out some arrangement between Swann and the police commissioners. Grant stressed the need to follow lawful procedures rather than resort to force to the new commissioners whom Swann had appointed. He made the same appeal to the old commissioners, though his aide Cyrus Comstock later complained that he may not have urged "the old commissioners & their friends quite so strongly as he ought" to submit peacefully, if force was used against them. It hardly mattered. Both sets of officials promised not to initiate violence. "Union men are satisfied with Grant's intentions," a reporter wrote, "but fear he will be overruled by the President."[34] He was, in fact, overruled by the governor. Grant had barely left before the governor wired the president asking whether federal troops would be sent to keep order. And that very day, Swann removed the police commissioners.

Grant had little doubt now that Swann intended to choose election judges "who will not scrutinize too closely the right of disfranchised rebels to vote. . . . He may bring on a terrible riot & civil war." On November 2, at the cabinet meeting, the general predicted a great likelihood that the governor's removals would mean violence in Baltimore. Indeed, he had fears that the administration's friends on the spot were aiming to create a situation in which federal forces would be thrown against the Republicans, so that "the radicals" would be goaded into firing on the American flag. Tensions ran high on both sides. Johnson himself got very excited and declared that Washington itself was in danger of "insurrection and violence," though from what source remained unspoken, and it was not a point that Grant took up. If there was an "insurrection" in Maryland—by which the president clearly meant a radical coup—Secretary of the Interior Browning wrote that Grant was "very obviously leaning to Radicalism and inclined to throw the blame on the Administration party. . . . All his sympathies are with the radicals."[35]

All Grant's sympathies, in fact, were with keeping the peace and avoiding any grounds for the president to use the military on Swann's side or to proclaim martial law—which was a real prospect. On November 3, his new appointees went to the sheriff's office to summon a posse to take possession of the commissioners' office and were arrested on the charge of attempting to incite riot. The county sheriff was arrested as well. A writ of habeas corpus was sought from the Maryland court of appeals, but until it went through the commissioners were held under a bench warrant in Baltimore's criminal court. Presiding Judge Hugh L. Bond made clear that he had a duty to keep the commissioners from disturbing the peace and that they must give bond for their good behavior. In other words, they must rely on an appeal to the courts for control of their offices—which almost certainly would postpone their being seated until the election was over.[36]

Swann hastened to Washington for military aid. On November 4, the secretary of war, attorney general, president, and general met again. The president presented Swann's plan for troops to be sent. Grant, Stanton, and the attorney general were said to have opposed any military interference and maintained that whatever action was taken must be left to the courts. Once more Grant proposed making a peace mission to Baltimore, and there he met with Swann's friends and Baltimore Republicans. Both sides promised to keep the peace, and a compromise was arranged, which allowed both sides to choose judges of election for every polling place, with the power to decide who could vote and who could not. Grant's appearance in Baltimore provoked reporters' curiosity, though he insisted that he had not come "in his official capacity, but as a citizen, desirous of preserving the peace of the city and willing to use his influence in compromising the difficulty." It was not, however, as a citizen that he was able to order six infantry companies on their way south from New York to disembark at Fort McHenry and to stay there until after the election.[37] "One thing is certain," the *New York Tribune*'s Washington reporter added, "Swann's pet plan of having martial law declared immediately has failed. He returned to Baltimore to-night. Gen. Grant and a portion of his staff also left here for Baltimore in the evening train. He will remain until after the election."

Neither side was happy and neither side abided fully by the deal, but Grant's larger purpose was achieved. There was no federal military presence on November 6 when the polls opened, no martial law, and no violence. The Union Board of Police Commissioners had control, and Swann's commissioners were under lock and key. Acting on information of an uprising in the works, the commissioners sent out a puissant body of patrolmen to invade the suspected hiding places. Some 6,000 muskets were seized, many of them found to be loaded and capped, 108 cases of arms were captured at an auction house, and other muskets were rounded up from stores and groggeries.[38]

Yet, in the end, the Unionist success only let them preside over their own ruin. Swann's friends won everything worth having. The legislature was about two-thirds Democratic and sure to repeal most of the restrictions on the suffrage. Swann, who had hoped to go to the Senate, would get his way—at least as far as being elected to it. In spite of the Unionist judges, twenty-one lawmakers from Baltimore were elected on the Democratic side. "The Police Board will of course be turned out," a reporter predicted. "If the Courts do not do it, the Legislature will." Swann crowed in a victory speech from the steps of the custom house that the results had vindicated his policy. And he extended his praise to Andrew Johnson. Had it been necessary, he assured listeners, Johnson would have sent U.S. troops to occupy Baltimore's streets—he knew this, having been in daily contact with the president, and could guarantee that "there was no hesitancy on the President's part."[39]

The president thought that he had had a narrow escape from a Radical coup. "I had forces here ready to put down any attempt at disturbance," he boasted later, "and when they found that out they didn't go very far." Republicans drew just the opposite conclusions. Had it not been for Stanton and Grant, editor John W. Forney later declared, "a bloody conflict would have taken place in the streets of Baltimore," the result of a deliberate presidential plan "to organize violence against Congress" and bring on a war of races. Radicals drew comfort from the larger implications. Grant was on their side, and, as long as he had command of the army, it could not be used easily by the president to turn out governments of which he disapproved or plant them in place. "Genl Grant is a block in his way, & without any doubt he had much rather have Lee in his place."[40] Then there was Grant himself. He kept his own counsel, but the events of the past month had disturbed him deeply. Then perhaps, but certainly later, he came to see Johnson's doings in the worst possible light.

The Maryland imbroglio had taught Stanton on whom he could rely—and on whom not. All plans to retire were set aside for the time being. Late in November, when congressmen trooped back to town, George S. Boutwell of Massachusetts, one of the leading radicals, received a note from the War Office. Stanton needed to see him at once. Closeted in a back room away from prying ears, the beleaguered secretary shared his fears. The "condition of affairs in the preceding weeks and months" had upset him more than at any time during the war. That nightmare, of a Johnson Congress, backed by bayonets, still haunted him. Orders had been sent to the army that had been not gone through either Grant or himself. This must never happen again; Congress must rein in Johnson's power to menace the republic. Boutwell set to work on amendments to the army appropriations bill that empowered the newly forged alliance of Grant and Stanton. The president was required to send orders to military officers only through channels, specifically through the secretary or through Grant. Any officer obeying orders that had not come from the general of the army committed a misdemeanor, and the general of the army would keep his headquarters in Washington. Not even the president could send him away without his own consent or the Senate's; there would be no compelling Grant to go on a mission to Mexico hereafter. Boutwell carried the amendments to the Appropriations Committee and saw to their addition to the appropriations bill that passed just at the session's close in early March. Republicans did not take the floor to explain their reasoning, though one Democrat declared that one explanation was obvious, their expectation that without it the president might use the army for a coup d'état.[41]

Only conjecture can spread the links further, to one protection that Stanton had never asked for: a Tenure of Office Act protecting presidential appointees from dismissal without the Senate's consent, including, apparently, the secretary of war himself. Many more important forces pressed the bill stripping Johnson of a power over appointments never denied any president before: the selfishness of spoilsmen, the determination to keep Johnson from appointing a "bread and butter brigade" from buyable Republicans that might turn his failed National Union movement into a serious political force, and the wish to keep one more power out of the hands of a potential dictator. But one road to the Tenure of Office Act is at least possible, the path that led, however windingly, from the tumultuous streets of Baltimore.

The President will doubtless be pressed by
extreme men to do some imprudent things,
but I have now no reason to suppose that
he will yield to the pressure.
—*Secretary of the Treasury Hugh McCulloch*

 *chapter* 9

IMPEACHMENT FEVERS, 1867

As revolution unfolded across the South, all lay quiet on the Potomac—at least comparatively speaking. The president made himself a nuisance to Republicans, congressmen passed new laws to limit his powers for mischief, and most of the majority probably felt like the preacher who remarked that, although he wished Andrew Johnson no harm, he would not mind if the Lord took a sudden fancy to him. Yet at year's end, Johnson was alive and kicking, in full possession of his faculties, unashamed and untamed. For all the predictions of alarmed conservatives the autumn before, Congress had failed to impeach Andrew Johnson. At first glance, impeachment might seem the great nonstory of the year.

But it was much more momentous than that. What failed to happen set other forces in motion, and it did nothing to ease the tensions between radicals and moderates, Congress and the president. If anything, it heightened them. The fear of impeachment, and of the conspiracies behind it on both sides, poisoned politics markedly and contributed to the Republican Party's shift away from radicalism. But quite possibly it also explains the one thing that historians think needs no explaining, because it did not exist: the comparative moderation of Andrew Johnson.

Moderate? Cautious? Andrew Johnson? Connecting those words with so reckless—or dauntless—a president flies in the face of all scholarly wisdom, not to mention common sense. Every time Congress adjourned, he would do something provocative.[1] *Le Monde*'s American correspondent, Georges Clemenceau, described the wearisome pattern. Republicans limited themselves "to binding Andrew Johnson firmly with good brand-new laws. At each session they add a shackle to his bonds, tighten the bit in a different place, file a claw or draw a tooth, and then when he is well bound up, fastened, and caught in an inextricable net of laws and decrees, more or less contradicting each other, they tie him to the stake of the Constitution and take a good look at him, feeling quite sure he cannot move this time. But then . . . Samson summons all his strength, and bursts his cords and bonds with a mighty effort, and the Philistines (I mean the radicals) flee in disorder to the Capitol to set to work making new laws stronger than the old, which will break in their turn at the first test."[2]

In fact, though it might have seemed otherwise to Congress, the bonds generally held. Rather than break them, the president only loosened them. Step-by-step, law-by-law, his own discretionary power was crimped and the power of commanders and of southern Republicans to shape Reconstruction was enhanced. More often than not, the president only threatened to break his bonds, or, when he had broken them, he sat down where he was and waited for Congress to bind him again.

Was this the best he could have done? Democrats did not think so. Some of them shook their heads at how often Johnson let "I dare not" wait upon "I would." He could have joined the Democracy openly, but he stood aloof. He could have swept the Republican officeholders out wholesale, but he held back. His cabinet could have been purged of Lincoln's last few advisers. Instead of taking Alaska, Seward could have taken his leave.[3] *Oughts* never turned to *shalls*. And when it came to thwarting Reconstruction, the president's thrusts were more symbolic than real.

Imagine the Johnson that never was, the Johnson being invoked by his chief defender in Washington and the administration's assumed mouthpiece, the *Washington Daily National Intelligencer*. In mid-September, the newspaper pointed out what no Democrat would have disputed: "The whole reconstruction scheme is equal, in treasonable essence and political crime, to the late rebellion itself." Momentous threats required drastic remedies. Now the South toiled under "naked military despotism," "the work of a great combination looking to the overthrow of the Constitution." The president could undo it all by drawing on his executive powers. His oath of office required him "to *preserve*, protect and defend the Constitution," and that duty was paramount. It trumped all specific limits and powers enumerated in the document, including any responsibility to execute what passed for laws.[4]

Such fire-breathing talk met the same welcome in some quarters that it always had. Letters to the president repeated the same old appeals: only a Caesar's boldness could save the republic. He must be not just an Andrew Jackson "but more than a Cromwell if necessary," a Missourian wrote, offering to call for volunteers "to defend the Union or the right." A proclamation must be issued, informing the people of the menace coming from Capitol Hill and summoning them to "independent action to set up "a Congress made up of representatives from all the States—for the purpose of maintaining the Constitution & preserving the Republic of the early fathers." By proclamation he could make the southern governors call fresh congressional elections. When the winners came north, he could have them sworn in himself. Only then would impeachment become impossible, a Kentuckian warned him. Firing the military department commanders would put freedom's enemies at bay. "Congress has the deer's heart and the woman's hand," a New Orleans conservative editor assured the president. "It has the courage of a braggart." The president must test that courage and make "conspirators . . . quail." He could do that using the army "to check anarchal legislation. It was intended by the framers of the Constitution that the president should use this power against enemies at home as well as enemies from abroad." Southern registration must reopen to let whites put themselves on the rolls. All the appointive offices must be scoured—the cabinet, too. Then the executive branch would "be prepared for any immergency which may arise on the re-assembling of Congress." Others warned that a conflict of arms for the South's electoral vote was sure to happen unless Johnson made "a timely display of a purpose and a power to intimidate the radical revolutionists."[5]

Compare the Johnson that could have been with the Johnson that was, in one minor incident, the Amnesty Proclamation of September 1867. It angered Republicans, as Johnson had expected it would, and, symbolically, it was a great boon to those former Confederates left out of earlier amnesty proclamations. Yet the Amnesty Proclamation did not do certain things that would have damaged Radical Reconstruction badly. Democrats argued that under the document's provisions every Confederate was wiped as clear of crime as if none had occurred. If none of them now could be treated as rebels or stigmatized as traitors, then all of them were eligible to register and vote. The disabilities in the not yet ratified Fourteenth Amendment keeping former Confederates from holding office had no force. The Reconstruction Acts' disfranchisements of those same Confederates became dead letter. The generals must reopen the registration lists in the South. They must enter the names of thousands of white conservatives barred from politics just weeks before. At a stroke, the potential white vote against holding constitutional conventions would have swollen into near-majorities. Inspired with new hope that they would have the numbers to carry the election, many more whites, never disfranchised but deeply disheartened, might have shown up to register or turned out at the polls to express their opinions.

Even if the conventions had met, they would have held a larger contingent of conservative delegates, enough to give the new constitution a different shape than that of the one they ended up having. But, at the very least, the elections for Reconstruction conventions could be delayed into the new year; reregistration would take weeks. By New Year's, the thundering will of an angry northern public, returned to its conservative instincts, could reinvigorate Democratic southerners to show up at the polls and either vote down the constitutional conventions or elect delegates aplenty. At first, just such possibilities occurred to Wall Street. "There is the d—l to pay on the street," a Treasury official wrote Secretary McCulloch. "Governments are down and gold is rampant. No cause can be assigned, other than the Presidential Proclamation, and the rascally articles in the Herald favoring practical repudiation."[6]

The speculators sweated for nothing. In spite of Secretary of the Navy Gideon Welles's advice that "relieving from *disfranchisement*" be specified, the wording changed by the time an official proclamation was published, and the White House gave Democratic interpretations of the Amnesty Proclamation no support. No fresh orders instructed the generals to reopen the registration. The attorney general issued no interpretations friendly to the conservative reading of the document. The elections for constitutional conventions stayed on schedule.

Late in the spring, the administration had tried to limit the Reconstruction Acts' disfranchisement, but in this case also it was significant how cautiously the president made his challenge. Attorney General Henry Stanbery's interpretation of the laws' meaning did truncate the acts badly, but the president and the attorney general acted with conspicuous reserve. The decision was not sent out as a military order but merely as a suggested reading of the law, authoritative but a little less than official. So generals like Philip Sheridan could continue to abide by their own interpretations of the statutes, fully aware that they would receive backing. Furthermore, the attempt to weaken the law was made by the attorney general and not by the president, protecting the latter from the risk of impeachment. At worst, he could be accused of having permitted the attorney general to give his opinion on the true meaning of an act that was, admittedly, vague in some particulars and confusing in others, a patchwork fabric. No Congress was going to bring on a constitutional crisis over exercising so obvious a legal function as that. But from the president himself came no orders, nor even suggestions, to the military, as to what they should do with the opinion.[7]

Johnson's restraint, comparatively speaking, deserves some reflection. Just on pragmatic grounds, his discretion was understandable during the spring of 1867. For one thing, an appeal to the people now lay nearly two years out of reach. There would be no state elections that summer to change the balance of power in the House. But quite reasonable prospects remained that southern conservatives would be able to temper the Reconstruction process to their own ends. The president could help the process by interpreting the Reconstruction Acts to allow the widest possible registration of white voters. More he need not do.

All those arguments for restraint weakened by the beginning of July. As Congress came back into session to declare just what it had meant by the disfranchising clauses of the original Reconstruction Acts, it must have been evident to the president that, whatever results would come out of the constitutional convention elections that fall, conservatives were not going to reap the benefits. They would be disfranchised out of their prospective majorities in some states, where the black and white Unionist vote that registered was nearly a majority in any case; they had never had a chance in states with a black majority, like South Carolina and Louisiana. Elsewhere, the white registration was low not because the registrars had excluded them from the franchise but because so many potential voters were not prepared to take the risk of being rejected or endure the shame of sharing in a new political system that they considered degrading and lawless. If Reconstruction were to be derailed, then, Johnson would have to take far more drastic steps than would have been necessary before. He must have generals supervising the political process who gave the conservatives encouragement, or at least who let them alone to use their economic and political influence against the Reconstructionists. The place to start that process would be taking control of the War Department and keeping a close relationship with the general of the army, Ulysses S. Grant, through whose orders the generals down south were controlled. Not surprising, as soon as Congress adjourned, the president asked for Secretary of War Edwin Stanton's resignation and, when he did not get it, suspended him from office until the Senate could come back into session and decide whether to make the removal permanent.[8]

All of the steps that Johnson could try would give conservatives a better chance of winning, but nothing more than that. Reconstruction could not be stopped. To open up the registration, he would need to fire generals and, if need be, cancel or postpone scheduled elections. Black voting still would happen, even then, and that almost certainly meant that the Radical Reconstructionists would carry up to half of the states. Far more drastic action, an open defiance of the very letter of the law, was the only way of getting the kind of results that Johnson wanted—stopping the "revolution."

But the president would not yet take those actions. For one thing, despite the inconsistencies in his constitutional readings and his headstrong, impulsive nature, Johnson believed that he was the protector and enforcer of the nation's laws. Within the narrowest interpretations he could make, the Reconstruction laws must be carried through, and Johnson would have thought long and hard before acting so out of the character that he saw himself playing, as the one true preserver of the Constitution and the laws. The president was no Cromwell, nor did he mean to be. He was not about to play the conservative usurper to rid America of radical usurpers.

A far better hope of rescue for the republic would come in forcing the Radicals to expose their true nature without disguise. The more he provoked them, the more radical they would grow and the more outrages they would commit. Eventually, a northern public would stand it no longer, and the political reaction that Johnson had been looking for would set in. Quite possibly the administration's real purpose in having the attorney general give his reading of the Reconstruction Acts' true meaning was to goad Congress into coming into extra session and to give the radicals the chance to hurt their cause still more by some foolish action. That, at least, was why Henry Stanbery actually welcomed the return of the members.[9]

In any case, the unfolding events in southern Reconstruction may well have forced the president into a fallback position. To protect the white South from radicalism was still his great desire, but as it became clear that he could not save the South and that the North was not about to rush to its rescue, he was restricted to lessening the damage that Radicals had inflicted. He could no longer save the South, but he could save the presidency and its reserve of powers. That was why his most aggressive and dramatic steps were those to assert presidential prerogatives: the right to have the cabinet officers he chose, to issue blanket pardons of former Confederates, and to execute the laws as he interpreted them, until Congress clarified their meaning.

Expediency, tactical maneuvering, principle: any and all can explain Johnson's cautious sort of recklessness. Still, there may have been another consideration, too. It was perfectly true that the House did not impeach in 1867. But throughout the year, the threat hung over the president's head, and it is at least possible that it shaped his behavior or, more precisely, his restraint. For Johnson overestimated wildly how strong radicalism was on Capitol Hill and badly overestimated what influence the Thaddeus Stevenses had over their colleagues. Convinced that they had total power through trickery, parliamentary tricks, and the use of the party lash, seeing every measure as radicalism incarnate, and unable to make distinctions between Republicans, he could not—until there was a formal vote on the impeachment resolutions in December—be sure that there would not be conviction, whatever the evidence was, of actual crimes.

In retrospect, the process of impeachment seems perfectly straightforward. The power had been used against federal judges in the past. But impeaching a president was something new, and historians may have missed the vast amount of doubt as to how it would work, not to mention the rich supply of constitutional misinformation that editors could draw on to enlighten their readers. What, precisely, were the "high crimes and misdemeanors" that opened a president to impeachment? Could he be removed for walking on the grass or for misgovernment? Would he be compelled to attend every day's sessions, like a prisoner in the dock? While the trial went on, did he forfeit his executive authority, and could Congress suspend him from his functions? And if so, could it do so by a simple majority vote? If convicted, did removal constitute the only punishment that the Senate could inflict, or could a joint resolution disfranchise him or open him to indictment and imprisonment? Only the full Senate could try him; but suppose one-third of the states were excluded: did it constitute a court? And could the president challenge its authority to put him on trial?[10] None of these questions had been put to the test, and on all there were different possible answers, some of them quite sinister in their implications.[11]

If the president imagined an unscrupulous opposition, the course of the impeachment investigation only confirmed his suspicions. Even as the House Judiciary Committee examined Johnson's actions for a usurpation of powers charge, other congressmen were on the track of more sensational possibilities. With so many members uneasy about proceeding, having the most cautious, judicious, and experienced directors was vital to success: somebody like "Judge" Luke Poland of Vermont, say, glacially austere and proper down to the last brass button on his small-coat, or Judiciary Committee chairman James F. Wilson, who ended up chairing the formal inquiry. But the real headlines went to two fiery spirits.

The more respectable of the two, James R. Ashley of Ohio, had spent ten years among the House radicals and done his state much service—not to mention future states: he headed the Territories Committee. No congressman had worked harder or more skillfully to put through the Thirteenth Amendment. Ruddy, bouncy, jovial, and generous, with a Byronic curl to his hair, he was quite well liked, so much so that his outbursts could be explained away as warmheartedness overheating his reason. Still, colleagues treated him warily. His enthusiasms ran roughshod over his judgment. Enemies accused him of secret, possibly crooked, deals for divvying up territorial offices (a congressional inquest cleared Ashley's name, but Democratic papers stuck to the original charges).[12] So Ashley lacked the ballast for heading an impeachment investigation, and his original resolution looked disturbingly open-ended, a fishing expedition into misconduct. A House Republican caucus modified the wording to keep the focus on the president alone and made sure that the Judiciary Committee handled the hearings. Ashley had no official standing there.[13] If moderates thought that they had frozen him out, they thought wrongly. He might not judge, but he was glad to prosecute.

But his cohort was worse. Benjamin Butler was a newcomer to the House, unversed in the informal etiquette of deference and mutual courtesy that freshmen needed to get along and much too experienced in blackguarding. A working-class Democrat turned radical in wartime, he had leaped onto the front pages as an intriguer against Lincoln and a supporter of emancipation. His conversion was genuine, but it earned him the hatred that every Democrat felt for a renegade and the mistrust that most moderate Republicans had for any new convert who, on joining the choir, hectors the rest for their halfheartedness. He made a coarse but extremely effective stump speaker. Bullies and prosecutors often do. Nobody could deny that he was quick-witted, a master of innuendo, who within weeks had turned himself into a virtuoso in parliamentary jiggery-pokery. As the Union general who occupied New Orleans, he had brushed aside rules that got in the way of doing his work, and his greatest contribution to freeing fugitive slaves—classifying them as "contraband of war," which federal authorities did not need to surrender to their Rebel owners—never quite escaped the look of a pettifogging lawyer's trick, which was what Butler had been, back in Massachusetts, and one of the best. Thus none of his qualities recommended him for so grave an undertaking as an impeachment investigation, but it was a demonstrable fact that his patriotism paid. His bunting factory held the contract for supplying the government with flags and would do so for the next sixty years. In wartime, he had shown a genius for appointing and protecting shakedown artists, inside speculators, grafters, and cotton smugglers. Nobody ever proved that Butler stole, but no white southerner doubted the stories of his stealing silverware from the aristocracy, and for the rest of his life hecklers would interrupt his speeches with shouts of "Spoons!"[14]

Under such leadership, impeachment got off track right away. Butler and Ashley had no interest in making a case for the charge of usurpation but went after the sensational: charges that the president had appeared drunk on the Swing around the Circle and that corruption lay at the bottom of the wholesale pardons issued in 1865. Rumor accused Andrew Johnson of an intimate role in Lucy Cobb's pardon brokering in the White House. One lobbyist supposedly boasted sending a thousand pardons south to his clients in a single month. The former chief of the secret service, Lafayette Baker, had been fined for false imprisonment in the Cobb case, and he made an eager witness against the president. Baker also had tales to tell about a letter that Johnson had written when he was military governor of Tennessee late in the war, which offered to carry the state over to the Confederacy. The letter had come from one John W. Adamson of Nashville, who, it would seem, had it abstracted from Johnson's desk. Adamson had the letter again, and a certain Mrs. Harris could back up everything that Baker said. Baker promised to retrieve the letter. Neither it, nor Adamson, nor Mrs. Harris ever put in an appearance, though Adamson had a reasonable excuse, having been dead for the last twenty years. Another Nashville witness revealed how the president had profited handsomely from restoring control of a Tennessee railroad to former Rebels. Conclusive proof to the contrary came from Secretary of War Edwin Stanton himself. Mare's nests heaped on mare's nests. Baker complained of the president's gullibility, not his corruption. Later evidence showed that the pardon broker had sent no pardons south that month at all. Exaggerating slightly, the committee minority later doubted that Baker ever got the facts right "in any one thing . . . even by accident."[15]

These charges dwindled to trivialities next to the most sensational. Accusing John A. Bingham of Ohio, the preeminent moderate on the Judiciary Committee, of having a personal interest in suppressing an investigation into Lincoln's murder, Butler persuaded the House to set up a select committee, chaired by himself, to uncover the truth. Democrats quickly pronounced the Assassination Committee well titled, raised as it was "for the purpose of assassinating the reputation of men." Its most treasured evidence was John Wilkes Booth's diary, now in government care. Eighteen pages, it would seem, had been cut from the book, pages that might prove a miscarriage of justice in the hanging of Mary Surratt, or perhaps, just perhaps, some connection with

Andrew Johnson. "Who spoliated that book?" Butler demanded. The answer, perhaps to his dismay, was that most likely Booth did. In any case, the pages (and dozens more) had been missing before it ever reached official hands.[16]

The Judiciary Committee issued its report, finding nothing, at the close of the Thirty-ninth Congress. A new hearing began in the Fortieth, and within three months it had run out of leads to follow. By then, Ashley's unofficial investigation had taken on a life of its own. Of Johnson's usurpation and his danger to a just and lasting peace down south, he was convinced from the first, and many of the corruption charges came from him. But he smelled something much more hideous. Sharing, as he admitted, in "the dark suspicion which crept over the minds of men as to his complicity in the assassination plot," he could not "banish from my mind, the mysterious connection between death and treachery which this case presents." Many months later, under prodding from Democrats, the congressman admitted that he had never found evidence "that would satisfy the great mass of men," especially those not sharing in his "theory about this matter"—which turned out to be Dye's theory of a southern plot to clean out every president that stood in its way. Ashley's whole point was to explain why he had refused to make public the farrago of allegations and hearsay that implicated the president. Far from letting his theory dictate his case, he had presented only evidence that would stand up to scrutiny.[17] But if proofs he never found, it did not come from want of looking.

Enter the peculiar Sanford Conover, lawyer, newspaper correspondent for the New York Tribune, onetime Confederate, and now inmate of Old Capitol Prison. Just after the war, Conover's supposed contacts with the clandestine Rebel operations in Montreal made him a prime witness for investigations into Lincoln's assassination. Conover—or James W. Wallace, an alias of his—claimed to have knowledge tying the crime to Jefferson Davis himself and could cite two corroborators, William Campbell and Joseph Snevel, who could back up his charges. His promises were as good as gold—fool's gold. Even before the trial of Booth's associates had ended, the press teemed with affidavits and letters showing Conover up for a liar, including one from the real James Watson Wallace. The confidential talks that Conover had held with Jacob Thompson in February 1865 were striking for two men who, according to one of Conover's own letters that fell into the hands of the press, still had never clapped eyes on each other a month later. Campbell and Snevel were made-up names for A. J. Hoare and William H. Roberts. In May 1866, they admitted their true identities and explained that Conover had paid them to give the false testimony that he concocted. For that matter, Conover was really one Charles A. Dunham.

Dunham admitted his true identity but denied suborning or forging. All he needed was to go to New York for the proofs of his innocence. With an officer to keep an eye on him, Dunham reached the city, slipped loose, and disappeared. Six months passed before he was caught. Under guard, he admitted to perjury. But others had put him up to it, he asserted, specifically Judge Advocate General Joseph Holt, and he had the letters to prove it. They made hot reading when the *New York Herald* printed them, as well they might. Dunham had invented them all, forging the most damning words he could against the whole Bureau of Military Justice. That was not known when Dunham came up for trial, but there was more than enough evidence to convict him of perjury and put him in jail to await final sentence.[18]

Dunham needed friends badly. Turning to Democrats in Congress, he told them that he knew shocking things about leading Republicans and that a pardon would unseal his lips. The congressmen fell for the bait. Primed to spot conspiracies, they would give anything for proofs. They signed a request for the perjurer's pardon. But, with no response from the White House, Dunham looked to the Republicans and offered the same bait: shocking things he knew that would tie Andrew Johnson into the assassination conspiracy. When Dunham's wife brought the offer to Ashley, it must have been music to his ears. Willingly, he hurried to Old Capitol Prison to learn more.

Dunham had letters between Johnson and John Wilkes Booth—or so said Dunham. Let the prison doors open, and all these proofs would be Ashley's to use in making his case. The congressman listened raptly but not without caution. What exactly did those letters say? Who had them now? Could Dunham write a memorandum of particulars? Ashley could not promise freedom once the "actual letters" were produced, but he promised to do what he could. He would even promise not to make the correspondence public without Dunham's consent. The agreement was good enough for Dunham to get to work preparing his summary. Ashley arranged for a special room, where the prisoner had all the pens, paper, and law books he needed and his wife's company throughout the day.

Spring passed, but the summary did not appear, nor did those incriminating letters. Dunham was stalling, ever more insistent on being set free before anything was delivered. Time ran out on April 25, when the court passed down a ten-year sentence for lying to the Judiciary Committee. In a panic, Dunham sent Ashley his statement about what the letters contained. Ashley hardly had to look at it to see that the document fell far short of the specific allegations he had been promised. It was too general to show anything and so worthless that Ashley never bothered to show it to the Judiciary Committee. Still guessing that there might be something to the story, he tried to delay Dunham's transfer to the Albany penitentiary while leads were followed up. The prisoner's claim that he had information useful for the trial of the last surviving member of the Booth conspiracy, John H. Surratt, seemed promising enough for Ashley to notify Albert G. Riddle, the government prosecutor in the case (the actual material turned out to be no good at all). Ashley and Butler tried to get information out of Surratt himself, and their go-between hinted that evidence linking the assassination to someone in higher office might be enough to save Surratt's neck from the noose. The man in whom the emissary confided, the physician at Old Capitol Prison, relayed the offer on to Johnson, who most likely assumed that it was authorized by Ashley and Butler. Neither congressman ever got to talk to Surratt, or, for that matter, to his sister, who might have passed on their offer, whatever precisely it was. Summer came. Still Ashley had nothing beyond Dunham's statements. Neither then nor later did he actually charge Johnson with a part in the Lincoln assassination or give Dunham's memoranda to the public.

By the time Congress came back into session in early July, Ashley was baffled. He had not quite figured out what should have been plain all along from Dunham's record—at least, not enough to keep from writing a letter to the prosecution, trying to help the prisoner escape hard labor in the penitentiary. The congressman had been conned, and worse still, by a pretty transparent scoundrel. Contact ended. "I have been too often imposed upon during the investigation in which I am engaged that I grow more cautious," he wrote a friend who had sent him some apparent evidence.

Dunham could see that the game was up—but only with that particular quarry. He could not face a prison sentence. He needed a pardon and induced District Attorney Riddle to write a letter in his favor to the president. His wife went to Judge Advocate Holt and convinced him to endorse the prosecutor's plea that Dunham not yet be moved. Holt did so, though he was careful not to vouch for Dunham's truthfulness and did not ask for or even hint at a pardon. When not even these letters seemed enough to postpone his transfer to the Albany prison, Dunham panicked. He wrote the president himself asking for a pardon and included a memorandum of allegations that, as the forger explained it, had been cajoled from him by Ashley and Congressman Benjamin Butler of Massachusetts. Knowing well the liar he was, they had made him invent evidence to implicate Johnson in the Lincoln assassination. They had promised him a pardon in return, or so he claimed.[19]

And what a tale they supposedly meant to link to Johnson! It would seem that the then vice president–elect had held a conference in his hotel room with

John Wilkes Booth, and that the arrangements had been made to kill Lincoln at the inaugural. Johnson's odd behavior on that day came from nervousness, wondering when the blow would fall. Dunham would be able to show that Booth had imparted all these facts just days after Lincoln's second term began. The supposed would-be assassin of Johnson had simply been to ward suspicion away from the soon-to-be president, Finding persons "of good standing and moral character to prove these matters," Dunham now declared that he had assured Ashley, would be easy for him. Along with his letter to the president, the convict enclosed a memorandum of the "facts," which each witness was expected to swear to, and a few notes from Ashley himself. Out of context, the notes were harmless enough, a request that Dunham state what he knew, a receipt for the material since sent, and the promise that none of the letters between Booth and Johnson would be used without Dunham's permission. But Dunham supplied the context. And once again, the same old lure was proffered to the president: all that the convict said, he could prove—but only after being set free.[20]

And, once again, the lure caught a gudgeon. Johnson showed Dunham's materials to a select group of cabinet officers. Only Postmaster General Alexander Randall had reservations about publishing the damning documents until evidence to back up Dunham's story could be found. Caution won out. Dunham's wife was asked to find out the names of witnesses from her husband, including of the two individuals who Dunham insisted had been quizzed by Ashley and himself and put through their paces, in preparation for playing their perjuring parts. The same catch to the offer arose that Ashley had met with already. No names would be forthcoming until Dunham had his pardon.

Corroboration always lay one condition ahead. At no time did anyone back up Dunham's charge that Ashley or Butler had sought anything but genuine letters to prove what they were sure was true. In fact, there was no evidence that Butler had visited Dunham at all. The only person who had heard any part of Ashley's private talks with Dunham was a prison warden, who testified that he had heard the congressman warn the prisoner "not to tell him anything which was not true." Two letters from a former cellmate did appear later, in which it appeared that Dunham had hinted to him that Ashley had been more eager for proofs than concerned with how true they were, though neither document actually accused Ashley of asking Dunham to make up evidence and both rested solely on Dunham's word about what had occurred behind closed doors. Against that, one might set the affidavit of an acquaintance of Dunham's, some months before, that, to drag Judge Advocate Holt down with him, the prisoner had arranged a scheme to have various people swear that

Holt had asked them to perjure themselves to secure Jefferson Davis's conviction for his part in the assassination. Ben Wood, the editor of the Copperhead *New York Daily News*, and Roger Pryor, the onetime fire-eating Virginia congressman and now a New York lawyer, had been part of the scheme and would handle the money to pay off the retinue of perjurers—at least so Dunham claimed. Other witnesses swore that Dunham's emissaries had approached them with promises of money, too, and some of them defended themselves as merely tipping the scales of justice back where they should have been all along. Sure that Jefferson Davis had been jailed unfairly and blaming Holt for it, they hoped to forestall any trial of the former Confederate president by discrediting the whole Bureau of Military Justice. Weaving Holt into the mesh of Ashley and Butler's supposed schemes would work just as well. Dunham would have more statements in the future, and they would grow even wilder. Ashley had also wanted fabricated proofs to connect the murder to Preston King, Johnson's former collector for the Port of New York, who had drowned himself two years before! A certain Harrison had all the documents Dunham needed! But nobody ever found this Harrison, and Dunham gave them no help in finding him. But, in one statement, Dunham remained unshakably consistent. "The public shall have the whole story in detail, . . . *as soon as I am at liberty.*" He was perfectly free some eighteen months later, but the public was never made the wiser.[21]

The Johnson administration showed much less discretion about going public with an accomplished liar's lies than Ashley or Butler had. Without corroboration and without making any effort to check for any, on August 10 the president gave the documents to the press. He also gave Dunham his pardon. To those prepared to see in Ashley a corrupt fanatic, or in impeachment a foul conspiracy on trumped-up charges, the documents were a godsend. Imaginative correspondents, if they wanted, could make the congressmen's failure to reveal their "evidence" against Johnson a crowning proof of their wickedness. Their scheme, aided, no doubt, by Riddle's and Holt's letters, had been to get the president to issue Dunham's pardon, at which time they would cry cover-up and broadcast their proofs. As for Montgomery Blair, he went further still, declaring that the real masterminds of Dunham's plot were Holt and Stanton, which to Blair was only natural—the two men (in his special take on history) favored the Rebellion and "encouraged its leaders in bringing it on."[22]

Butler and Ashley had given the whole impeachment process a discreditable, even a ridiculous, face. The charges, they never actually leveled, were so ill-founded that any cause the two congressmen espoused was sure to be tainted. The president never saw them as the marginal players they were. To him and his supporters, they were the vanguard of a larger radical conspiracy, ready to invent any excuse for impeaching him and, that failing, any method for ousting him. Anticipating impeachment from the moment the Fortieth Congress met in special session, Johnson could not be sure that the Butlers and Ashleys would not muster the numbers they needed to impeach. Repeatedly, he would make sure that he had at least some political cover. The price of getting rid of Stanton was that it would have to be done under the terms of the Tenure of Office Act rather than by making an outright challenge of the law's constitutionality, and that General Ulysses S. Grant would be put in charge of the War Department until the Senate had decided the case. To keep Grant on his side, the president could not afford to dismiss all the generals immediately or appoint open enemies of Reconstruction. In any case, the military commanders could only be replaced, not eliminated entirely. No elections were canceled and no registration of voters was revolutionized in conservatives' favor.

Any commander would have the potential power to crimp or hinder Reconstruction. But that very much depended on putting the most conservative officers in charge, which was more than Johnson was prepared to do just yet. The apolitical men and the centrists had always reflected mainstream military sentiment. Most generals, even if they could not be ordered by the secretary of war ad interim, looked to him for advice and approval, counted on his backing, and adjusted their own plans to fit his suggestions. Even the most conservative of the commanders, Winfield Scott Hancock, did not go far in defying Grant. He issued a proclamation declaring the supremacy of civil law, but that was the policy that other commanders had upheld, even if they did not actually issue proclamations to that effect. And when he found that he could not get his way at headquarters, Hancock quit, after scarcely four months on the job.[23]

However much the president saw himself as acting with commendable restraint, the removal of Stanton and of two of the least conservative district commanders and the issuing of the Amnesty Proclamation, all coming within a month, could be seen quite differently. The old fears of Johnson reawakened, not as strongly as in 1866—nobody really thought that he could find members enough to form a Congress of his own—but with a nagging regularity. "People say that Johnson's more intimate pals talk as if he contemplated a coup d'etat—a purging of Congress after the manner of Cromwell," New York lawyer George Templeton Strong confided to his diary. ". . . One might be pardoned for hoping he would undertake some great crime and outrage, if one were sure he would be hanged for it." Fortunately, Strong allowed, having a man like General Grant running the War Office reined the president in.

"Amphitheatrum Johnsonianum." Thomas Nast, *Harper's Weekly*, March 30, 1867. Emperor Andrew watches with satisfaction the slaughter of black southerners by Confederates and the New Orleans police in the arena. Again, his evil genius, Seward, stands at his ear. Wreaths on the columns honor the butcheries in Memphis and New Orleans, and conservatives and Copperheads lurk in the shadows. But there are two differences from the year before. The cartoon no longer doubts where Stanton stands: he turns away in disgust. In the lower left-hand corner, General Philip Sheridan, later removed as district commander over New Orleans, draws the sword, presumably to slay the emperor and stop the massacre. General Ulysses S. Grant stays his friend's hand, but from his posture and Sheridan's expostulating look, the cartoonist makes clear that he does so only because the time to do summary justice has not yet come. Read literally, one might see the cartoon as an invitation to regicide.

Without it, no one could guess "what wild revolutionary scheme" might be hatched.[24]

But Grant himself was growing more and more uneasy. A few days after the Amnesty Proclamation, he wrote Philip Sheridan: "I do not know what to make of present movements in this Capitol but they fill me with alarm." Sheridan knew what he meant plainly enough. He, too, anticipated "greater evils." In all the struggles with the president, "no other thought has entered my mind, except to be able to use it [Sheridan's authority] to assist you, should the trouble which I sometimes fear, *may again come to distract the country*," he wrote back. "I am afraid to say on paper all I fear and apprehend," Grant wrote General Sherman in mid-September, "but I assure you that were you present there is no one who I would more fully unburden myself to than yourself, or whose advice I would prise more highly."[25] Warily, he watched the creation of a state militia in Maryland. Governor Swann wanted it equipped with cannon; Grant refused to provide any. "I have a mind to write to the Governor of Maryland and notify him that I am fully aware of what is going on, and intend to keep my eye upon it," he remarked.

By early September, nerves were frayed worse than ever. People in Boston were asking, "What are we coming to in political affairs?" one newspaper mused, not referring to the fall campaign. Everywhere, people could be found who thought the country very close to "a fresh outbreak of civil war." Approvingly, the *New York Herald* described "the executive plan" as based on "the Bonaparte method, — the overthrow of Congress and the absorption of its powers within the Executive, — in fact, a dictatorship." A *Boston Post* correspondent, after chatting with the president, published his private warnings that Johnson would use force if Congress tried to suspend him during an impeachment trial. "As you remarked that the papers had been too timid in stating [your views and purposes], I was impressed with the idea that I could not state them too plainly," he wrote Johnson, and presented them "in the best way to make them impressive. . . . Your friends every where were delighted."[26]

One of the crests in the waves of anxiety came early in November when a certain "H. S." offered a closely reasoned argument in the *Washington Daily National Intelligencer* for the illegality of the two extra sessions already held by the Fortieth Congress. The *Intelligencer* was the mouthpiece of the administration, with White House familiars on its staff, and its every phrase was suspected to be authoritative. The fact that the attorney general had the same initials as the letter writer misled readers into assuming that Henry Stanbery would issue these views as an official legal opinion within days. Since the president had not authorized the Fortieth Congress to assemble at any time other than the one set down in the Constitution, there had been no lawful assemblage, and thus the Second and Third Reconstruction Acts and the appropriations bills to finance military overlordship were null and void. It did not take much foresight to predict that the president would use this excuse to wipe Reconstruction off the books completely. The legal argument was so implausible that even Democratic organs like the *New York World* dismissed it at once. If "H. S." was right, then the First Congress had violated the Constitution several times. But the whole framework of government rested on that body's actions — all of the important cabinet departments had been created in that extra session. Further exegesis was hardly needed, the *World* concluded. What good could come of bayoneting "the legs of a theory after the breath is out of its body?" Within a day, the *Intelligencer* admitted that Stanbery had not so much as seen, much less written, the letter, though it asserted that the views mirrored his own.[27]

For the *Intelligencer*, the article was one foray among many. Midway through September, it declared that there were Radical plans in the works for a coup d'état, which would rely on General Grant to "usurp supreme power in respect to the ten States now under military rule, and precipitate a contest upon the point at Washington." Not that Grant would go along with the conspirators, it cautioned; but the opening round would come if the general resisted the president's interpretation of the Reconstruction laws or blocked his implementation of them.

Armies were on the march! Private, partisan armies! One such army, it was alleged, was the Grand Army of the Republic, a secret-oath-bound organization, with 200,000 or so members. What were its designs? Why were its inner workings secret, if there was no sinister purpose, one revolutionary and unlawful? The *Intelligencer* spotted the real purpose: a conspiracy to force Congress to overthrow the executive branch when it reconvened in November 1867 "at the word of command from the revolutionary leaders." A Republican win in the large states that fall would be the signal for the coup. The prospect was "sufficiently probable to alarm every man in that State who owns a Government bond, or has a dollar to lose by the hazards of revolution."[28]

Those fears affected the president himself. In late October, he noticed that black private militia had been raised in Washington, D.C. Apparently, he suspected them of being an army in readiness for a military coup, orchestrated by Congress. He ordered General Grant to have them disbanded and suppressed. Grant did not oblige him, and, as further investigation showed, most of those militia companies were fraternal and mutual self-help organizations for former Union veterans. The members had no arms except those they owned themselves. Most, indeed, had no arms at all.[29]

In so fretful an atmosphere, uncertainties as to how impeachment might play out worried both sides. A peaceful resolution seemed probable but not certain, and as the autumn campaign began, the question became even more worrisome. From the first, conservatives had hinted that the Jacobins on Capitol Hill would not just offer articles of impeachment. Instead, aware that they lacked the votes to convict in the Senate, they would pass a bill suspending the president until a verdict was reached. Johnson would be as good as removed — his powers would be stripped from him and radicals could put off any trial at all until the presidential term ended in 1869.[30]

But a suspension bill had no chance of passing the Senate. Indeed, it had very few advocates in the House.[31] But to Johnson it seemed a probability. Cautiously he began to feel out members of his cabinet for advice on what to do. Should he resist suspension? Should he use force to counter the attempt to oust him from the White House without the formalities of a trial and conviction? The cabinet overwhelmingly favored resistance. Throughout October, the question kept recurring of who could be put in charge of the War Department, once Grant vacated the position — someone who would assure the army's support, if a clash with Congress came. On October 8, a few cabinet officers discussed the possibility of giving the job to retiring governor Jacob D. Cox of Ohio. But Welles's fear was that Cox might weaken if Congress and General Grant "resorted to revolutionary measures, which from certain indications are not improbable," and proposed Frank Blair Jr. instead — a man "who, with some infirmities, had courage and energy to meet any crisis." The president liked the idea and toyed with putting old Thomas Ewing into the cabinet as a way of assuring the loyalty of Ewing's son-in-law, William Tecumseh Sherman. Without this incentive, Sherman might be likely to side with his friend Grant.

At length, at Welles's behest, the president sought out Grant for some clarification of views. Grant could not have failed to notice the plots and threats against him, Johnson began. The president must "resist invasions and usurpations" of the Constitution and the rights of the executive. What if attempts were made to depose or arrest him before a trial or conviction took place? Would Grant obey his orders? Grant's answer was conditional but comforting. He said that he assumed he would obey orders and promised advance warning if his mind changed, the better "to make arrangements." Within days, word came that Boutwell declared no intention of having the president arrested before impeachment and conviction and insisted that no such act would be legal. This, Welles was sure, could not be by chance. Boutwell surely had intended otherwise, and thus, naturally, Grant must have spoken to him and told him that he would not be party to any such movement—an astonishing inference that the secretary of the navy hastened to pour into the president's ear that very afternoon. He "seemed struck with my explanation." Already the president had prepared a letter to his cabinet, discussing the prospects for a revolutionary crisis. A month later, just as Congress reassembled, the cabinet met to discuss what he should do in the event that efforts began to suspend the president. Grant was the first to speak, declaring that any such suspension would be ex post facto law, though he qualified this remark by adding that his view would be different if the Supreme Court upheld such action or if the Constitution were amended to allow suspension of an officer. Others would not even add such qualifications. Gideon Welles was in favor of the president resisting, regardless of law or court decision.[32]

Word of these talks leaked out to Republicans—though, as always happened with cabinet discussions, in a much cloudier version. From the *New York Herald* came a two-column special letter in September from its Washington correspondent. Johnson, it seemed, meant to use force to resist not just suspension but impeachment itself. "He holds that a mere difference of opinion as to the constitutionality of a law between himself and Congress is neither treason, bribery, nor other high crime or misdemeanor," the reporter informed readers. "He holds, therefore, that he cannot be impeached, suspended or removed from office."[33] Republicans predicted that if the Senate did try him and convict him he would not abide by its judgment. And why should he? If he doubted the legality of the House and Senate as presently constituted, the Senate had no power to try him, and the House had no power to prosecute him. No verdict would be valid, any more than a trial by a petit jury in which four of the twelve jurors had been shut out of the courthouse until the trial ended would be legal.

The president might not talk so boldly, but other Democrats did. "The Radical oligarchy now controlling the Rump Congress mean revolution," roared former senator James Wall of New Jersey. "They fully intend to absorb within themselves, as the central directory of the nation, the executive and judicial powers." Now impeachment loomed, and Republicans meant to depose Johnson before conviction, indeed, before the trial could begin. The president must not allow himself to be packed off so ignominiously! He must "meet them at the threshold of their traitorous revolutionary attempt with all the powers with which the Constitution of the country has invested him."[34] It would not take a fevered imagination to guess that Wall was proposing that the president use the army to counter the Congress—and that guess would most likely have been right. Wall still grieved that General McClellan had missed his chance in 1862 to march the army to Washington and disperse the government.

Praising Johnson for opposing "a revolutionary Congress," one correspondent reminded him in November that the "very existence of the Republic now depends on your being firm, with an army at Washington to sustain not only yourself, but the Constitution, against the, perhaps, coming desperate efforts of Congress to sustain themselves, for despotic power, over the will of the people." Impeachment must be resisted with force; the president must refuse to recognize any court that did not represent all the states in the Union. What if the conflict meant a "trial of arms," one admirer assured Johnson. What fighting talent could the radicals count on? Grant was a "great bubble filled with the empty breath of popular applause." Butler, Banks, Schenck, Garfield—all were unfit even to handle a brigade under fire. In the crisis, the "military talent of the country" would fight in the ranks of those who sustained the Constitution and the laws—thus exclusively on the president's side. Better still, the author of the letter added that his old war wound was healing fast. "There will be no chance of actual collision between Congress and yourself before November or December and long before that time I will be ready for the saddle or the field."[35]

Primed with such fears, radicals found it easy to see what they expected to find. They looked at the expansion of the Maryland state militia and surmised that this was part of Johnson's plan, an army that he could call on to throw out Congress or to resist charges of impeachment, lodging himself behind their muskets. In particular, people who spent a great deal of time in counties near Washington reported a common opinion there "that the president intends to resist impeachment by force, and that nearly all the rebel militiamen confidently expect to be called upon." Those fears found new voice in the November issue of the *Atlantic Monthly*. There, in "The Conspiracy at Washington," readers were advised that they stood at the edge of the abyss, on the verge of a crisis that would make the Rebellion look paltry. A coup like Louis Napoleon's in 1851 was in the offing.[36]

Compared to the scare of the previous year, however, the Republicans were hardly able to make the hairs on the back of their followers' necks prickle. For one thing, the dread event had been too long in the offing. Johnson had had many more opportunities far more advantageous in the past, when he had a large political backing up north and more discretion in dismissing officeholders. He could have made a clean sweep of generals occupying the southern states and put in obstructionists. He could have violated the Tenure of Office

Act by firing Secretary of War Stanton rather than suspending him until the Senate reconvened, as the law required. As secretary of war ad interim, there would have been tools much more useful to his hand than General Ulysses S. Grant and shoulder-strappers whose devotion to his cause had been made starkly clear. Coming up with an army of former Confederates and southern state militias to impose his will might have been feasible in 1866. Now, with governors subject to removal at the district commander's discretion, there was small chance of that happening. Johnson might sow the dragon's teeth, but what would the harvest be?[37]

Among the new skeptics of talk of a new civil war was General Grant himself. As he was about to open the newspaper one morning, one of his in-laws, "in his usual rebel style[,] was predicting all sorts of disasters to the Country and that in the next fight a Million of men would go from the North to help the South." Dryly, Grant told him that he thought so, too, but that that million of men "would go with brain in their heads, money in their pockets, strength and energy in their limbs, and would make the South bloom like the rose until the old inhabitants would wonder why they had not done so before."[38]

Common sense should have pointed in other directions than hysterics. The idea that the president would use force to take control of the Fortieth Congress when it met in November and would seat southern representatives elected by his conservative governments to sit in the Thirty-ninth Congress could not be taken seriously. The time for doing so was long past. When the Fortieth Congress organized in March 1867, the president might have acted. For that reason, the *Boston Advertiser* admitted, "that occasion was universally felt to be critical. We might then very easily have had rival organizations and a grave dispute as to the true legislative succession." Even in July, Johnson could have attempted the trick—it would have been the best possible time. The country would have had less warning, and, with so many Republicans not showing up for the extra session, the administration's friends would have had a fighting chance "of seriously disputing the ground with Congress than now exists." But to presume that Johnson would do it in November, and do it with General Grant running the army, and do it after he had all but admitted the legality of the present Congress's membership by signing bills and returning vetoes, presumed an unpredictability and inconsistency even beyond his bounteous capacity.[39]

One by one, the possibilities that even Andrew Johnson could undo Reconstruction were vanishing. By year's end, it seemed quite clear that, however much the president had reined in the most notable of his generals and cooled their ardor, he had not been able to slow the process of Reconstruction. Every single southern state holding an election so far had voted for a Reconstruction convention; and in every state but one, Republicans had won overwhelming majorities of the delegates.

The further Reconstruction progressed, the more outlandish the cries of alarm sounded. By Election Day, at least some Republicans were voicing an open skepticism. The plots kept coming, one after the other, like the procession of spectral kings in *Macbeth*, but each one, by dissolving, made successors look more insubstantial. At one time, the *New York Evening Post* complained, northerners were told that Johnson would march to the Capitol and disperse the Rump Congress—later, that he would refuse to recognize Congress as nothing more than "a mere debating society." Now Johnson meant to make a new cabinet of Copperheads and Confederates. Every day a plausible new scenario was sketched out. But nothing happened. Maybe nothing ever would. The fears looked more like bloviation to the editors, and, more than that, they looked like it to the people.[40]

For if there was one thing clearer than anything else in the 1867 elections, it was that the Republican fearmongering was not working. Northern voters were growing tired of Reconstruction, and many of them were getting alarmed. With the South on its way to reconstructing, radicals with "all sorts of isms and extremes" had applied their energies into remaking the North. In a country longing for peace, all the most unsettling elements—from the do-gooders in Maine and Massachusetts talking about stiffer liquor laws, which, to hear Democrats tell it, would invade "every man's apple orchard and kitchen pantry," to the equal rights advocates in New York and Ohio pushing for Negro suffrage at home and disfranchisements for white soldiers who had left the service before their time, to the campaigners for giving women the vote in Kansas, to the tub-thumpers for impeachment—all clamored on the Republican side.

But quite a few voters thought that these elements needed a rebuke. In a year when no congressional seats and (except in Ohio and California) no senators would be lost, moderate Republicans could afford to give one. A Boston Republican compared the voters' response to the Scots prayer that the Lord hold a sinner over the mouth of Hell and give him a good shake—but not quite let him drop in. Democrats took quite another message from the returns. Their argument that the real danger to liberty lay with the Republicans was taking hold. Reconstruction was repudiated. "New York is back at the old mooring ground, anchored fast to the constitution," an Alabama paper exulted, "and New Jersey is by her side."[41]

Democrats had not yet recognized the sea change in Republican feeling, but the evidence was apparent by November on the front page of any city newspaper and in any tabulation of election returns across the North. The real force reining in a Radical Reconstruction did not come from the generals at all, nor from Andrew Johnson. It came from a northern electorate growing more and more detached from the Reconstruction issue, more and more distracted by other local issues, and increasingly restless with a process down south that seemed to be stumbling—not into conservatism but into precisely the opposite kind of extremism. Perhaps a lasting southern Reconstruction might have come with more radical generals in command, a more generous budget for the Freedmen's Bureau, replacement of conservative white authorities with radical ones chosen by black and white loyalists, and some confiscation of the big planters' property. But the elections of 1867 suggest that if southern Radicals had really been given full, free rein, northern Republicans would have been even more vulnerable and their defeats that much greater. Republicans themselves saw that the immoderation of their friends down south, not the moderation of their demands, was what alarmed northerners most. The pressure on the southern constitutional conventions to back away from wholesale white disfranchisement, and from radical experimentation, intensified.

When an impeachment resolution reached the House floor in December, even its sponsors knew that it was doomed. Lafayette Baker's testimony discredited impeachment with every charge he made. His brain, the *New York Evening Post* commented, proved "a storehouse of mare's nests," rivaling Wilkie Collins in plots, Dickens in grotesque characters, and the lurid supposed confessions of nuns in sensation. Sift the witnesses' statements as editors might, they found none of the "most startling revelations" that impeachers had promised. The conspiracies to throw out Congress, to bring on a new reign of terror, which reputable magazines had been assuring readers did exist, the statements of senators that they had the highest authority for saying that a coup like Oliver Cromwell's was in the offing and that Johnson had guilty knowledge of Lincoln's murder, all proved after exhaustive study to have nothing more than rumor behind them. Take the worst that the witnesses could produce, and the supposed army gathering in Maryland to reopen a rebellion melted like smoke. Ashley was completely discredited himself. "Toledo has been a perfect roar of laughter ever since the collapse of his wind bag caused by the publication of his testimony," a local resident gloated. The fears that had given impeachment so much of its pressing importance melted along with it. Was this, then, the best that Johnson's enemies could do? It was not good enough for a House majority. In vain, George Boutwell pleaded at the least for a censure resolution. By a wide margin, the House made clear that it would not impeach until Johnson broke some law, and, as radicals admitted, they could prove no such offense.[42]

This is not to say that hysterics did not continue in some quarters. They did. Radicals looked with foreboding on a president, set free at last from the fear of removal and already, who, in his annual message, hinted that under certain circumstances he might feel himself free to violate the law. "I give this country and republican institutions four years more of trial," former Confederate vice president Alexander Stephens told an interviewer in early March 1868. "This madness for centralization, this consolidated despotism, if achieved, will be the downfall of freedom." Radicals had "almost, if not quite, absolute dominion," the *Augusta Constitutionalist* lamented. One party went about its mission, usurping power, and the other tamely submitted, hoping for something to turn up, an "astonishing condition of affairs." What the *Constitutionalist* was really saying, as one northern editor pointed out, was that it was distressed that the northern people had not begun war in the streets over policy differences.[43]

But there was only one place where that war could be declared. The larger story of 1867 was that from the White House no call to battle had come. "The President will doubtless be pressed by extreme men to do some imprudent things," Secretary of the Treasury Hugh McCulloch had written a subordinate in October, "but I have now no reason to suppose that he will yield to the pressure." Quite a few of Johnson's opponents had realized it, too, by year's end. Yet McCulloch's insertion of the word "now" made his words a bit less heartening than they may have been meant to be. Perhaps the cabinet minister himself felt a lingering uncertainty as to what, precisely, the president really did intend to do.[44] Four months later, McCulloch found out.

What good did your moderation do you?
If you don't kill the beast, it will kill you.
— *Thaddeus Stevens*

chapter **10**

IF YOU DON'T KILL THE BEAST
Impeachment at Last

On February 25, 1868, the republic ended not with a whimper but with a bang. "War! War!! War!!!" screamed the headlines on the *Houston Telegraph*'s extra edition. "The President Impeached! — The First Gun Fired! — Three Women Murdered! — Thirteen Killed! — Thirty-seven Wounded — Andrew Johnson a Prisoner! — General Thomas Killed! — Stanton's Leg Broken! — War Department Burned! Sherman with the President! — Grant Declares Himself Dictator! — Secretary Seward Resigned! — Civil War Inevitable!!" Readers snatching up the paper would learn that the president had summoned the military and ordinary citizens to recapture the unfortunate General Lorenzo Thomas, only to be captured on the second charge by forces obeying Congress. Fleeing town on horseback, the secretary of war had fallen off, breaking his leg. All newspaper offices but one had been closed by the new military dictator, but General William Tecumseh Sherman had called for 300,000 ninety-day troops to restore the president's authority. "The greatest excitement prevails," the *Telegraph* confided.[1] So it must have, at least among its readers.

Reality had thrills enough. February 21 had seemed to be a routine Friday in the Senate, at least until just before two o'clock. Amid the murmur of oratory, the president's private secretary entered the chamber with a sealed envelope and brought it to the front. Curious at its contents, Radical Republican Zachariah Chandler strolled to the desk of the president pro tempore. One glance was all it took to send him rushing over to his friend and colleague Charles Sumner, dragging him back to see for himself. Other senators ran forward. Congressmen visiting the chamber ran to the House bursting with the news. The president was sending in the name of Adjutant General Lorenzo Thomas for secretary of war ad interim and appointing General George Thomas as head of a new army department to be located in Washington. Edwin M. Stanton, who had refused to resign, and who, barely five weeks before, the Senate had insisted could not be removed, was to be ejected. Thomas was to occupy the War Office at once. The aging desk soldier was soon boasting all over town his intent to "kick out" his predecessor.[2]

An order to take forcible possession would have been shocking even without a long background of suspicions and fears, but it came at the end of six months of wrangling and a year's worth of tension. In March 1867, Congress had passed the Tenure of Office Act to protect officials needing Senate confirmation from presidential removal. Any man that a president had appointed he could suspend from office during a congressional recess, but the Senate could reinstate the officeholder when it came back into session. The act included cabinet officers, and, so most Republicans thought, it meant Stanton above all. The legal provisions had the cloudiness about them that lawmakers often produced when trying to reach consensus, and this was certainly the case in determining whether "Mars" (Stanton) at the War Office was actually covered. But Johnson himself had as good as admitted it when he availed himself of the statute's provisions the August before and, instead of firing him, suspended Stanton. In the face of the Senate's response, it seemed clear to the president's enemies that he had done the one thing moderates had insisted he must do to permit impeachment: he had broken the law. From the War Office, Stanton sent news that Thomas had come to announce his intention to take possession. Should he give up peacefully?[3] Conservative Republican senators quickly told him to hold onto the place "to the point of expulsion," and within hours the full Senate had passed a resolution denying Johnson's power to remove the secretary.

As representatives huddled and conferred about the exciting news on the House floor, Thaddeus Stevens, leaning on the arm of his old rival, John Bingham of Ohio, was everywhere, always with the same reminder. "Didn't I tell you so?" he demanded. "What good did your moderation do you? If you don't kill the beast, it will kill you." Burrowing through his desk, "Honest John" Covode of Pennsylvania pulled out an impeachment resolution, prepared long since. "At last he has thrown us an open defiance," Michigan congressman Austin Blair wrote an old acquaintance. "We have no choice left but to take up his glove and now one or the other of us must go to the wall." "We are in the midst of a revolutionary crisis," the president's newspaper defender, the *Washington Daily National Intelligencer*, announced, as word of the attempt on Stanton's office reached it. Action had to be taken against "the reckless and wicked projectors of this new rebellion."[4]

"Rebellion" certainly was not what Johnson had had in mind. The president himself would argue after the fact that all he had wanted was a legal case that could be taken to the courts to challenge the Tenure of Office Act's constitutionality—and, at the same time, to assert that the act did not cover Stanton and therefore that it could not have been violated at all. Just because the two explanations conflicted with each other and both conflicted with the president's actions until then did not mean that Johnson did not believe one, the other, or both. And forcing a chief executive to put up with a cabinet officer with whom he was not on speaking terms was a distasteful business. Quite a few members knew how difficult Stanton could be, and had he resigned many of them would have thought good riddance—at least, if Andrew Johnson had not been president. But within three days, the House had voted for impeachment, with no Republican votes against it, and all the betting favored the Senate's convicting Johnson within the month. How could they have done so?

Popular historians since that time have known exactly what Republicans must have felt: Radicals must have exulted even as they raged at the president's presumption. At last they had the president where they wanted him! Congressmen out to make their branch all powerful saw a chance to gut the presidential office.[5] Republicans knew that with Johnson gone the worst obstacles to their agenda would be removed. In fact, the impeachers had many different emotions, though the exultation seems the hardest to find. Undoubtedly, Republicans were furious, especially the moderates. They had run out of patience with the president, and certainly exasperation and weariness with the constant struggle against a pesky executive made them ready, for the moment, to put aside all doubts about whether Johnson may have had a plausible defense. Still, though the risk to southern Reconstruction could not have been far from the impeachers' minds, reference to it appeared surprisingly little in their speeches. Nor did any of them argue for congressional supremacy over the executive branch. Instead, they stood on the most conservative grounds: the need to uphold the majesty of the rule of law against one who would violate the law and create a unitary executive, able to thwart or ignore any law he pleased. Not Congress, but the president, had been the real usurper.[6] He, not the Republicans, had been the pushiest refashioner of what the framers of the Constitution had set down.

In fact, the speed with which impeachment sailed through the House spoke to the story of the crisis that is often dismissed. There was not just anger but, especially among radicals, a lingering fear: fear of a coup, of a new civil war, of rival armies, one serving the president and one serving Congress. Fear may not have been as strong as two years before, but vestiges remained. Johnson's attempt to remove Stanton came at the end of a series of maneuvers that took very little imagination to read in the most alarming terms.

By January, the president was aware that the Senate would most likely order Stanton's retention in the War Office. His plan had been that General Grant, as secretary of war ad interim, would refuse to give up the keys when ordered to do so. Grant's popularity might be enough to force Congress to back off. Republicans would think twice before they hauled the man most likely to be their presidential nominee into the courts. If they did, the administration would be able to challenge the constitutionality of the Tenure of Office Act, and in any case, while the courts decided, the president's supporters would be in possession. As soon as Grant had served his purpose, Johnson would get rid of him and pick another secretary more willing to do his bidding. The president no more trusted Grant than Grant trusted the president. He was using the general—nothing more. It could not have escaped his notice that the person likeliest to be fined and jailed would be Grant, not himself, and that, at the very least, it would soil the general as a candidate almost beyond scouring.

Unfortunately for the president, Grant realized it, too. Days before the Senate acted on Stanton's case, he let the president know that he could not break the law. Talked into holding off his final decision and informing Johnson when he did and striving to work out some deal that might both satisfy the president and reassure the Congress, the general ran out of time. When news of the Senate's decision came to him, Grant resigned the keys and left the War Office. Before he could reach the president to inform him of what had taken place, Stanton was behind his old desk again.[7]

A court case would still have been quite possible, if that had been the president's first goal. He could have simply refused to recognize Stanton as secretary or he could have had the Treasury refuse to honor his requisitions. In fact, Johnson was not at all interested in choosing a successor for Stanton who might have reassured the Congress and eased "Mars" into the resignation that both men had been wanting for so long. All Grant's efforts to find some face-saving deal were brushed aside; all his attempts to stay on good terms with Johnson went for nothing. What followed was a month of inspired leaks

"Ides Febrvarii, MDCCCLXVIII." *Harper's Weekly*, February 22, 1868. Johnson, Welles, and Seward, despoilers of the temple of the republic, are turned aside from their purposes by the determination of General Grant. The general is cloaked in Law and stands on Truth. The cartoonist's point seems to be that by permitting Secretary of War Stanton's return to office, Grant protected rule by law. Any other course would have been the triumph of "Conspiracy" and "Anarchy."

from the White House to make it seem as if Grant had double-crossed his commander in chief and an exchange of letters in which Johnson did his best to show up the general as a liar, humiliated before the whole cabinet for his perfidy. There is not much doubt about how Grant read the affair; if he had suspected that Johnson was a dangerous man, interested only in seizing control of the army, he now knew it for certain — and in fact continued to believe it for the rest of his life.[8]

But the president's next actions seemed more alarming still. Working to find some way around the system, the president looked anew to General Sherman, whose sympathies were completely against Congressional Reconstruction. In mid-February, Johnson proposed a new army department, the Army of the Atlantic, with Sherman at its head. Headquartered in Washington, such a department would be sure to run afoul of Grant. Perhaps the president meant no more than mischief in setting Grant and Sherman against each other. Sending in Sherman's nomination as general of the army, a rank held by Grant only, he may simply have been acting out of spite. Or it may have been meant as a veiled warning that when the crisis came there would be more than one military chieftain for soldiers to rally behind. "This would set some of them thinking," Johnson told his private secretary.

Indeed it did. Considering the president's past reputation, that thinking must have been of the most bloodcurdling sort. The orders had all the look of the administrative beginnings for a rival military force, able to protect Johnson against a War Department and a regular army commanded by General Grant that would take the side of Congress. Perhaps Johnson meant it to protect himself from a Republican plot to arrest him and take over the government when impeachment came. But the steps could have been equally consistent with plans for a coup.

Sherman would have none of it. He had fled Washington, relieved to escape the snarl between his friend and his commander in chief. Now, like a thunderclap, came news that he had been put into a position where his authority was sure to collide with just about every other figure involved in running the army. By now, he, too, may have had a glimmering suspicion of more sinister schemes afoot. "The President would make use of me to beget violence, a condition of things that ought not to exist now," he wrote his brother, the very influential conservative Republican senator John Sherman. There was something pertinacious and disturbing about Johnson's failure to hear the general's insistence again and again that he would take no such position and his refusal to heed any of the point-blank letters that he had sent. Now it had come as orders. But Sherman was not to be put on the spot. He begged off the command of any new Department of the Atlantic and, even before it was offered to him, urged senators not to approve the brevet general's rank that press reports had assigned to him. As he noted, with what must have been an affected naïveté, the army already had its headquarters—and a department that centered its authority there. Rather than accept any such orders, Sherman would resign from the service.[9]

Thwarted, the president then looked to an alternative, one equally independent of Grant's control. He nominated for brevet general rank George M. Thomas, who, unlike Sherman, might be thought to have no qualms about coming to Washington at the same rank that Grant enjoyed and clashing with him for control of the army: Thomas and Grant had been on notoriously uneasy terms with each other since the war. As a congressman explained it, Johnson could only mean to create a new department "for headquarters, and some general of the highest rank known to the law, always present, and pliant, or devoted enough to execute his orders, whether lawful or unlawful; ready at the word of command to prevent by force a man declared by the solemn judgment of the Senate to be Secretary of War from entering his Department, or by force [to] eject a Secretary of War when he will not abdicate at the illegal summons of the President."[10] And, precisely at that moment, the president called in Adjutant General Lorenzo Thomas and offered him Stanton's place as secretary of war ad interim.

The whole thing smelled fishy. Johnson's actions still could be seen as an effort to bring the Tenure of Office Act into court for an appeal. But other, less aggressive, ways would do that, and the president's methods could also be read, with very little glossing on the facts, in a much more sinister way. Over the last few months, he had dropped hints of a readiness to use force on his own behalf. In early January, he had had a long talk with a correspondent for the *New York World*, the national voice of the Democratic Party, and sure to be widely reprinted. Once more he lugged out his references to "headlong spirits" in Congress fomenting a "revolution" and warned that the effect might be "more damaging than that of the last civil war." Asked what he would do in reply, Johnson gave an answer as ominous as it was vague. "Special measures" would meet "special occasions," but this the president would say: he trusted "the *good sense of the army*" and relied on the people. "I believe in the young men — they will not permit a revolution to be accomplished, *even though it may be necessary for the people to take the matter into their own hands*." Soberly, John Sherman congratulated his brother on escaping from "the worst complication we ever had." No one disputed the president's right to bring a court case against Stanton's right to the office. But forcible removal of a man in office was "a trespass, an assault, a riot, or a crime, according to the result of force." And it made no sense. The president had means of testing his right of removal without military action. The courts were open.[11] Control of the War Office itself was not necessary for a secretary of war to function.

Dangerous questions would not die: Why did Johnson want control of the War Office itself and not just the dismissal of Stanton? Why had he created a separate military department in Washington, and what did he expect it to do? Why had he permitted Lorenzo Thomas to use force as a means of challenging the law? Some Republicans thought they knew the answers, not just in general but in specific. Could Johnson have wanted the War Department to get hold of government arms, in order to equip Maryland's militia? That militia, reportedly, could match the army stationed in Washington, and it was only a few hours away. Maryland's governor was said to have offered the president troops to sustain his position.[12]

Those fears gave special emphasis to the president's summoning of General William H. Emory to the White House. Emory commanded the troops in Virginia, Maryland, and the District. His garrison would be enough for ousting Stanton or even for taking the Capitol, if that was Johnson's intention — and alarmists thought that it might be. According to one report, the president had tried to see whether Emory would provide him with troops and met with a firm refusal. The general declined to produce any men without explicit orders from his superior, General Grant. Balked at that level, the president then applied to one of Emory's subordinates, Colonel Wallace, commander of the Twelfth U.S. Infantry in Washington, only to meet the same demurral: no troops would be furnished except on command of his immediate military superiors. All the same, General Grant had removed the Twelfth Infantry from its responsibility guarding the War Office and replaced it with the Fifth U.S. Cavalry, his own bodyguard and far more trustworthy in a pinch. The president's best hope now would be to replace Emory, and the very man for the job was General Gordon Granger, commander of the Twenty-fifth Infantry and known for his ardent support of Johnson's Reconstruction policy. The news, therefore, that Granger had been in council with Johnson only seemed to confirm the other rumors.

Journalists had some basis for their stories, but not much. The president had indeed called in General Emory and had contacted Wallace, as he admitted, but only to find out about troop movements ordered by General Grant. He had made no effort to shake their loyalty, or so he claimed, although sources pretending to be in the know assured Republican correspondents that that claim was false.[13]

The coup, if such it was, never happened, of course. George Thomas was no more ready to involve himself in a power struggle than Grant had been — he sent in an immediate refusal of the promotion. And Emory made it quite clear to the press that he would take orders only from his immediate superior officer, General Grant. As for Lorenzo Thomas, after demanding to take over the War Office and being asked to return later, when Stanton could decide on what to do, he put his energies into a wild evening of partying and boasting about his plans, only to be arrested over breakfast, haled into court, and forced to give bond to keep the peace. There would be no court case, and though Thomas did sit in cabinet meetings for the next few months, he was treated dismissively as a coxcomb and a nuisance, fit to be ignored except when he appeared among his colleagues fuddled by drink.

None of this could have been known on that February weekend, and in view of Johnson's course, nothing seemed absolutely impossible. Soon Stanton was bombarded with telegrams, telling him to hold on. Sumner's was the briefest: "Stick!" he wired. But others took the time to urge that force be met with force and made the assumption that the president did mean to apply more. "Don't surrender the office," J. M. Howard wrote him. "If force is employed against you, repel it—stand firm!" By refusing to surrender his place, the secretary would ensure that "any revolutionary violence" would have to be committed by the president, trying to take over the War Office, and not by Congress in trying to restore it.[14]

Assuring banker Jay Cooke that the excitement over Stanton's removal was overblown, his confidential reporter found that the "coolest heads" in the Capitol assumed that the president was just trying to test the secretary of war's rights in the courts. "I don't see any indication that *force* will be used to oust Mr. Stanton," he added.[15] But others did, at least in the first few days of the impeachment crisis. Guards were stationed around the War Department, and Stanton's right to hold the place was protected at gunpoint by his newly appointed armed escort of Republicans. After feeding on Rebel and Democratic cant about the "Rump Congress," "a body hanging upon the verge of the Government," and echoing it himself, what could be more natural than for the president to believe those words and fling aside the law that the Rump Congress had made, or to believe that he would find allies aplenty if he tried? "Today but for Congress there would be war," the *Philadelphia Press* announced. If the House had not acted at once to set impeachment in motion, the rolling drum would have been the president's recruiting sergeant for a new rebellion. When hopes of using the regular army melted away, Secretary of the Navy Gideon Welles was rumored to have offered some 200 Marines to break down the barriers protecting the War Office, little counting on the undoubtedly loyalty of their commander (Welles never considered offering anything of the kind).[16]

Years later, the memory of the putsch that never came to shove still stirred in the more Radical Republicans. Writing to back up allegations that General Grant had suspected the president of planning a coup d'état, former congressional delegate N. P. Chipman asserted that many insiders felt that the country had stood on the verge of civil war or revolution and had evidence to back this up. "I sat up with Mr. Stanton several nights during the 'siege of the War Dept' by Pres't Johnson," he recalled, "& had a force of men, members of the Grand Army of the Republic, in readiness at an agreed signal to come to the rescue should Mr. Johnson attempt to resort to force, as we all expected he would, & I knew what Mr. Stanton thought then of Johnson's purposes. I know all felt that it was a period of supreme danger to the country & that Mr. J. was in a temper to resort to force & only lacked the organization on which to call." Without

Grant's firmness and without Stanton's refusal to vacate the War Office, Chipman insisted, the president would have tried the military overthrow of Congress. It was also a fact that on the morning of February 22 Grant had issued an order reminding post commanders of the recent act of Congress requiring that all U.S. Army orders pass through his hands first and that only those directives coming by way of his own office be obeyed. To radical reporters, this could only mean that he was taking steps against a potential coup on the president's part.[17]

How often such fears had come up over the last two years! Now, even more levelheaded Republicans, if only momentarily, glimpsed indications that the long-dreaded scenario might be upon them. Hastening to Washington, *Chicago Tribune* publisher Joseph Medill found residents even more excited than at the fall of Richmond. "The course of the President is regarded as a preliminary act of dictatorship," he wrote, "—as a preparatory step in the direction of restoring the rebels to power and trampling upon Congress." Who doubted that as soon as the army had been brought under his sway, Johnson would order General Grant's arrest, one Illinois congressman asserted. "If he can turn out the heads of Departments, he can turn us out, and with the Army at his back he is determined to do it. What follows? With the entire control of the Army, we are in the hollow of the hand of this unscrupulous usurper— this man who stops at no constitutional impediment, and who either knows or fears no law." If not now, the president would bring on conflict later, when Congress was not in session. Controlling the army, he could force the South's electoral votes to be counted, every one of them, for whatever candidate he chose, and base it on illegal elections that his Democratic friends had held. "Lincoln was murdered, and other distinguished patriots may be," Congressman William D. Kelley of Pennsylvania cried. "It is known that men ascend to power over bloody steps, and that they may do it in this country and yet be tolerated."[18]

Moderates mastered their fears faster than did radicals, and as they did so, they found less reason than ever to trust the judgment and sanity of their own colleagues. Still, even if nothing outrageous was intended, those who had watched the president in action over the last three years could not put anything past him and were ready to respond in kind. "He is the most dangerous man that ever occupied the Chief Magistracy," an army officer wrote in his diary from Virginia. "That he meditated a coup d'etat and the forcible vindication of his constitutional theories as a bid for the Democratic nomination for the Presidency appears plain. That he will be brought to justice appears equally plain." If "the gentlemen, with the President at their head force it upon us," a Tennessee Unionist promised, "we can only promise to do as we did before, to meet the enemy on the field of battle, face to face, and ask that a just God protect the right."[19]

Panic dispelled over time, but it still held enough force to affect the range of charges that the House managers met to draw up against Johnson. Some of the articles rested on the charge that the president meant to use force against Stanton. The ninth charge concerned Johnson's interview with General Emory. At Congressman Benjamin Butler's behest, another article charged the president with encouraging rebellion against Congress in his speeches made on the Swing around the Circle. But the great catchall article, the one that radicals saw as the surest to win the two-thirds vote required for conviction, was the eleventh. Its strength lay in its mixture of offenses, some criminal and others not so, all bound together by a larger premise that Johnson had shown, not by his words alone but also by his actions, that he did not believe there was a legal Congress. To take just one example, when the president sent a telegram south, discouraging ratification of the proposed Fourteenth Amendment, he had promised that the country would not sustain "any set of individuals" in such a revolutionary measure. Referring to Congress as a "set of individuals" implied that it had no more authority than a mob. Interestingly, Article Eleven's sponsor was not the radical Thaddeus Stevens, who had just barely won a place among the House managers at all; John A. Bingham of Ohio, the leader of the managers and the longtime bane of the House radicals, had proposed it.[20]

To the most ardent Democrats, as to Republicans, there was no doubt that now the crisis had come when the republic really would meet its long-promised end. America had reached "the days of Cromwell and Charles I and [James] II," Congressman James Brooks of New York exclaimed. Before them opened "the scenes of the French Revolution," "the worst of all tyrannies ever created." There would be no fair trial, Democrats agreed. None was intended. Then America would be run by a Committee of Public Safety, as the French Jacobins had had in their revolution. Conjuring up the first French constituent assembly, overthrown by sans-culottes and fanatics, lobbyist Sam Ward saw "more volcanic danger" than even when South Carolina left the Union. No way remained for defeating "the conspirators except by a bloody & long protracted contest," Connecticut editor A. E. Burr fumed. As soon as impeachment concluded, other high-handed measures would follow to overthrow American institutions, California congressman James A. Johnson announced. "By civil war the Republican party can now destroy our institutions." The president's secretary, the president himself, and some Democratic newspapers looked to the future and saw military despotism in the works. If the conspirators boasted truly, a newspaper warned, "the Dictator will be on the throne in a few weeks' time."[21] From the *Philadelphia Age* came the insistence that no impeachment, by any rules, would be lawful, because the Congress was not lawful. The southern states remained unrepresented. As a "fragmentary and unconstitutional body," the House had no authority to impeach anyone—a position that James Brooks, House minority leader, came very close to endorsing himself.[22] Despairing, Thomas Bayard wrote his father, Senator James Bayard, that the country was gone for good. All he could hope for was that "the Revolution may be perfected *rapidly* as a *slow* death is to be avoided."[23]

Down south, diehard opponents of Reconstruction barely concealed their hopes that civil war would break out and allow them a chance by force of arms to put the president back on top. They predicted a violent collision in Washington and taunted Republicans that this time the South was sure to win. The crisis would come when the House suspended Johnson from office and Johnson appealed to the bayonet to keep hold of his powers. He would not need the army; volunteers would respond to his call from all across the north. On the floor of the Mississippi constitutional convention, jubilant conservatives announced that they could rally 100,000 men in that state alone to march on Washington, and all the more confidently because the wire service had just informed them that the president had arrested General Grant and thrown him into jail. "Now or never, is the only safe motto," an admirer wrote the president just before the trial began. ". . . Kentucky is impatiently waiting for you to lead off and give her the rallying cry to stand by you and the Constitution at all hazards."[24]

As rumors flew, excitable northerners awaited the call to arms. From Elmira, New York, came word that "some of the most rabid are preparing for war," though the writer guessed that if bloodshed became a real possibility the saber-rattlers would "be most earnest in the procuring of sutlerships, &c." But passions stirred everywhere. "There was great excitement here today over the news from Washington," an Illinoisan wrote Congressman Elihu Washburne. "I tell you it reminds us of Fort Sumpter times. Everybody is for fight." As grand commander of the Grand Army of the Republic, General John A. Logan was the recipient of many telegrams from various posts, assuring him that their members stood ready to come to the capital, armed and ready for action, in a few days.[25] All over the United States, commanders of the Grand Army of the Republic stood behind Congress, the *Atchison (Kans.) Daily Champion* reminded its readers. Did Rebels want another fight? This time the South would be stripped as bare as it had been before the Creation. Another midwesterner favored slaughtering the northern Democratic leaders first, "as you would wolves."[26]

Democrats themselves were of mixed minds. Most counseled acceptance of this latest usurpation by radical conspirators. Others called for an open fight. How far they would reenact the original, time would tell, but this James Brooks of New York could promise: "If you proceed further, if as threatened, you suspend him! if you throw him out of office by any other process than impeachment, I tell you in behalf of thousands and tens of thousands and hundreds of thousands and millions of the people of this country we will never, never, so help me God! never, never submit." If he were the president's lawyer, Judge George W. Woodward of Pennsylvania told the House, he would advise Johnson to deny that Congress had any jurisdiction and issue a proclamation announcing that he would never defer "to the irregular, unconstitutional, fragmentary bodies who propose to strip him of it. Such a proclamation, with the Army and Navy in hand to sustain it, would meet a popular response that would make an end of impeachment and impeachers."[27] A New Yorker told the president to insist on seating twenty southern senators in the tribunal that was to try him, but if he failed to accomplish this, to pronounce the body null and void. "We must defend that Blessed instrument with our Blood if it is requisite for us to do so." Let him dismiss the House and justify this action to the people by informing them that the Republicans had begun a revolution.[28] Ohio Democrats talked of sending the state militia to offer the president its services—which, with a Republican as governor, suggested the rich fantasy life of professional politicians. Not since 1861 had there been such a readiness to sign up, and the disappointment went deep when the president's will faltered.[29]

Wild reports spread. The Senate buzzed like an upset hive at the news that two bottles of nitroglycerine had been discovered in a passageway of the capitol, and a large crowd gathered to watch them be disposed of. (A newspaper correspondent disposed of some of them by uncorking one bottle and taking a long swig—it proved to contain bourbon. By that time, unfortunately for them, most of the Democratic congressmen had fled the building, having been first out the door.) When Charles Sumner presented a petition asking that Congress abolish the presidency, Democratic editors took it as the opening shot in a campaign already under way to replace presidents with a congressional commission. The secretary of war, the *Hartford (Conn.) Daily Times* informed readers, was "favorably considering a proposition to seize the Supreme Court by military power—and remove—by that power—the McCardle case from the court."[30]

The first days after Johnson's action were filled with false reports that the president meant to apply force. On Saturday, word came that the president was writing a proclamation, asking the country to rescue him in his hour of peril. (No such proclamation ever appeared.) "Keep your office strongly guarded," New York lawyer Edwards Pierrepont wrote the beleaguered secretary of war. "There is a plan, not by soldiers, but by ruffians with secret arms, to take possession of your office and put Thomas in. Believe this and act upon it."[31] Democrats in Philadelphia's fourth ward were reported to have met and resolved "to send a fighting delegation to Washington to sustain the President." Rumor transformed this into the news that "four hundred armed toughs" were on their way down to "overawe Congress." On Sunday, the Maryland militia paraded through Baltimore, 14,000 strong, or so the news dispatches related, and an advance on Washington was "freely talked of in that city." (Maryland never acted, perhaps because, as the governor later pointed out, guns for equipping militia had never been sent from Washington. There was also nothing to Senate secretary John W. Forney's story that Confederate raider John S. Mosby was raising armies on his own in the counties just across the border from the District.) From Pennsylvania and Illinois, the governors offered troops to Congress, offers that only added to "a wide-spread apprehension."[32]

Time weakened but did not end the wild conjectures. As the opening day for the impeachment trial neared, the *New Orleans Times* informed readers that the radicals were assembling a military force to hold the Capitol against armed attack. Patrols marched the Washington streets, and companies of infantry from across the North had been ordered to the District. Bridges over the Potomac were held by pickets every night, and four detachments of artillery were placed in strategic spots. The preparations were not defensive; they were precautions as the revolutionaries readied their next move. A bill was in the works, the *Times* asserted, to choose a new chief justice in the event of a vacancy; and now that it was plain that the chief justice might not rule as radicals wanted him to, during the impeachment trial, this measure was as good as the announcement of a vacancy about to be made, if need be "with bayonets." At the War Office, Stanton had heard that a surprise foray would be made, and he moved in companies of infantry to reinforce nearby military installations, the better to cope with an invading army. A picket guard manned the building's entry, and the secretary stopped taking his daily walks. But he could not have felt easy. Within the week, stories were afloat that the president was consulting with Major General Winfield Scott Hancock, in town after resigning his southern command and known to be ambitious. That feared rival military district was about to be created, and one of the most conservative officers was to be put in charge.[33]

But Democratic leaders had no intention of getting themselves involved in the affair. They were tired of expecting more from Johnson than he would deliver, and they fully expected him to fall short again. Besides, by promising to back the president's hand they emphasized their own readiness for treason, and in a presidential year, too. The Democratic national committee had been meeting in Washington when the president ordered Stanton's removal. Members did not let the news disturb their supper. Even banter about Johnson's "inconceivably stupid blunder" occupied their minds for only a few moments. From the start of the crisis, the least militant Democrats were members of the House and Senate. Their advice to the president had been all on the side of caution, if only because they really believed that General Grant would use the army to crush out trouble at the first opportunity. A quick ouster would be far worse than conviction after a prolonged trial, and the more rashly the president acted, the swifter the axe would fall.[34] This was purely a Republican fight, Francis Kernan wrote to Samuel J. Tilden from upstate New York. Let the president face off against "the men who elected him." By March, even the sensationalist *Chicago Times* had grown sick of the fevered reporting. "The country is not 'glowing like a furnace,'" it informed readers, whatever the *New York World* might pretend. "We are not in the midst of a revolution, 'which may become sanguinary.'" Impeachment was like "a last year's almanac—out of date, useless, and almost forgotten."[35]

Nor did the army show the slightest desire to join a revolution. District commander Edward O. C. Ord, whose sympathy for Mississippi Reconstruction had been glacial, let General Grant know that even he could be relied on, in case of an armed clash. Nine-tenths or more of the officers, he guessed, would stand with Congress, himself included. But military men "had better let the politicians fight out their own battles."[36]

Many, perhaps most, Republicans, had never expected a coup at all, even among those who conjectured that it was conceivable. Exasperation, mingled with contempt, made for a strong enough emotion to turn Republicans into impeachers and would-be convicters, but it was a far cry from the alarm that their radical colleagues were voicing. After the first few days of the crisis had passed, the clamor of impending civil war died away. Not that all Republicans trusted the president's intentions even then. To those still distrustful, the real explanation was that when he looked for armed force to back him up, he could not find it; this was why he protested that he wanted "'legal relief,' wouldn't hurt anybody at all, &c. &c. None so peaceful as those who can't help themselves!" the *Lewiston (Maine) Evening Journal* jeered. Republicans quickly realized that northern Democrats, too timid to do more than skulk in wartime, were not going to seize muskets now that the Confederate army was disbanded.[37] Having circulated among his constituents, a Pennsylvania congressman admitted that he could not find apologists for the president, even among Democrats. If war came, he could muster "a grand division of drilled soldiers," ready to defend the Union, the Constitution, and Congress, in six hours; "the nullifiers and obstructionists" could not gather "a corporal's guard" in six weeks. John Sherman foresaw a quiet, orderly trial and a quiet ejection, if the Senate brought in conviction. But his prediction came more than a week after Johnson's first move had been followed by no others, and he did not know what Thomas A. R. Nelson, the president's counsel and friend, later admitted: that Johnson agreed with Judge Woodward's view that there was no legal House with the authority to impeach, no lawful Senate with the right to convict, and that his obedience to the court was proof of his extraordinary "forbearance" for the republic's sake.[38]

A few newspapers noticed the admission, but by that time the impeachment trial had nearly closed, with the evidence creating more doubts than fears among Republicans. The worst physical force between Stanton and Thomas had come when the secretary ran his fingers through his would-be successor's hair, just before they shared a bottle of whiskey with each other. Thomas may have boasted to a fellow Delawarean that he would kick Stanton out of the office, but the vaporings of a hard-drinking old dandy were a far cry from action, much less the kind of specific orders from the president that the impeachers needed, in order to prove that Thomas was doing Johnson's bidding. The sillier Thomas looked—and he was at his muzzy-minded, gabby worst under cross-examination—the harder it became to treat the attempted ouster of Stanton seriously. In the end, all the managers had were remarks from a private citizen from Delaware to show violent purposes. If they produced only such a "needle in a hay-stack" and shaped it into "the sharp point of their case," one of the president's counsel joked, senators could feel sure that there was "no bristling of bayonets under the hay-mow."

Conspiracy and the threat of a coup were the basis for many of the articles. Without proof for either, the charges tottered. Even before the House passed the ninth article of impeachment, charging the president with trying to order General Emory to disobey the chain of command set up by Congress, Emory's own testimony had torn it to pieces. The articles charging that Johnson meant to use force against Stanton found so many doubters on the Republican side that the impeachers dared not bring them to a vote; the tenth article, imputing to the president's speeches in 1866 an intention to treat the Congress as an illegal body, disappeared into the prosecutors' fulminations against bad manners and disrespectful treatment of the legislative branch. Even Article Eleven, the one deemed most likely to succeed, had to be read for the parts that did not relate to criminal conspiracy. With Article Ten lost beyond recovery, the Swing around the Circle no longer could bolster the claim that Johnson believed that no legal Congress existed, and the managers did not dare allow cabinet officers into the witness chair, for fear that they would add to the proof that Johnson may have meant to test the Tenure of Office Act in the courts all along. Thaddeus Stevens, in his argument, might assure senators that impeachment, unlike an ordinary criminal trial, needed no proof of intent—the acts alone sufficed to justify removal.[39] But most senators needed more than that, just as they needed more than unindictable offenses, whatever Ben Butler would say. A week before the Senate voted, it was clear that most of the articles had no chance at all. The sturdiest was Article Eleven, but its conspiratorial framework made it weaker, not stronger. Its catchall nature had become a fatal vulnerability, requiring those who voted for it not only to ask whether the president had broken the law but also whether these reflected that unproven, darker purpose. When the chief justice ruled that the article had to be voted on as a whole and not item by item, he cost impeachment one vote, which, as it turned out, was one more than could be spared.

The key to the president's acquittal, though, came in a deal brokered behind the scenes to arrange a safe replacement for Stanton in the War Department. General John G. Schofield had conservative leanings, but his loyalty to the Reconstruction Acts had not been as much in question as had been that of Winfield Scott Hancock and certainly his name had never surfaced as a possible accomplice in any presidential coup. He was a friend of General Grant and had won his explicit approval.[40] Johnson had his doubts—just a week before he had declared Schofield to be as bad as the worst of the radical generals, and he still thought him "cold and selfish." But pressure had come from Senator James W. Grimes of Iowa, one of the doubtful Republicans, and he spoke for others nearly as uneasy as himself. Seizing on the opportunity of reassuring a few Republican senators that not only would it be right to acquit Johnson but that it would also be safe, the president's attorney, William M. Evarts, had opened negotiations. No settlement could stick without the consent of General Grant, by now the inevitable nominee for president of the Republicans, and Schofield got it not just in one meeting but in two, however grudgingly made. Grant even admitted that, should the president be convicted, Schofield would be the ideal head of the War Department under a Republican successor. On the other side, it became clear that Grimes and his friends would not trust anything but Johnson's explicit promise, given personally, regarding Stanton's replacement.

So informed, editor John F. Coyle of the *Washington Daily National Intelligencer* invited Grimes and the president to a dinner party. "At the end of the wine and walnuts the other guests withdrew and the promise necessary to secure the vote of Senator Grimes was given," Coyle boasted; but, as he added, Johnson kept his word, refraining even from uttering spiteful remarks about Edwin M. Stanton. (Other, more reliable sources, had the same two negotiators but located the event at the rooms of Maryland senator Reverdy Johnson.)[41] For moderates, the deals (and there were others) were much more reassuring than simply a change of men in the War Department. The president had effectively renounced any intention to use the army to overthrow the Reconstruction laws.

Though nobody actually mentioned it, the senators may also have thought that Johnson's most likely opportunity for mischief had passed as well. Given the chance to rule on the constitutionality of the Reconstruction Acts, the Supreme Court had given it a pass, and, perhaps significantly, in part because the administration's counsel had not pressed the judges to act. By the time the jurists returned to session, new civil governments would be running, recognized by Congress. The Court would have a perfect justification then for doing nothing: there would be no military regime to disband, and settled constitutional law required that once Congress had decided that a state government was the lawful one the Court had no power to decree otherwise. Without that postponement of a decision until after the election, General Frank Blair later charged, "Mr. Johnson would have been condemned, and not even one of the seven radical Senators would have been found in Congress to save him."[42]

The healthiest sign may have been the one thing that no one at the time so much as whispered, that acquittal had been forced by fear of a coup. Sixteen years later, the *Brooklyn (N.Y.) Daily Eagle*, resting its evidence on what reporters at the time supposedly knew but never dared say, claimed that if the Senate had voted for conviction, Johnson "would have cleaned out Congress with trusty troops, who were available under willing officers for that purpose. The intention was known to at least some Republican Senators." Those who were "behind the scenes" believed that fear of what would result influenced at least two votes to acquit. "It is known two more could have been had and would

"The Political Death of the Bogus Caesar." Thomas Nast, *Harper's Weekly*, March 13, 1869. The word "Bogus" is especially interesting: it may indicate that Johnson was no threat to the republic after all. Nast probably expected Johnson's conviction. Apparently most cartoonists did: a number of humor magazines had cartoons celebrating or mourning his removal that came out just in time for the acquittal verdict. But this cartoon, based on a famous picture by Gérôme of Julius Caesar's assassination, probably was no leftover—it was saved until the president's term ended. The assassins depicted are the managers: George Boutwell, John A. Logan, John Bingham, James Wilson, Benjamin Butler, and Thomas Williams. One figure is leaving—Thaddeus Stevens—who by the time Nast's cartoon appeared had died. On the wall are the words "Treason Is a Crime and Must Be Punished," an ironic reference to Johnson's own statement—before he began handing out pardons by the thousands.

have been had if they had been needed."[43] No private account, no newspaper reporter, backed up that memory. Johnson had no "trusty troops," no "willing officers." When the House tried to find the "true inwardness" of acquittal, it dredged up every rumor for public display. It discovered corruption in poker games and subornation in dinner parties. But with Ben Butler roaring, bullying, sweating, and distorting every fact he could find, not even the most ardent impeachers gave the slightest hint of thinking that the president had any such intention.

The senators who voted to acquit believed that Andrew Johnson was no longer a menace to the republic. He was simply a pest. But the knowledge that the president would not be armed in the future, that he had taken the last step necessary to show that he would be nothing more than an irritant to lawmakers, must have made Republicans' decisions easier. They had guarantees now that there would be no nasty surprises in the future. On May 16, when the vote came on the most feasible article of impeachment, the nineteen senators voting to acquit were just enough to save him.

Impeachment ended many of the worst fears that had bedeviled both sides. On the one side, it became nearly impossible even for radical Republicans to conceive of Andrew Johnson as plotting a future coup. He no longer had time. His chance of winning the Democratic nomination for president existed only in his own imagination. Seven southern states were mostly reconstructed and within a few weeks of being restored to Congress. Johnson's ability to forestall Reconstruction would be taken from him. With the departure of the military commanders and the restoration of civil rule, his ability to meddle with the process would be gone forever.

Indeed, it was clear by then that the meddling that Johnson had done had proven fruitless, at least in stopping Reconstruction for good, though it had emboldened the terrorists and hobbled the government's response to them. Unionists were paying in blood for their new order, and they blamed it on what Johnson had done. Still, most Republicans saw light dawning ahead, once the right kind of civil authorities took control. In every state, a majority of voters turning out had ratified the state constitutions that Republicans had drawn up. The white officials who could have been his allies were winding down in their last days in office. No longer would they be able to summon state militias to sustain presidential treason. On the contrary, before the summer was out, the arsenals and armed might of the southern states, such as it was, would have Republican commanders and radical recruits. All of this had become clear only during the impeachment trial, and, perhaps, it had happened only because of it. For three months, the president had been helpless to act,

as helpless as if he had been suspended from office, by the political consider-
ations that any bold step carried with it.[44]

For another thing, it was clear now, if it had not been before, that the
president lacked a Napoleonic nerve. His Brumaire had come—and he had
retreated into legalisms and professions of lawful intentions. The summons
that could have gone forth to the South never sounded. By April, even Johnson must have realized that the real reason why Democratic troops in the
North had rattled their sabers so long and so loudly was that they had found
it healthier than actually drawing them.

Indeed, the very notion of "true inwardness" during the trial had shifted
markedly away from Napoleons and Caesars at all. Conspiracy theorists were
talking much more about corruption; and the postscript to the impeachment
trial was an attempt to determine how the president had bought himself free
of conviction and what interests had profited from executive favors in return.
What spoils had been handed out? What Indian agencies and kickbacks to
whiskey distillers had enriched the president's special defenders? What secret
funds had been raised?

There were many reasons for the shift, which was just beginning: the expanded role of the "independent" big-city presses, with their own built-in distrust of politicians in general and of any self-proclaimed tribunes of the people
aside from themselves, the suspicion of profit takers, which always grew as
economic prospects shrank for everybody else, and the thundering rhetoric of
Democrats against the banks and bondholders—all played their part. The old
vision of how politics actually worked would survive, but it was taking second
place to the search for thief and pirate in high places. When impeachment
managers had to take time out from the trial to answer the charge that they
had been willing to exchange Johnson's acquittal for a favor on behalf of shady
speculators, when Republican newspapers lost interest in their junior senator's
vote from outrage at a swindling Indian land-cession treaty, the stark moral
alternatives of the trial took on a blurred—or, perhaps, smudged—quality.

By year's end, the press was teeming with tales of corruption and swindle.
The saturnalia revealed the failings of the Johnson administration, of course;
Republican editors never forgot to make that point. Crooked whiskey distillers,
acting with revenue officers' apparent collusion, could be blamed on the Treasury Department, as could customhouse defaulters, but nobody claimed that
Johnson himself had shared in the stealing.[45] Nobody would have dreamed
of it. Indeed, reporters saw a wider malaise, beyond any one man's misdeeds.
America itself seemed to have grown sordid. The new press scapegoats were
men on the make, not Caesars clutching at power. The new villains' energies

turned not to threatening the republic but rather to raiding the treasury. It was easy to raise a sense of outrage or disgust against such people, but fear came less readily. The danger was a different kind, a threat to American morals and public ethics, but one wholly consistent with the survival of republican institutions and curable by the very agencies that it had thrived under, government by the consent of the governed. To accuse men of ambition was one thing; to accuse them of selfishness and avarice was quite another.

Fears lingered of a congressional coup in action. Sober conservative Republicans like Charles Francis Adams looked on the impeachment trial's results with despairing eyes. The "best balanced system" of government stood in danger of overthrow by "the consequences of human passions," he wrote sourly. "You think the present case temporary—it seems to me . . . a precursor to similar and worse struggles." Nothing in public affairs gave him "a single gleam of hope for the future." Even more moodily, his son, John Quincy Adams II, wrote to his father that America's time was running out. If "the people decline to return to the constitution next fall I do not regard our system of government worth ten years purchase," he warned.[46]

But other Democrats did see a turning point of sorts. Had "a factious and revolutionary Congress" succeeded, a Tennessean wrote the president, there would have been "a desperate struggle with anarchy and violence. Your defeat would have resulted either in civil war or despotism, or perhaps both." The point, however, was that the Congress had failed, and it had failed because of what Democrats had insisted could not possibly happen. Republican senators had voted their conscience and fended off conviction. Within days, Ben Wade, who just weeks before had been reported as filling his cabinet and preparing to assume power, found his last hope snuffed out. The Republican national convention handily defeated his bid for second place on the ticket.[47] Impeachment was gone for good; Thaddeus Stevens would go to the grave with his purpose unfulfilled.

The apocalypse had not been cancelled due to lack of interest. It would linger, ever finding a welcome place in some Democrats' minds. Thomas F. Bayard would be mourning the pending death of the republic for years. But the vision of an all-powerful, radical-dominated Congress no longer had the ability to disturb their rest the way it had until now. The idea of a South permanently kept out of the Union so that Republicans could control the electoral college or of a lasting military rule in the South had become increasingly implausible. It would take new menaces to make Americans' flesh creep.

But then, after all, it was an election year.

I look for a war the most terrible in its results
that has ever cursed any people or country.
—*Governor Robert K. Scott*

chapter 11

LET US HAVE PEACE

It did not take Democrats long after impeachment's failure to realize that Andrew Johnson's acquittal had gained them nothing beyond the potential impact that ten months more of legalism and obstruction would have on using the government's force against night-rider terrorism down south. In spite of the rising menace of the Ku Klux Klan, Reconstruction was stronger than when the trial began. General Grant still ran the army, and a cautious moderate, General John Schofield, administered the War Department. The votes for acquittal had carried with them an unspoken deal that the president would not obstruct the Reconstruction laws. But there was not much left of the Reconstruction laws to resist. At midyear, every state but three had completed the process of writing new constitutions and electing new civil governments. Republicans headed them all. And Negro suffrage in the South was now not so much a fear as a fact. Instead of sustaining what had been, Democrats would have to knock down what now was. Only much more radical methods than before could bring the conservative social order of 1865 back to life.

The readmission of the southern delegations to Congress therefore forced Democrats to a reckoning at the worst possible time, six months before the presidential election. Were they to stand firm, even when doing so made them look like revolutionaries? Or should they discard their beliefs to fit the new realities?

Manton Marble, of the *New York World*, made a tentative effort to bring his party around to the latter. If the party stood by its principles, it was sure to fall with them, and Reconstruction would go on anyhow. As things stood, all the power lay with Republicans and with the new state governments. Democrats could rail against them all they pleased, but it was a condition, and not a theory, that they must meet. Would "indignation at a brutal murder restore the victim to life?"

All reasonable routes of escape had been closed, the *World* argued. No longer should Democrats deceive themselves with dreams that the Supreme Court would overthrow Reconstruction. The judges had dallied too long. Now any decision would come too late for any real effect. Within a year, at most several, every single southern state would have fulfilled the terms of the Reconstruction Acts and been readmitted. Since the acts were no longer in force, the Court could not rule on their constitutionality. Not even the conservative judges would issue a decision overturning the state governments in operation. Judging whether a government was legal was Congress's responsibility, and it had made its decision when it admitted senators and congressmen.

With a great deal of luck, Democrats might win the House; with even breaks, they could carry the presidency in 1868. But it would be foolish of them to hope that the Reconstruction Acts could be repealed. The Senate stood in their way. The Senate was so lopsidedly Republican that Democrats at the earliest might be able to win it five years hence. Even if repeal passed, what, in the end, could it accomplish? No act of Congress could overturn state governments already recognized as legal. If lawgivers in Washington could set up and dispense with recognized state governments as they pleased, then the states became creatures of the national authority, to be dismissed like servants whenever their master wanted ones better able to cringe and fawn before him.

Democrats were helpless to achieve the greatest good, then, and their refusal to accept the new order of things would only bar them from lessening Radical wrongs. Were white southerners prepared to deny that the governments were valid? If so, then they could not conscientiously vote in the elections, because any election an illegal authority called was illegal. That fall, every one of them would have to stay home, and then Republicans would sweep the South and lock up the electoral college. The only practical chance for saving white civilization was in voting the rascals out, but if the machinery of elections had no legal force, how could white southerners even start the redemption of their section? By what authority could they elect a legislature that would call new constitutional conventions? What lawful power existed in the state to hold an election to ratify new, conservative constitutions? And on what grounds would any such election be valid? By remaining as sticklers for constitutional niceties, conservatives would forfeit everything substantial that they might gain for the empty honor of having been true to their principles.

That same practicality dictated how Democrats must face Negro suffrage. Let them complain as they would that blacks could not vote—they *were* voting and *would* vote, though at peril of their lives. Let conservatives boast that the Constitution was on their side—election returns showed that the people were not. Democrats would need voters from outside their ranks to win. By definition, these had to be people ready to give the Republican side the benefit of the doubt. "If the South will not be prevailed on to convert some of the negroes, it must permit us to convert some of the Northern Republicans," the *World* lectured. "To proselyte either, we must recognize the existing state of facts."[1]

Such a changed outlook needed a new kind of Democratic presidential candidate, and the *World*'s editor found him on the Supreme Court. Dignified, talented, and upright, Chief Justice Salmon P. Chase never doubted that he would make a better president than any other man in his lifetime, and he had pulled every wire within reach to get there. Dreams stirred in him, of redeeming the Democracy from its southern masters, to make it, for the first time, truly the party of equal rights. His willingness to support the *Milligan* decision, which overturned the use of military courts in wartime where civil courts still functioned, his known uneasiness with the Reconstruction Acts, and, most of all, his clear sympathy with Andrew Johnson during the impeachment trial had made him just the kind of radical Republican that Democrats might accept as a nominee. But ever since he had been jeered as "the attorney-general for fugitive negroes" before the war, Chase had been the embodiment of the antislavery cause at its most compassionate. As one of the founders of the national banking system, Chase would inspire trust among conservative business men. Under such leadership, the Democrats could give irrefutable proof that they posed no threat to a decent, safe Reconstruction.[2]

It was not to be. The *World* could parse constitutionalism or it could remind the Democrats of practical realities, but it could not overcome that instinctive sense among the rank and file that the Republicans had already revolutionized government and that one of the agents of this revolution had been Chase himself. Unless drastic action was taken, the usurpers would get away with their ill-gotten gains. They would have rigged the system to keep themselves on top and position themselves for new and worse power grabs in the future. Reconstruction must be defeated and the white South must be given its voice in the nation's councils again.[3] That would take bold leadership and bolder constitutional thinking than before. Just standing where they had stood until now put

"Dignity and Impudence." Thomas Nast, *Harper's Weekly*, October 24, 1868. General Frank Blair is impudence, the dog with the "War" collar; Grant is the mastiff with the word "Peace" on his collar.

the Democrats in the role of revolutionaries, who were forced to overthrow established authority. Instead of halting a process still under way, they would need to reverse it—a far more difficult proposition, as southern conservatives had already found.

The boldest solution came from General Frank P. Blair Jr., the hard-drinking scion of an indomitable clan. Blair had become one of the earliest leaders in the Republican Party of Missouri, as outspoken in his detestation of slavery as he was of blacks in general. By the war's end, Blair had drifted back to the Democrats, and as Missouri reconstructed, he had turned into one of the most intemperate opponents of the so-called Radicals. He brought court cases against their requirement for loyalty oaths for jurors and denounced the disfranchisement of former Rebels and Confederate sympathizers. Well before the presidential race began, Blair had become a voice for those Union soldiers who felt that they had won over traitors in the South only to be forced to take up the fight on traitors in the North.[4]

As the Democracy pondered its choices for president, Blair made himself conspicuously available. His fevered imagination did not need the regular stimulation of strong drink. He was a man who, in the euphemism of the day, "saw things." But, unlike the others, he was all too ready to take up arms against a sea of troubles. As early as the winter before, he had tried to convince old friends that a military record was essential in any Democratic nominee for president. "Consider for a moment what would have been the position of affairs if instead of Andy Johnson we had a man of military experience & approved leadership in the White House. Would he have been impeached? Would Grant & the army have disobeyed his orders? But nobody expects Andy to resist—nobody wants him to resist—& nobody would help him if he did— and all simply because he has shown himself to be [a military] incompetent." Democrats must not let themselves be put in such a position again! The man they needed for president must be one who would be ready to see that he was not cheated out of an election, one who could "rally his followers to resist any fraudulent or unfair count of the votes," and one whose soldier's credentials made him a credible leader in the fight that was sure to follow. Blair saw in himself that coming man.[5]

Far more than did General Winfield Scott Hancock, Blair preached open war on the new Republican order. Just a few days before the national convention opened, he issued a public letter to a Missouri Democrat, Richard Brodhead, explaining what the party must do if it came to power. A Democratic president could not persuade a Republican Senate, but he could make it more Democratic by unseating the southern Republicans elected by usurping governments. And those governments down south, Blair asserted, were usurpers. Let the president simply declare the Reconstruction Acts null and void, send in the army to undo the governments, and disperse Republican authorities. White southerners could erect governments in place of the radical ones. If the Democrats in the North carried most of the seats in the House—as they certainly would—they would admit the congressmen that the white conservative governments had chosen. Faced with a Democratic president unafraid to use the army to get his way, the Senate would submit at once. In one great stroke, the Constitution would be restored to its old status.[6]

Many southern Democrats hailed the Brodhead letter as the kind of frank speaking they had long hoped for. Blair's manliness made him tower above the shufflers and trimmers; he, surely, uttered what the rank and file felt. Almost all Democrats shared Blair's feelings, the *Louisville (Ky.) Courier* announced. The president had a duty to use all of his power, without restraint, to enforce the Constitution. Andrew Johnson's chief weakness lay in his timidity. He could have backed himself up with armed force. Boldness would have cowed Radicalism completely. More conventional means offered only illusions of rescue. "Radical usurpation renders a settlement of the difficulty through . . . the courts impracticable," the *Courier* explained.[7]

Blair had thrown down the gage not just to the Republicans but also to palterers within the party. By that time, even the *New York World* had backed away from accommodation. Abandoning the Reconstruction issues, Democrats would need to fight on some other grounds. But doing so would have been even more dangerous than Blair's program. They could talk about cutting government expenses and the national debt, but that was sure to open a discussion of the need to tax government bonds and to expand the money supply. Then western and eastern Democrats would take after each other, hammer and tongs. Whatever its disagreement about tactics, those in the party seethed at the enormities of Radical Reconstruction. None of them liked Negro suffrage, and as an issue, race-baiting was just too good to give up. As the bondholders' candidate, Chase would have been impossible, and the more ground he gave on the Reconstruction issue, the clearer it became that at his most conservative, he stood leagues away from the Democratic position. The chief justice might sell his soul for the presidency but not his core principles.[8]

So when the Democratic national convention assembled in New York on Independence Day, in 1868, delegates were in no mood for halfway measures. The platform denounced Reconstruction as illegal, unconstitutional, and void. Chase's candidacy made a promising beginning—over and over. But the real momentum lay with George F. Pendleton, Ohio's favorite son and a sharp critic of eastern financial policy. Delegates out to rein in the national banks and pay the war debt in paper money liked no other candidate better. They could not get Pendleton the two-thirds vote needed, and they were not about to let any other aspirant have it either. In the confusion, a delegate proposed the presiding officer, New York's former two-term governor, Horatio Seymour. Seymour could satisfy the Peace Democrats ranged behind Pendleton, and he might just carry the one state that Democrats could not do without. Seymour was horrified. Shy, self-doubting, worried for his health, and not welcoming a bruising campaign, he tried to beg off. His friends hustled him out of the hall before delegates took him at his word. With a civilian heading the ticket, a Union soldier seemed indispensable as a running mate. The Confederate South wanted Blair and got him.[9]

Democrats could make their campaign seem conservative in only one way: by painting the extremism and menace of Reconstruction in such lurid colors that any solution, any form of redress, would look like a restoration of sanity by comparison. Blair's letter only increased the need to make the campaign into a crusade to save human liberty. Oratory spangled with the old historical favorites: Oliver Cromwell, the French Revolution, Jacobins, the guillotine, the outlawing of Christianity, and the deliberate resolve of the Republicans that they would accept civil war rather than compromise. Those who feared that the future would bring a wiping out of America's republican form of government could rest easy, the *St. Paul (Minn.) Daily Pioneer* announced. "*They are already accomplished facts.* We still preserve the *forms* of elections. But they are only forms to blind and hoodwink the people."[10]

Reconstruction was not over. Democrats insisted that it was only a first step. The ancient republican tradition taught that the spirit of revolution was insatiable. If it slumbered, it did so only to gain strength. If it paused, it did so just before stepping up the pace. After the election, the whole program that Republicans had approved would be thrown out and something far more radical would be adopted. Lands would be confiscated, every single white former Confederate would be disfranchised, the congressmen so recently admitted would be expelled again, and military rule would be imposed for the next twenty years. Worse, the fetters laid upon the limbs of southern states would be matched with others for the North. Military despotism ruled the South now, Frank Blair shouted. "And, my friends and fellow-citizens, if they establish it in the ten Southern States, why not in ten more States? Why not in all of the other States?" "We are to strike at the head of this conspiracy, for there is a conspiracy against the liberties of the people to overthrow the Constitution," former Senator George Pugh informed his hearers. "It is a conspiracy to destroy and lay waste one-half of this Union, and then destroy and lay waste our half." Whites would be driven out of the South and off the Pacific Coast, where Negro and Chinese commonwealths would rise. State lines would disappear and separate races would merge into one mongrel breed. Had not an old antislavery fanatic predicted that Grant's election would "melt the millions into one indissoluble whole"? Who knew better the true inwardness of the Republican program?[11]

The only question was into what new, sinister shape the fragments of the republic would be hammered. "Until recently, I have anticipated only a military despotism as the next turn of affairs," a Democrat wrote the presidential nominee. Other onlookers predicted the anointment of an emperor and speculated that white southerners would insist upon it, as the alternative to free governments chosen by Negro rule. Early in September Alexander Stephens gave an audience to a *New York Herald* reporter. Emaciated and pale, his lips twitching nervously, he seemed a near invalid from neuralgia and other ailments. But to hear him tell it, the republic was much worse stricken than himself. Despotism was coming. Ulysses S. Grant was "just the man for a *coup d'etat.*" If he was elected, "I never expect to see another Presidential election." General Grant wanted empire, Frank Blair declared, not least because such a government "would give additional consequence to military men."[12] Any such attempt, Democrats promised, would happen over their dead bodies and over plenty of others'. "*The Constitution cannot be destroyed in peace,*" Ben Hill of Georgia wrote in a public letter to the North. "Wake your people from this fatal delusion before it is too late. *I cannot tell when or how or between whom war will come*. But it will come." It would make the Civil War seem a modest fracas by comparison. "A *united* North will not again wage battle against a *divided* South."[13]

Some Democrats were ready to fight immediately. A suggestion that Republicans might cancel the popular elections down south and let the legislatures choose presidential electors stirred promises of bloody resistance. "They talk about war," Joseph "Old Saddle-bags" McDonald of Indiana thundered. "I say to them that if that infamous attempt to defraud the American people out of their rights be foisted on this country, there will be war. [Several voices: "Let it come."] If they are determined to grasp power in this country . . . and attempt to turn the tide in that way—if our candidate is elected by a majority of the legal voters, he will be President; if he don't there will be a fight over it."[14]

In such a context, Blair's proposal for unsettling Reconstruction seemed far less momentous. It could even be shown to be a necessary preliminary for the return to normalcy. Democrats protested that the Brodhead remedy need not end in violence, but they never renounced using force as a possibility if the republic could be saved in no other way. Even if the army could not be counted on, General Thomas Ewing was not concerned about the outcome. "General Blair at the head of the militia will be a match for General Grant at the head of the regular army," he announced. Democratic marchers sang with gusto a song that did not take much interpreting to sound alarming:

> And Blair will act his part,
> With candor true and just
> The power of the usurper
> We'll crush beneath the dust.[15]

A few southern papers were franker still. "It will not be long ere the Democrats and Radicals of the North become involved in a bloody internecine strife," a Tuscaloosa editor gloated. "Nor will it be much longer before the carpet-baggers and scalawags of the South are hung, wherever found."[16]

Republicans were not slow to see that the Brodhead letter, "which secured him the rebel support in the New York Convention[,] will go far to defeat his & Seymour's election." It did not help matters when a promoter ran a booming business selling photographs of Seymour, Blair, and John Wilkes Booth at the Missouri Democratic convention. Let Horatio Seymour try to steer the debate to finance and taxes, "A Veteran Observer" wrote in the *New York Times*. "He might as well whistle against the wind. . . . The rebels have beat the drum of rebellion, and the Copperheads are marching to its music—that is the whole of it."[17]

The apocalypticism of the Democratic campaign helped Republicans immensely. Their main problem had been in trying to defend Negro suffrage. Doing so had made it easier to paint them as being very far from moderate and possibly fanatical. They could not deny that most of the North—and even a minority of Republicans—wanted to reserve the franchise for whites. They also could not deny that their own shock troops, the radicals, wanted and expected to extend the vote to blacks not just in the South but everywhere and that this would be much more controversial than giving it to them only in the distant, formerly Rebel, provinces of the South. Now, however, there did not need to be very much talk about racial equality or any defense of the Republican record. The attack on Negro suffrage, when it came, would focus on the electorate recently enfranchised down south, where it could be portrayed by Republicans as a safeguard to loyalty in the nation at large—and therefore as much more acceptable than it would have been on its own merits.[18]

Now they could make themselves the party of maintaining the status quo. Grant's letter, with its words "Let us have peace," was just what was wanted, and campaign banners echoed the sentiment in endless diversity: "Grant us Peace" and "We are tired of War." The election of Grant meant the start of an "Era of Good Feelings," the *Marietta (Ohio) Register* promised. Far from fanatical notions, he was moderate and modest, the last man to embroil the country in war or put it to needless expense. With his inauguration, the country would find repose. But elect Seymour and Blair, and nothing would result but the reopening of settled questions, terrible confusion, and inevitable civil war.[19]

Republicans could form a campaign around Blair's threats, and well they knew it. In the West, some Republicans circulated photographs of Blair as campaign documents. By themselves, the pictures were reminder enough of what was at stake in the election.[20] Democrats promised peace indeed, Carl Schurz told Chicagoans. There were just a few preliminaries before they could deliver it, a "trifle": the armed overthrow of southern state governments and a Senate coerced into submission. What else could the Democratic platform mean but that? "This is not a quiet legislative process." It was "counter-revolution in the fullest sense of the term" and, other speakers warned, race war.[21]

Democratic victory might well mean the restoration of the Confederacy. Every southern comment that could be tortured into wistfulness for disunion got generous play up north, no matter how far out of context it was. "The country is far too large to remain very long under one government," the *Memphis*

Appeal insisted, "and the day will come when the South will be independent." (Alarmed by similar statements, Democratic managers forced Albert Pike, the fire-eating editor, to announce his immediate retirement.)[22] No man should be deceived, Oliver Morton told an Indianapolis crowd. Blair was the choice of unreconstructed Rebels. General Preston, a former Confederate officer from Kentucky, had placed him in nomination. General Wade Hampton, a fellow Confederate veteran from South Carolina, had seconded the nomination. If he was chosen on any single proposition, it was his vow "again to bring war upon us." "Every Democrat or rather Rebel believes that they will immediately take possession of the State Government under their old Constitution and drive all Northern men from the State or shoot them down where they are," South Carolina governor Robert K. Scott informed the local army commander. "And the native Loyal men have nothing to hope for. . . . I look for a war the most terrible in its results that has ever cursed any people or country. . . . These threats are now only being whispered all over the South, but so loudly that the air has become vocal with the sound."[23]

It took Democrats little time to see what a liability the Brodhead letter might be. Alarmed, Democratic national chairman August Belmont watched "our Southern friends . . . making a sad mistake by their speeches on the basis of Blair's foolish letter. Their threats of revolutionary reaction must hurt us badly." On July 12, 1868, the *New York World* promised that Blair's statement would "ring out in tremendous response from millions of hearts throughout the North and West." Apparently, it rang with quite the wrong tremendous response, for the very next day the *World* hastened to assure readers that there was not the slightest danger of Blair doing anything if he came into power. He was harmless. As vice president, he could do nothing to put his theories into practice. Indeed, Blair would be an element of safety. Who in their right mind would kill Seymour—and what Congress would dare impeach him—knowing that Blair was next in line?[24]

By mid-September, with it quite clear that this was not palliation enough, the *World* emphasized that anything Blair had written before the convention was irrelevant. All his statements must be superseded by the platform, and the platform had no such doctrines. There would be no violence, and Blair expected none. The moment Republicans were beaten at the polls, the Democratic program would go into effect.[25] This was not at all comforting, for the platform was itself open to extremely dangerous readings, as the *World* must have known. Still, an ambiguous statement was better than a blatant call for violence, and that was the best that the *World* could do.

Democrats struggled to set themselves free or give the platform a less inflammatory meaning. Even Republicans admitted that the Reconstruction Acts were unconstitutional, Henry C. Murphy explained to a Brooklyn audience. The courts had the right to declare acts of Congress and the legislature unconstitutional; they did it "every day." That was all that would happen here, and without violence. The laws would be obeyed until a court found them void, the *Detroit Free Press* insisted. And, freed from the intimidating presence of usurping lawmakers, judges would do so speedily.[26] Even more consoling was former Attorney General Stanbery's reading of the platform. The Reconstruction Acts would not be voided but would be repealed by the Congress, allowing an orderly transition from the pretended state authority to the real, constitutional government.

The most passive rendering of Blair's nullification came from George Ticknor Curtis, a legal scholar and an old hanger-on of Daniel Webster. His scenario offered the most attractive alternative. No doubt the next Congress would have to accept the southern governments as legitimate, he conceded; certainly the Court could not strike them down. But national authority had no obligation to go beyond a bare recognition. Democrats, when they took over the national government, could simply refuse to do anything to recognize or to prop up the southern state governments. "There need be no violence, no revolution and no disturbance. The whites and the blacks will be left to settle the question for themselves, and among themselves."

And then what would happen to the governments that were in place? Let no one assume that voiding the Reconstruction Acts would turn the clock back to 1860, Henry C. Murphy of Brooklyn insisted. Things would return only to the way they had been in 1866, with slavery abolished, secession renounced, and the Thirteenth Amendment on the books. Dismissing talk of former Confederates wiping out Republican authorities at gunpoint, former Confederate vice president Alexander Stephens explained that the conservatives would try nothing so hasty. As soon as the courts had given their ruling, white southerners would call constitutional conventions and write up new fundamental documents, to be ratified by the people. Negro suffrage itself would be adjusted by requiring all voters to pass an educational test. Curtis envisioned a round of negotiations, leading to consensus and mutual consent. The "moral influence" of Americans condemning the Republican policy would inspire "the intelligence of both races" to agree on the terms by which they would live together henceforth.[27]

What could be less threatening? Or more unrealistic? As Republicans pointed out, Stanbery's plan for repeal by Congress was based on wishful thinking. No revolution at the polls could possibly bring in a Democratic Senate, and Democratic control of the House was extremely unlikely. How could repeal affect state governments already in operation? That same wishful thinking also undercut the argument that the Supreme Court would "at one breath clear away the cloud that has rested over the Executive, the Congress, and the States." Democrats' contentions to the contrary, the judges had given no indication that they would overthrow Reconstruction, and what little chance there was that they might interfere was lost finally when the states' representatives were readmitted to Congress.

But even leaving aside these practical realities, and even assuming that Congress could induce the Republican governments to dissolve and disperse, what constitutional state government would be restored? The governments established before had been created by Andrew Johnson, acting on his military authority. With no sanction from Congress, with no constitutional basis for the provisional governors who had set the machinery running, these regimes really did fit the Democratic catchphrase "unconstitutional, revolutionary, null, and void." Instead of returning the southern states to a constitutional basis, then, the Democratic platform would replace one alleged usurpation with another that was just as illegal.[28]

As for the negotiated settlement, Curtis's imagination devised a political context that could not possibly exist. It proposed fantasies—that only "intelligent" citizens would have any say in the final outcome and that whites, having long resisted any impartial suffrage that took away some of their own rights to vote, would consent to it now. The idea that harmonious negotiations could convince blacks to "settle the question" the way whites wanted, in a section of the country where most whites believed that blacks had no right to vote at all, was fantastical. If the electorate voted for a Democratic president that fall, Curtis had predicted, all of the "conditions and restrictions" that Reconstruction imposed "will fall practically dead." So they would—and so would thousands of Republican voters and officeholders. With the Klan rampaging, that was happening to many of them already. Only a theorist could have believed that a southern governor, having seen the Democrats take the presidency but not the Congress, and with a popular majority at the polls eight months behind him, would peacefully surrender his place or call new elections not stipulated in the state constitution.[29]

No bloodshed would take place unless Republicans resisted the will of the people, Democratic editors warned; it was they, not the Democrats, who were threatening civil war if they did not get their way. George F. Pendleton was almost as loose-lipped, dangerously so, when he spoke to Democrats in Pittsburgh. Blair's advice that the federal government sweep away the Reconstruction governments was "a very good way" of restoring constitutional supremacy, he allowed, but it was quite unnecessary, at a time when the southern regimes were so weak. Remove the military props from them, and they could not stand for a minute. The November elections would be enough to make them dissolve without a finger being lifted by the incoming administration. Any Republicans who thought to resist the majority needed to be advised not "to dig their graves and uniform themselves in their winding sheets." That sounded like a promise that any blood that was shed would be Republican blood, and would be on their heads, if they resisted the Democratic program.[30]

All roads therefore led back to the methods that Blair had proposed in the Brodhead letters. It would take the raw use of force to sweep the Reconstruction governments away, and Democrats knew it; indeed, Blair was told frankly by Seymour's closest confidant that his understanding of what was wrong and what was to be done was not in dispute. But it would never do to say so until *after* the election.[31] Newspapers other than the *New York World*, which were considerably less wise, never dropped their belief in the Brodhead letter as true gospel. "We are in the midst of a great revolution," Robert Toombs thundered to the Georgia Democratic convention. The election might end it peacefully, but if not, "then the true men of the South will rally once more around their now folded banner, and will try the issue at the cartridge box." Northern men would join them and, "if necessary, lead your battalions." Breathing nothing but good will, General John B. Gordon assured southern blacks that his people wanted peace, not war—but on their own terms. "If you turn a deaf ear to the Southern man these green leaves that now clothe the forest will not grow red with another autumn before they will be drenched with your blood and mine," he added, invitingly. White southerners boasted that they understood Blair perfectly. As soon as Republicans were defeated, they would rid themselves of the reconstructed governments and install their immediate predecessors. If the army's help was needed, Seymour would send it.[32]

All of the attempts to explain away Blair's plans had one particular drawback: Blair himself. The more "the American Robespierre" tried setting the record straight, the clearer it became that Republicans understood him perfectly. His letter of acceptance protested that he had never actually said, "Let us have war"—such an appeal was a shameless Republican paraphrase. His policy alone could give the South a lasting peace.[33] "It was the duty of the President to trample these laws in the dust," he insisted, "because they were unconstitutional and had been declared so by the Supreme Court." The appeal to the Court, then, had already happened. So had the appeal to the people. Their vote for Democratic nominees for county and state office was as good as a vote to void the Reconstruction Acts. The presidential election would clinch things. By insisting on enforcing the Reconstruction Acts over the last ten months, Republicans had gone right against what "the people" demanded, in no muted tones. That was the real revolutionary act. Nothing else could have been expected from a "usurping Congress," nay, a "fragment of a Congress," phrases that ominously revived the notion that no law that had been passed while southern representatives were absent had any validity. "Blair is good as far as he goes," a cautious Democrat commented, "but he goes too far."[34]

Nor was the suggestion that Blair was only the vice presidential candidate much consolation. A man like Seymour, unable to say no to a presidential nomination that he desperately protested that he did not want, would hardly have the fiber to resist men of reckless determination at his elbow. Pleasant, plausible, and smooth, Horatio Seymour had made a career out of a "sickly shrinking from great responsibilities," including the presidential nomination, which he lacked the courage to admit that he was seeking and then lacked the resolution to refuse. Such a man was made to act as the tool of stronger wills. At just the right time, Seymour would retreat to Newport to nurse his delicate constitution in the surf, or to the Wisconsin pine woods to breathe the robust air of the West. Those of a fiercer disposition would handle the stern business. So forceful and desperate a figure as Blair would "bend or break" Seymour "like a reed across his knees." Seymour was made to be broken. His health was frail. So, it was whispered, was his mental health. Madness galloped through his family, grazing every member, sending mobs of kinfolk into lunatic asylums or suicides' graves. Who was to say that Seymour was up to the strain? If something should happen to incapacitate him — stroke or self-destruction — then Blair would take over the presidential chair. But he would not stay seated for long — there would be plenty for so ambitious a man to do, when he buckled on the sword of commander in chief.[35] And who could be sure, Republicans asked, that this was not what southern Democrats were counting on? Presidents had been put out of the way before when they no longer suited the South's convenience. Who was to say that Blair might not, in the future, have friends who stood ready to spare Seymour the trials that life in the White House was sure to entail?[36]

Blair was just bloody-minded enough to do such a thing himself. In one campaign speech, he predicted that Grant would never leave the White House alive, appealing to the old fear of a military dictator who would never freely surrender power once he had it, the twice-told terror of a Caesar awaiting his chance. But Republicans heard his words quite differently. What they heard was a threat that if Grant were elected the assassins would be sent to finish him

"Wilkes Booth the Second." Thomas Nast, *Harper's Weekly*, November 7, 1868. Mark M. "Brick" Pomeroy, the "red-hot" Democratic editor and Copperhead who had called for some Brutus to pierce Lincoln's heart, leads a masked Frank Blair in an assassination attempt on General Grant. Pomeroy did make such threats. Blair did not. What the candidate meant to convey was his fear that, having entered the White House, Grant would never yield power as long as he lived.

off.[37] Brick Pomeroy's newspaper made the threat explicit: if Grant won the White House, Grant must die.[38] Who was to say that the Ku Klux Klan might not do for its friends what it had done to its enemies, on the South's behalf?

Behind Blair, though, was the most basic and deadliest form of corroboration. White southerners did not need to denounce Reconstruction as lawless and void. They only had to act that way. They did not need to promise bloody revolution — so many of them were already delivering its first installment. Night riders hauled out state legislators for whippings, showed their displeasure for Republican speeches by burning down their houses, and "Ku Kluxed" troublesome editors. The "reign of terror" in Louisiana cost hundreds of Republican lives. Schools, churches, homes, and printing offices were sacked. Benjamin F. Randolph, at the forefront of South Carolina's Union League movement, was gunned down in broad daylight on a railroad platform, soon after the leading Democrat in the county had advised his followers to dig Randolph's grave if he dared come there campaigning. Gleefully, the *Tuscaloosa (Ala.) Independent Monitor* reported that five "notoriously bad negroes" had been discovered "swinging by the necks to limbs in the woods" for "making threats against the whites" in one Alabama county. In Georgia, federal officers compiled a list of more than 300 racial killings since the beginning of the year, with the pace quickening as the election approached. "Harry McDaniels, a coloured member of the Legislature from this County[,] was severely wounded in the shoulder," a South Carolina politician wrote the governor early in November; "the same party of Rowdies it is supposed, went to 3 or 4 coloured person's houses at one Place they taken out the coloured man of the House and Beaten him severely and at two other Places taken the men women and children out and then ransacked the House making threats to the coloured people if they voted or left home on Election day that they (the Coloured people) would be murdered."[39]

Republicans could not have asked for better evidence of the revolutionary character of the Democratic threat. And they could trace the malign spirit straight back to the words of the platform and the Brodhead letter. The one reflected the other precisely. "Blair has in advance declared war," Governor Robert K. Scott of South Carolina warned General George Meade; "he has plainly told us that the Reconstruction of Congress is revolutionary and must be set aside. The leading men in the Rebellion understand him to mean that it must be done by force if need be and they are prepared to act his declaration. They boldly say that if the Democratic Party are successful they will take charge of affairs of state and drive all Northern men from the South." Already, the true revolutionaries had identified themselves. Democrats responded that the blame for the violence lay with those who had brought white southerners to so fierce a resistance. To insist that good treatment of the white South depended on it acting with good will reversed the order of things; it reminded one newspaper of the child that complained to his mother, "Make Bill behave himself. Whenever I hit him on the head with the hammer he hollers!"[40]

As the backlash set in, Democratic managers thought twice about the southern orators they had brought north to plead their cause. Democratic papers stopped publishing speeches down south, because they were so likely to remind people of the "red-hot" Reconstruction plank in the platform, the one live plank that everyone wanted to discuss. Packages of campaign documents spread across the North were complete in every particular but one: the Brodhead letter was left out. In some states, the Democratic central committee refused even to publish Blair's more temperate letter of acceptance.[41] "General Grant cannot 'Let us have peace,'" the *New York World* insisted. His kind of peace was the triangular, steel, bayonet-shaped kind. Senator Ben Wade had said it perfectly when he joked that Grant would bring peace even if he had to fight for it. But Horatio Seymour would "bring peace and not a sword. To him the talk of pacification would be easy, for neither party policy nor personal surroundings would constrain him." Moderates feared that Democrats would "precipitate the country into another war," a former senator told a crowd. "Well, you may count me out. I do not want to see another war as long as I live, or at least until this debt is paid." So desperately alarmed were Democrats at the prospect of being painted as the real extremists that they tried every-thing—even, on occasion, using the voice of sweet reason. If Grant's motto was "Let us have peace," the *Chicago Times* contended, the Democracy's was, "Let us be friends": friends north and south, but also friends regardless of party. Considering the level of debate past and yet to come, that appeal was the most discordant note of the whole campaign.[42]

The returns from the October state elections showed Democrats that they would need more than fair words. The results had been heartbreakingly close. Still, defeat was defeat. Those conservative Republicans that the Democracy had been counting on simply had not shown up. From Pittsburgh, a Democrat complained that Seymour's name had sparked no enthusiasm—except among Republicans, whom it had inspired to turn out at the polls in record numbers and to expand their majorities. Locally, Blair's nomination had cost hundreds of votes, and from Ohio came the same complaint.[43]

For months, there had been knots of grumbling Democrats, especially in Ohio, where some of Chase's old backers, like Alexander Long and Henry Reed of the Cincinnati *West and South*, had never made their peace with Sey-mour or stopped forecasting defeat. If only Seymour could be dropped, they argued, the party might well have a chance. It might even get the chief justice's open support (Chase had made no endorsement of either candidate yet), espe-cially if he were made the nominee instead. And Chase was good for hundreds of thousands of Republican votes. By early September, the clamor had turned into an intrigue, in which a few leading Democrats mulled over how they could remove the name at the head of the ticket and replace it with another. As the returns came in from the "October states," editor Manton Marble joined the movement. Now he used his *New York World* to urge a "bold stroke of policy." His editorials were vague on the specifics but put more emphasis on changing the tail of the ticket than the head. Victory still beckoned, Marble wrote, if the party pushed aside "any impediment to success which can yet be removed." Other Democratic opinion makers now felt free to go public with their ideas.[44] When the *Washington Daily National Intelligencer* gave support to Marble's call, it seemed to place the president's own endorsement on the plan.

Only desperation made the scheme look feasible. Two groups were at work, apparently together but in fact at cross-purposes. Those who wanted Seymour gone had no objection to Blair. Those who wanted Blair gone were not all of them ready to sacrifice Seymour. To have the national committee revise the ticket, to take it out of the hands of the national convention, was as unrepublican an act as the old congressional caucus system. Parties were built on morale and a high turnout. Shaking up the ticket now would be an admission that the party had gone wrong to begin with. It would allow Republicans to declare that Blair and Seymour were so dangerous that not even their own party could trust the nation in their hands.

Changing the ticket also opened the party to deeper and more destructive unknowns. If Chase were put on the ticket, would he accept the platform? Or would that have to be scrapped as well? And if Chase were chosen, especially in light of his small number of votes at the Democratic national convention, all of the other favorite sons and contenders who had outpolled him would feel miffed and their followers would be incensed. Indeed, many of those supporting the change of ticket hoped that their own choice would be the one. The more vocal members of the party wanted no change at all and were aghast at the crawfishing that the *New York World* was engaging in. Those rejecting the dumpers were not just indignant. They saw a Republican plot, with Marble taking pay à la Benedict Arnold. "Traitor, fool, renegade, tool of a wicked power," Brick Pomeroy's *New York Democrat* screamed, "uncover your head, take off your shoes, for the place where thou dost stand is holy ground. Your fire will die out, but the bush of Democracy will live for pilgrims to rest under the shade thereof, after turning aside to spit on your graves!"[45]

In the end, all prospective gains were only fairy gold, melting away at the touch. It was just possible that the Democrats would accept Seymour's resignation and then find themselves without any candidate whatsoever. Shy about going onto the ticket in the first place, the candidate now leaped at the chance of getting off it again. If there was any change at the other end of the ticket, he would retire as well. There could be no partial reconstruction of the Democratic team. The scheme perished in a chorus of abuse. "But wait until their Bull

Run comes off two weeks from today," a Republican predicted to William E. Chandler, "and the waters of Salt River will be crowded with their canoes."[46]

November's returns bore this writer out. White voters gave Seymour a narrow lead, to be sure—and had the southern states all been admitted that lead would have increased considerably. But with Negro suffrage, Grant had a safe margin nationally. In the North, his victory was beyond contest. The closeness itself gave a misleading impression of public opinion. Without Democratic fraud in New York and the intimidation of black voters in Georgia and Louisiana, Grant would have had an electoral landslide. Take away Klan intimidation in the upper South, and his popular margin would have been unassailable on any terms. If the Election Day gains of 1867 had been the first wave of a public reaction against Reconstruction, as conservatives claimed, the tide had crested and was on the ebb.

It was Seymour's loss, but Blair's defeat, and conservative Republicans told the Democratic leadership so. Everywhere, another party insider mourned, Democrats had to keep explaining away Blair, and they could never do it well enough to repair the damage. His letter "outraged the good sense of every American citizen who loves the Constitution and laws, and who hates civil war and anarchy," the *Detroit Free Press* admitted. His cure for Reconstruction was more appropriate for a Mexican general than for an American statesman. But that, after all, was only to be expected: Blair's nomination had been part of a secret design by George Pendleton's friends, who, unable to rule the party, decided to ruin it! Glumly, Justice David Davis looked back on a campaign that had begun with such promise. The people had been ripe for change, and if only the Democrats had chosen a candidate who had acted with the Republicans during the war as standard-bearer (he had his colleague Chase in mind, of course) the Republican Party would have shattered to bits. But a weakling who could not say no to a nomination he never wanted had been deemed "the *man* for the crisis." Then, "as if the very Devil was in it—Frank Blair, a common Loafer, with no moral character, with his revolutionary letter to Broadhead, is nominated by southern men, who go home & make speeches to infuriate the Northern people." "You should be *kind to Blair*," W. H. Kemble, the Republicans' campaign manager for Pennsylvania, wrote Congressman Elihu Washburne, "—he did us a vast service."[47]

But Grant had done them an even greater service. Obviously, it was because of his candidacy, the nominee above politics, that Republicans had been able to overcome a strong Democratic challenge. Even running against Seymour, a more radical candidate most likely would have lost. Desperate for some excuse to put the radicals out, the *New York Journal of Commerce* had lost hope as soon as the Democratic ticket had been announced. Conservative Republicans and Democrats stood on common ground, it insisted, now that the results were in. But Democrats had thrown away the chance to bring them over. It had embraced radicalism itself, a radicalism every bit as dreadful as Thaddeus Stevens's brand. Given the choice between Blair and repudiation and a general who kept the radicals and congressional leadership at arm's length, conservatives made the natural decision. Now, the *Journal* predicted, Grant would chart his own course. Peace, reunification, and reconciliation would be his watchwords. The Sumners and the Butlers, who had never trusted him, would have to take the back seat. The *Journal of Commerce* and Democratic newspapers, which peddled the same line after the election, had every reason to let the wish father the thought, but moderate Republicans were saying the same. The renunciation of radicalism, which had been the centerpiece of their campaign, stayed at the forefront in editorials once the returns were in. This time, there would be no goading force from the South to impel the party towards radicalism, as there had been in 1866. What Grant had promised was not more reconstructing but that tinkering with the southern states was at an end. The new administration promised to bring peace and stability. It was created to preserve and protect the present order of things, not to build anew. With help from Blair, Republicans had been able to position themselves as true conservatives, but to do so, they had had to mortgage their future, promising that if the Congressional Reconstruction program failed to provide a full measure of equal rights there would be no new dispensation, no innovation beyond the larger outline of what had been laid down already.[48]

The campaign, then, strengthened a trend already well under way among Republicans—to make themselves the party that maintained, sustained, retained, contained. Instead of promising new advances, the "party of moral ideas" billed itself as the preserver of what had already been won.[49] Even in defending Reconstruction, the argument made most often was not that it promoted justice but that it preserved the nation and fulfilled the promise of the war that there would be a lasting Union. To undo this might well thrust blacks back into slavery. But, more important, it would undo the work already done and restore the anarchy, the chaos, that the country was eager to get past. It was in this response to the weariness of the country and in a promise not to make Reconstruction any more wearisome—or perhaps not to dwell very much longer on issues that by now were growing tiresome—that Republicans made their case. In effect, the party promised no new adventures, no fresh innovations. It was there to react to events, not to initiate ones. For Republicans, the election seemed to be the moment when Reconstruction was set on the path from which there could be no turning back. But they were wrong to think it the end of the beginning. The terms on which they had won their victory, instead, made it the beginning of the end.

Now let not Nature's hand
Keep the wild flood confined! let order die!
And let this world no longer be a stage
To feed contention in a lingering act;
But let one spirit of the first-born Cain
Reign in all bosoms, that, each heart being set
On bloody course, the rude scene may end,
And darkness be the burier of the dead!
—*Shakespeare*, Henry IV, Part 2,
act 1, scene 1, lines 154–60

chapter 12

THE WOLF WHO CRIED WOLF

Early in 1875, the *Nation*, America's foremost magazine of opinion, took readers on a trip down memory lane, straight into never-never land. Had it been only seven years ago that the country had seemed poised on the edge of overthrow? A glance at the daily press around the time of Johnson's impeachment would "furnish food for exceeding merriment." Leaders of Republican opinion had cried out at presidential crimes that "actually beggared description." This "greatest criminal of this or any other age" menaced the republic. And what had come of it? The House had impeached, the Senate had let the "Tennessean Catiline" off. Now Johnson, after having left Washington as meekly as his ego would permit, was coming back, a senator-elect "amidst the good-humored laughter of the people whose ruin he was accused of compassing." The whole uproar had passed off like a raucous dinner party, leaving the guests with throbbing "but wiser heads. . . . There has rarely been a more amusing episode in the history of any people, nor a better illustration of the way in which an incident of really trifling importance can be worked up by the effects of unscrupulous politicians, supported by unscrupulous newspapers, so as to wear the look of irretrievable disaster."[1]

Edwin L. Godkin, the *Nation*'s editor, did not bother to ask how the American people could have been so gullible. The blindness of partisanship, the madness of the crowd: both of these he had seen over and over, in his ten years on the job. The electorate was made to be fooled. But there was more, that vital missing ingredient. In 1867, a new war of North against South, of northerner against northerner, of black against white, seemed quite possible. Memories of the last war were too fresh and the proofs of real conspiracies were too compelling to disregard what might be clues to the crisis yet to come. That confidence that the republic was meant to last, united and free, needed time to root itself deeper. The outcry may have been wrong, but it was not so foolish as a decade of peace made it seem.

For that matter, if Godkin had glanced at something more recent than yellowing newspapers — the files of the *Nation*, say, from the past year — he might have found cries of alarm more decorously done, but no less misplaced, than the ones he dismissed so easily. Just a month before, soldiers had intervened in Louisiana's legislature, in "the most outrageous subversion of parliamentary government by military force yet attempted in this country." But not the first: every allegation of intimidation let partisans overturn duly elected authorities to put in ones they liked better. Let lawmakers get away with it, and "of course the State government becomes an expensive and useless mockery." "Half the Union" saw the president simply as a military commander and a supplier of troops, and white southerners openly begged for military rule rather than the governments they endured. No "thoughtful man" could help feeling anxious. Readers of ancient or medieval history need not look here for the "nature of the subtle and slow process by which popular governments have been destroyed." They could find it in the apologists for General Grant's administration.[2]

The editor was no fool and no natural alarmist, but he reflected not the return of common sense and perspective to American public affairs so much as a shift in what kind of threats the state was perceived as facing. If he exaggerated badly by missing quite obvious facts — that intimidation and violence really had robbed certain states of a republican form of government and that the enthusiasm for military rule was much more a rhetorical flourish than a genuine wish for a southern Caesar — Godkin, too, had his thinking shaped by a larger context of government interferences. No more than the impeachers of 1867 could he see clearly into the future, and it may be unreasonable to expect it of him.

The sense of crisis, clearly, did not end with General Grant's election. It did not end at all, in fact. Reconstruction was itself one prolonged crisis, an unsettling rather than a settling. The Republican governments were not stable and never became secure. But over the next eight years much of the power went out of the language of conspiracy. What brought about the change? At least two things: the Democratic Party and the white South had to prove to the American electorate that they were no menace to the Union, and the Republicans had to raise doubts that they might be.

Democrats had been working to reassure the electorate all along. They had tried to win over Union war heroes; they ran generals for Congress and for governor. The White Boys in Blue countered Grant's veterans.[3] With the defeat of Seymour and Blair, efforts intensified for what came to be called the "New Departure."

Mythology credits the New Departure to the Ohio Democrats in 1871 and to the work of the irrepressible Copperhead, Clement Vallandigham. But observers at the time knew differently. They understood Ohio's action to be important not so much for how it led the way as that it gave a sign of how far the revolution had spread. For Ohio was one of the last great northern bastions of diehard sentiment. New York had come to the New Departure in 1870, and, as John Quincy Adams II pointed out, Massachusetts had put an even more explicit acceptance of the New Departure in its 1869 Democratic platform.[4]

Some of the force behind conversion was cold calculation. In the southern states, where most black voters lived, the Democracy had made its official peace with Negro voting, though always with the unspoken condition that blacks would vote Democratic. Democrats had staged barbecues and hosted biracial rallies, even endorsed some blacks as independent candidates for office. "At any hour during the day, on almost any street corner of Selma, Democrats . . . drank with negroes, walked arm-in-arm with negroes, rode in carriages with negroes," a Republican editor jeered after one local election, "—and all this was done in the most public manner." Where blacks outnumbered whites, there was nothing else that even "the bowie-knife, draw-poker, blood-drinking democrats of old chivalry antecedents" could do—at least unmasked and by the light of day.[5]

For their northern associates to hold firm looked at best unrewarding and at worst silly. When the Fifteenth Amendment became part of the Constitution in 1870, it seemed sillier still. "What would be the effect of a policy of acceptance of the inevitable Colored Cuss," New York congressman Samuel S. "Sunset" Cox wrote privately: "He is here! in Senate and as a voter, and he will soon be everywhere whether we like it or not. . . . I think it's foolish—we are,—not to look into the *Whites* of his eye, 'Squar!'" Some of the Democratic change of tactics came from a belief, still quite real, that the republic was in grave danger and that the only way to protect the country from that danger was to give ground. Centralization continued. "Unless prompt and stern resistance is interposed, everything will be national, and nothing local," the *New*

York World cried. Faced with a peril so great, "how weak to pother and worry over the negro question! It is the over-strained mule of an advancing army, and must be left behind, if need be, to perish and die. Democrats must take a stand in this momentous struggle on the Constitution as it *is*, with *all* the amendments, how many soever there be."[6]

Plenty of Democrats did not share Marble's impatience. Still convinced that the aim of the Reconstruction Acts had been a conspiracy to seize and hold power, they wanted to hold firm to principle. Rightly, they doubted the trade-off. In return for the promise of unknown numbers of black votes for the Democracy, the party was dampening the ardor of thousands of Democrats, who would stay at home rather than vote to stultify themselves. A paper in Alabama had "heard of condensed milk, potatoes, meats, &c., but condensed radicalism is the latest thing out." The editor was perfectly willing to pass the plate. "It is put up by a few democratic editors expressly for their democratic friends who were unable to swallow the article in its crude state." Alongside local organizations that worshipped "straight African, wool, heels and scent," an unfriendly witness could name other Alabama precincts that "[vomited] the colored brother and "stigmatize[d] any white man that dallie[d] with dusky balloters."[7]

As it happened, Democrats had very good reasons for embracing the New Departure that had nothing to do with race; and historians who concentrate on the race issue understand the implications down south better than those up north. For the real purpose was not to accept equality so much as to prove to a white northern electorate that the Democracy was housebroken—that it was entirely safe to entrust it with the government.

The Klan violence raging across the Cotton South made this all the more necessary. Unquestionably, Democrats gained considerably by the terrorism down south. But by excusing the Klan, they also added to their reputation as the party of disorder and revolution. The Klan became a liability in the North and even in some places in the South. By focusing attention on Republican sins and by making general statements in favor of the maintenance of order, Democrats could control the political damage. They could argue that the terrorism was needed not to wipe out Reconstruction so much as to eliminate the robbers.[8] Indeed, the Klan could serve their purposes very well by showing that in the most important conservative function the Republican Reconstruction governments had fallen short of their intentions—they were not able to keep peace and order. Democrats could do both—and without putting the Union at any risk.

For this purpose, they could point to the states that had been "redeemed."

Beyond question, those states were a terrible thing for freedmen and loyalists. But the level of violence and disorder after the Redemption of the upper South was nearly invisible to newspaper readers: the savagery that would follow the Deep South's Redemption was yet to come. School systems were cut back but not wiped out. And nowhere did the Redeemed South give the least sign that it was working toward the creation of a new Confederacy. The New Departure, then, could be tested most clearly where Democrats had the chance to shape policy as they wished. As far as northern reporters could see, they had done a decent job of it. Taxes fell, states' credit ratings improved, violence subsided, and schools stayed open. But the crucial thing was to prove that the Democrats were not revolutionary. No state militia drilled in preparation for another war. No Union veteran coming south was in danger of being molested as long as he kept his politics to himself.[9]

Charles Nordhoff, *New York Herald* special reporter, reflected that changed image of the southern Democrats, the so-called Redeemers. Touring the Cotton South in the spring and summer of 1875, he found reassuring signs in all the redeemed states. His first point was the vital one: there was not the slightest chance of another war. No white southerner wanted it or dreamed of it or would join it if some hothead began it. There was no deep white race prejudice against blacks—no terrorism—no violence. All of the government's protection of southern Republican governments had not made them stable. It had subverted government and the established order. But their successors had done everything that government should do and without endangering the Union at all.[10]

Nordhoff misread how far blacks' rights were protected in the Democratic South, just as he exaggerated the misrule of the Republican states. But in his emphasis on loyalty he was accurate. The white South had made its own New Departure, as former Confederates tried to come to terms with the war and with what it meant. With increasing persuasiveness, they sold the North on the idea that they had returned to the Union for good. "No man who is not a fit subject for the lunatic asylum has any other thought, expectation, or wish than that the Government of the United States and the Union under it should exist for all time to come," a Virginia congressman asserted. The cult of the "Lost Cause" had begun almost before the armies trudged home, and by the 1870s it had wrapped most of the leading Confederate generals in cloaks of romance. South as well as north, veterans' societies had turned parades into pageants and Memorial Day into a reminder of the nobility of the war's sacrifices and of why *their* side had been right all along. Yet celebrate the Confederacy as they would, white southerners made equally clear that the Lost Cause was just that, *lost*, and that they had no intention of reviving it except in cultural display. They were honoring the South within the Union, not the South outside of it. Given the chance to display their readiness to conciliate the North, they did so with apparent heartiness at centennial celebrations of the American Revolution. Neglected just after the war, the Fourth of July again became a day honored in the white South.[11]

One of the great set pieces for displaying the spirit of conciliation was delivered just after the death of Senator Charles Sumner in 1874. Many speeches honored the Radical Republican's idealism, but the address most remembered came from Lucius Q. C. Lamar of Mississippi, a onetime member of the Confederate Congress and now a member of the U.S. House. He emphasized Sumner's belief "that all occasion for strife and distrust between North and South had passed away." Did not many among his listeners believe so, too, and rightly? "The South—prostrate, exhausted, drained of her life-blood . . . yet still honorable and true—accepts the bitter award of the blood arbitrament without reservation, resolutely determined to abide the result with chivalrous fidelity." She suffered in silence. A North "elated by success" had the generous heart it had always had and "yet, as if mastered by some mysterious spell," held back in distrust and doubt. "Would that the spirit of the illustrious dead whom we lament today could speak from the grave to both parties to this deplorable discord in tones which should reach each and every heart throughout this broad territory: 'My countrymen! *know* one another and you will *love* one another.'"[12]

Lamar meant no more than that the white North "know" the former Confederate South, and he was careful to omit the still greater final cause of "this great champion of human liberty," a bill ending racial discrimination in public accommodations and schools, which the Mississippian's particular "South" abominated. But his words were also an assurance that the South sued rather than commanded. It had thrown itself back into the Union so unconditionally that it would accept being wronged without complaint rather than redress it with arms.

In a far less forgiving spirit, Ben Hill of Georgia rose in January 1876 to repel slurs on the character of Jefferson Davis. His speech breathed defiance to the Republicans. "With masters enslaved, intelligence disfranchised, society disorganized, industry paralyzed, States subverted, Legislatures dispersed by the bayonet," the people knew what the majority party's "grace and magnanimity" amounted to, he snarled. To Reconstruction's creators, the South conceded nothing. "Martyrs owe no apologies to tyrants." Even Hill's fellow Democrats shrank back from so truculent a speech, and Hill tamed it for the *Congressional*

Record. And yet, at least in its milder form, the diehard's message was Lamar's: the South would work out its destiny within the Union and Constitution, not out of it. "There are no confederates in this House," Hill announced; "there are now no confederates anywhere; there are no confederate schemes, ambitions, hopes, desires or purposes here." Let Radicals do their worst, break every pledge that the Founders gave, trample the Constitution freely, and commit wrongs till they were "like the stars of heaven or the sands of the seashore, without number; but know this, for all your iniquities the South will never again seek a remedy in the madness of another secession. [Continued applause.] We are here; we are in the house of our fathers, our brothers are our companions, and we are at home to stay, thank God. [Much applause.]"[13]

Against such protestations, much of the force went out of the Republican appeal. Bloody shirt oratory could still argue that southern Democrats carried elections by fraud and force and that Confederate brigadiers would march back to Washington to rule the North and pay off their wartime losses.[14] But the claim that treason would break up the Union made a harder sell every year, and it was that fear of revolution that had kept the Republican Party out of harm's way.

That was ironic. By 1876, revolution was not only possible. It had happened, and a reign of terror had happened too. Without it, neither Lamar nor Hill would have found their way from the House into the Senate. A genuine conspiracy had worked the overthrow of Reconstruction in some of the Deep South and had weakened it everywhere else. Indeed, the conspiracy had been palpable before Ulysses S. Grant took the presidential oath. Terrorism took different names: the Ku Klux Klan, the Council of Safety, the Knights of the White Camellia.[15] Everywhere, it undermined the newly installed Republican governments in the South. More than that, the Klan aimed to restore if not slavery in law then a slavery in fact, in which blacks could count themselves fortunate to have schools or churches of their own.

That the terrorism sought to narrow black freedom was plain enough from the first. Black men were killed for intimacy with white women or for familiarity with white neighbors. "The colored people dare not dress up themselves and fix up, like they thought anything of themselves, for fear they would whip us," a Georgia woman complained, and she had grounds: night riders had beaten her twice that year. Blacks working for a country shopkeeper who was high in the local Klan learned from him what it took to be left alone. "He said if I always raised my hat to the people when I passed, and was always polite to them, I would not be bothered," one explained. Everywhere, Klan raids took guns away from those that had them. Schoolhouses and churches were favored targets, as they had been since emancipation. In Walton County, Georgia, the Klan informed the public that Negro schools must close. A teacher's books were burned, and the invaders boasted that "they would just dare any other nigger to have a book in his house."[16]

The likeliest victim was a black who for one reason or another had become "too big a man." That meant, economically, ones who were not dependent on the planters. Many raids were directed at blacks who owned land or blacks who were allowed to rent it from white owners or blacks who asked for more than the penury of a sharecropper's contract. In Georgia, black tenants were driven from the land just before harvest and told not to come back to collect their share of the crop. Others were warned not to seek employment from any other landlord without permission. Prayer meetings were targeted, a Georgia farmer complained. "They supposed the negroes would get together and talk politics, and in that way . . . found out too much to work for nothing."[17]

Blacks were visited and ordered to vote Democratic. When they refused or cast "a damned Radical ticket," they were beaten or killed. Republican organizers were murdered, too. In Alabama, Republican lawmakers were hauled off of railroad cars and whipped and could only get back to the next session of the legislature when the governor produced a military convoy for them. A Georgian was flogged with leather belts and left for dead because he had named his son after Foster Blodgett, a Republican leader and president of the state railroad. Because of night riders and whippings, counties where Republicans had scored big majorities in the state election eight months before gave General Grant miniscule support in November. One vote was cast for him in Columbia County—1,221 votes fewer than Republicans had cast earlier. In eleven counties, he did not get a single vote. The more exclusively political it was, the more whites applauded the terrorists as insurgents, doing what any people had the right to do, against an illegitimate government. "I tell you, sir, that we've borne it as long as we can, and now it's got to stop," a South Carolinian told one northern reporter. "The niggers have got to let men of property and intelligence hold the offices, or they've got to leave this part of the country."[18]

Along with it went what historians easily could describe as a conspiracy of silence. Conservative newspapers, having built up the fame of the Klan with more glee than seemed politically expedient, turned around and began to deny that the violence had any political implications at all. If the Klan invaded the house of a crippled black Baptist preacher unable to walk or feed himself, lugged him out into his yard at midnight and lashed him with a buggy whip, this could be explained by the victim's alleged encouragement of black arsonists, and not by his place as a leader of the black community.[19]

To justify Klan violence, newspapers, after the fact, had to find a reign of terror, to which the whites were responding, the better to blame both sides equally, or, more often, to find outrages that would shove any discussion of white marauding off the front page and out of the public mind entirely. The movement, editors insisted, was really only a counterpart of the intimidating, revolutionary black Union Leagues. It was vital to fight "that secret negro conspiracy which has for its object the establishment of negro domination." The hanging of Jim Williams, a South Carolina militia captain, and the pinning of a note to the corpse reading "Capt. Jim Williams on his big muster" was only to be expected for a man who, it was later charged, had vowed to "kill from the cradle up" (though Williams had never got around to killing anyone). To hear the *Livingston Journal* tell it, the Ku Klux Klan raids in the county simply were responding to an imminent threat:

> Gangs of from 25 to 75 negroes have night after night, for weeks, in succession, been kept under arms in thickly populated neighborhoods. Armed gangs of the kind mentioned have held secret [Union League] meetings in this town, and continued in session until midnight. Parties of armed negroes have marched through the county . . . in broad daylight, at the order of one man—their object being left for the public to conjecture. Threats have been made to reduce our town to ashes, if our citizens did not conduct themselves as the self-constituted commanders prescribed.

In time, conservative newspapers stopped reporting incidents at all, as if they had never happened, and blamed the killing of Republicans on other Republicans pretending to be Democratic terrorists or acting as agent provocateurs to give the organization a bad name. The Klan had never existed; it was "the getting together of honest folks . . . to keep the turbulent and unruly within bounds," and the Grand Dragon had disbanded it.[20]

In the most narrow sense of the word, there was no one actual conspiracy, just little conspiracies. Personnel and purposes changed from one incident to the next. Klans were by no means the only sources for white violence. Church and school burnings, beatings, and killings had been common before the Klan was formed, and many of the attacks took place without any of the paraphernalia of the secret order. By late 1866, the Freedmen's Bureau counted thirty-three blacks murdered in Tennessee since the war's end; it counted twenty-nine in Arkansas and twenty-four in South Carolina. But the figures were too low. In Louisiana at about the same time, General Joseph A. Mower could count seventy such killings, which, he thought, amounted to barely half the actual total. Reconstruction saw a series of race riots, in which the Klan played

"Too Thin, Massa Grant." Matt Morgan, *Frank Leslie's Illustrated Newspaper*, September 14, 1872. Morgan suggests that the Klan was a myth, a scare deliberately manipulated by President Grant to keep blacks loyal to the Republican ticket. He was wrong in every detail, but it was the line that most Democrats (and a number of disaffected Republicans) were taking. The cartoonist, imported from England to match Nast's powerful Republican attacks, barely lasted out the 1872 campaign.

no visible role and where the killings went on without any masks. Some of them had prior planning and arrangements. In a few cases, the murders were done in cold blood, after the fighting had ended. But others were spontaneous eruptions. Even before the Klan's creation, federal officers were seeing a new kind of violence in the South, a mingling of the old slave patrols with the bushwhacking gangs that had preyed on Confederate and Unionist civilians alike in wartime. Without property value, former slaves no longer were worth enough to the white community to deserve any protection. Organized bands, calling themselves "rangers," "moderators," or "nigger killers," had gone riding through Kentucky, to drive out freedmen. Mississippi, too, had its "regulators," and in some localities, the banded anarchs gave themselves titles and official chains of command.[21]

In later years, when the "redemption" of the South from Negro rule and carpetbaggery had become the founding legend of postwar politics, chroniclers worked to trace a Klan pedigree for great political figures on the Democratic side. Whole structures of command were devised, the better to give the organization that kind of solid hierarchical form that the New South wanted to imagine had always been the way politics and society at their best ran, with the "best men," the "respectables" and the statesmen, commanding and controlling the yeoman farmers and the vulgar herd and never, of course, being part of the crimes of the Klan. Even Robert E. Lee was a supposed member. Republicans would have loved to have believed it to be true — a terrorist organization, intended to overthrow free government and headed by future senators and governors. Evidence is scanty for most of the big names tossed about. The Klan was not a conspiracy led by only planters and gentlemen, sending submissive poor whites to do their dirty work. Doctors and lawyers wielded whip and pistol, and the typical Klan leader was as likely to be a middling member of society as not. When it came to killing, there was no real contrast between the flower of chivalry and men, as one black put it, "not worth the bread they eat."[22]

There were guiding hands and plans laid — there had to be. The Klan worked in small groups, and raiders preferred to strike neighborhoods where the victims were less likely to recognize them. That took some forethought about where to go and who to raid. But above the county level, the lines of hierarchy turned into cobwebs, if they were to be seen at all. Local Klans were founded with encouragement from the state level but left alone thereafter. In many places, Klans were founded by locals acting on their own, who never bothered to make any connection to the larger brotherhood. If anything, the real creators of Klan chapters were not the Kleagles and Grand Dragon but the newspapers that romanticized and mythologized the Klan from the first. The high command did not plan strategy, specify targets, define goals, or steer the movement in certain directions. If there was a pattern beyond local action, it was of a movement that the organizers could start up but then find themselves unable to stop. The Klan might flare up to apply itself against Republicans and carry an election, and it was usually at the start of a campaign that a previously quiet area descended into chaos. Or a Klan group might start as a response to the governor mustering blacks into the state militia. But when the original provocation passed, or when Republicans had won the election and the initial impetus for the Klan no longer existed, the chaos did not end. Indeed, it intensified and diffused against an ever-wider range of targets, often to the irritation and sometimes the alarm of those who had invoked its presence in the first place.[23]

The Klan terror, in short, worked on a freelance basis, through whites in the secret order at least pretending to be acting on their own. The attacks were all political in a broad sense. Every killing or beating sent a message to those who had escaped attack—a message of how easy it would be for them to get out of line in their behavior and how small an infraction could provoke a midnight visit. All the same, who was struck and why had a random quality. In that respect, the conservative newspapers were right: many of the attacks were a settling of scores, though of course the offense given was one that could not be endured without retaliation precisely because the perpetrator was a black, a Republican, or both. That diffuse agenda was one reason why Republicanism managed to survive at all. A well-orchestrated campaign to finish off party organizers would have been far more efficient. Instead, Klan violence took in a host of targets, and many of the victims were blacks who, for some individual fault, had brought down the wrath of the white community.

"The wrongs these freedmen suffer are unheard of," Freedmen's Bureau agent William C. Morrill wrote General George Meade in November 1868, "and I don't see how human nature can stand it without fearful retaliations. Even Major Wilson last night said, 'G—d d—n it[,] I wish I had a company of cavalry and a roving commission[;] I'd like to shoot about a hundred.'" When public authority failed to grant them protection in 1868, the blacks of Stewart County, Georgia, took steps of their own. Matches were cheap, and "those who have inflicted injury upon some poor innocent colored man" found their homes and barns going up in flames, as one white Republican reported. In Blount County, Alabama, white Union veterans set up an "anti-Ku-Klux" group, ready to mete out blow for blow, death for death, unless the beatings and school burnings stopped. Occasionally blacks fought back, drove their attackers off, and wounded or killed night riders. Every black meeting after midnight, whether in arms or not, served as a threat and a warning to white neighborhoods that terrorism might not go unpunished. Whites were always ready to play up the prospect of black violence. It became a stock-in-trade for Democratic reporters to the northern press.[24] But even more-sympathetic white witnesses expected that outrages would be paid in kind. Some white northerners expected it, even wanted it, as a sign that black people were worth protecting and that they were doing something for themselves. "If people are killed by the Ku-Klux," a northerner asked North Carolina judge Albion W. Tourgee, "why do they not kill the Ku-Klux?" Surely the failure to act showed those under attack to be unworthy of their rights, unmanly in ways that no southern white would tolerate.

But the firepower on either side was desperately uneven from the first, and the examples of black resistance need to be taken in context. For blacks in the Louisiana sugar country, still working in gang labor and living in close quarters to one another, mobilization for defense was feasible. They might be attacked in open daylight by a superior white force, but the midnight night raiders stood a good chance of being beaten back. For the cotton sharecropper, off on his own in the countryside, help was too far away to call upon and would arrive too late. He, at least, was the soft target for Klan violence, just as schoolhouses and churches were. Let him repel an attack one night; he could not fend it off every night from then on, as long as he lived, and what courage he showed would be repaid fatally, if not to himself, then to members of his family, less able to protect themselves.[25] A black military presence could never match the guns in the hands of onetime Confederates, as well they knew. They lacked the military experience, and their shotguns were a poor match for the single shot Winchester rifles and the six-shooting pistols that their enemies carried. One only had to imagine the effect that a private black brigade would have had, if it went from door to door, hauling out and meting out summary punishment to individual whites who had been part of a Klan raid. It never happened, because it was perfectly plain that in open, battlefield conditions, no black force could possibly prevail; and in its wake, as happened in so many set-tos, the survivors would be hunted down, and their kin and their friends and any bystanders of their race would be marked for death.

For good reason, then, the moment new state governments were established, black and white Republicans besieged Congress with pleas for a distribution of arms, the better to equip effective loyal militias. Wary of putting guns into the hands of military units yet unmade, and even more chary about passing them to what might well be black infantry in a presidential election year, Congress held back. They knew how inflammatory the dread of a black uprising could be, three years after the war's end, and how passionately the Democrats would evoke it. It would cost votes up north, and if it roused white southerners, it could set off that prospect, still very real in white minds, of a war of races. The governors of Florida, Louisiana, and Arkansas all tried vainly to borrow guns from northern state authorities in the summer of 1868. Eventually, Governor Powell Clayton's emissary ended up buying rifles and ammunition for Arkansas in New York. The shipment never made it to Arkansas; a tugboat with sixty to seventy armed and masked Democrats waylaid the ship bearing it before the goods reached Little Rock. Florida governor Harrison Reed went to New York in person to buy the weaponry, but Klansmen got to them before they could reach Tallahassee. In the upper South, where white Unionists were strongest and where most former Union soldiers of southern origin lived, state militia had the best chance of being organized. That was because a white native militia could do what no governor would dare send a black militia to do. In Tennessee and Arkansas, the militia rousted out the Klan and destroyed it. Texas governor Edmund G. Davis formed a State Police, two hundred strong, and arrested suspects by the thousands. The Klan never recovered. The Democrats, after having shouted themselves hoarse with indignation, organized the Texas Rangers on the same plan and staffed it with as many white former State Policemen as they could enlist.[26] Such exemplary authorities showed up the other governors and added to northern complaints that southern officials really could do more to save themselves.

They neither could nor did. "Put on your iron glove," a Republican begged South Carolina's governor. But the only glove Robert K. Scott had ready at hand would be black militia companies. Sending them out arresting white suspects was almost sure to make white violence worse, or lead to a battle like the one in Chester. "It should have been called rather a massacre of the blacks," a reporter commented, "for the timid, ignorant negroes, after firing one volley, threw away their guns and ran, the whites pursuing them and killing all they could." Sheriffs dared not arrest and grand juries feared to prosecute.[27] Klan violence carried Georgia for Seymour in 1868 and helped him win Louisiana. It so diminished the black vote in Alabama and North Carolina that the Republicans lost both in 1870, though they would make a comeback. Every other state withstood the onslaught. After Congress passed the Third Enforcement Act in 1871, giving the president broad powers to take political violence into federal court, prosecutions wiped out the Klan wherever it lingered.[28] But after three years of relative peace, the threat to Republican authorities took new shape, this time as paramilitary clubs, the so-called White Leagues. They did not strike by night. They paraded by day, rode through black communities firing off their guns by night, and, given the chance, overawed black Republicans at the polls. In September 1874, they took on the Metropolitan police in Louisiana and forced Governor William Pitt Kellogg's resignation; President Grant had to send the army to put him back into office again. Against the coup in upcountry parishes, he could do nothing.[29] In Alabama, the white militia had everything their own way that fall, especially after they rode into black neighborhoods stripping colored households of their pistols, shotguns, and ammunition to forestall "insurrection." "One black fellow of this town actually had the temerity to propose a negro company" to match the white one, a Tuscumbia man remarked, "and the whites came to the conclusion that he ought to be killed for thinking of such a thing." Thinking was as far as such a proposal would get. The governor was not about to commission or arm anyone.[30] A year later, White League threats and violence broke up Mississippi Republican meetings and carried the election. In 1876, mounted and armed Red Shirt legions hurrahed for Wade Hampton in South Carolina and made clear that they would see him sworn in one way or the other. Wherever the White Leagues mustered, beatings and killings happened. An uprising in Coushatta, Louisiana, ended in the capture and butchery of parish officials; a quarrel over roadside privileges in Hamburg, South Carolina, ended in a siege, with six blacks shot down in cold blood and more felled as they ran.[31]

This was revolution, ever more open and bold. Yet from the North the outcry rose ever fainter. How could it have happened? There were, in fact, many good reasons beyond the obvious one, which was that to most northerners, a black life was not worth as much as a white one. After years of crying wolf and no wolf coming, Republican leaders found it harder to arouse their audiences. By the mid-1870s, so many outrages had been proven exaggerated or fabulous that northerners had an excuse not to believe the real ones.[32] And many of them did not want to believe. Ever since the war, they had wanted the Union to be as it had been — or, rather, as it always should have been, with North and South together. From veterans on both sides, from the Lamars and the Hills, came the language of reconciliation, making every southern outrage an all-the-less-welcome piece of news. The cruelties inflicted on former slaves had stirred indignation after the war not simply because of the injustice but also because Republicans made the treatment of blacks a test of white southerners' acceptance of the unwritten terms of peace that the North demanded. Blacks had been given the vote not simply to protect themselves but to make sure that there would be enough voters to make loyal governments in the South. Take away the fear of another war and the doubts about southern loyalty, and at least one of the forces committing northerners to "the second American revolution" was gone. They could be angry at wrongs done to black Republicans; they were losing the ability to be afraid, as well. For many northerners, that was not enough.

Extraordinary government action had taken a political toll, and the frustrations of propping up southern Republican governments gave Democrats a more compelling case that the real threat to constitutional government lay with the emergency powers that the national government had taken on in wartime. By 1872, sending soldiers to guard the polls that Andrew Johnson had only toyed with in Maryland had become common Republican practice. Aware as he was of the distrust a military chieftain in the White House would excite and inclined as he was to the old Whig idea that presidents should execute the law and leave most of the policymaking to Congress, General Grant involved himself in southern affairs as little as he could. Virginia Conservatives ratified the Reconstruction constitution in July 1869 and swept the Radicals from power forever. Tennessee conservatives allied themselves to the Republican governor in a factional fight, carried the state election, and immediately called a constitutional convention that would put the governor out of office and a Radical comeback out of reach. When North Carolina governor William W. Holden battled the Klan, he looked in vain to Washington for support.[33] Not until 1871 did the president ask Congress for legislation that would give him the power to take on the terrorists. Always, national authority served as a last resort, not as a first. But those last resorts just kept happening, and from 1872 on they marred every election season. Voters grew tired of having to bail out southern governments. Onetime supporters of Reconstruction fell away, protesting that they had never intended the national government to intrude itself forever.

The very use of federal military force could give short-term relief to state governments in trouble. But it did not make them stronger. Rather, it reinforced the arguments that Democrats had made from the first, that they were pretend governments unable to survive on their own. The more the national government tried to do, the more the state governments looked like paper cutouts and invented entities, scarecrows all dressed up with government apparatus but without the essential thing on which authority had to rest—the consent of the governed.

They had unwitting accomplices: those authorities themselves. Under fire from whites who never accepted them as legitimate and accepted violence as the best way of restoring lawful government, the Republicans in power used every technicality and argument to tweak election results to go their way. Fearful of defeat, Georgia's governor Rufus Bullock came to Washing-

"The Republic on the Brink. U.S.G. [Grant] — 'Push her off, gents. I'll kick the other thing over. We must have things our own way.'" Matt Morgan, *Frank Leslie's Illustrated Newspaper*, November 9, 1872. "King Grant," shabby and drunk, aided by Senators Roscoe Conkling, Oliver Morton, Zachariah Chandler, and Simon Cameron, prepares to kill liberty and popular government. The cartoonist may have reacted to allegations of vote fraud in Cameron's Pennsylvania, but the landslide reelecting Grant was far beyond what ballot-box manipulators could have managed.

ton to have the state remanded to military supervision and re-reconstructed. Months later, he showed up again to lobby for a two-year delay in the state elections.[34] Driven from power, Virginia Republicans looked to Congress to undo the 1869 election and remand the state to military rule. Tennesseans pressed to have Congress nullify its readmission of that state, now more than three years past. Do that, one predicted, and "all midnight masked violence will cease! — *but not else.*" All of these efforts with the exception of Bullock's first failed, although in Bullock's second venture defeat came only after a bruising struggle in the House. But to moderate Republicans the very attempts on behalf of "contemptible jackasses" were alarming. If states restored to their full privileges could be undone — if elections could be set aside when they inconvenienced Republicans — then no state had any rights that the national government was bound to respect.[35] Such states were not sovereignties. They were congressional puppets.

Elsewhere, Republicans applied every technicality to stay in power. Alabama's 1870 election was close, and the legislature was split between two parties. Apparently beaten, Governor William H. Smith went to court to challenge the returns and to keep lawmakers from counting the vote. Backed with federal troops, Smith kept his rival, Robert B. Lindsay, from moving into the executive offices. For several weeks, two men played governor before Smith gave way. Two years later, federal troops had to keep the peace as both parties contested the statehouse and assembled their own legislatures. In 1873, Texas Democrats won the governorship, or supposed they had. The Republican state supreme court found technical reasons to void the election, and party leaders persuaded the sitting governor to hold on while they sought soldiers to back up his claim. Republicans took over the capitol basement to house their own legislature, and Democrats clambered up a ladder to the second floor to organize a general assembly all their own. Even in Mississippi, the best-governed of the "carpetbag" states, there was a brief, disturbing flurry when it seemed as if the losers, who claimed to be truer Republicans than the winners, meant to "Mexicanize" their government by trying to cancel the election a week before the polls opened.[36]

Troubles in Louisiana never ceased from troubling. The laws that made Governor Henry Clay Warmoth so formidable made his presence an impediment to every ambitious man. Anyone as powerful as the executive had to be obeyed or broken, and Republicans did break Warmoth, for all his influence. In doing so, they split their party organization. Ward club meetings broke up in rows, often with the professional help of New Orleans roughs hired to wallop the opposing faction. The police did their best — to outdo the musclemen at their own game. By the time the Republican convention met in August 1871, bribery, brass knuckles, and brawling had confused things irretrievably. Most election districts sent double delegations, each swearing that the other was fraudulent. When the legislature came into session early in the following year, there was a near revolution, with attempts to impeach the governor, abductions of senators to prevent a quorum, and guns facing off against guns in the assembly chamber. As both sides mustered armed men, the U.S. Army intervened to protect Warmoth's government and ordered all other forces dispersed.

A tumultuous Republican convention chose William Pitt Kellogg for governor, amid jeers and fistfights. Warmoth had lost control of his own party. He joined the Democrats and threw his influence behind their nominee. Both parties did plenty of cheating. "Warmouth being the bolder, abler and shrewder man, had all the power or influence given him by the infamous 'Election law,' was master of the situation," a conservative commented, "and Mr. Kellogg stood no chance of being 'counted in,' unless he appealed to his antidote, to his election law, as passed for him specially by Congress, and had a new count! And such a count! . . . Enough to say that not having the election returns before them, the Returning Board discarded Arithmetic, and used all the unknown quantities of Algebra."[37]

Nothing could result from this but two governors, two legislatures, and plenty of impeachments to go around. Shortly after midnight on December 6, 1872, two companies of federal soldiers took over Mechanic's Institute, where the legislature was to meet. The city awoke to find cannon and bayonet protecting the Kellogg legislature in session. Kellogg's success lasted because federal guns were at his disposal, and he served out his entire term. But successes have rarely been so empty or so catastrophic. Within weeks, rival military forces had armed in New Orleans and in upcountry parishes there were struggles for control, with all claiming that right and law were exclusively on their side and, among conservatives, at least, by the growing conviction that they could make a plausible enough claim of legitimacy to find apologists—even Republican apologists—across the North. In Grant Parish, such a struggle ended in a massacre.[38]

Finally, there was Arkansas. In a state that one reporter thought should have a whiskey bottle, a pistol, and a bowie knife on its official seal, Republicanism had an almost porridgelike fluidity. Radicals turned into conservative darlings, proscriptive Unionists turned into reconciliationists the moment they found that white Confederate votes could shift the balance of power. There was one constant factor: Governor Powell Clayton's struggle for dominance.

In 1872, the factional feuds split the party into Minstrels, Clayton's friends, and Brindletails, his foes. Democrats backed Joseph Brooks, the Brindletail nominee, for governor, against Elisha Baxter, the Minstrels' choice. Baxter won the election, though only after such an irregular count that thousands of voters refused to recognize his right to the office. Conservatives felt especially bitter, but as the new governor demonstrated his sympathy with their ideas, they changed their minds. And so did Republicans. So many legislators were graced with offices that the General Assembly was depopulated and changed from Republican to Democratic control. Everyone knew that when the legislature met in 1874, it would call for a constitutional convention to remove the last vestiges of Radical rule. Democrats who had stood by Brooks took up Baxter's cause. Minstrel Republicans wavered in their support for the man they had elected and toyed with the idea of proclaiming Brooks the lawfully elected governor. If the Reconstruction programs—if Republican government itself—were to be saved, no time could be lost.

On April 15, 1874, without the governor's lawyers present to contest the decision, a circuit court judge ruled that Brooks had won the election seventeen months before and had legal title to the executive office. Chief Justice John J. McClure administered the oath of office in secret. Then, with a few dozen armed men behind him, Brooks marched into the statehouse to demand possession. A dumbfounded Baxter was ejected. In response, he marshaled a host of armed desperadoes all his own. For a month, the state was in a tumult as both sides claimed the right to govern and raised their own militias to enforce their wills. At one governor's direction, a supreme court justice was kidnapped. At another's command, arms from the state armories were passed out to followers. Most Democrats supported Baxter and most Republicans favored Brooks, but the lines were by now so tangled that no allegiance made much sense. Blacks fought blacks and whites battled whites. "Perhaps a more whimsical, rattling, roaring farce has never been put upon the reconstruction stage," said one newspaper. Only with the Grant administration's intervention did Baxter prevail, and he immediately turned the state over to the Democrats.[39]

Governments that could not keep order without outside aid, states that chose governors in twos, authorities dependent on force, technicality, and judicial caprice—none of this fit the promise of Radical Reconstruction. It came closer to the fears that conservatives had of what would happen once the national government started tinkering with the system the Founders had made. Traitors no longer endangered republican institutions. But Americans had good reason to worry about its protectors. So, in early 1875, when the Grant administration sought one last round of intervention—to give Arkan-

"A Threatened Military Execution." Joseph Keppler, *Frank Leslie's Illustrated Newspaper*, February 1875. With Philip Sheridan commanding the firing squad, Grant orders Arkansas executed, just as Louisiana had been. Neither ended up happening. Louisiana's murder consisted of the army's insistence on unseating five Democrats from seats in the Assembly after a very irregular proceeding had awarded them the places. However much the president would have liked to overturn the Democratic government in Arkansas, Republicans refused to give him the authority.

sas back to Joseph Brooks, to police Louisiana's tumults, and to add to the government's powers to oversee southern elections—Republicans wanted an end to the whole thing. "Bayonets in Louisiana," the *New Haven (Conn.) Register* shrieked. "A Sovereign State Throttled by the Military Power. A Legally-Elected legislature Dispersed. The Beginning of the End." "If Caesar attempts to wrap the purple about him," Senator Eli Saulsbury of Delaware thundered, "I say in the name of public liberty let the American people tear the robes from him." The old analogies to Cromwell and Napoleon and the coup on the 18th Brumaire were trotted out again—but this time not against Johnson but against Grant. In fact, Johnson, grayer but not wiser and newly returned to Washington as a senator, uttered some of them himself. In his last speech, the old appeals lived again. "Save the Constitution," Johnson urged, "bring the Government back to it, or the time will come—God forbid it, but I fear it will come—when the goddess of Liberty will be driven from this land staggering over fields of blood and carnage to witness the loss of representative government."[40]

Andrew Johnson died that summer and was buried with the flag for a winding-sheet and his much-worn copy of the Constitution for a pillow, and thus he never saw that promised end.[41] Nobody did, though they kept looking for it. Even before Grant took office, Democrats had been trying to build him up as a would-be emperor. His every involvement in the South set off alarms anew, and by 1874 the president's silence about whether he would accept a third term stirred cries that he was the coming Caesar. Republicans worried that it might be true. Some of them still worried, even after Grant made clear that he had no such intentions.[42]

The idea that he might use the patronage to win a third nomination was a plausible one, at least. But seeing Grant as a conspirator against liberty took rather more imagination. By 1875, the public had his measure: a quiet, plodding man, free from imagination, slow to act, with terrible judgment about whom to trust. In six years, the tools that a dictator would need most, money and military support, had grown scarcer. The administration had cut taxes and reduced the army to bare-bones level. By his gingerly move toward civil service reform, Grant had even shown a willingness to part with some of his power over the spoils system. His administration may have been bungling, ham-handed, corrupt, and inefficient. Stories of waste and mismanagement were legion. Scandals infected just about every department of government. Grant's Washington made a sordid picture, but it was nowhere near as likely to excite fear as to cause disgust and contempt. Public men were not about to steal the people's liberties—not when they already had their hands full from stealing the people's money. "This political contest is something more than a fight about a white hat and a played-out cigar," an orator pleaded in 1872. But he needed to plead: for all the talk of liberty at risk, voters that year were roused to an unprecedented apathy—and gave the cigar (Grant) a landslide over the white hat (Horace Greeley). "We have sometimes thought that if the whole constitution were abolished by an edict from Washington, the country would hardly give a sign of disapproval, providing always that the money market was kept steady," a Missouri newspaper commented.[43]

One thing remained to give the coup d'état the coup de grâce. On Election Night, 1876, Democrats went to bed sure that they had carried the presidency

"Constancy." Thomas Nast, *Harper's Weekly*, April 10, 1875. As former president Johnson's maiden speech to the Senate showed, his basic outlook had not changed at all. The notable change was in Nast. No longer a menace, "King Andy" had been diminished to a rather comic eccentricity. In old age, Nast told his biographer that when Johnson saw one of his later cartoons he declared that he forgave Nast everything he had ever drawn about him—which does not sound much like Johnson.

for Governor Samuel J. Tilden of New York. Next morning they woke to find that his victory depended on a solid South. In three states, Louisiana, Florida, and South Carolina, Republicans claimed to have won, and they ran the Returning Boards that would count the votes and, more important, decide which votes counted. Believing that their enemies had bullied, killed, and cheated their way to within an inch of the presidency, supporters of Rutherford B. Hayes meant to hold that inch. Both sides cried foul and charged bribery, fraud, and intimidation, and both were most likely right. With Congress deadlocked about counting the electoral votes, threats of violence filled the air. Counting Hayes in would kill the republic, Tilden's supporters cried. "Goodbye Free Government, free elections, free speech and free press, as well as all civil liberties if the people submit to it," one Democrat stormed. Editor Henry Watterson of the *Louisville Courier-Journal* called for 100,000 unarmed men to march on Washington and enforce Tilden's right. The slumbering fears that saw Grant as Caesar awoke. The time was perfect for him to declare an emergency and use the army to proclaim himself head of state until a new election could pick a winner—an election that, naturally, would never happen. There would be two chief executives, others predicted. That long-promised next civil war loomed, weeks away.[44]

And, in the end, what did all the hue and cry amount to? Grant did call on the army—but only to keep order. Tilden buried himself among the law books looking up precedents. Those crying "Tilden or Blood" got neither one. Southern Democrats made clear that if their northern allies wanted a new war, they should count them out: "They have no idea of war, don't want war, and I think if left to themselves would soon subside and await the declaration quietly," T. J. McLain assured Congressman James A. Garfield. Northerners failed to rally either—100,000 unarmed Tilden supporters stayed home. The last thing insiders on both sides wanted was their own friends' maneuvers behind the scenes. They worked out a deal, giving the problem of awarding presidential electors to a special Electoral Commission that by happenstance ended up tipped Republicans' way, eight to seven. House Democrats put on a show of outrage and filibustered the count as long as they could. But not long enough, and Hayes was inaugurated quietly.[45] If the republic could weather a crisis like this without Caesar or the Confederates putting in an appearance, it could stand just about anything. When the last troops marched out of South Carolina, removing federal protection from the last vestige of the state's Republican government, it carried the last vestige of the postwar period's alarms with it. And the rest was silence.

"I think th' country is goin' to th' divvle," said Mr. Hinnissy, sadly.

"Hinnissy," said Mr. Dooley, "if that's so I congratylate th' wurruld."

"How's that?" asked Mr. Hinnissy.

"Well," said Mr. Dooley, "f'r nearly forty years I've seen this country goin' to th' divvle, an' I got aboord late. An' if it's been goin' that long an' at that rate, an' has got no nearer thin it is this pleasant Chris'mas, thin th' divvle is a divvle iv a ways further off thin I feared."

—Finley Peter Dunne, "National Housecleaning"

THE DOG THAT BARKED
TOO MUCH AT NIGHT

One of the most famous Sherlock Holmes stories has as its clue the curious behavior of the watchdog that failed to bark at night; this book may be seen as the story of watchdogs who barked all the time and, because they set up such a steady yammering, ended up not heard by later historians and by a growing number of their own contemporaries. No sentinel is likely to be believed if he supposes every bush a bear, and there comes the moment when the things he feared rise before him, and he gives the alarm—and no one comes. One irony of Reconstruction was that fears that were never more than fond fancies were roused so well that when they had been laid to rest and other terrors rose the will to believe was gone.

That may give a clue to the larger failure of Reconstruction as a "second American revolution." Henceforth, Republican administrations' dealings with the South would be based on the promise "let us have peace." Necessarily, then, presidents could not intervene without provocation. They gave up their ability to set the pace of change; they would let southerners, black and white, Republican and Democrat, set it for them and define what their obligations were. The Republican Party had chosen to surrender the initiative. It would never really get it back.

THIS FORMULATION, THOUGH, assumes what we cannot assume, that most Americans saw the main purpose of Reconstruction as a second American revolution at all. In that sense, it would indeed prove a failure—though that failure seemed less clear, unambiguous, and complete in 1877 than in retrospect. But in another quite conservative sense—which we cannot capture because the phantasmagoria, the midnight fantasies, and the stump speech terrors of the late 1860s seem like no more than fustian to people for whom the securing of the Union was sure, certain, and complete and must have seemed so, from the surrender of Kirby-Smith's army, if not those of Lee and Johnston—Reconstruction had not failed at all. Its goal was to assure that the main purpose of the war would be fulfilled—of a Union held intact forever: of a North and South able to work together, a Union free of slavery, where sectional rivalries would not burst out in internecine war or in vaunting appeals to state sovereignty, backed by armed force.

That may explain, too, why the second American revolution was defeated by the very success of Reconstruction. The terrors of a Confederacy reborn, of secret armies of traitors, were the strength of the Union movement in the North, but they depended on voters believing in them. The fears would be there for a generation longer. But, increasingly, they lost their audience, and the more fearful prospects became increasingly unlikely. As they did so, Republicans had to look to backup threats, not quite so dire. There would be wild allegations of Confederate plots to destroy the North by lowering the tariff. Or that Texas would split itself into five states, giving the South dominance of the Senate. Or that the Confederate war debt would be paid simply by declaring that no Rebel debts could be paid because there *were* no Rebels any more. Everyone was loyal, and everyone's losses could be reimbursed. But none of these struck the same kind of alarm.

The defense of equal rights depended, in effect, not on a sense of justice alone but also on a sense of urgency and the need for protections for the Union. By 1875, it was plain to any thinking person—which is to say just about anyone who was not a newspaper editor—that the Union would not be undone, that, however much they prided themselves on their southernness, white southerners would never go out of the Union, would never seek a new war. Every dedication of a Confederate war memorial added to that sense. Nostalgia was not a danger, and there was nothing more soothing than ceremonies, all done in the spirit of elegy, for a Lost Cause—a cause recognized as lost beyond recovery.

But does not the panic of 1865, 1866, 1867, 1868 ad infinitum suggest another lesson? It may well be that the moderates had a stronger case than we have

"Farewell, a Long Farewell, to All My Greatness." Thomas Nast, *Harper's Weekly*, March 13, 1869. It was not a king but a cardinal, Wolsey, in Shakespeare's *Henry VIII*, who uttered Johnson's line. Nor was it the end of Johnson's greatness. Later generations of biographers would portray him as a hero battling against a sea of fanatics and Negro lovers and, indeed, as the true heir of Abraham Lincoln's policies.

perceived. In their desire to make southern reconstruction and restoration as quick as was practicable and to keep federal intervention at a minimum, they recognized that drastic remedies have toxic side effects.[1] The more the Constitution was stretched, bent, and scrutinized for loopholes and the longer the sectional crisis went on, the harder it became to return to some kind of political normalcy and to political discourse as comparatively reasoned debate. Every drastic measure gave opponents an excuse for drastic countermeasures. Any polity seen as illegitimate almost invites illegitimate means for its overthrow. Certainly that was among the stronger reasons why "respectable" white southern politicians could apologize for, wink at, or participate in the atrocities of the Ku Klux Klan. They were not just restoring a social system based on white supremacy and near-peonage for black tenant farmers; they were undoing governments made by unconstitutional laws passed by an illegal Congress and based on an electorate that to white conservative minds never had any legitimate right to share power.

The consequences of too quick a reconstructing and too weak a federal involvement were terrible ones for "America's unfinished revolution." Arguably they were one reason why it was unfinished. Not all fears were false, nor were all those that proved unfounded so foolish, so unreasonable. As the Klan violence proved over and over, there were conspiracies afoot, murderous plots to overthrow freedom and to subvert state governments. But the moderates were right to worry about the radical alternative, of a system where emergencies were normal and fear, not trust, was the basis of policymaking, of a system where parties saw their opponents as enemies of the republic, to be eliminated by any means possible. Fear bred a dangerous kind of politics and, ultimately, one that was uncontrollable. Reconstruction on terms fitting our own ideas of justice was attainable, for a price; but the price may well have been a republic likely to endure.

In a way, the nightmare-mongers had been right all along. They had blamed events, from the decrees of a feckless king to the defiance of a reckless president, on sinister, unseen forces. Unseen forces there were: fear and suspicion, misapprehension and resentment over a constitutional order gone forever with the war. They sat in council at Washington and stalked the southern countryside. For them there needed be no Reconstruction, no restoration. And from them, there would be no Redemption.

Notes

ABBREVIATIONS

ADAH   Alabama Department of Archives and History, Montgomery
AMA   American Missionary Association Records
BaltSun   *Baltimore Sun*
BRFAL   Bureau of Refugees, Freedmen, and Abandoned Lands
CG   *Congressional Globe*
ChaCou   *Charleston (S.C.) Daily Courier*
ChMer   *Charleston (S.C.) Mercury*
ChN&C   *Charleston (S.C.) News and Courier*
ChiTi   *Chicago Times*
ChiTrib   *Chicago Tribune*
CinCom   *Cincinnati Commercial*
CinEnq   *Cincinnati Enquirer*
CinGaz   *Cincinnati Gazette*
ClPD   *Cleveland Plain Dealer*
DetFP   *Detroit Free Press*
HL   Huntington Library, San Marino, California
H. Rept.   House Report
HSP   Historical Society of Pennsylvania, Philadelphia
ISHS   Illinois State Historical Society, Springfield
IoSDAH   Iowa State Department of Archives and History
Ku Klux Testimony   Testimony for H. Rept. 22, "Affairs in the Late Insurrectionary States"
LC   Library of Congress
LLIU   Lilly Library, Indiana University, Bloomington
LSU   Hill Library, Louisiana State University, Baton Rouge
MDAH   Mississippi Department of Archives and History, Jackson
MHS   Massachusetts Historical Society, Boston
MemApp   *Memphis Daily Appeal*
NHHS   New Hampshire Historical Society, Concord
NYDaN   *New York Daily News*
NYEP   *New York Evening Post*
NYH   *New York Herald*
NYPL   New York Public Library, New York
NYSL   New York State Library, Albany
NYTi   *New York Times*
NYTrib   *New York Tribune*
NYW   *New York World*
OHS   Ohio Historical Society, Columbus
PhilA   *Philadelphia Age*

PROLOGUE

1. *ClPD*, October 11, 1866, among many other newspapers.

2. "Impeachment of the President," H. Rept. 7, testimony: 45–51, 419–20.

3. Indeed, Michael Les Benedict pointed the way toward the origins of this book in one of his voluminous endnotes in *Compromise of Principle*, 434–35. But the scholarly attention to fear of renewed civil war dates back further, to William A. Russ's article, "Was There Danger of a Second Civil War during Reconstruction?" 39–58. Russ and I would agree in answering no; whether Republicans believed that there was such a danger and in some cases felt it a serious danger is another matter.

4. Hofstadter, *Paranoid Style in American Politics*, 3–40.

5. The phrase "unfinished revolution" can be found in Foner, *Reconstruction*, which remains, for our time, the irreplaceable guide to the era. The words, "second revolution" were common enough. For an example, see "Northern Illinois," editorial in *ChiTrib*, October 18, 1864.

CHAPTER 1

1. Lorant, *Glorious Burden*, 68.

2. "Con-g-ss Embark'd on Board the Ship Constitution of America Bound to Conogocheque by way of Philadelphia" and "The Grand National Caravan Moving East," in Reilly, *American Political Prints*, 6–7, 54–55.

3. David Brion Davis, *Fear of Conspiracy*, 11.

4. A comprehensive compendium of conspiracy theories has appeared in a two-volume reference work. See Knight, *Conspiracy Theories in American History*.

5. Haynes, *Invisible Power*, xiii–xvi; Hibbard, *Charles I and the Popish Plot*, 188–93, 198–203, 232–38.

6. Miller, *Popery and Politics in England*, 154–88, 214–16; Kenyon, "Birth of the Old Pretender," 418–26.

7. Wood, "Conspiracy and the Paranoid Style," 401–41; Bailyn, *Ideological Origins of the American Revolution*, 35–50; Cruickshanks, *Political Untouchables*, 42–47.

8. Scott, *Commonwealth Principles*, 19–40.

9. Bailyn, *Ideological Origins of the American Revolution*, 85–90, 110–26, 145–48; David Brion Davis, *Fear of Conspiracy*, 23–28, 30, 33; Davidson, *Propaganda and the American Revolution*, 125–27.

10. For inquisitions into secret traitors in the Revolution, see Paltsits, *Minutes of the Com-*

missioners, 1:9–61. For later fears, see David Brion Davis, *Fear of Conspiracy*, 36–52; Stewart, *Opposition Press of the Federalist Period*, 428–29, 442–44, 492; and, most comprehensive, Knox, "Conspiracy in American Politics," 1–45.

11. On the uses of republican vocabulary, see Hess, *Liberty, Virtue, and Progress*; Wilentz, *Chants Democratic*; Holt, *Political Crisis of the 1850s*; and Howe, *Political Culture of the American Whigs*. On the mixing of liberal and republican traditions, see Kloppenberg, "Virtues of Liberalism," 9–33; Ross, "Transformation of Republican Ideology"; and Banning, "Jeffersonian Ideology Revisited," 3–19.

12. Victor E. Piollett to William Bigler, November 21, 1864, Bigler MSS, HSP; *Bradford Reporter* (Towanda, Pa.), September 20, 1848; *Erie (Pa.) Observer*, March 25, 1848; *Easton Whig and Journal*, June 21, 1848; J. Muir to William S. Meredith, September 11, 1849, Meredith MSS, HSP; *ClPD*, September 25, 1850. On the persistent refusal to accept a two-party system's legitimacy, Neely, *Union Divided*, 4–6, 120–25, should not be overlooked.

13. John W. Andrews to Thomas Ewing, March 2, 1861, Ewing MSS, LC; Miles, "Whig Party and the Menace of Caesar," 361–79.

14. John E. Wool to Nathaniel P. Banks, January 6, 1861, Banks MSS, LC; *Columbus Ohio State Journal*, September 20, 28, October 12 (Arnold), 1850; *ClPD*, September 23, October 2, 1850.

15. On Whig fears and the evidence on which many of them had good reasons for feeling concern, see Howe, *Political Culture of the American Whigs*, 87–92; Howe, *What Hath God Wrought*, 411, 421–30; Brown, *Politics and Statesmanship*, 24–30; and Kruman, "Second American Party System," 523–24. For Democratic fear of power being concentrated, the following remain especially valuable: Thornton, *Politics and Power*; and Watson, *Jacksonian Politics and Community Conflict*.

16. *Philadelphia Daily News*, February 10, 1854; *Galena (Ill.) Weekly North-Western Gazette*, October 1, 1850; note also Diggins, *Lost Soul of American Politics*, 105–9, 118.

17. David Brion Davis, *Fear of Conspiracy*, 82–83, 92–94.

18. Freehling, "Spoilsmen and Interests," 25–42; Ford, "Republican Ideology in a Slave Society," 405–24; *ChMer*, July 10, 11, 1860; Howe, *Political Culture of the American Whigs*, 43–68 (on John Quincy Adams); Shields, *Line of Duty*; *CinGaz*, October 9, 1856.

19. Hartnett, *Democratic Dissent*, 85–86; Anbinder, *Nativism and Slavery*; Whitney, *Defence of the American Policy*, 229.

20. O. Freeman to Thomas Ewing, May 1, 1854, Thomas Ewing MSS, LC. That there was a Slave Power, if not a conspiracy, is fully substantiated in Richards, *Slave Power*. On the specifics of the conspiracy theory, see ibid., 1–27; Gienapp, "Republican Party and the Slave Power," 53–74; and Gienapp, *Origins of the Republican Party*, 356–62.

21. *CG*, appendix, 36th Cong., 1st sess., p. 355; Pfau, "Place of Conspiracy"; James Anderson to Stephen A. Douglas, December 25, 1857, Douglas MSS, University of Chicago; Foner, *Free Soil, Free Labor, Free Men*, 87–101; *CinGaz*, June 24, 1856.

22. Bergeron, *Papers of Andrew Johnson*, 10:492; James Walker to James Buchanan, August 17, 1856, Buchanan MSS, HSP; *ClPD*, August 21, 26, October 6, 1846, July 23, September 23, 1856; *Nashville Republican Banner and Nashville Whig*, July 28, 1855.

23. Thornton, *Politics and Power*, 212–20; *ChMer*, July 11, 18, 27, August 2, 1860; "Independent," *ChaCou*, August 30, 1860; Carey, *Parties, Slavery, and the Union*, 166–67.

24. Johnson, *Toward a Patriarchal Republic*, 45; Carey, *Parties, Slavery, and the Union*, 239–

41; "Terrorism for the South," in *ChMer*, July 30, 1860; Thornton, *Politics and Power*, 217–21; *ChaCou*, September 17, 1860. That distrust of white southerners has its fullest and most eloquent coverage in William W. Freehling's two exhilarating volumes, *Secessionists at Bay* and *Secessionists Triumphant*.

25. "Lyrics to the South," *ChMer*, July 24, 1860.

26. Barney, *Road to Secession*, 154, 158.

27. Craig M. Simpson, *Good Southerner*, 204–18; William C. Davis, *Rhett*, 380–81; Freehling, *Secessionists Triumphant*, 211–21.

28. Freehling, *Secessionists Triumphant*, 330–31, 336–37, 367–71; Johnson, *Toward a Patriarchal Republic*, 34–36, 43–45; *ChMer*, July 4, 20, 24, 1860; *ChaCou*, September 12, 21, 28, October 13, 1860; Barney, *Road to Secession*, 148–50, 158; *CG*, 36th Cong, 2d sess., appendix, 298 (March 2, 1861).

29. Channing, *Crisis of Fear*, 22–55; Barney, *Secessionist Impulse*, 166–80; *ChaCou*, August 29, October 10, 1860; Link, *Roots of Secession*, 178–95, 214–17; Baum, *Shattering of Texas Unionism*, 58–59.

30. *ClPD*, August 10, 1860; see also *NYTrib*, June 4, 1861.

31. *PhilPr*, July 2, 1860.

32. Perkins, *Northern Editorials on Secession*, 51–53, 71–73; *ClPD*, September 11, 13, 1860; *PhilPr*, June 30, 1860.

33. Johannsen, *Stephen A. Douglas*, 777; "Occasional," *PhilPr*, August 22, 1860.

34. Stampp, *And the War Came*, 7–10; Vallandigham, *Life of Clement Vallandigham*, 208–9; E. Peshine Smith to Henry C. Carey, March 2, 1854, Carey MSS, HSP. On the ex-Democratic exceptions, see Foner, *Free Soil, Free Labor, Free Men*, 179–81.

35. *CinGaz*, August 2, 29, 1860; *Indianapolis Daily State Sentinel*, November 2, 1860.

36. Stampp, *And the War Came*, 13–15; *Indianapolis Daily Journal*, November 10, 1860; Alfred Brooks to Henry C. Carey, December 25, 1860, Carey MSS, HSP.

37. Wakelyn, *Southern Unionist Pamphlets*, 18–23, 246; Brownlow, *Sketches of the Rise*, 92–94, 158–76; *CG*, 39th Cong., 1st sess., 156 (January 9, 1866), 501 (January 30, 1866).

38. See William W. Freehling's compelling dissection of the South Carolina secession moment, in *Secessionists Triumphant*, 398–412.

CHAPTER 2

1. Nevins and Thomas, *Diary of George Templeton Strong*, 3:67 (December 1, 1860), 87–88 (January 9, 1861).

2. Ibid., 3:99 (February 13, 1861). Rumors of a plan to seize Washington were plentiful enough to inspire a congressional hearing, which found nothing. For a lingering belief in some plot to seize Washington, see Nicolay and Hay, *Abraham Lincoln*, 3:135–38, 3:143–44.

3. Nevins and Thomas, *Diary of George Templeton Strong*, 3:69–90 (January 15, 1861), 3:93 (January 26, 1861). On Mayor Fernando Wood's intentions, see McKay, *Civil War and New York City*, 33–37.

4. Nevins and Thomas, *Diary of George Templeton Strong*, 3:67 (December 1, 1860), 3:102 (February 23, 1861), 3:107 (March 7, 1861); *Diary of a Public Man*, 38–40. On the facts of Lincoln's journey, see Nicolay and Hay, *Abraham Lincoln*, 3:302–16. The story about Wigfall is discredited in King, *Louis T. Wigfall*, 105–6.

5. Craig M. Simpson, *Good Southerner*, 241–42, 247–51.

6. John A. Trimble to Horatio Seymour, March 17, 1863, Trimble MSS, OHS; J. J. Bingham to Charles Lasselle, May 10, 1864, Lasselle MSS, Indiana State Library, Indianapolis; *Luzerne (Pa.) Union*, October 5, 1864.

7. *CinGaz*, November 3, 4, December 15, February 26, 1863; *CG*, 37th Cong, 3d sess., appendix, 67 (January 27, 1863).

8. *Philadelphia Public Ledger*, October 7, 1864; Silbey, *Respectable Minority*, 18–23; Vallandigham, *Life of Clement Vallandigham*, 138–40.

9. Silbey, *Respectable Minority*, 66–70, 94–96.

10. Clement Vallandigham to John A. Trimble, January 1864, Trimble MSS, OHS.

11. *Albany (N.Y.) Atlas and Argus*, February 3, 1862; *PhilA*, August 26, September 24, 1863, September 29, 1864, January 26, 1865; *CinEnq*, April 12, 26, May 2, 15, 1862. For rebuttal of the disunion charges, see 36th Cong., 2d sess., 1393 (March 2, 1861). For a nuanced evaluation of disunionism, even among abolitionists, see the unsurpassable Kenneth M. Stampp, *And the War Came*, 247–50.

12. *PhilA*, September 23, 1863; Klement, *Copperheads in the Middle West*, 17–18; *New York Weekly News*, November 17, 1863; *CinEnq*, April 2, 9, 24, 28, May 18, 1862; *CinGaz*, October 1, 1862.

13. *CG*, 37th Cong., 3d sess., appendix, 67 (January 27, 1863); Vallandigham, *Life of Clement Vallandigham*, 179–204; *New York Weekly News*, June 9, 1863; *CinEnq*, April 16, 1862.

14. Lawson, *Patriot Fires*, 101–24.

15. Ibid., 90–97.

16. *Uniontown (Pa.) Genius of Liberty*, October 20, 1864; *ISRSpr*, November 4, 1864.

17. Wubben, *Civil War Iowa and the Copperhead Movement*, 113–15, 166–69; *PhilA*, September 2, 1863; *Luzerne (Pa.) Union*, November 9, 1864.

18. Neely, *Fate of Liberty*, 51–138; Wubben, *Civil War Iowa and the Copperhead Movement*, 53–57, 64–69; Klement, *Copperheads in the Middle West*, 18–23; *CG*, 37th Cong., 3d sess., appendix, 67 (January 27, 1863); *PhilA*, June 2, 1863; *CinEnq*, April 9, 16, 24, 28, May 18, 1862.

19. *CG*, 38th Cong., 2d sess., 859 (February 17, 1865); *New York Weekly News*, November 28, 1863; Wagandt, *Mighty Revolution*, 156–81.

20. John Vanhook to John G. Davis, October 29, 1863, Davis MSS, Indiana Historical Society, Indianapolis; *Boston Daily Advertiser*, October 25, 1864; C. M. Gould to Samuel S. Cox, October 16, 1864, Cox MSS, Brown University, Providence, R.I.; *Luzerne (Pa.) Union*, November 30, 1864.

21. M. Birchard to Samuel S. Cox, March 10, 1864, Cox MSS, Brown University, Providence, R.I.; J. D. Stiles to Lewis Coryell, July 1, 1863, Coryell MSS, HSP; James W. Wall letter, in *PhilA*, October 26, 1863; *New York Weekly News*, June 9, 1863.

22. *Luzerne (Pa.) Union*, August 31, 1864; D. A. Farley to John G. Davis, November 18, 1863, Davis MSS, Indiana Historical Society, Indianapolis. For similar warnings of ruin, see *Uniontown (Pa.) Genius of Liberty*, August 25, 1864.

23. *Luzerne (Pa.) Union*, November 2, 1864.

24. Dyer, *Secret Yankees*, 33–35; Klement, *Dark Lanterns*, 7–14; *ChMer*, August 1, 1860; *NY-Trib*, January 5, 1861.

25. Roland, *Albert Sidney Johnston*, 249; Gilbert, "Mythical Johnston Conspiracy," 165–73; *CinEnq*, April 4, 5, 7, 1862; Klement, *Dark Lanterns*, 15–16.

26. For Clement Vallandigham's dissection of the Sons of Liberty's purposes and impact, see his speech, reprinted in Vallandigham, *Life of Clement Vallandigham*, 381–85.

27. *CinGaz*, October 1, 2, 1862, February 26, 1863; *NYTrib*, August 8, 1862.

28. *CG*, 37th Cong., 3d sess., appendix, 67 (January 27, 1863); *CinGaz*, October 29, 1862, February 19, 26, 1863; Klement, *Dark Lanterns*, 64–75; Thornbrough and Corpuz, *Diary of Calvin Fletcher*, 8:5–6 (January 2, 1863), 8:10 (January 5, 1863), 8:12 (January 7, 1863), 8:16 (January 11, 1863), 8:17–20 (January 11, 1863); Patrick and Willey, *Fighting for Liberty and Right*, 62 (January 24, 1863).

29. Thornbrough and Corpuz, *Diary of Calvin Fletcher*, 8:105 (April 6, 1863), 8:143n (May 21, 1863).

30. Klement, *Dark Lanterns*, 151–68; Churchill, "Highest and Holiest Duty of Freemen," 198–200.

31. *Malone (N.Y.) Palladium*, September 1, 1864; *Sacramento Daily Union*, October 18, 24 (quote), 1864; *Boston Daily Advertiser*, October 13, 1864; Klement, *Dark Lanterns*, 176–77.

32. Churchill, "Highest and Holiest Duty of Freemen," 173–79, 202; *Dayton (Ohio) Daily Empire*, October 31, 1864; *ISRSpr*, October 18, 1864; *Malone (N.Y.) Palladium*, September 1, 1864; *CinEnq*, April 19, 1862. On the alarm the plank raised, see *Philadelphia Public Ledger*, October 7, 1864.

33. *Dayton (Ohio) Daily Empire*, November 15, 1864; Klement, *Copperheads in the Middle West*, 237; *PhilA*, November 5, 1864.

34. *Sacramento Daily Union*, July 28, 1864.

35. Salmon P. Chase to George S. Denison, November 11, 1864, Denison MSS, LC.

36. Klement, *Copperheads in the Middle West*, 242–43; Wagandt, *Mighty Revolution*, 260–63; *Dayton (Ohio) Daily Empire*, November 11, 1864; *PhilA*, November 4, 1864; *Boston Daily Advertiser*, October 25, November 10, 1864; William P. Davis to John G. Davis, October 24, 1864, Davis MSS, Indiana Historical Society, Indianapolis.

37. *Dayton (Ohio) Daily Empire*, November 15, 1864; *PhilA*, April 12, 1865; W. D. Latshaw to John G. Davis, May 12, 1865, Davis MSS, Indiana Historical Society, Indianapolis.

38. "Agate," *CinGaz*, April 17, 1865; ibid., May 1, 1865.

39. Turner, *Beware the People Weeping*, 46.

40. Nevins and Thomas, *Diary of George Templeton Strong*, 3:582 (April 15, 1865).

41. Turner, *Beware the People Weeping*, 94–95; Diary, Samuel P. Richards MSS, May 14, 1865, Atlanta Historical Society; Miers, *When the World Ended*, 92; Samuel L. M. Barlow to Montgomery Blair, April 21, 1865, Barlow MSS, HL.

42. Thomas and Hyman, *Stanton*, 421–22; Turner, *Beware the People Weeping*, 45–46; J. H. Dillon to Samuel L. M. Barlow, May 10, 1865, Barlow MSS, HL; Cadwallader manuscript, 802–4, ISHS; Leonard, *Lincoln's Avengers*, 10, 53–54, 63–65.

43. Turner, *Beware the People Weeping*, 125–37; for one use of that tainted evidence, see "Argument of John A. Bingham, Special Judge Advocate," 64, 72.

44. Leonard, *Lincoln's Avengers*, 112, 202–7, 220–21; Logan, *Great Conspiracy*, 643–44.

45. "Agate," *CinGaz*, April 17, 1865; J. B. Bacon to Benjamin F. Butler, April 20, 1865, George S. Boutwell to Butler, April 20, 1865, Butler MSS, LC; Turner, *Beware the People Weeping*, 69–70.

46. Turner, *Beware the People Weeping*, 61–62, 136–37; Leonard, *Lincoln's Avengers*, 34–35; *Pottsville (Pa.) Miners' Journal*, April 29, 1865. For lasting suspicions that Rebels and Val-

landigham "'[gave] it to him,' and that he died of it," see *Steubenville (Ohio) Weekly Herald*, September 19, 1866.

47. Singer, *Confederate Dirty War*, 118–40; Guttridge and Neff, *Dark Union*; Higham, *Murdering Mr. Lincoln*.

48. "Argument of John A. Bingham, Special Judge Advocate," 53–62; Headley, *Confederate Operations*, 264–80; Singer, *Confederate Dirty War*, 51–99.

49. Crist, *Papers of Jefferson Davis*, 11:160; Turner, *Beware the People Weeping*, 94–96.

50. Kauffman, *American Brutus*, 128–29.

51. Ibid., 142, 212–13, 251.

52. Ibid., 399–400.

53. Turner, *Beware the People Weeping*, 96–97; Rubin, *Shattered Nation*, 126–30.

54. Scarce, but not nonexistent. See Nevins and Thomas, *Diary of George Templeton Strong*, 3:586 (April 16, 1865); and Wubben, *Civil War Iowa and the Copperhead Movement*, 199.

55. Turner, *Beware the People Weeping*, 97–99; Nevins and Thomas, *Diary of George Templeton Strong*, 4:159 (October 31, 1867); *St. Lawrence (N.Y.) Plaindealer*, March 19, October 1, 1868; *Jamestown (N.Y.) Journal*, October 30, 1868; *NYTrib*, July 14, 1868; *Kennebec Journal* (Augusta, Maine), April 22, 1868; *PhilPr*, November 2, 1868; *Tuscaloosa (Ala.) Independent Monitor*, February 19, 1868. On Dean, see *St. Louis Missouri Republican*, July 29, 1868.

56. Logan, *Great Conspiracy*, 559–62.

CHAPTER 3

1. Rable, "Despair, Hope, and Delusion," 129–55; *Raleigh (N.C.) Sentinel*, November 3, December 24, 27, 28, 1864; Anderson, *Brokenburn*, 316.

2. Miers, *When the World Ended*, 90.

3. "Agate," *CinGaz*, April 10, 1865; "Two Diaries from Middle St. John's, Berkeley, South Carolina, February–May 1865," published by the St. John's Hunting Club, 1921, p. 41.

4. Miers, *When the World Ended*, 95, 97; Childs, *Private Journal of Henry William Ravenel*, 228, 232; Towles, *World Turned Upside Down*, 474; Anderson, *Brokenburn*, 313, 335. On the backdrop and larger meaning of the rumors, see Rubin, *Shattered Nation*, 124–25.

5. Mott, *American Journalism*, 360–65; Summers, *Press Gang*, 11–24.

6. Fitzgerald, *Urban Emancipation*, 53–55; O'Donovan, "Transforming Work," 179.

7. O'Donovan, "Transforming Work," 193.

8. Carter, *When the War Was Over*, 195–97; Grimsted, *American Mobbing*, 116–17, 136, 171–77. For the many-headed aspects of racial contempt and fear, see Wood, *Black Scare*, 1–39.

9. Rose, *Rehearsal for Reconstruction*; McFeely, *Yankee Stepfather*, 97–106.

10. *New Orleans Tribune*, November 19, 1865; *Augusta (Ga.) Loyal Georgian*, January 27, 1866; Smith, Smith, and Childs, *Mason Smith Family Letters*, 236; Rawick, *American Slave*, 6 (Alabama and Indiana narratives), 344–45; William Henry Trescot to his wife, March 11, 20, 1866, Trescot MSS, South Caroliniana Collection, Columbia. On the corrective lectures given the freedmen, see "Reports of Assistant Commissioners of the Freedmen's Bureau," Sen. Exec. Doc. 27, 14, 82.

11. R. Plumb to James A. Garfield, December 12, 1865, Garfield MSS, LC; O'Donovan, "Transforming Work," 191.

12. Hahn, "Extravagant Expectations," 122–42; Childs, *Private Journal of Henry William*

Ravenel, 258; see also Mahaffey, "Carl Schurz's Letters from the South," 241; James L. Orr to Andrew Johnson, January 19, 1866, in Registers and Letters Received by the Commissioner of the BRFAL, reel 24; "Reports of Assistant Commissioners of the Freedmen's Bureau," Sen. Exec. Doc. 27, 14, 85.

13. Carter, *When the War Was Over*, 191–93; Dennett, *South As It Is*, 56, 190; Berlin, *The Black Military Experience*, 748. The quintessential source on the scare of 1865 is Carter, "Anatomy of Fear," 145–64.

14. *NYDaN*, November 27, 1865; H. L Jaragin, James H. Rives, Randos Sherrod, W. M. Conner, and others, to Benjamin G. Humphreys, October 31, 1865, Governor's Papers: Humphreys MSS, MDAH.

15. Berlin, *The Black Military Experience*, 748; *MemApp*, November 22, 1865; Carter, *When the War Was Over*, 194–95; "Bolivar" to William Sharkey, September 4, 1865, Governor's Papers: Sharkey MSS, MDAH.

16. Litwack, *Been in the Storm So Long*, 425, 428; W. P. Coleman to J. Madison Wells, October 25, 1865, Union Provost Marshal's Files of Papers Relating to Two or More Civilians, reel 65, National Archives; "Druid," *NYDaN*, November 7, 11, 1865; Andrews, *South since the War*, 179; *BaltSun*, December 4, 22, 1865.

17. "J. G. S.," *NYDaN*, October 10, 1865; *BaltSun*, November 25, 28, December 23, 25, 1865; Towles, *World Turned Upside Down*, 490.

18. Litwack, *Been in the Storm So Long*, 426; A. C. Smart to Major-General Gillmore, August 26, 1865, Union Provost Marshal's Files of Papers Relating to Two or More Civilians, reel 64; Samuel Matthews to John H. Matthews, November 19, 1865, Matthews MSS, MDAH.

19. Dennett, *South As It Is*, 78; Myers, *Children of Pride*, 1296, 1366; Williams, *Papers of William Alexander Graham*, 6:329.

20. Litwack, *Been in the Storm So Long*, 426.

21. Carter, *When the War Was Over*, 202–4; Litwack, *Been in the Storm So Long*, 426; Crouch, "Spirit of Lawlessness," 224; Schurz, *Reminiscences*, 3:170–72.

22. Litwack, *Been in the Storm So Long*, 426–27; Trowbridge, *The South*, 408.

23. *MemApp*, November 24, 1865; *NYW*, November 7, 1865.

24. *BaltSun*, November 9, 1865; *ChaCou*, November 24, 1865; *MemApp*, November 19, 22, 1865; *NYW*, November 8, 1865.

25. *NYW*, October 11, November 29, 1865.

26. *NYDaN*, November 1, 1865; *MemApp*, November 22, 25, 1865; *BaltSun*, November 11, 16, 1865; *ChaCou*, November 23, December 19, 1865; Bergeron, *Papers of Andrew Johnson*, 9:422.

27. Semmel, *Jamaican Blood and Victorian Conscience*, 15–18, 46–55; Oliver, *Jamaica*, 172–85; *NYTrib*, November 27, December 18, 1865; *NYEP*, November 23, December 4, 1865. The "fiends" appear in "Astille's" letter from Jamaica, *NYDaN*, October 31, 1865.

28. Wood, *Black Scare*, 120–21; Carter, *When the War Was Over*, 200–201; *NYH*, December 1, 1865; *Nashville Daily Union and American*, December 17, 1865; *ChaCou*, December 19, 1865; "Leo," *ChaCou*, January 5, 1866; *ChMer*, November 27, 1866.

29. *Christian Recorder* (Philadelphia), July 1, 1865; *NYTrib*, December 8, 1865; Trowbridge, *The South*, 138; S. G. Wright to Whipple, December 4, 1865, AMA: Mississippi; Mahaffey, "Carl Schurz's Letters from the South," 242.

30. Berlin, *The Black Military Experience*, 752–54; Carter, *When the War Was Over*, 197–98; Alvan C. Gillem to Joseph Fowler, December 19, 1865, Fowler MSS, SHC.

31. Dennett, *South As It Is*, 176, 240–41.

32. Andrews, *South since the War*, 179; *Nashville Daily Press and Times*, January 3, 1866; A. Warren Kelsey to Edward Atkinson, November 13, December 6, 1865, Atkinson MSS, MHS.

33. *ChaCou*, January 5, 1866; *Nashville Daily Press and Times*, January 2, 1866.

34. Litwack, *Been in the Storm So Long*, 429–30; *NYTrib*, January 1, 1866; "Reports of Assistant Commissioners of the Freedmen's Bureau," Sen. Exec. Doc. 27, 14, 65, 97; *MemApp*, December 26, 1865; *BaltSun*, December 27, 28, 1865.

35. Greenawalt, "Virginians Face Reconstruction," 454; Nicholson Diary, January 22, 1866, MDAH.

36. *Augusta (Ga.) Loyal Georgian*, January 20, 1866.

37. Thomas J. Wood to Benjamin G. Humphreys, January 8, 1866, Governor's Papers: Humphreys MSS, MDAH; "Reports of Assistant Commissioners of the Freedmen's Bureau," Sen. Exec. Doc. 27, 65; Berlin et al., *Free at Last*, 523–24.

38. Zuczek, *State of Rebellion*, 20; Smith, Smith, and Childs, *Mason Smith Family Letters*, 251; *Nashville Daily Union and American*, December 14, 1865; *NYTrib*, November 28, 1865; Dennett, *South As It Is*, 275; Rufus Saxton to Oliver O. Howard, December 19, 1865, Registers and Letters Received by the Commissioner of the BRFAL, reel 24; Oscar J. E. Stuart to Benjamin G. Humphreys, n.d. [late 1865], Governor's Papers: Humphreys MSS, MDAH.

39. Hahn, "Extravagant Expectations," 147–54; *MemApp*, December 24, 1865; *BaltSun*, December 21, 1865; Litwack, *Been in the Storm So Long*, 428.

40. A. C. Smart to Major-General Gillmore, August 26, 1865, Union Provost Marshal's Files of Papers Relating to Two or More Civilians, reel 24; Berlin, *The Black Military Experience*, 748. On the Black Codes' gun ownership provisions, see Roberta Sue Alexander, *North Carolina Faces the Freedmen*, 49; *NYTrib*, January 25, 1866; and Shofner, *Nor Is It Over Yet*, 54–55. On the confiscation of freedpeople's guns, see "Reports of Assistant Commissioners of the Freedmen's Bureau," Sen. Exec. Doc. 27, 6; and *Augusta (Ga.) Loyal Georgian*, February 3, 1866.

41. J. H. Johnson to General John Ely, March 8, 1866, Registers and Letters Received by the Commissioner of the BRFAL, reel 28; Dennett, *South As It Is*, 193–94; see also Ash, *Middle Tennessee Society Transformed*, 197, 203.

42. Crouch, "Spirit of Lawlessness," 217–32; "Reports of Assistant Commissioners of the Freedmen's Bureau," Sen. Exec. Doc. 27, 8, 78–79, 83; William Goodloe to C. B. Fisk, January 31, 1866, Records of the Assistant Commissioner for the State of Tennessee, BRFAL, reel 10; Stuart Barnes to Colonel O. Brown, December 30, 1865, in Registers and Letters Received by the Commissioner of the BRFAL, reel 25; A. Warren Kelsey to Edward Atkinson, November 13, 1865, Atkinson MSS, MHS.

43. Litwack, *Been in the Storm So Long*, 429; *Jackson (Miss.) Daily Clarion*, April 29, 1868; *New Orleans Daily Picayune*, January 8, 15, 1868; Saville, *Work of Reconstruction*, 144. For a black plot to create a "Santo Domingo" in Louisiana, see *Montgomery (Ala.) Mail*, October 10, 1867.

44. Bergeron, *Papers of Andrew Johnson*, 13:257.

45. Ku Klux Testimony: Alabama, vol. 3, H. Rept. 22, part 10, 42d Cong., 2d sess., 1662, 1687; *Jackson (Miss.) Daily Clarion*, April 28, 1868; *MemApp*, September 30, 1868; *NYW*, December 30, 1867; J. J. Bailey to Robert M. Patton, September 16, 1867, Patton MSS, ADAH. On the

fire engine, see M. G. Candee and C. C. Colton to — Adams, [July 22, 1867], Swayne MSS, ADAH.

46. Snay, *Fenians, Freedmen, and Southern Whites*, 69–70; Saville, *Work of Reconstruction*, 145–47; *Raleigh (N.C.) Sentinel*, August 15, 1866; Frank B. Conner to Lemuel P. Conner, May 16, 1867, Conner MSS, LSU; F. C. Hall to Robert M. Patton, July 3, 1867, Patton MSS, ADAH.

47. "S.," *NYW*, December 13, 1867; "Ubique," *NYTi*, December 7, 1867, January 6, 1868; Saville, *Work of Reconstruction*, 149; Ku Klux Testimony: Georgia, vol. 1, H. Rept. 22, part 6, 42d Cong., 2d sess., p. 108.

48. There were, of course, other reasons for secrecy. See Snay, *Fenians, Freedmen, and Southern Whites*, 70–79.

49. Milledge Bonham to Robert K. Scott, August 19, 1868, Governor's Papers: Scott MSS, South Carolina State Archives, Columbia; *Tuscaloosa (Ala.) Independent Monitor*, August 4, 1868; Gilbert Pillsbury to Franklin J. Moses, March 16, 1868, Scott MSS, OHS; Fitzgerald, *Union League Movement in the Deep South*, 67–69.

50. A. M. Dorman to Wager Swayne, June 14, 1867, Swayne MSS, ADAH; "Y. S.," *CinGaz*, December 18, 1867; *NYW*, December 13, 14, 17 (*Montgomery Mail* quotation), 23, 1867.

51. (*Mobile (Ala.) Nationalist*, May 17, 1866. For another "negro riot," in Savannah, where the rioters committed the outrage of holding a meeting in their church and disturbed the peace by trying to defend themselves when police with guns and knives broke into the building and began killing them, see *CinGaz*, February 26, 1868.

52. Ash, *Middle Tennessee Society Transformed*, 195, 240; *Memphis Daily Avalanche*, August 22, 1866.

53. Perman, *Reunion without Compromise*, 145–46; Bergeron, *Papers of Andrew Johnson*, 9:164.

CHAPTER 4

1. Childs, *Private Journal of Henry William Ravenel*, 228–30; Anderson, *Brokenburn*, 340.

2. Patrick and Willey, *Fighting for Liberty and Right*, 335; Nevins and Thomas, *Diary of George Templeton Strong*, 3:598 (May 15, 1865); see also Silber, "Intemperate Men, Spiteful Women, and Jefferson Davis," 295–303.

3. *NYW*, March 14, 1864; John McKim to J. Miller McKim, March 10, 1866, McKim-Maloney-Garrison MSS, Columbia University, New York.

4. Brownson, *American Republic*, 310–11. More than any other source, McKitrick, *Andrew Johnson and Reconstruction*, 93–119, has informed this chapter.

5. *Memphis Daily Avalanche*, August 25, 1866; *ChaCou*, June 12, 1866; McKitrick, *Andrew Johnson and Reconstruction*, 97–98.

6. *CG*, 39th Cong., 1st sess., 151 (January 9, 1866); *ChiTi*, September 8, 1866; *CinEnq*, August 5, 10, 1867; William Bigler to J. D. Stiles, May 14, 1865, Bigler MSS, HSP; Bergeron, *Papers of Andrew Johnson*, 9:309.

7. Belz, *Reconstructing the Union*, 209–10; McKitrick, *Andrew Johnson and Reconstruction*, 101–2, 108–10; Burgess, *Reconstruction and the Constitution*, 36–37; *CG*, 39th Cong., 1st sess., 156 (January 9, 1866).

8. *ChiTi*, August 11, 1866; *NYW*, February 20, 1864 (quote), July 20, 21, September 19, 1865;

CG, 39th Cong., 1st sess., 445 (January 26, 1866), 467 (January 27, 1866); *Hartford (Conn.) Daily Times*, April 1, 1868; James Dixon to William M. Grosvenor, December 15, 1865, Grosvenor MSS, Columbia University, New York.

9. McKitrick, *Andrew Johnson and Reconstruction*, 99–101; *CG*, 39th Cong., 1st sess., 467 (January 27, 1866); *CG*, 40th Cong., 2d sess., 2736 (June 1, 1868); *CinGaz*, July 22, 1865.

10. See Boutwell, *Reminiscences of Sixty Years*, 2:105. For an endorsement, made slightly conditional, note the speech of Halbert E. Paine of Wisconsin, *CG*, 39th Cong., 1st sess., 564–65 (January 31, 1866).

11. *CG*, 39th Cong., 1st sess., 142–45 (January 8, 1866), 562–64 (January 27, 1866); *NYTrib*, December 6, 1865; Burgess, *Reconstruction and the Constitution*, 56–60; Sumner, "Our Domestic Relations."

12. Belz, *Reconstructing the Union*, 133–35; *CG*, 39th Cong., 1st sess., 900 (February 17, 1866); *NYEP*, September 25, 1865; *ChaCour*, July 31, 1865.

13. Bancroft, *Speeches, Correspondence, and Political Papers of Carl Schurz*, 1:407; *CinGaz*, June 15, 17, 1865; see also *Nation*, February 28, March 7, 1867; *Boston Evening Transcript*, August 19, 1865; defense of Johnson by John A. Bingham of Ohio, in *CG*, 39th Cong., 1st sess., 157 (January 9, 1866); and the detailed argument by Samuel Shellabarger, in ibid., 143 (January 8, 1866).

14. Belz, *Reconstructing the Union*, 168–69, 206–8; *CG*, 39th Cong., 1st sess., 27 (December 12, 1865).

15. *CG*, 39th Cong., 1st sess., 290, 295 (January 18, 1866), 901 (February 17, 1866); *NYTrib*, November 25, 1865; *CinGaz*, June 6, 1865.

16. Vorenberg, *Final Freedom*, 33; Trefousse, *Radical Republicans*, 301–2, 316; *CinGaz*, November 16, 1865.

17. Belz, *Reconstructing the Union*, 235–39; Cox and Cox, *Politics, Principle, and Prejudice*, 139–43. The president's presumed role and the divergence between conservative and radical Republican constitutional theories have their best exposition in Benedict, *Compromise of Principle*, 122–26.

18. *NYEP*, November 20, 1867; Vorenberg, *Final Freedom*, 30, 41–42, 133. This caution applies (though with much less force) to radicals like Charles Sumner of Massachusetts. Charles Sumner to Francis Lieber, May 2, October 12, 1865, in Palmer, *Selected Letters of Charles Sumner*, 2:300, 2:337.

19. Bogue, *Earnest Men*, 305–10.

20. Cox and Cox, *Politics, Principle, and Prejudice*, 134–37.

21. Ibid., 57–58; *CG*, 39th Cong., 1st sess., 153, 156–57 (January 9, 1866).

22. *CG*, 39th Cong., 1st sess., 151 (January 9, 1866); *CinCom*, September 18, November 19, 1865.

23. *NYDaN*, April 14, 1866.

24. Perman, *Reunion without Compromise*, 173–79. The phrase comes from "Brick" Pomeroy's *La Crosse (Wis.) Daily Democrat*, July 11, 1866, one of the most widely quoted northern Democratic newspapers in the South.

25. On Stevens's response to the Caledonia's destruction, see W. A. McGinley to Edward McPherson, May 18, 1865, McPherson MSS, LC; Korngold, *Thaddeus Stevens*, 214–15.

26. Morse, *Diary of Gideon Welles*, 2:571 (August 7, 1866); Stewart, "Journal of James Mallory," 229; *Pittsburgh Daily Post*, October 9, 1866.

27. Donald, *Charles Sumner and the Rights of Man*, 139–40; *CinEnq*, July 30, 1867; Woolfolk, *World's Crisis*, 501–4; *ChaCou*, December 29, 30, 1865.

28. *NYW*, September 17, 1866; *PhilA*, September 29, 1864; *CG*, 39th Cong., 1st sess., 199 (January 11, 1866); *CinEnq*, July 30, 1867; *Hartford (Conn.) Daily Times*, March 31, 1868.

29. "Druid," *NYDaN*, October 30, 1865; *Raleigh (N.C.) Sentinel*, August 29, 1866; N. G. Smiler to Charles Mason, February 22, 1866, Mason MSS, IoSDAH; *ChiTi*, November 6, 1866; *Hartford (Conn.) Daily Times*, April 1, 1868 (Voorhees quote).

30. M. C. Johnson to Benjamin G. Humphreys, December 29, 1866, Governor's Papers: Humphreys MSS, MDAH; *Hartford (Conn.) Daily Times*, March 31, 1868; *ChaCou*, January 3, 1866; Woolfolk, *World's Crisis*, 634.

31. Note, for example, *ChaCou*, December 29, 1865; *MemApp*, February 3, 1866; *Raleigh (N.C.) Sentinel*, July 19, 1866; and *PhilA*, January 25, February 5, 12, 1867.

32. *Alexandria Gazette and Virginia Advertiser*, November 1, 1866; Morse, *Diary of Gideon Welles*, 2:635 (December 7, 1866); Bergeron, *Papers of Andrew Johnson*, 9:164, 9:233; O. R. Boyles to Thomas A. R. Nelson, January 22, 1866, Nelson MSS, McClung Historical Collection, Knox County Public Library System, Knoxville.

33. Woolfolk, *World's Crisis*, 509–12; Morse, *Diary of Gideon Welles*, 2:571 (August 4, 1866); *Raleigh (N.C.) Sentinel*, August 31, 1866.

34. "Leo," *ChaCou*, April 6, 1866; Donald, *Charles Sumner and the Rights of Man*, 143–46, 230–36, 247–54.

35. *Indianapolis Daily Herald*, May 31, 1866; *Raleigh (N.C.) Sentinel*, June 23, August 21, 29, 31, September 1, 14, 1866; Roark, *Masters without Slaves*, 183–84.

36. This extreme phrase came from Peace Democrat C. C. Burr, a New Jersey editor and publicist, at the Jefferson birthday anniversary dinner in 1866. See *NYDaN*, April 14, 1866.

37. *Nashville Daily Press and Times*, August 23, 1866; W. B. Wood to Robert M. Patton, May 17, 1866, Patton MSS, ADAH; "Leo," *ChaCou*, May 14, 1866; "Sumter," *ChaCou*, May 10, 1866; Perman, *Reunion without Compromise*, 195.

38. Gideon Welles to Mark Howard, December 12, 1865, Howard MSS, Connecticut Historical Society, Hartford; *Erie (Pa.) Observer*, September 7, 1867; *NYW*, September 1, 1868; *Hartford (Conn.) Daily Times*, March 16, 1868.

39. *CG*, 39th Cong., 1st sess., 3–4 (December 4, 1865); *Concord Monitor*, March 2, 1868.

40. Vorenberg, *Final Freedom*, 77, 110–11, 134–35; *CG*, 39th Cong., 1st sess., 400–402 (January 30, 1866); *Raleigh (N.C.) Sentinel*, September 14, 17, 29, 1866.

41. *CG*, 39th Cong., 1st sess., 355 (January 22, 1866).

42. *ChMer*, November 21, 1866; "Letter from MM. deGasparin, Martin, Cochin, and Laoulaye, to the Loyal Publication Society of New York" (n.p., 1866), p. 8, in John Sherman Pamphlet Collection, RBHL; *CinGaz*, April 18, 1865; *NYW*, March 2, 1867.

43. *PhilA*, January 5, 25, February 4, 1867.

44. *NYW*, July 20, November 9, 1865; *DetFP*, November 3, 1865; *Nashville Daily Union and American*, December 9, 1865; Bergeron, *Papers of Andrew Johnson*, 11:339–40; *Augusta (Ga.) Loyal Georgian*, January 27, 1866.

45. *CinGaz*, August 9, 18, 1866.

46. *ChaCou*, January 1, 1866; *Baton Rouge Tri-Weekly Advocate*, May 12, 1866; *CinGaz*, May 23, 1866; *NYDaN*, April 10, 1866; *NYW*, April 9, 1866.

47. *MemApp*, February 3, 1866; *Louisville (Ky.) Daily Courier*, April 9, 1866; *ChaCou*, April

11, August 2, 1866; *Baton Rouge Tri-Weekly Advocate*, April 14, 1866; *NYDaN*, April 7, 11, 28, 1866.

48. *NYTrib*, July 3, 1865; see also Hamilton, *Correspondence of Jonathan Worth*, 1:536.

49. *MemApp*, February 3, 1866; Bergeron, *Papers of Andrew Johnson*, 11:339.

50. *CinGaz*, September 25, October 7, 1865; Carter, *When the War Was Over*, 228–30. In fact, most of the southerners elected had been, at best, Johnny-Rebs-come-lately. Some had been peace candidates. Only one in eleven had stood with the secessionists before Lincoln's election; half had balked until their states left the Union. And three of the governors elected eventually joined the Republicans.

CHAPTER 5

1. "J. Q.T.," *CinCom*, May 19, 1866.

2. Charles Nordhoff to Godwin, February 16, 1869, Bryant-Godwin MSS, NYPL; Jacob D. Cox to James Monroe, November 21, 1866, Cox MSS, Oberlin College, Oberlin, Ohio.

3. Milton, *Age of Hate*, 74–90. Johnson's life gets its best treatment in Trefousse, *Andrew Johnson*; but no one should miss the keen-eyed, unsparing overview in McKitrick, *Andrew Johnson and Reconstruction*, 85–92.

4. Bergeron, *Papers of Andrew Johnson*, 3:64, 3:256.

5. "Gath," *ChiTrib*, April 10, 1869.

6. Trefousse, *Andrew Johnson*, 189–91; Henry L. Dawes to his daughter, December 8, 1866, Dawes MSS, LC; "Gath," *ChiTrib*, April 10, 1869.

7. Elbert B. Smith, *Francis Preston Blair*, 381, 385–86; Morse, *Diary of Gideon Welles*, 2:364 (August 21, 1865).

8. Cox and Cox, *Politics, Principle, and Prejudice*, 53–58; "Douglas," *ChaCou*, July 28, 1865; Elbert B. Smith, *Francis Preston Blair*, 221–25, 334–40; Morse, *Diary of Gideon Welles*, 2:248–49 (February 22, 1865), 2:369–71 (August 30, 1865).

9. Bergeron, *Papers of Andrew Johnson*, 8:247. Blair certainly had tried to draw Democratic support for the amendment. See Vorenberg, *Final Freedom*, 183–85.

10. Bergeron, *Papers of Andrew Johnson*, 8:516–23.

11. Cox and Cox, *Politics, Principle, and Prejudice*, 214–15; McKitrick, *Andrew Johnson and Reconstruction*, 312, 517.

12. Morse, *Diary of Gideon Welles*, 2:244 (February 21, 1865), 2:247–48 (February 22, 1865), 2:331–32 (July 11, 1865), 2:405 (December 28, 1865), 2:437 (February 22, 1866).

13. Morse, *Diary of Gideon Welles*, 2:447, 2:449 (March 9, 1866); Niven, *Gideon Welles*, 515–17, 534.

14. Morse, *Diary of Gideon Welles*, 2:330 (July 10, 1865), 2:363–64 (August 19, 1865), 2:369 (August 30, 1865).

15. Bergeron, *Papers of Andrew Johnson*, 10:406.

16. Bowen, *Andrew Johnson and the Negro*, 48–52; for fuller coverage of Johnson's views toward blacks before the war, see Bowen, "Andrew Johnson and the Negro," 28–49.

17. Or so one of those friends told Congressman William D. Kelley of Pennsylvania. See *CG*, 40th Cong., 2d sess., 1347 (February 22, 1868).

18. McKitrick, *Andrew Johnson and Reconstruction*, 88–89; Bergeron, *Papers of Andrew Johnson*, 9:154–55, 9:245.

19. Benedict, *Compromise of Principle*, 140–45; Morse, *Diary of Gideon Welles*, 2:387 (December 3, 1865).

20. *ChiTrib*, December 24, 1865, January 19, 1866; *NYTi*, December 15, 1865; *NYTrib*, December 15, 1865; *CG*, 39th Cong., 1st sess., 74 (December 18th, 1865), 111–12 (December 21, 1865), 145 (January 8, 1866), 182 (January 10, 1866), 293–96 (January 18, 1866).

21. *CG*, 39th Cong., 1st sess., 78–79 (December 19, 1865); Palmer, *Selected Letters of Charles Sumner*, 2:353–54.

22. Morse, *Diary of Gideon Welles*, 2:395 (December 11, 1865), 2:398 (December 18, 1865), 2:417 (January 15, 1866).

23. Morse, *Diary of Gideon Welles*, 2:387 (December 3, 1865), 2:412 (January 8, 1866), 2:437–38 (February 22, 1866), 2:452 (March 10, 1866), 2:544 (June 30, 1866), 2:555 (July 18, 1866), 2:635 (December 7, 1866).

24. *CinGaz*, February 8, 1866; Philip Ripley to Manton Marble, February 8, 1866, Marble MSS, LC; *NYW*, February 10, 1866. A dramatic rendering of the set-to appears in Oakes, *Radical and the Republican*, 249–55.

25. *NYTi*, December 25, 1865; *NYTrib*, December 25, 1865; McKitrick, *Andrew Johnson and Reconstruction*, 175–84; Lionel A. Sheldon to James A. Garfield, January 19, 1866, Garfield MSS, LC.

26. "The offspring of an intrigue," Welles thought—for which no proof exists. Morse, *Diary of Gideon Welles*, 2:385 (December 1, 1865), 2:410 (January 3, 1866).

27. Morse, *Diary of Gideon Welles*, 2:387 (December 3, 1865), 2:432 (February 13, 1866). Johnson's fear was based on a misreading of the Constitution. For the misreading and a clarification, see *Indianapolis Daily Herald*, January 17, 1866; *ChiTrib*, March 17, 1866; *Balt-Sun*, November 28, 1865; *CG*, 39th Cong., 1st sess., 153 (January 9, 1866), 468 (January 27, 1866).

28. Trefousse, *Andrew Johnson*, 226–33; Benedict, *Compromise of Principle*, 126–31, 144–45.

29. McKitrick, *Andrew Johnson and Reconstruction*, 179–82, 255–57, 315–18; Cox and Cox, *Politics, Principle, and Prejudice*, 130–39.

30. McPherson, *Political History of the United States of America*, 45.

31. Sumner, "One Man Power vs. Congress," 12–15; William Bigler to J. D. Stiles, May 14, 1865, Bigler MSS, HSP. See also Palmer, *Selected Letters of Charles Sumner*, 2:298–300. For an evaluation of the two men's dealings that gives Johnson every benefit of the doubt, see Milton, *Age of Hate*, 176–78.

32. Wendell Phillips to Moncure Conway, September 12, 1865, McKim-Maloney-Garrison MSS, Columbia University, New York; "The Dangers of the Hour: An Address Delivered at Concert Hall, Philadelphia, March 15, 1866, by Hon. Wm. D. Kelley" (Washington: Chronicle Book and Job Print, 1866), in John Sherman Pamphlet Collection, RBHL; Benedict, *Compromise of Principle*, 103–8.

33. Benedict, *Compromise of Principle*, 109–10; Wendell Phillips to Moncure Conway [probably October 1865], Conway MSS, Columbia University, New York.

34. Benedict, *Compromise of Principle*, 127–31; *Kennebec Journal* (Augusta, Maine), June 23, 1865; William Dennison to Jacob D. Cox, July 19, 1865, Cox MSS, Oberlin College, Oberlin, Ohio; Schurz, *Reminiscences*, 3:157; Boutwell, *Reminiscences of Sixty Years*, 2:103; Donald, *Charles Sumner and the Rights of Man*, 225–29, 236–38.

35. Benedict, *Compromise of Principle*, 155–56; McKitrick, *Andrew Johnson and Reconstruction*, 279–91; Bergeron, *Papers of Andrew Johnson*, 10:120–27.

36. Maslowski, *Treason Must Be Made Odious*, 53–90.

37. Hugh McCulloch to H. H. Van Dyck, February 24, 1866, McCulloch MSS, LLIU; James Rood Doolittle to Orville H. Browning, October 7, 1866, Browning MSS, ISHS; "R.J. H.," *Milwaukee Sentinel*, March 2, 1866.

38. Bergeron, *Papers of Andrew Johnson*, 10:145–57; *NYH*, February 23, 1866.

39. Morse, *Diary of Gideon Welles*, 2:439 (February 23, 1866); Ezra Fogg to Thomas Jenckes, February 23, 1866, Jenckes MSS, LC. For a sharp rebuff to the assassination and annihilation charges, see L. Maria Child, "The President of the United States," *Independent* (New York), March 8, 1866.

40. Joseph H. Geiger to John Sherman, February 24, 1866, Craft J. Wright to Sherman, February 27, 1866, John Sherman MSS, LC; M. S. Wilkinson to Henry S. Lane, March 14, 1866, Lane MSS, LLIU; Del Mussey to William Henry Smith, February 23, 1866, Smith MSS, OHS; James Parton to Benjamin F. Butler, March 16, 1866, Butler MSS, LC.

41. Hunt, *Israel, Elihu, and Cadwallader Washburn*, 119; John Wien Forney to Wayne MacVeagh, March 4, 1866, MacVeagh MSS, HSP.

42. O. White to John Sherman, March 4, 1866, John Sherman MSS, LC; Lewis Barker to William Pitt Fessenden, March 8, 1866, Fessenden Family MSS, Bowdoin College Library, Brunswick, Maine.

43. *CinCom*, April 21, 1866; John L. Potter to Elihu B. Washburne, March 4, 1866, Washburne MSS, LC; *Pottsville (Pa.) Miners' Journal*, March 10, 1866.

44. McKitrick, *Andrew Johnson and Reconstruction*, 298–319; Cox and Cox, *Politics, Principle, and Prejudice*, 192–206; *CinGaz*, March 19, 1866; *CG*, 40th Cong., 2d sess., 1348 (February 22, 1868); *CinCom*, March 1, 1866.

45. *NYW*, March 31, April 2, 1866; "Druid," *NYDaN*, April 7, 1866; John P. Verree to Elihu B. Washburne, April 12, 1866, Washburne MSS, LC. On the possible coup, see *CinGaz*, March 19, 1866; *ChiTrib*, March 29, 1866; *NYTrib*, April 6, 1866.

46. *ChiTrib*, March 31, 1866; *Baton Rouge Tri-Weekly Advocate*, April 14, 1866; "Mack," *CinCom*, April 2, 4, 6, 1866.

47. "Mack," *CinCom*, April 6, 1866; *Baton Rouge Tri-Weekly Advocate*, April 21, 1866.

48. Bergeron, *Papers of Andrew Johnson*, 10:455. On the Memphis and Norfolk riots, see *NYDaN*, May 15, 1866.

49. *CinCom*, March 3, May 1, 1866; *Independent* (New York), March 22, 1866; *NYTrib*, April 6, 1866; Bergeron, *Papers of Andrew Johnson*, 10:529; *NYDaN*, May 30, 1866.

50. On proposals for a Johnsonian coup, see *NYDaN*, December 8, 1865, April 7, 9, 11, 13, 17, 19, 26, 28, 1866.

51. *Louisville (Ky.) Daily Courier*, April 9, 1866; "Sumter," *ChaCou*, April 11, 1866; *NYTrib*, April 6, 1866.

52. Childs, *Private Journal of Henry William Ravenel*, 278; "Leo," *ChaCou*, April 9, 1866.

53. Thomas Affleck to his sons, February 12, 1867, Affleck MSS, LSU; "Leo," *ChaCou*, April 9, 1866; *CinCom*, April 21, 1866; Bergeron, *Papers of Andrew Johnson*, 10:410–11; *Rutland (Vt.) Weekly Herald*, May 3, 1866.

54. William Pitt Fessenden to William H. Fessenden, March 31, 1866, Fessenden Family MSS, Bowdoin College Library, Brunswick, Maine; "Sumter," *ChaCou*, April 11, 1866.

1. On the making of the Fourteenth Amendment, see McKitrick, *Andrew Johnson and Reconstruction*, 336–55; and Benedict, *Compromise of Principle*, 69–70, 182–87.

2. Thorndike, *Sherman Letters*, 276.

3. *PhilA*, July 19, September 7, 1866; Morse, *Diary of Gideon Welles*, 2:555 (July 18, 1866); *Boston Post*, October 31, 1866; M. Y. Johnson to Charles Mason, September 1, 1866, Mason MSS, IoSDAH.

4. Turner, *Beware the People Weeping*, 65; *CinGaz*, July 3, 1866. Similar conspiracy theories can be found expressed in *NYTrib*, May 16, 1868; *Milwaukee Sentinel*, March 5, 1866; *Milwaukee Wisconsin*, June 30, 1866, citing Dye's book; and *Findlay (Ohio) Hancock Jeffersonian*, October 5, 1866.

5. *Washington Chronicle*, January 13, 1866 (attack on Wade); *CinGaz*, July 3, 4, 1866; *Indianapolis Daily Journal*, September 11, 1866; *Steubenville (Ohio) Weekly Herald*, September 19, 1866.

6. *Pottsville (Pa.) Miners' Journal*, April 28, 1866; *CinCom*, October 30, 1866. For similar allegations, which the speaker claimed to have believed in 1866, see *CG*, 40th Cong., 2d sess., 1347 (February 22, 1868); and, more obliquely, ibid., appendix, 108 (February 24, 1868). See also the assertions of one Republican speaker, recalled two years after by the skeptical *Memphis Daily Post*, May 22, 1869. For a proper rebuke of the charges, see *CG*, 40th Cong., 2d sess., appendix, 54–62 (December 5, 1867), 199 (February 24, 1868).

7. *CinEnq*, July 23, 1866, August 12, 1867; *Richmond (Va.) Daily Dispatch*, July 7, 1866.

8. *CinEnq*, July 23, 1866; *La Crosse (Wis.) Daily Democrat*, July 20, 1866; *Indianapolis Daily Herald*, September 10, 1866; *PhilA*, September 25, 1866; *CinGaz*, September 11, 1866; L. M. Smith to Benjamin F. Butler, November 15, 1866, Butler MSS, LC; *Findlay (Ohio) Hancock Jeffersonian*, October 5, 1866; *CinCom*, October 3, 1866.

9. Henry Cooke to Jay Cooke, June 13, 21 (quote), 1866, Cooke MSS, HSP; "Mack," *CinCom*, June 18, 1866; "D.W. B.," *Independent* (New York), July 26, 1866.

10. Williams, *Diary and Letters of Rutherford B. Hayes*, 29; *CinGaz*, July 18, 1866; Henry L. Dawes to Electa Dawes, July 12, 1866, Dawes MSS, LC; "R. V. W. S." to Thurlow Weed, July 12, 1866, Weed MSS, University of Rochester, Rochester, N.Y.

11. *CinGaz*, July 16, 1866; Henry L. Dawes to Electa Dawes, July 15, 17, 1866 (quote), Dawes to Electa Dawes, July 19, 1866, Dawes MSS, LC.

12. *Nashville Daily Press and Times*, July 12, 16, 1866.

13. *CinGaz*, July 12, 13, 14, 18, 1866; *Nashville Daily Press and Times*, July 5, 9, 1866; — to Elihu B. Washburne, July 14, 1866, Washburne MSS, LC.

14. Hollister, *Life of Colfax*, 287; *Nashville Daily Press and Times*, July 17, 20, 21, 1866; McBride, "Blacks and the Race Issue," 125–27.

15. Morse, *Diary of Gideon Welles*, 3:554–55 (July 17, 1866); "Y. S.," *CinGaz*, July 23, 1866.

16. The bias of the southern dispatchers for the Associated Press was well known to Republican editors and frequently commented on. See *ChiTrib*, August 4, 1866; see also Henry R. Gardner's letter to his parents, July 31, 1866, printed in Shewmaker and Prinz, "Yankee in Louisiana," 293.

17. *New Orleans Times*, July 31, August 1, 2, 1866; "S.," in *NYW*, August 13, 1866.

18. Reynolds, "New Orleans Riot of 1866 Reconsidered," 26.

19. *NYW*, August 6, 13, 1866; *Raleigh (N.C.) Sentinel*, August 6, 1866; Charles Leaumont testimony, "New Orleans Riots," H. Rept. 16, 255. The *New Orleans Times* declared that Dostie, in his dying statement, had admitted to planning to cause a bloodbath. The actual words it quoted, "I had reason to be apprehensive—to fear a bloody attack," might be open to other interpretations. *New Orleans Times*, August 2, 1866.

20. *New Orleans Times*, July 18, August 1, 3, 1866; *Pittsburgh Daily Post*, August 10, 1866; *PhilA*, February 13, 1867. The authoritative book on the New Orleans riot remains Hollandsworth, *An Absolute Massacre*, readable and swift paced, although, in its brief coverage of the Washington connection, in my opinion hasty in dismissing the congressmen's denials of involvement after the fact.

21. W. R. Fish to Nathaniel P. Banks, July 8, 1866, Banks MSS, LC; *New Orleans Times*, July 24, 28, 1866; "New Orleans Riots," H. Rept. 16, 263, 501–2, 540–41; *Pittsburgh Daily Post*, August 10, 1866; Edward Durell to his sister, July 28, 1866, Durell MSS, New-York Historical Society, New York.

22. The statement, reported by the *New Orleans Times*, July 18, 1866, may be made up, but it reflects Stevens's line on the Lincoln experiment from the first. Howell later testified that Stevens had been cool to the plan, but only because he preferred his own bill, already framed, to remake the state government. See Howell testimony, "New Orleans Riots," H. Rept. 16, 57.

23. "New Orleans Riots," H. Rept. 16, 23, 53, 57, 500; *New Orleans Times*, July 21, 22, 24, 1866. On Republicans' position and intentions, see "A.," in *Boston Daily Advertiser*, May 1, 1866; Thomas J. Durant to Henry Clay Warmoth, December 9, 1865, February 14, March 2, 1866, Warmoth MSS, SHC; Lionel A. Sheldon to James A. Garfield, December 16, 1865, Garfield MSS, LC; Uzee, "Beginnings of the Louisiana Republican Party," 209; and, most significant, *New Orleans Times*, July 21, 1866.

24. Testimony of Rufus K. Howell, "New Orleans Riots," H. Rept. 16, 49.

25. Ibid., 49; ibid., majority report, 22; *Pottsville (Pa.) Miners' Journal*, August 11, 1866; Vandal, "Origins of the New Orleans Riot," 149.

26. "New Orleans Riots," H. Rept. 16, 278–79.

27. John Gibbons to Nathaniel P. Banks, July 30, 1866, Banks MSS, LC.

28. B. Dally to Nathaniel P. Banks, July 31, 1866, Banks MSS, LC; Shewmaker and Prinz, "Yankee in Louisiana," 294; C. C. Morgan to Benjamin F. Butler, August 9, 1866, Butler MSS, LC.

29. *New Orleans Times*, August 2, 1866; *New Orleans Tribune*, September 2, 1866; *PhilA*, February 8, 13, 18, 1867; "New Orleans Riots," H. Rept. 16, 259; Reynolds, "New Orleans Riot of 1866 Reconsidered," 17–18.

30. Morse, *Diary of Gideon Welles*, 2:567 (August 2, 1866), 2:569 (August 3, 1866), 2:573 (August 6, 1866).

31. *ChiTrib*, August 21, 25, 27, 1866; McKitrick, *Andrew Johnson and Reconstruction*, 426–27.

32. Benedict, *Compromise of Principle*, 206.

33. *Baltimore American and Commercial Advertiser*, August 27, 1866.

34. Patton, *Unionism and Reconstruction in Tennessee*, 109–10.

35. Thomas B. Alexander, *Political Reconstruction in Tennessee*, 125–26; Bergeron, *Papers of Andrew Johnson*, 10:430, 10:512–13, 10:752–53, 11:90, 11:126–27.

36. — to Elihu B. Washburne, July 14, 1866, Washburne MSS, LC; *CinGaz*, July 13, 20, 1866; *Memphis Daily Avalanche*, August 21, 24, 40, September 11, 1866; *Nashville Daily Press and Times*, July 26, August 6, 9, 13, September 6, 1866; Bergeron, *Papers of Andrew Johnson*, 11:50.

37. Parrish, *Missouri under Radical Rule*, 88–97; W. M. Stone to Richard J. Oglesby, July 19, 1866, Oglesby MSS, ISHS; J. W. Strong to John D. Strong, October 3, 1866, Strong MSS, ISHS; *Memphis Daily Avalanche*, September 5, 1866; *Nashville Daily Press and Times*, August 22, 1866; S. T. Glover to Orville H. Browning, December 29, 1866, Browning MSS, ISHS.

38. Dearing, *Veterans in Politics*, 84–100; *Richmond (Ind.) Palladium*, October 4, 1866.

39. Dearing, *Veterans in Politics*, 105–6; *Indianapolis Daily Journal*, September 22, 1866; M. Y. Johnson to Charles Mason, September 1, 1866, Mason MSS, IoSDAH.

40. Randall, *Diary of Orville Hickman Browning*, 2:94 (September 21, 1866); Dearing, *Veterans in Politics*, 107; *PhilA*, October 9, 1866; *Indianapolis Daily Journal*, September 15, 19, 20, 1866.

41. Dearing, *Veterans in Politics*, 107–8, 119; *Boston Post*, October 31, 1866; M. Y. Johnson to Charles Mason, September 1, 1866, Mason MSS, IoSDAH.

42. John R. Cravens to Henry S. Lane, August 23, 1866, Lane MSS, LLIU; W. M. Stone to Richard J. Oglesby, July 19, 1866, Oglesby MSS, ISHS; Coulter, *William G. Brownlow*, 317; *Nashville Daily Press and Times*, August 4, 1866.

CHAPTER 7

1. *Kennebec Journal* (Augusta, Maine), September 7, 1866. Blair got his numbers wrong. There were 153 Republicans in the House. Only if Democrats picked up 30 seats in the North and admitted a solid Democratic South could they hope to control the chamber.

2. William Dickson to Robert M. Patton, July 29, 1866, Patton MSS, ADAH; *Rutland (Vt.) Weekly Herald*, July 26, 1866; McKitrick, *Andrew Johnson and Reconstruction*, 403–10; Bergeron, *Papers of Andrew Johnson*, 10:714.

3. McKitrick, *Andrew Johnson and Reconstruction*, 411–16; Benedict, *Compromise of Principle*, 194–95; *Nashville Daily Press and Times*, August 23, 1866.

4. *PhilNAm*, September 26, October 1, 1866; *Indianapolis Daily Journal*, September 15, October 8, 1866; *Baltimore American and Commercial Advertiser*, November 13, 1866; *Albany (N.Y.) Evening Journal*, September 13, 1866; Thomas H. Duval to Elisha M. Pease, August 9, 1866, Pease MSS, Austin Public Library, Austin, Texas.

5. Benedict, *Compromise of Principle*, 200–201; *NYTrib*, September 6, 7, 8, 1866; *ChiTrib*, September 7, 1866; *BaltSun*, September 7, 1866.

6. McKitrick, *Andrew Johnson and Reconstruction*, 428–37; *NYH*, August 31–September 4, 1866. The speeches, as published in the *New York Herald*, a newspaper sympathetic to Johnson and relatively complete in its coverage, show that the political content in his extemporaneous remarks broadened and sharpened as he moved through upstate New York, which may explain why it was not until the train crossed into Ohio that the unpleasantness began.

7. McKitrick, *Andrew Johnson and Reconstruction*, 436n; *Indianapolis Daily Journal*, September 13, 1866.

8. St. Louis speech in *CinCom*, September 10, 1866; Cincinnati speech (on the 8 million

hangings) in *Louisville (Ky.) Journal*, September 13, 1866; *CinEnq*, September 13, 1866; Clinton Fisk to Oliver O. Howard, September 10, 1866, Howard MSS, Bowdoin College Library, Brunswick, Maine.

9. *Findlay (Ohio) Hancock Jeffersonian*, September 7, 1866; *CinGaz*, August 27, 1866; Comitatus, *Reconstruction on "My Policy,"* 18.

10. *NYH*, September 6, 1866; *Albany (N.Y.) Evening Journal*, September 13, 1866; *Baltimore American and Commercial Advertiser*, November 13, 1866; *Indianapolis Daily Journal*, September 24, 25, 1866; *NYTrib*, October 29, 1866; *CinGaz*, September 11, 1866.

11. *NYTrib*, October 17, 1866; *Richmond (Va.) Daily Dispatch*, September 17, 20, 26, October 6, 1866.

12. *Elmira (N.Y.) Daily Advertiser*, October 11, 1866; *Richmond (Ind.) Palladium*, October 11, 1866; H. H. Van Dyck to Hugh McCulloch, October 11, 1866, McCulloch MSS, LLIU; Henry Cooke to Jay Cooke, October 11, 1866, Cooke MSS, HSP.

13. Henry D. Cooke to Jay Cooke, October 12, 1866, Cooke MSS, HSP; *NYW*, October 12, 1866; *CinCom*, October 16, 1866; "Impeachment Investigation," 40th Cong., 1st sess., H. Rept. 7, 45–51.

14. Henry Cooke to Jay Cooke (three letters), October 11, 1866, Cooke MSS, HSP; *Indianapolis Daily Journal*, September 24, 1866; *ChiTrib*, October 24, 1866; *Albany (N.Y.) Evening Journal*, September 13, 1866; *CinCom*, October 15, 1866; *Philadelphia Daily News*, October 10, 1866; *NYW*, October 12, 1866.

15. *NYTi*, September 28, 1866; *Findlay (Ohio) Hancock Jeffersonian*, October 5, 1866; *PhilA*, October 5, 1866; *CinEnq*, July 19, 1866; *Auburn (N.Y.) Daily Advertiser*, October 8, 1866.

16. *CinCom*, October 1, 1866; *Belleville (Ill.) Advocate*, October 5, 1866; *Indianapolis Daily Journal*, September 15, 26, 1866; *ChiTrib*, October 10, 1866; *Albany (N.Y.) Evening Journal*, September 13, 1866; *CinGaz*, October 2, 1866; *NYW*, July 11, 1866; *Malone (N.Y.) Palladium*, September 27, 1866.

17. Bancroft, *Speeches, Correspondence, and Political Papers of Carl Schurz*, 1:398; *Findlay (Ohio) Hancock Jeffersonian*, October 5, 1866.

18. James Speed to Henry S. Lane, August 6, 1866, Lane MSS, LLIU; Robert Dale Owen to Nathaniel P. Banks, July 18, 1866, Banks MSS, LC; Lucius Fairchild to —, September 15, 1866, Fairchild MSS, SHSW; *Auburn (N.Y.) Daily Advertiser*, November 2, 1866. For assurance that the North would crush such a rebellion, see *CinGaz*, July 20, September 28, 1866; *Cadiz (Ohio) Republican*, October 10, 1866; and *Rutland (Vt.) Weekly Herald*, September 20, 1866.

19. Bancroft, *Speeches, Correspondence, and Political Papers of Carl Schurz*, 1:414–15.

20. *Albany (N.Y.) Argus*, October 26, 1866; *Cadiz (Ohio) Sentinel*, September 26, October 3, 1866; *NYW*, July 20, September 18, 1866; *ChaCou*, September 27, October 1, 1866.

21. *ISRSpr*, November 3, 1866; *PhilA*, September 25, October 5, 6, 1866; *Philadelphia Daily News*, October 5, 1866; *Cadiz (Ohio) Sentinel*, October 3, 1866; *DetFP*, October 10, 1866; James B. Wall to Manton Marble, October 5, 1866, Marble MSS, LC. The same course may have been what Philadelphia's former mayor was driving at in a letter after the election. See Richard Vaux to William Bigler, December 23, 1866, Bigler MSS, HSP. An even more violent invitation to the president to "welcome the traitors with bloody hands to hospitable graves" appeared in the *Houston Telegraph*, quoted in *CinGaz*, September 20, 1866.

22. *Bangor (Maine) Whig and Courier*, October 9, 1866.

23. *CinGaz*, July 6, September 29, 1866; *Rutland (Vt.) Weekly Herald*, July 26, September 20, 1866; *Independent* (New York), July 26, 1866.

24. Morse, *Diary of Gideon Welles*, 2:556 (July 19, 1866); *Indianapolis Daily Journal*, September 19, 1866; *Cadiz (Ohio) Sentinel*, October 3, 1866; *Findlay (Ohio) Hancock Jeffersonian*, July 27, 1866; *Kennebec Journal* (Augusta, Maine), November 2, 1866.

25. Thomas Affleck to his sons, November 26, 1866, Affleck MSS, LSU; *Richmond (Va.) Daily Dispatch*, November 5, 1866.

26. Bergeron, *Papers of Andrew Johnson*, 11:322.

27. Ibid., 11:419.

28. Benedict, *Compromise of Principle*, 201–2; *ISRSpr*, September 28, 1866; *Peoria (Ill.) Daily National Democrat*, November 1, 1866.

29. County-by-county returns appear in the *Tribune Almanac, 1867*.

30. Samuel S. Cox to Manton Marble, October 1866, Marble MSS, LC; *NYTrib*, November 19, 1866; *NYTrib*, November 16, 1866; *Raleigh (N.C.) Sentinel*, November 12, 1866; *Richmond (Va.) Daily Dispatch*, November 12, 1866; Henry L. Dawes to Electa Dawes, December 7, 1866, Dawes MSS, LC.

31. *New Orleans Times*, November 9, 13, December 9, 13, 1866; *ChMer*, November 23, 24, 1866; *ChaCou*, October 5, 11, 1866; Hamilton, *Correspondence of Jonathan Worth*, 2:859–60.

32. *Richmond (Va.) Dispatch*, September 17, 1866; *New Orleans Times*, December 4, 1866; Samuel Shellabarger to James M. Comly, December 29, 1866, Comly MSS, OHS; R. Mills to Elisha M. Pease, November 24, 1866, Thomas H. Duval to Pease, November 20, 1866, Pease MSS, Austin Public Library, Austin, Texas.

33. Reuben Tomlinson to J. Miller McKim, October 25, 1866, McKim MSS, Cornell University Library, Ithaca; *(Mobile (Ala.) Register*, quoted in *NYW*, October 29, 1866; O. A. Pegram to James L. Orr, February 18, 1867, Governor's Papers: Orr MSS, South Carolina State Archives, Columbia.

34. *CG*, 39th Cong., 2d sess., 1847–52 (February 26, 1867).

35. Benedict, *Compromise of Principle*, 216–43; Perman, *Reunion without Compromise*, 270–72; John Forsyth to Manton Marble, March 5, 1867, Marble MSS, LC.

36. *NYW*, April 4, 1868; *Zanesville (Ohio) Daily Signal*, February 28, 1867; Childs, *Private Journal of Henry William Ravenel*, 304 (February 15, 1867).

37. Bancroft, *Speeches, Correspondence, and Political Papers of Carl Schurz*, 1:437–39; *NYW*, January 30, 1868.

38. *NYW*, February 28, 1867, April 4, 1868; *Zanesville (Ohio) Daily Signal*, March 14, 1867.

CHAPTER 8

1. *Indianapolis News*, October 24, 1885.

2. See Hyman, *Stanton*, 499; *Brooklyn (N.Y.) Daily Eagle*, July 26, August 3, 1885; *Indianapolis News*, October 23, 24, 1885. Washburne claimed that since Grant was sharing quarters with him at the time he certainly would have known if the general had felt any such fears. Letters from Grant and his aides at the time, however, make clear that Washburne misremembered: Grant was in Washington and Washburne in Galena that fall, and Washburne had been out of town since the end of July. Of course, that fact in itself does not disprove Washburne's essential point. See Simon, *Papers of Ulysses S. Grant*, 16:298–99, 16:342, 16:349.

3. Horace White to Elihu B. Washburne, March 25, 1866, John P. Verree to Washburne, April 12, 1866, L. H. Funk to Elihu B. Washburne, September 1, 1866, Washburne MSS, LC.

4. "R. J. H.," *Milwaukee Sentinel*, March 2, 1866; Morse, *Diary of Gideon Welles*, 2:573–74 (August 6, 1866), 2:580–81 (August 17, 1866), 2:611 (October 5, 1866); *NYW*, August 21, 24, 1866.

5. Thomas and Hyman, *Stanton*, 491, 493.

6. Brooks D. Simpson, *Let Us Have Peace*, 118–27; Brooks D. Simpson, "Grant's Tour of the South Revisited," 425–48. Simpson's account of Grant's postwar relations with the president and secretary cannot be improved on and, for precise accuracy throughout, far surpasses Thomas and Hyman's invaluable and convincingly sympathetic biography of Stanton. Sharp glints of insight also stud William S. McFeely's (necessarily shorter) account, in *Grant*, 252–57.

7. Benjamin F. Butler to Horace Greeley, September 20, 1866, Greeley MSS, LC, cited in Brooks D. Simpson, *Let Us Have Peace*, 152–53; Thomas and Hyman, *Stanton*, 503.

8. *CinCom*, March 6, 1868.

9. Brooks D. Simpson, *Let Us Have Peace*, 148–51.

10. "Impeachment of the President," H. Rept. 7, testimony, 833–34. See *Indianapolis News*, October 23, 24, 1885; Brooks D. Simpson, *Let Us Have Peace*, 153.

11. Brooks D. Simpson, *Let Us Have Peace*, 154.

12. *Baltimore American and Commercial Advertiser*, January 10, 26, 27, 1866.

13. Baker, *Politics of Continuity*, 153; *ChiTrib*, October 24, 1866; *Baltimore American and Commercial Advertiser*, July 2, August 24, 25, September 8, October 23, November 1, 1866.

14. *BaltSun*, October 8, 9, 11, 1866; *Baltimore American and Commercial Advertiser*, October 9, 17, 19, 1866.

15. *NYTrib*, October 16, 18, 1866; *Baltimore American and Commercial Advertiser*, October 16, 17, 19, 20, 1866.

16. *NYTrib*, October 19, 1866; *ChiTrib*, October 24, 1866; *CinCom*, October 26, 1866; George W. Lee to William H. Seward, October 22, 1866, Seward MSS, University of Rochester, Rochester, N.Y.

17. Special Washington correspondence, *NYTrib*, October 22, 1866.

18. *NYTrib*, October 22, 24, 1866.

19. *BaltSun*, October 23, 1866; *Baltimore American and Commercial Advertiser*, October 23, 1866.

20. "Mack," *CinCom*, January 6, 1868; Andrew Johnson to Edwin M. Stanton, October 25, 1866, in Bergeron, *Papers of Andrew Johnson*, 11:386.

21. Brooks D. Simpson, *Let Us Have Peace*, 154–55; William Tecumseh Sherman to James G. Blaine, November 21, 1885, Blaine MSS, LC.

22. This, in a somewhat more sinister casting, is the surmise of Stanton's biographers. See Thomas and Hyman, *Stanton*, 503. On Sherman being groomed for the post, see *BaltSun*, October 27, 29, 1866.

23. Brooks D. Simpson, *Let Us Have Peace*, 155; Simon, *Papers of Ulysses S. Grant*, 16:337–38.

24. If so, he must not have read an up-to-date newspaper. The *NYTrib* had rumors that Senator Cowan had been offered the War Department position and that Stanton had announced his intention to leave as soon as he finished his annual report. The stories were actu-

ally denied in newspapers October 18, though papers added that Stanton would soon resign and offered the significant addition that General Sherman's appointment to the position was probable. See *NYTrib*, October 16, 18, 1866.

25. Brooks D. Simpson, *Let Us Have Peace*, 155; Simon, *Papers of Ulysses S. Grant*, 16:337-38; Morse, *Diary of Gideon Welles*, 2:621 (November 17, 1866).

26. "Impeachment of the President," H. Rept. 7, testimony: 840-41; Simon, *Papers of Ulysses S. Grant*, 16:346-47; *BaltSun*, October 24, 1866; *NYTrib*, October 24, 1866. According to the paper's correspondent, Swann also conferred with Grant, which Grant in his letter to Johnson of October 24, 1866, corroborates.

27. Morse, *Diary of Gideon Welles*, 2:621 (November 17, 1866); Boutwell, *Reminiscences of Sixty Years*, 2:109. Grant described his response as declining as "respectfully as I could." Simon, *Papers of Ulysses S. Grant*, 16:357.

28. Simon, *Papers of Ulysses S. Grant*, 16:349.

29. Ibid., 16:350-54.

30. The refusal was made in response to one more request from the president, this time issued through the secretary of war. Grant's reply went into the circumstances of his earlier refusal in enough detail that the letter may have been meant for Stanton's eyes, as a reassurance that he would not be left unsupported by Grant's departure and as one more incentive to keep the secretary from resigning. Simon, *Papers of Ulysses S. Grant*, 16:357.

31. Ibid., 16:339-40, 16:359; Bergeron, *Papers of Andrew Johnson*, 11:417; Brooks D. Simpson, *Let Us Have Peace*, 155-58.

32. *NYTrib*, October 27, 29, 1866.

33. *BaltSun*, October 27, 1866; *Baltimore American and Commercial Advertiser*, October 23, 26, November 1, 2, 1866; *NYTrib*, November 2, 1866.

34. "Impeachment of the President," H. Rept. 7, testimony: 842-43; Brooks D. Simpson, *Let Us Have Peace*, 159; *NYTrib*, November 2, 1866.

35. Brooks D. Simpson, *Let Us Have Peace*, 160.

36. *NYTrib*, November 5, 1866.

37. Simon, *Papers of Ulysses S. Grant*, 16:362-63; Brooks D. Simpson, *Let Us Have Peace*, 160.

38. *NYTrib*, November 6, 1866.

39. *Baltimore American and Commercial Advertiser*, November 7, 10, 12, 13, 1866; *NYTrib*, November 6, 1866.

40. "Mack," *CinCom*, January 6, 1868; "Occasional," *PhilPr*, March 18, 1868; Samuel Harris to Zachariah Chandler, November 5, 1866, Zachariah Chandler MSS, LC; Brooks D. Simpson, *Let Us Have Peace*, 160-61.

41. Boutwell, *Reminiscences of Sixty Years*, 2:107-8; *CG*, 39th Cong., 2d sess., 1354 (February 19, 1867).

CHAPTER 9

1. See Benedict, *Compromise of Principle*, 246-51, 252-53, 255-56; McKitrick, *Andrew Johnson and Reconstruction*, 490, 493-94; and, much more sympathetically to Johnson, Sefton, *United States Army and Reconstruction*, 135-37.

2. Clemenceau, *American Reconstruction*, 102-3.

3. Bergeron, *Papers of Andrew Johnson*, 13:3; Morse, *Diary of Gideon Welles*, 3:195 (September 4, 1867), 3:203–5 (September 20, 1867).

4. *Washington Daily National Intelligencer*, September 16, 20, 1867.

5. Bergeron, *Papers of Andrew Johnson*, 13:26, 13:132, 13:152.

6. Perman, *Reunion without Compromise*, 323–24; *CinEnq*, September 26, 1867; Bergeron, *Papers of Andrew Johnson*, 13:175–76; Morse, *Diary of Gideon Welles*, 3:197 (September 7, 1867), 3:198 (September 9, 1867), 3:199 (September 11, 1867); H. H. Van Dyke to Hugh McCulloch, September 9, 1867, McCulloch MSS, LLIU.

7. *NYEP*, August 30, 1867; Sefton, *United States Army and Reconstruction*, 128–35; Morse, *Diary of Gideon Welles*, 3:94 (May 14, 1867), 3:96 (May 21, 1867).

8. Perman, *Reunion without Compromise*, 322–35; Sefton, *United States Army and Reconstruction*, 153–60.

9. Henry Stanbery to Orville H. Browning, June 30, 1867, Browning MSS, ISHS.

10. "Druid," *NYDaN*, April 2, 1866; Richard Jones to "my dear children," April 10, 1866, Wheeler Family MSS, ADAH; Childs, *Private Journal of Henry William Ravenel*, 295 (September 19, 1866); *NYW*, September 7, 1866; *ClPD*, October 5, 1866; *CinGaz*, August 11, 1866.

11. Benedict, *Impeachment and Trial of Andrew Johnson*, 23–36. On the argument for conviction without actual crimes, see *PhilNAm*, April 4, 7, 1868; and "Puritan" to William Pitt Fessenden, May 15, 1868, Fessenden Family MSS, Bowdoin College Library, Brunswick, Maine. On the need to disqualify from office, see Neal Dow to William Pitt Fessenden, April 6, 1868, ibid.

12. Horowitz, *Great Impeacher*, offers a sympathetic evaluation and a convincing vindication from corruption charges on pp. 80–83. For personal descriptions, see Duvergier de Hauranne, *Frenchman in Lincoln's America*, 2:342; Rutherford B. Hayes Diary, 7 (December 1, 1865), Hayes MSS, RBHL. For the distrust, see "Star" to Jay Cooke, January 4, 1867, Cooke MSS, HSP.

13. *Kennebec Journal* (Augusta, Maine), February 1, 8, 1867.

14. Summers, *Era of Good Stealings*, 6–7, 14–15, 26, 174–77.

15. Dorris, *Pardon and Amnesty*, 146–51; "Impeachment of the President," H. Rept. 7, minority report (Wilson), 96–101, 110–11; Milton, *Age of Hate*, 409.

16. "Impeachment of the President," H. Rept. 7, minority report (Wilson), 104; Eisenschiml, *Why Was Lincoln Murdered?*, 138–44. The authoritative evaluation of the so-called diary is Kauffman, *American Brutus*, 271–73, 380.

17. Horowitz, *Great Impeacher*, 131; "Impeachment of the President," H. Rept. 7, testimony: 1199–1201.

18. Turner, *Beware the People Weeping*, 208–9, 213–19; Leonard, *Lincoln's Avengers*, 83–86, 103–4, 150–53, 167–68, 216–27.

19. *CinGaz*, August 13, 14, 1867; "H. V. N. B.," *CinGaz*, August 23, 1867; "Impeachment of the President," H. Rept. 7, testimony: 1201–7; Horowitz, *Great Impeacher*, 135–37.

20. *NYH*, August 10, 1867.

21. Leonard, *Lincoln's Avengers*, 268–69; Horowitz, *Great Impeacher*, 138–39.

22. *CinGaz*, August 25, 27, 1867; *CinEnq*, August 12, 1867; *NYW*, August 19, 1867; Turner, *Beware the People Weeping*, 222. Needless to say, the entrapment charge rested on conjecture only, and Blair's allegations were crazy.

23. Mantell, *Johnson, Grant, and the Politics of Reconstruction*, 32–37, 75–76; Sefton, *United States Army and Reconstruction*, 154–57; Jordan, *Winfield Scott Hancock*, 202–11.

24. Nevins and Thomas, *Diary of George Templeton Strong*, 4:149–50 (September 3, 13, 1867).

25. "Dixon," *Boston Daily Advertiser*, September 16, 1867; Simon, *Papers of Ulysses S. Grant*, 17:317–18, 17:343. On Johnson's potential use of the Maryland militia, see Nevins and Thomas, *Diary of George Templeton Strong*, 4:151 (September 25, 1867).

26. *Boston Daily Advertiser*, September 2, 1867; Bergeron, *Papers of Andrew Johnson*, 13:125.

27. *NYW*, November 18, 19, 1867; *CinEnq*, November 20, 21, 1867. The real "H. S." was an official in the Treasury Department's law office.

28. *Washington Daily National Intelligencer*, September 14, October 7, 1867.

29. Bergeron, *Papers of Andrew Johnson*, 13:209; Simon, *Papers of Ulysses S. Grant*, 18:22–24.

30. Nevins and Thomas, *Diary of George Templeton Strong*, 4:123 (January 30, 1867); *CinEnq*, September 28, 1867.

31. *CinEnq*, November 20, 25, 26, 1867. Boutwell dismissed such ideas out of hand. "Oh, there is no fear of suspension," he told a reporter. "That's clearly unconstitutional."

32. Morse, *Diary of Gideon Welles*, 3:237–38 (November 30, 1867).

33. *Boston Daily Advertiser*, September 14, 1867.

34. *NYW*, September 19, 1867.

35. Bergeron, *Papers of Andrew Johnson*, 13:49, 13:208.

36. *CinCom*, September 27, 1867; *Boston Daily Advertiser*, August 29, 1867; John W. Forney to William Pitt Fessenden, October 21, 1867, Forney MSS, LC.

37. *NYEP*, October 24, 1867.

38. Simon, *Papers of Ulysses S. Grant*, 18:34.

39. *Boston Daily Advertiser*, September 2, 1867.

40. *NYEP*, October 24, 1867.

41. Benedict, "Rout of Radicalism," 334–44; *NYEP*, September 14, 1867. On Republican interpretations of the returns, see Henry D. Cooke to Jay Cooke, October 12, 1867, Cooke MSS, HSP; Henry A. Smythe to William E. Chandler, October 16, 1867, William E. Chandler MSS, LC; Thomas Russell to Nathaniel P. Banks, October 11, 1867, Banks MSS, LC; and *Boston Daily Advertiser*, November 7, 1867. On the Democratic response, see *(Mobile (Ala.) Daily Advertiser and Register*, November 8, 21, 1867; and *NYW*, November 15, 16, 1867.

42. Benedict, *Impeachment and Trial of Andrew Johnson*, 73–88; *NYEP*, December 2, 1867; "Mack," *CinCom*, December 7, 1867; *Boston Daily Advertiser*, December 2, 1867; G. E. Welles to Robert K. Scott, December 6, 1867, Scott MSS, OHS.

43. *CinCom*, March 16, 26, 1868.

44. Hugh McCulloch to Van Dyke, October 11, 1867, McCulloch MSS, LLIU.

CHAPTER 10

1. Quoted in the *Washington Weekly Chronicle*, March 21, 1868.

2. *NYTrib*, February 22, 1868; Benedict, *Compromise of Principle*, 297; Benedict, *Impeachment and Trial of Andrew Johnson*, 105–8.

3. Thomas and Hyman, *Stanton*, 584–85; *NYTrib*, February 22, 24, 1868.

4. Benedict, *Compromise of Principle*, 297–99; Clemenceau, *American Reconstruction*, 153 (March 6, 1868); Austin Blair to Mason W. Tappan, February 23, 1868, Tappan MSS, NHHS; *Washington Daily National Intelligencer*, February 21, 1868.

5. As in, for example, Bowers, *Tragic Era*, 176–78; Milton, *Age of Hate*, 303–4.

6. Benedict, *Impeachment and Trial of Andrew Johnson*, 36–45, 108–11.

7. William G. Moore Diary, January 9, 1868, Johnson MSS, LC; Brooks D. Simpson, *Let Us Have Peace*, 226–35; Simon, *Papers of Ulysses S. Grant*, 18:105–10, 116–22, 124–27.

8. Thomas and Hyman, *Stanton*, 571–74; Simon, *Papers of Ulysses S. Grant*, 18:108; "D.W. B.," *Independent* (New York), January 30, February 20, 1868; William G. Moore Diary, January 26, 1868, Johnson MSS, LC; Brooks D. Simpson, *Let Us Have Peace*, 235.

9. *NYTrib*, February 20, 21, 1868; Simon, *Papers of Ulysses S. Grant*, 18:139–43; Thorndike, *Sherman Letters*, 305; Marszalek, *Sherman*, 374; William Tecumseh Sherman to Andrew Johnson, February 14, 1868, Johnson MSS, LC.

10. *CG*, 40th Cong., 2d sess., 1388 (February 24, 1868).

11. Thorndike, *Sherman Letters*, 311.

12. *Providence (R.I.) Evening Press*, February 25, 1868. In reality, the militia was, as a Republican newspaper charged, "a humbug and a nuisance," utterly unfit for action. *Baltimore American and Commercial Advertiser*, February 24, 25, June 18, 1868.

13. *ChiTrib*, February 23, 1868; *NYTrib*, February 24, 1868; Thomas and Hyman, *Stanton*, 592.

14. J. M. Howard to Edwin M. Stanton, February 21, 1868, Charles Sumner to Stanton, February 21, 1868, Stanton MSS, LC; *NYTrib*, February 24, 1868.

15. "Star" to Jay Cooke, February 21, 1868, Cooke MSS, HSP.

16. Thomas and Hyman, *Stanton*, 587–88; *CG*, 40th Cong., 2d sess., 1367 (February 24, 1868); *PhilPr*, February 22, 1868; *NYTrib*, February 24, 1868.

17. N. P. Chipman to Whitelaw Reid, February 6, 1886, Reid MSS, LC; *NYTrib*, February 24, 1868.

18. *ChiTrib*, February 23, 28, 1868; *CG*, 40th Cong., 2d sess., 1345, 1348 (February 22, 1868), 1361 (February 24, 1868); *Lewiston (Maine) Evening Journal*, February 26, 1868.

19. Muggleston, "Freedmen's Bureau and Reconstruction in Virginia," 66–67; *CG*, 40th Cong., 2d sess., 1396 (February 24, 1868).

20. *NYTrib*, March 4, 1868; for the "set of individuals" remark, see John A. Bingham's argument, in *Supplement to the Congressional Globe in the Proceedings of the Senate Sitting for the Trial of Andrew Johnson, President of the United States*, 403.

21. *MemApp*, February 27, 1868; Sam Ward to S. L. M. Barlow, February 25, 1868, Barlow MSS, HL; A. E. Burr to Gideon Welles, February 26, 1868, Welles MSS, Connecticut Historical Society, Hartford; *CG*, 40th Cong., 2d sess., 1385 (February 24, 1868); *Hartford (Conn.) Daily Times*, February 22, 25, 27, 1868.

22. *PhilA*, February 25, 1868; *CG*, 40th Cong., 2d sess., 1336, 1341 (February 22, 1868). For other arguments about the illegality of the Senate and the House, see Bergeron, *Papers of Andrew Johnson*, 13:601–2, 13:611; and *CG*, 40th Cong., 2d sess., 1384–85 (February 24, 1868), 1519–20 (February 29, 1868). Judge Woodward of Pennsylvania, a stickler for precision, explained that an "incomplete Congress" did have the power to make laws. Legislative powers were quite different from those exercising criminal jurisdiction, such as impeachment. Also

a stickler for not getting into trouble, the judge had his remarks inserted in the *Globe*, rather than speaking them—the one factor that may have saved him from expulsion. See *Washington Weekly Chronicle*, February 29, March 14, 1868; and *CG*, 2530–31 (May 18, 1868).

23. Thomas F. Bayard to James A. Bayard, March 27, 1868, Bayard MSS, LC.

24. "Stone Mountain," *NYTi*, March 3, 1868; W. F. Leake to Thomas Ruffin, February 29, 1868, Ruffin MSS, LC; "Hampden," *CinCom*, March 9, 26, 1868; Bergeron, *Papers of Andrew Johnson*, 13:601–2, 13:706–7.

25. Hector M. Seward to William H. Seward, February 25, 1868, Seward MSS, University of Rochester, Rochester, N.Y.; A. A. Terrell to Elihu Washburne, February 24, 1868, Washburne MSS, LC; Lucius Fairchild to Schuyler Colfax, February 27, 1868, Fairchild MSS, SHSW; John S. Wilcox to Richard J. Oglesby, February 26, 1868, Oglesby MSS, ISHS; *CinCom*, February 25, 27, 1868.

26. *Atchison (Kans.) Daily Champion*, February 25, 1868; R. J. Jenkins to Elihu Washburne, February 26, 1868, Washburne MSS, LC; *Washington Daily National Intelligencer*, February 25, 1868. On the GAR's role, see also A. L. Chatham to Elihu Washburne, February 24, 1868, Washburne MSS, LC; and Bergeron, *Papers of Andrew Johnson*, 13:593.

27. *CG*, 40th Cong., 2d sess., 1336–37 (February 22, 1868), 1385 (February 24, 1868); Bergeron, *Papers of Andrew Johnson*, 13:579, 13:588, 13:655; H. H. Boyce to William H. Seward, February 25, 1868, Seward MSS, University of Rochester, Rochester, N.Y.

28. Richard E. Lewis to Andrew Johnson, March 11, 1868, Johnson MSS, LC. For similar appeals to Johnson to take charge of the army, see also H. H. Boyce to William H. Seward, February 25, 1868, Seward MSS, University of Rochester, Rochester, N.Y.; and, more indirectly, Ethan A. Allen to Johnson, March 31, 1868, S. J. Anderson to Johnson, March 31, 1868, George Robertson to Johnson, March 31, 1868, in Bergeron, *Papers of Andrew Johnson*, 13:702–6.

29. *CinCom*, March 6, 1868; A. E. Burr to Gideon Welles, February 26, 1868, Welles MSS, Connecticut Historical Society, Hartford.

30. *CinCom*, March 21, 1868; *Hartford (Conn.) Daily Times*, February 29, March 3, 1868. The McCardle case threatened to bring on a Supreme Court challenge to the Reconstruction Acts.

31. Gorham, *Life and Services of Edwin M. Stanton*, 2:443.

32. Morse, *Diary of Gideon Welles*, 3:291 (February 24, 1868); *Washington Weekly Chronicle*, March 21, 1868; *NYTrib*, February 24, 1868; *Decatur (Ill.) Republican*, May 7, 1868; *PhilPr*, April 9, 1868; *CinCom*, February 24, 25, 1868; "Star" to Jay Cooke, February 24, 1868, Cooke MSS, HSP.

33. *New Orleans Times*, March 28, 1868; "Occasional," *Washington Weekly Chronicle*, March 21, 1868; *NYH*, March 20, 25, 29, 1868.

34. *ChiTrib*, February 23, 1868; *NYTrib*, February 24, 1868; Gambill, *Conservative Ordeal*, 113.

35. See also Orville E. Babcock to Edward Lee Plumb, February 25, 1868, Plumb MSS, Stanford University, Palo Alto, Calif.; Francis Kernan to Samuel J. Tilden, March 7, 1868, Tilden MSS, NYPL; *NYW*, February 26, 1868; and *(Mobile (Ala.) Nationalist*, March 12, 1868.

36. Simon, *Papers of Ulysses S. Grant*, 18:89.

37. *Lewiston (Maine) Evening Journal*, February 25, 1868; Edwards Pierrepont to John A. Dix, February 25, 1868, Dix MSS, Columbia University, New York.

38. *CG*, 40th Cong., 2d sess., 1366, 1368, 1391 (February 24, 1868); Thorndike, *Sherman Letters*, 314; *Washington Weekly Chronicle*, May 2, 1868.

39. *Supplement to the Congressional Globe in the Proceedings of the Senate Sitting for the Trial of Andrew Johnson, President of the United States*, 320–23.

40. Morse, *Diary of Gideon Welles*, 3:338–40 (April 25, 27, 1868).

41. William Moore Diary, April 23, 1868, Johnson MSS, LC; McDonough and Alderson, "Republican Politics and the Impeachment of Andrew Johnson," 177–83; Cox, *Union—Disunion—Reunion*, 592–94; "Van," *Hartford (Conn.) Daily Courant*, May 16, 1868; *CinGaz*, May 16, 1868.

42. Fairman, *Reconstruction and Reunion*, 391–95, 467–78; *PhilPr*, March 30, 1868. See Frank Blair Jr. speech, *NYH*, October 28, 1868.

43. *Brooklyn (N.Y.) Daily Eagle*, July 26, 1885.

44. *ChiTrib*, May 13, 15, 1868; Mantell, *Johnson, Grant, and the Politics of Reconstruction*, 89–93.

45. Summers, *Era of Good Stealings*, 30–45; *Atchison (Kans.) Freedom's Champion*, June 1, 1868; *NYTrib*, May 27, 28, July 4, 1868.

46. Charles Francis Adams to Charles Francis Adams Jr., April 24, May 2, 1868; John Quincy Adams II to Charles Francis Adams, May 26, 1868, Adams Family MSS, MHS.

47. W. W. Duffield to Andrew Johnson, May 27, 1868, Francis Fellows to Johnson, May 28, 1868, Johnson MSS, LC; Mantell, *Johnson, Grant, and the Politics of Reconstruction*, 98–100.

CHAPTER 11

1. *NYW*, June 3, 8, 17, 22, 1868.

2. Niven, *Salmon P. Chase*, 425–30; Blue, *Salmon P. Chase*, 286–89.

3. For resistance to the *New York World*, see *Montgomery (Ala.) Mail*, June 20, 21, 1868; *Louisville (Ky.) Daily Democrat*, June 5, 1868; and *Richmond (Va.) Dispatch*, June 17, 1868.

4. Parrish, *Missouri under Radical Rule*, 56–59, 70–74.

5. William Ernest Smith, *Francis Preston Blair Family in Politics*, 392–97.

6. Blair's letter was no unconsidered outburst. He had been formulating these thoughts privately for months. See William Ernest Smith, *Francis Preston Blair Family in Politics*, 389–90, 405–8.

7. *Louisville (Ky.) Courier*, September 24, 1868.

8. *NYW*, June 15, 20, 1868; "Leo," *ChaCou*, June 22, 1868; William M. Browne to Samuel L. M. Barlow, June 24, 1868, Barlow MSS, HL; Blue, *Salmon P. Chase*, 289–91.

9. Mantell, *Johnson, Grant, and the Politics of Reconstruction*, 121–28.

10. *ChiTi*, August 30, 1868; *Mobile (Ala.) Daily Register*, September 21, 1868; *Ithaca (N.Y.) Democrat*, August 13, 1868; *St. Paul (Minn.) Daily Pioneer*, October 22, 1868.

11. *Rochester (N.Y.) Daily Union and Advertiser*, October 31, 1868; *CinEnq*, October 6, 9, 1868; *Illinois Democrat* (Champaign), July 17, 1868; *ChiTi*, October 20, 1868; *DetFP*, October 7, 1868; *Indianapolis Daily Journal*, August 17, 1868.

12. *ISRSpr*, July 28, 1868; Morris S. Miller to Horatio Seymour, August 1, 1868, Seymour MSS, NYSL; *New York Sun*, October 29, 1868; *Louisville (Ky.) Courier*, September 6, 1868; James R. Doolittle to Manton Marble, January 27, 1868, Marble MSS, LC; *Rochester (N.Y.)*

Daily Union and Advertiser, October 27, 1868; *ChiTi*, October 30, 1868; *Rochester (N.Y.) Daily Democrat*, October 31, 1868.

13. *Louisville (Ky.) Courier*, July 26, 1868; *NYTrib*, October 2, 1868 (Hill's letter).

14. *Indianapolis Daily Journal*, August 18, 1868.

15. *Ithaca (N.Y.) Democrat*, August 13, 1868; *NYW*, August 14, 1868; *Jamestown (N.Y.) Journal*, October 30, 1868; *Indianapolis Daily Journal*, August 13, 1868; *Albany (N.Y.) Morning Express*, October 3, 1868; *NYTrib*, August 28, 1868; *ChiTi*, September 30, 1868.

16. *Tuscaloosa (Ala.) Independent Monitor*, August 25, 1868.

17. C. F. Burnham to James S. Rollins, September 8, 1868, Rollins MSS, Missouri Historical Society, Columbia; *NYTi*, September 21, October 5, 1868; *Troy (N.Y.) Daily Times*, August 21, 1868; Benjamin F. Butler to Haskins Taylor, August 15, 1868, Butler MSS, LC.

18. *NYTi*, October 10, 1868.

19. *Peekskill (N.Y.) Messenger*, October 8, 1868; *CinGaz*, September 10, 1868; *Marietta (Ohio) Register*, October 1, 1868; *Bridgeport (Conn.) Evening Standard*, November 3, 1868; *Oneida (N.Y.) Dispatch*, July 31, 1868; *Poughkeepsie (N.Y.) Daily Eagle*, November 3, 1868.

20. *Indianapolis Daily Journal*, August 1, 1868.

21. *Oneida (N.Y.) Dispatch*, August 7, 1868; *St. Louis Daily Democrat*, October 9, 19, 1868; *Cazenovia (N.Y.) Republican*, August 19, 1868.

22. *St. Lawrence (N.Y.) Plaindealer*, October 15, 1868; *Jamestown (N.Y.) Journal*, October 30, 1868; *Auburn (N.Y.) Daily Advertiser*, August 24, September 4, 1868; *Oneida (N.Y.) Dispatch*, October 9, 1868.

23. *Indianapolis Daily Journal*, July 30, 1868; Robert K. Scott to General E. R. S. Canby, September 8, 1868, Scott MSS, OHS.

24. August Belmont to Manton Marble (n.d., but probably August 1868), Marble MSS, LC; *NYW*, September 18, 1868; *Carthage (Ill.) Republican*, July 21, 1868.

25. *NYW*, September 19, 22, October 21, 1868; see also *NYTi*, reply, September 21, 1868.

26. *NYTi*, October 6, 1868; *ChiTi*, October 23, 1868; *DetFP*, August 21, 1868.

27. *NYTi*, October 6, 1868; *Louisville (Ky.) Courier*, September 6, 1868; *NYW*, June 29, 1868.

28. *Albany (N.Y.) Morning Express*, October 1, 1868; *Milwaukee Sentinel*, October 21, 1868; *NYTi*, October 6, 1868; *NYTi*, October 6, 1868.

29. *NYW*, June 29, 1868; *Auburn (N.Y.) Daily Advertiser*, August 24, 1868.

30. *NYW*, September 23, 1868; *ChiTi*, September 24, 1868; *CinEnq*, October 7, 1868.

31. Frank Blair Jr. to Francis P. Blair, August 7, 1868, Blair-Lee MSS, Princeton University Library, Princeton, N.J.

32. *Pottsville (Pa.) Miners' Journal*, September 26, 1868; *PhilNAm*, October 9, 1868; *NYTi*, September 29, 1868; *Auburn (N.Y.) Daily Advertiser*, July 8, 29, October 5, 1868; *Peekskill (N.Y.) Messenger*, October 15, 1868; *Newark Daily Advertiser*, August 6, 1868; *Kennebec Journal* (Augusta, Maine), August 5, 19, 1868; *NYH*, September 15, 1868 (Gordon's speech); Hawkins Taylor to Benjamin F. Butler, August 12, 1868, Butler MSS, LC.

33. *NYH*, October 28, 1868; Coleman, *Election of 1868*, 267. For examples of that Republican paraphrase, see *Oneida (N.Y.) Dispatch*, July 31, 1868. Blair's nickname is in the St. Louis *Daily Democrat*, October 8, 1868.

34. *Indianapolis Daily Journal*, July 23, August 1, 1868; *ChiTi*, October 22, 1868; *NYTi*, September 29, 1868; *St. Louis Daily Democrat*, July 23, 1868; *Milwaukee Sentinel*, October 21, 1868.

For a foreign reporter's judgment that Blair's campaign tours and speechifying were doing the Democrats "immeasurable harm" by "their exaggerations and ridiculous flights of oratory," see Clemenceau, *American Reconstruction*, 252.

35. *Jamestown (N.Y.) Journal*, August 7, 1868; *ChiTi*, September 21, 1868; Bancroft, *Speeches, Correspondence, and Political Papers of Carl Schurz*, 1:461–62; "Gath," *ChiTrib*, July 20, 1868; *Marietta (Ohio) Register*, October 15, 1868; *St. Louis Daily Democrat*, July 4, 1868; *Cazenovia (N.Y.) Republican*, August 19, 1868.

36. *St. Louis Daily Democrat*, July 4, August 13, 1868; *NYW*, September 23, November 2, 1868; *Indianapolis Daily Journal*, July 23, 30, August 1, 13, 18, 1868; *NYH*, October 28, 1868 (Blair's speech); *Nation*, October 22, 1868; *NYTrib*, July 10, August 1, 6, 1868; *CinCom*, October 13, 1868 (Henry Ward Beecher's speech).

37. *St. Louis Daily Democrat*, October 18, 19, 1868; *Cattaraugus Republican* (Ellicottville, N.Y.), October 29, 1868.

38. *PhilPr*, November 2, 1868; *NYTrib*, October 23, 1868; *Newark Daily Advertiser*, October 19, 1868.

39. Trelease, *White Terror*, 110–17; *Alabama State Journal* (Montgomery), November 10, 12, 18, 1868; "Report of Outrages Committed upon Citizens of the State of Georgia from Jan. 1st to Nov. 15th, 1868," Governor's Papers: Rufus Bullock, Georgia Department of History and Archives; *Tuscaloosa (Ala.) Independent Monitor*, September 1, 1868; Laurence Cain and others to Robert K. Scott, November 2, 1868, Joseph Crews to Scott, November 2, 1868, Governor's Papers: Scott MSS, South Carolina State Archives, Columbia.

40. Robert K. Scott to George Meade, September 16, 1868, Scott MSS, box 2, folder 1, OHS; *Troy (N.Y.) Daily Times*, August 20, 1868; *DetFP*, September 3, 1868.

41. *Troy (N.Y.) Daily Times*, August 14, 21, 1868; *New York Journal of Commerce*, October 22, 1868.

42. *DetFP*, October 4, 1868; *NYW*, September 24, October 20, 27, 1868; *Erie (Pa.) Observer*, September 10, 1868; *ChiTi*, August 6, 1868.

43. *NYW*, October 15, 1868; A. M. to Manton Marble, October 16, 1868, James T. Noble to Marble, October 16, 17, 1868, Marble MSS, LC.

44. McJimsey, *Genteel Partisan*, 130; *NYW*, October 20, 1868; Samuel L. M. Barlow to Samuel J. Tilden, October 15, 1868, Wilbur E. Storey to Tilden, October 16, 1868, Alexander Delmar to Tilden, October 16, 1868, Tilden MSS, NYPL.

45. Edward Hamilton to Manton Marble, October 16, 1868, Marble MSS, LC; *CinEnq*, October 16, 1868; Coleman, *Election of 1868*, 352–53.

46. Samuel J. Tilden, Augustus Schell, August Belmont to Wilbur F. Storey, October 17, 1866, Tilden MSS, NYPL; Henry B. James to William E. Chandler, October 20, 1868, William E. Chandler MSS, LC.

47. Hiram Ketchum to Samuel J. Tilden, November 12, 1868, Tilden MSS, NYPL; S. B. Norton to Horatio Seymour, November 8, 1868, Seymour MSS, NYSL; *DetFP*, November 5, 6, 1868; James T. Henry to Manton Marble, November 10, 1868, Marble MSS, LC; Fairman, *Reconstruction and Reunion*, 548–49; W. H. Kemble to Elihu Washburne, November 4, 1868, Washburne MSS, LC.

48. *New York Journal of Commerce*, August 4, October 22, November 5, 6, 1868; T. J. Barnett to Samuel L. M. Barlow, November 6, 1868, Barlow MSS, HL.

49. For the explicit recognition of the conservative appeal and the success of using Blair's

threats as a campaign issue, see Marston Robie to Benjamin F. Butler, August 4, 1868, and Butler's reply (written on the back), Butler MSS, LC; *Bridgeport (Conn.) Evening Standard*, November 3, 1868; *NYH*, October 7, 1868.

CHAPTER 12

1. "An Instructive Retrospect," *Nation*, February 11, 1875. Others reflected a similar incredulity. See McCulloch, *Men and Measures*, 394; McClure, *Recollections of Half a Century*, 68; and Julian, *Political Recollections*, 317.

2. *Nation*, October 8, 29, 1874, January 7, 21, 1875.

3. S. M. Johnson to Samuel J. Tilden, May 26, 1868, Horatio Seymour to Tilden, October 2, 1868, N. E. Paine to Tilden, August 12, 1868, Tilden MSS, NYPL; *DetFP*, October 7, 1868.

4. Grossman, *Democratic Party and the Negro*, 17–24; *Nation*, October 21, September 16, 1869; *NYW*, June 3, 1870; *ClPD*, June 2, 1871.

5. Perman, *Road to Redemption*, 16–21; *Charleston (S.C.) Republican*, January 26, 1870; *Alabama State Journal* (Montgomery), December 15, 28, 1870; *NYH*, July 11, 12, 1871.

6. Samuel S. Cox to Manton Marble, February 27, 1870, Marble MSS, LC; *NYW*, April 27, 1871; G. L. Miller to J. Sterling Morton, July 28, 1870, Morton MSS, Nebraska State Historical Society.

7. James B. Ball to Thomas F. Bayard, June 28, 1870, Bayard MSS, LC; *NYH*, July 21, 1871; *Alabama State Journal* (Montgomery), August 21, 1870.

8. Perman, *Road to Redemption*, 63–65; "Affairs in the Late Insurrectionary States," H. Rept. 22, minority report, 122–25, 232–33, 508–9, 583–84.

9. Foner, *Reconstruction*, 421–25; "Avery," *CinCom*, October 14, 1869.

10. Charles Nordhoff to Whitelaw Reid, April 14, 1875, Reid MSS, LC. That he was misled was not lost on contemporaries. See *Washington Chronicle*, May 26, June 2, 1875.

11. Maddex, *Virginia Conservatives*, 121–22; Blight, *Race and Reunion*, 70–97.

12. *Jackson (Miss.) Weekly Clarion*, May 7, 1874; Murphy, *L. Q. C. Lamar*, 116–17. For the prototype for his Sumner speech, see Mayes, *Lucius Q. C. Lamar*, 182.

13. *CG*, 44th Cong., 1st sess., 345–51 (January 11, 1876). On contemporary reactions and Hill's heavy editing, see *ChiTrib*, January 12, 15, 1876; Burwell B. Lewis to Robert McKee, January 19, 1876, McKee MSS, ADAH.

14. *Bangor (Maine) Whig and Courier*, October 19, 1876; *Indianapolis News*, August 26, 1876; P. B. S. Pinchback to Henry Clay Warmoth, May 6, 1876, Warmoth MSS, SHC.

15. Zuczek, *State of Rebellion*, 53–61, 88–93; Hyde, *Pistols and Politics*, 164–69; *NYTrib*, April 28, 1871.

16. Trelease, *White Terror*, 138, 288–89, 294–96, 319–21.

17. Foner, *Reconstruction*, 429; *NYTrib*, June 14, 1871; Trelease, *White Terror*, 139, 229–30, 288, 321, 354.

18. *NYTrib*, April 28, May 12, June 14, 1871; Hyde, *Pistols and Politics*, 168–72; Trelease, *White Terror*, 118–19, 122, 228–29, 235, 287.

19. *ChaCou*, July 29, 1870; Trelease, *White Terror*, 70–71, 371–72; "Affairs in the Late Insurrectionary States," H. Rept. 22, majority report, 44–47.

20. Trelease, *White Terror*, 65–65, 76–77, 205, 207, 237, 247–49, 259, 367; John Christopher to Robert K. Scott, March 12, 1871, Governor's Papers: Scott MSS, South Carolina State Ar-

chives, Columbia; for the many excuses, see "Chester," *NYW*, March 15, 1871; "S. D.," ibid., May 18, 1871; *NYTrib*, April 27, 1871; "H.W.R.," *NYTi*, April 22, 1871; and *NYH*, May 29, June 20, 1871.

21. Escott, *Many Excellent People*, 128–29; Zuczek, *State of Rebellion*, 18–20, 29–35; Hyde, *Pistols and Politics*, 160; Trelease, *White Terror*, xliii–xlvi.

22. Foner, *Reconstruction*, 431–33; Escott, *Many Excellent People*, 155–57.

23. Trelease, *White Terror*, 28, 40–42, 62, 78–79, 258–59.

24. W. C. Morrill to "dear general," November 2, 1868, Governor's Papers: Rufus Bullock MSS, Georgia Department of History and Archives, Atlanta; O'Donovan, "Transforming Work," 418–19; *NYH*, September 12, 1868.

25. Foner, *Reconstruction*, 436–38; Rodrigue, *Reconstruction in the Cane Fields*, 176–77.

26. Singletary, *Negro Militias and Reconstruction*, 28–29; Trelease, *White Terror*, 155–58; Nunn, *Texas under the Carpetbaggers*, 43–45, 74; Moneyhon, *Republicanism in Reconstruction Texas*, 139, 142–43.

27. A. W. Spies to Robert K. Scott, March 8, 1871, Governor's Papers: Scott MSS, South Carolina State Archives, Columbia; E. L. Mann to Robert K. Scott, June 13, 1870, Scott MSS, OHS; *NYTrib*, April 28, 1871.

28. Gillette, *Retreat from Reconstruction*, 25–27, 42–55. But see the skeptical Zuczek, "Federal Government's Attack on the Klan," 47–64.

29. Hyde, *Pistols and Politics*, 185–87.

30. William H. Black to David P. Lewis, August 25, 1874, C. J. Atkinson to W. L. Bragg (n.d., ca. September 17, 1874), Edward Turner and Jackson Turner to Lewis, August 21, 1874, Lewis MSS, ADAH; *NYH*, September 11, 1874.

31. Current, *Those Terrible Carpetbaggers*, 312–27; *Charleston (S.C.) News and Courier*, July 10, 11, 1876; Zuczek, *State of Rebellion*, 163–64.

32. Rogers, *Black Belt Scalawag*, 106–15; Zebulon L. White to Whitelaw Reid, October 9, November 28, 1874, Reid MSS, LC.

33. Gillette, *Retreat from Reconstruction*, 76–94.

34. Foner, *Reconstruction*, 452–54; Gillette, *Retreat from Reconstruction*, 87–89.

35. *NYTrib*, August 13, 1870; Jesse H. Moore to Richard J. Oglesby, January 2, 1870, Oglesby MSS, ISHS; William A. Buckingham to Henry P. Farrow, September 8, 1870, Farrow MSS, University of Georgia Library, Athens. On Tennessee, see W. H. Stilwell to Eaton, March 15, 28, 1870, Eaton MSS, Hoskins Library, University of Tennessee, Knoxville.

36. Gillette, *Retreat from Reconstruction*, 94–99; Moneyhon, *Republicanism in Reconstruction Texas*, 193–94; Harris, *Day of the Carpetbagger*, 478–81.

37. Taylor, *Louisiana Reconstructed*, 226–27; David F. Boyd to William Tecumseh Sherman, December 27, 1872, Fleming Collection, LSU.

38. Gillette, *Retreat from Reconstruction*, 105–12; Taylor, *Louisiana Reconstructed*, 245, 268–71; Thomas Ellis to E. J. Ellis, November 16, 1872, E. John Ellis to Thomas Ellis, December 7, 1872, Ellis Family MSS, LSU.

39. Gillette, *Retreat from Reconstruction*, 136–38; Current, *Those Terrible Carpetbaggers*, 266–68, 299–301; "H. V. R.," *CinCom*, May 12, 15, 19, 23, 1874; *NYTrib*, May 11, 1874.

40. Gillette, *Retreat from Reconstruction*, 120–35; *New Haven (Conn.) Register*, January 5, 1875; *NYH*, March 23, 1875; *ChiTrib*, March 23, 1875; Bergeron, *Papers of Andrew Johnson*, 16:744.

41. Milton, *Age of Hate*, 672.

42. *Harrisburg (Pa.) Patriot*, November 2, 1872; Augustus Schell to William A. Graham, September 19, 1872, Graham MSS, SHC; Summers, *Era of Good Stealings*, 249–55.

43. McFeely, *Grant*, 320–31, 404–16, 427–36; *CinGaz*, October 3, 1872; *CinEnq*, August 19, 1872; *St. Louis Missouri Republican*, October 30, November 7, 1872.

44. Polakoff, *Politics of Inertia*, 201–313; Summers, *Era of Good Stealings*, 287–91; A. H. Parsons to Samuel J. Randall, January 1, 1877, S. Griffin to Randall, December 17, 1876, A. H. Light to Randall, December 14, 1876, Randall MSS, Rare Book and Manuscript Library, University of Pennsylvania, Philadelphia; *Savannah Morning News*, August 22, 1876; *NYH*, December 1, 1876; *Mobile (Ala.) Register*, November 21, 1876; James S. Phillips to John Sherman, December 7, 1876, John Sherman MSS, LC.

45. Summers, *Era of Good Stealings*, 291–97; T. J. McLain to James A. Garfield, January 8, 1877, Garfield MSS, LC.

CODA

1. Jacob Dolson Cox to James A. Garfield, April 10, 1866, Garfield MSS, LC. The point was not unique. See reporter "Marco's" notes on a speech from future Indiana senator Joseph McDonald at New Albany on June 28, 1866, in *CinGaz*, July 3, 1866.

Bibliography

MANUSCRIPT COLLECTIONS

Albany, New York
    New York State Library
        Edwin D. Morgan MSS
        Horatio Seymour MSS
Athens, Georgia
    University of Georgia Library
        Henry P. Farrow MSS
Atlanta, Georgia
    Atlanta Historical Society
        Samuel P. Richards MSS
    Georgia Department of Archives and History
        Governor's Papers: Rufus W. Bullock MSS
Austin, Texas
    Austin Public Library
        Elisha M. Pease MSS
Baton Rouge, Louisiana
    Hill Library, Louisiana State University
        Thomas Affleck MSS
        Lemuel P. Conner MSS
        Ellis Family MSS
        Walter L. Fleming Collection
Bloomington, Indiana
    Lilly Library, Indiana University
        Henry S. Lane MSS
        Hugh McCulloch MSS
Boston, Massachusetts
    Massachusetts Historical Society
        Adams Family MSS
        Edward Atkinson MSS
Brunswick, Maine
    Bowdoin College Library
        Fessenden Family MSS
        Oliver Otis Howard MSS
Chapel Hill, North Carolina
    Southern Historical Collection, University of North Carolina
        Joseph Smith Fowler MSS
        Elliott-Gonzales MSS
        William A. Graham MSS
        Henry Clay Warmoth MSS

Chicago, Illinois
  University of Chicago
    Stephen A. Douglas MSS
Columbia, Missouri
  Missouri Historical Society
    James S. Rollins MSS
Columbia, South Carolina
  South Caroliniana Collection, University of South Carolina
    William H. Trescot MSS
  South Carolina State Archives
    James L. Orr MSS
    Robert K. Scott MSS
Columbus, Ohio
  Ohio Historical Society
    James M. Comly MSS
    Robert K. Scott MSS
    William Henry Smith MSS
    John A. Trimble MSS
Concord, New Hampshire
  New Hampshire Historical Society
    William E. Chandler MSS
    Mason W. Tappan MSS
Des Moines, Iowa
  Iowa State Department of Archives and History
    Charles Mason MSS
Fremont, Ohio
  Rutherford B. Hayes Memorial Library
    Rutherford B. Hayes MSS
    John Sherman Pamphlet Collection
Hartford, Connecticut
  Connecticut Historical Society
    Mark Howard MSS
    Gideon Welles MSS
Indianapolis, Indiana
  Indiana Historical Society
    John G. Davis MSS
  Indiana State Library
    Thomas A. Hendricks MSS
    Charles Lasselle MSS
Ithaca, New York
  Cornell University Library
    J. Miller McKim MSS
Jackson, Mississippi
  Mississippi Department of Archives and History
    Governor's Papers: Adelbert Ames MSS

       Governor's Papers: Benjamin G. Humphreys MSS
       Governor's Papers: William G. Sharkey MSS
       James and Samuel Matthews MSS
       Flavius W. Nicholson Diary
Knoxville, Tennessee
   Calvin M. McClung Historical Collection, Knox County Public Library System
       Thomas A. R. Nelson MSS
   Hoskins Library, University of Tennessee
       John Eaton MSS
Lincoln, Nebraska
   Nebraska State Historical Society
       J. Sterling Morton MSS
Madison, Wisconsin
   State Historical Society of Wisconsin
       Lucius Fairchild MSS
Montgomery, Alabama
   Alabama Department of Archives and History
       Governor David P. Lewis MSS
       Robert McKee MSS
       Governor Robert Patton MSS
       Governor William H. Smith MSS
       Wager Swayne MSS
       Wheeler Family MSS
New York, New York
   Columbia University
       Moncure Conway MSS
       John A. Dix MSS
       William M. Grosvenor MSS
       McKim-Maloney-Garrison MSS
   New-York Historical Society
       Edward Durell MSS
   New York Public Library
       Bryant-Godwin MSS
       Samuel J. Tilden MSS
Oberlin, Ohio
   Oberlin College
       Jacob Dolson Cox MSS
Palo Alto, California
   Stanford University
       Edward Lee Plumb MSS
Philadelphia, Pennsylvania
   Historical Society of Pennsylvania
       William Bigler MSS
       James Buchanan MSS
       Henry C. Carey MSS

Jay Cooke MSS
Lewis Coryell MS
Wayne MacVeagh MSS
William S. Meredith MSS
Rare Book and Manuscript Library, University of Pennsylvania
Samuel J. Randall MSS
Princeton, New Jersey
Princeton University Library
Blair-Lee MSS
Providence, Rhode Island
Brown University
Samuel S. Cox MSS
Rochester, New York
University of Rochester
William Henry Seward MSS
Thurlow Weed MSS
San Marino, California
Huntington Library
Samuel L. M. Barlow MSS
South Bend, Indiana
Notre Dame University
William Tecumseh Sherman MSS
Springfield, Illinois
Illinois State Historical Society
Orville H. Browning MSS
Sylvanus Cadwallader MSS
Richard J. Oglesby MSS
John D. Strong MSS
Lyman Trumbull MSS
Washington, D.C.
Library of Congress
Nathaniel P. Banks MSS
Thomas F. Bayard MSS
James G. Blaine MSS
Benjamin F. Butler MSS
William E. Chandler MSS
Zachariah Chandler MSS
Henry Laurens Dawes MSS
George S. Denison MSS
Thomas Ewing MSS
John Wien Forney MSS
James A. Garfield MSS
Horace Greeley MSS
Thomas Jenckes MSS
Andrew Johnson MSS

Manton Marble MSS
Edward McPherson MSS
Whitelaw Reid MSS
Thomas Ruffin MSS
John Sherman MSS
Edwin M. Stanton MSS
Elihu Washburne MSS

NEWSPAPERS AND MAGAZINES OF OPINION

Alabama State Journal (Montgomery)
Albany (N.Y.) Argus
Albany (N.Y.) Evening Journal
Albany (N.Y.) Morning Express
Alexandria Gazette and Virginia Advertiser
Atchison (Kans.) Champion
Auburn (N.Y.) Daily Advertiser
Augusta (Ga.) Loyal Georgian
Baltimore American and Commercial Advertiser
Baltimore Sun
Bangor (Maine) Whig and Courier
Baton Rouge Tri-Weekly Advocate
Boston Daily Advertiser
Boston Evening Transcript
Boston Post
Bridgeport (Conn.) Evening Standard
Brooklyn (N.Y.) Daily Eagle
Cadiz (Ohio) Republican
Carthage (Ill.) Republican
Cattaraugus Republican (Ellicottville, N.Y.)
Cazenovia (N.Y.) Daily Republican
Charleston (S.C.) Daily Courier
Charleston (S.C.) Mercury
Charleston (S.C.) News and Courier
Charleston (S.C.) Republican
Chicago Times
Chicago Tribune
Christian Recorder (Philadelphia)
Cincinnati Commercial
Cincinnati Enquirer
Cincinnati Gazette
Cleveland Plain Dealer
Columbus Ohio State Journal
Dayton (Ohio) Daily Empire
Decatur (Ill.) Republican

Detroit Free Press

Elmira (N.Y.) Daily Advertiser

Erie (Pa.) Observer

Findlay (Ohio) Hancock Jeffersonian

Galena (Ill.) North-Western Gazette

Harrisburg (Pa.) Patriot and Union

Hartford (Conn.) Daily Times

Illinois Democrat (Champaign)

Illinois State Journal (Springfield)

Illinois State Register (Springfield)

Independent (New York)

Indianapolis Daily Herald

Indianapolis Daily Journal

Indianapolis Daily State Sentinel

Indianapolis News

Ithaca (N.Y.) Democrat

Jackson (Miss.) Weekly Clarion

Jamestown (N.Y.) Journal

Kennebec Journal (Augusta, Maine)

La Crosse (Wis.) Democrat

Lewiston (Maine) Evening Journal

Louisville (Ky.) Daily Courier

Louisville (Ky.) Daily Democrat

Louisville (Ky.) Daily Journal

Luzerne (Pa.) Union

Malone (N.Y.) Palladium

Manchester (N.H.) Daily Union

Marietta (Ohio) Register

Memphis Daily Appeal

Memphis Daily Avalanche

Memphis Daily Post

Milwaukee Sentinel

Milwaukee Wisconsin

Mobile (Ala.) Daily Register

Mobile (Ala.) Nationalist

Montgomery (Ala.) Mail

Nashville Daily Press and Times

Nation (New York)

Newark Daily Advertiser

New Orleans Picayune

New Orleans Times

New Orleans Tribune

New York Daily News

New York Evening Post

New York Herald

New York Journal of Commerce
New York Times
New York Tribune
New York World
Oneida (N.Y.) Dispatch
Peekskill (N.Y.) Messenger
Peoria (Ill.) Daily National Democrat
Philadelphia Age
Philadelphia Daily News
Philadelphia North American and United States Gazette
Philadelphia Press
Pittsburgh Daily Post
Pottsville (Pa.) Miners' Journal and Pottsville (Pa.) General Advertiser
Poughkeepsie (N.Y.) Daily Eagle
Providence (R.I.) Evening Press
Raleigh (N.C.) Sentinel
Richmond (Va.) Dispatch
Richmond (Ind.) Palladium
Rochester (N.Y.) Daily Democrat
Rochester (N.Y.) Daily Union and Advocate
Rutland (Vt.) Weekly Herald
Sacramento Daily Union
St. Clairsville (Ohio) Gazette
St. Lawrence (N.Y.) Plaindealer
St. Louis Daily Democrat
St. Louis Missouri Republican
St. Paul (Minn.) Daily Pioneer
Springfield (Mass.) Republican
Steubenville (Ohio) Herald
Troy (N.Y.) Daily Times
Tuscaloosa (Ala.) Independent Monitor
Uniontown (Pa.) Genius of Liberty
Washington (D.C.) Chronicle
Washington (D.C.) National Intelligencer

U.S. GOVERNMENT DOCUMENTS

Congressional

Congressional Globe
"Affairs in the Late Insurrectionary States." H. Rept. 22, 42nd Cong., 2nd sess.
"Impeachment of the President." H. Rept. 7, 40th Cong., 1st sess.
"New Orleans Riots." H. Rept. 16, 39th Cong., 2nd sess.
"Reports of Assistant Commissioners of the Freedmen's Bureau." Sen. Exec. Doc. 27, 39th
    Cong., 1st sess.

Supplement to the Congressional Globe in the Proceedings of the Senate Sitting for the Trial of Andrew Johnson, President of the United States. 40th Cong., 2nd sess.

Military

Records of the Assistant Commissioner for the State of Tennessee, Bureau of Refugees, Freedmen, and Abandoned Lands. National Archives. Microfilm edition.

Registers and Letters Received by the Commissioner of the Bureau of Refugees, Freedmen, and Abandoned Lands. National Archives. Microfilm edition.

Union Provost Marshal's Files of Papers Relating to Two or More Civilians. National Archives. Microfilm Edition.

CONTEMPORARY ACCOUNTS, POLEMICS, AND MEMOIRS

Anderson, John Q., ed. *Brokenburn: The Journal of Kate Stone, 1861-1868.* Baton Rouge: Louisiana State University Press, 1955.

Andrews, Sidney. *The South since the War, As Shown by Fourteen Weeks of Travel and Observations in Georgia and the Carolinas.* Boston: Ticknor and Fields, 1866.

"Argument of John A. Bingham, Special Judge Advocate." Washington: Government Printing Office, 1865.

Bancroft, Frederic, ed. *Speeches, Correspondence, and Political Papers of Carl Schurz.* Vol. 1. New York: G. P. Putnam's, 1913.

Bergeron, Paul H., ed. *Papers of Andrew Johnson.* 16 vols. Knoxville: University of Tennessee Press, 1991.

Berlin, Ira, ed. *The Black Military Experience*, Series II of *Freedom: A Documentary History of Emancipation, 1861-1867.* Cambridge: Cambridge University Press, 1982.

Berlin, Ira, Barbara J. Fields, Steven F. Miller, Joseph P. Reidy, and Leslie S. Rowland. *Free at Last: A Documentary History of Slavery, Freedom, and the Civil War.* New York: New Press, 1992.

Boutwell, George S. *Reminiscences of Sixty Years in Public Affairs.* Vol. 2. New York: McClure, Phillips, 1902.

Brownlow, William G. *Sketches of the Rise, Progress, and Decline of Secession; With a Narrative of Personal Adventures among the Rebels.* Philadelphia: George W. Childs, 1862.

Brownson, Orestes A. *The American Republic: Its Constitution, Tendencies, and Destiny.* New York: P. O'Shea, 1866.

Childs, Arney Robinson, ed. *The Private Journal of Henry William Ravenel, 1856-1887.* Columbia: University of South Carolina Press, 1947.

Clemenceau, Georges. *American Reconstruction, 1865-1870, and the Impeachment of President Johnson.* New York: Dial Press, 1928.

Comitatus, Zedekiah, M.P.E.C. (pseud.). *Reconstruction on "My Policy," or, Its Author at the Confessional."* Skaggaddahunk (N.Y.?): Scantlewood, Timberlake, 1866.

Cox, Samuel S. *Union — Disunion — Reunion: Three Decades of Federal Legislation, 1855 to 1885.* Providence: J. A. and R. A. Reid, 1886.

Crist, Lynda Lasswell, ed. *Papers of Jefferson Davis.* Vol. 11. Baton Rouge: Louisiana State University Press, 2003.

Davis, David Brion, ed. *The Fear of Conspiracy: Images of Un-American Subversion from the Revolution to the Present*. Ithaca, N.Y.: Cornell University Press, 1971.

Dennett, John Richard. *The South as It Is, 1865–1866*. Edited by Henry M. Christman. Athens: University of Georgia Press, 1965.

The Diary of a Public Man and a Page of Political Correspondence. New Brunswick, N.J.: Rutgers University Press, 1946.

Duvergier de Hauranne, Ernest. *A Frenchman in Lincoln's America*. Vol. 2. Translated and edited by Ralph H. Bowen. Chicago: Lakeside Press, 1974.

Hamilton, J. G. de Roulhac, ed. *Correspondence of Jonathan Worth*. Raleigh: Edwards and Broughton Printing Co., 1909.

Hollister, Ovando J. *Life of Colfax*. New York: Funk and Wagnall's, 1886.

Julian, George W. *Political Recollections, 1840–1872*. Chicago: Jansen, McClurg, 1884.

Logan, John A. *The Great Conspiracy: Its Origin and History*. New York: A. R. Hart, 1886.

McClure, Alexander K. *Colonel Alexander K. McClure's Recollections of Half a Century*. Salem, Mass.: Salem Press, 1902.

McCulloch, Hugh. *Men and Measures of Half a Century*. New York: Charles Scribner's, 1888.

McPherson, Edward. *The Political History of the United States of America during the Period of Reconstruction*. Washington, D.C.: Solomon and Chapman, 1875.

Miers, Earl Schenck, ed. *When the World Ended: The Diary of Emma LeConte*. New York: Oxford, 1957.

Morse, John T., Jr., ed. *Diary of Gideon Welles*. 3 vols. Boston: Houghton Mifflin, Riverside Press, 1911.

Myers, Robert Manson, ed. *The Children of Pride: A True Story of Georgia and the Civil War*. New Haven, Conn.: Yale University Press, 1972.

Nevins, Allan, and Milton Halsey Thomas, eds. *The Diary of George Templeton Strong*. 4 vols. New York: Macmillan, 1952.

Nicolay, John G., and John Hay. *Abraham Lincoln: A History*. Vol. 3. New York: Century, 1917.

Palmer, Beverly Wilson, ed. *The Selected Letters of Charles Sumner*. 2 vols. Boston: Northeastern University Press, 1990.

Paltsits, Victor Hugo, ed. *Minutes of the Commissioners for Detecting and Defeating Conspiracies in the State of New York*. 3 vols. Albany: State of New York publisher, 1909.

Patrick, Jeffrey L., and Robert J. Willey, eds. *Fighting for Liberty and Right: The Civil War Diary of William Bluffton Miller, First Sergeant, Company K, Seventy-fifth Indiana Volunteer Infantry*. Knoxville: University of Tennessee Press, 2005.

Perkins, Howard Cecil, ed. *Northern Editorials on Secession*. 2 vols. New York: D. Appleton-Century, 1942.

Randall, James G., ed. *The Diary of Orville Hickman Browning*, vol. 2 of *Collections of the Illinois State Historical Library*. Springfield: Trustees of the Illinois State Historical Library, 1933.

Rawick, George P., ed. *The American Slave: A Composite Autobiography*. Westport: Greenwood, 1972.

Reilly, Bernard F., Jr. *American Political Prints, 1776–1876*. Boston: G. K. Hall, 1991.

Schurz, Carl. *Reminiscences of Carl Schurz*. Vol. 3. New York: McClure, 1908.

Simon, John Y., ed. *Papers of Ulysses S. Grant*. 28 vols. Carbondale: Southern Illinois University Press, 1967–.

Smith, Daniel E. Huger, Alice R. Huger Smith, and Arny R. Childs, eds. *Mason Smith Family Letters*. Columbia: University of South Carolina Press, 1950.

Sumner, Charles. "The One Man Power vs. Congress! Address of Hon. Charles Sumner, at the Music Hall, Boston, October 2, 1866." Boston: Wright and Potter, State Printers, 1866.

Thornbrough, Gayle, and Paula Corpuz, eds. *The Diary of Calvin Fletcher*. Indianapolis: Indiana Historical Society, 1981.

Thorndike, Rachel Sherman, ed. *The Sherman Letters*. New York: Charles Scribner's, 1894.

Towles, Louis P. Towles, ed. *A World Turned Upside Down: The Palmers of South Santee, 1818-1881*. Columbia: University of South Carolina Press, 1996.

Tribune Almanac, 1867. New York: Tribune Publishing Co., 1867.

Trowbridge, John T. *The South: A Tour of Its Battle-Fields and Ruined Cities, a Journey through the Desolated States, and Talks with the People*. Hartford, Conn.: L. Stebbins, 1866.

Vallandigham, James L. *A Life of Clement Vallandigham*. Baltimore: Turnbull Brothers, 1872.

Wakelyn, John L., ed. *Southern Unionist Pamphlets and the Civil War*. Columbia: University of Missouri Press, 1999.

Whitney, Thomas R. *A Defence of the American Policy*. New York: De Witt and Davenport, 1856.

Williams, Charles R., ed. *Diary and Letters of Rutherford B. Hayes*. 5 vols. Columbus: Ohio State Archaeological and Historical Society, 1922–26.

Williams, Max R., ed. *The Papers of William Alexander Graham*. Raleigh: North Carolina Department of Cultural Resources, 1976.

Woolfolk, L. B. *The World's Crisis*. Cincinnati: Miami Printing and Publishing, 1868.

SECONDARY BOOKS

Alexander, Roberta Sue. *North Carolina Faces the Freedmen: Race Relations during Presidential Reconstruction, 1865-1867*. Durham, N.C.: Duke University Press, 1985.

Alexander, Thomas B. *Political Reconstruction in Tennessee*. Nashville, Tenn.: 1950.

Anbinder, Tyler. *Nativism and Slavery: The Northern Know Nothings and the Politics of the 1850s*. New York: Oxford University Press, 1992.

Ash, Stephen V. *Middle Tennessee Society Transformed, 1860-1870: War and Peace in the Upper South*. Baton Rouge: Louisiana State University Press, 1988.

Bailyn, Bernard. *The Ideological Origins of the American Revolution*. New York: Knopf, 1968.

Baker, Jean H. *The Politics of Continuity: Maryland Political Parties from 1858 to 1870*. Baltimore: Johns Hopkins University Press, 1973.

Barney, William L. *The Road to Secession: A New Perspective on the Old South*. New York: Praeger, 1972.

———. *The Secessionist Impulse: Alabama and Mississippi in 1860*. Princeton: Princeton University Press, 1974.

Baum, Dale. *The Shattering of Texas Unionism: Politics in the Lone Star State during the Civil War Era*. Baton Rouge: Louisiana State University Press, 1998.

Belz, Herman. *Reconstructing the Union: Theory and Policy during the Civil War*. Ithaca, N.Y.: Cornell University Press, 1969.

Benedict, Michael Les. *A Compromise of Principle: Congressional Republicans and Reconstruction, 1863–1869*. New York: Norton, 1974.

———. *The Impeachment and Trial of Andrew Johnson*. New York: Norton, 1973.

Blight, David W. *Race and Reunion: The Civil War in American Memory*. Cambridge, Mass.: Belknap Press of Harvard University Press, 2001.

Blue, Frederick J. *Salmon P. Chase: A Life in Politics*. Kent, Ohio: Kent State University Press, 1987.

Bogue, Allan G. *The Earnest Men: Republicans of the Civil War Senate*. Ithaca, N.Y.: Cornell University Press, 1981.

Bowen, David Warren. *Andrew Johnson and the Negro*. Knoxville: University of Tennessee Press, 1989.

Bowers, Claude G. *The Tragic Era: The Revolution after Lincoln*. Cambridge, Mass.: Riverside Press, 1929.

Brodie, Fawn. *Thaddeus Stevens: Scourge of the South*. New York: Norton, 1959.

Brown, Thomas. *Politics and Statesmanship: Essays on the American Whig Party*. New York: Columbia University Press, 1985.

Burgess, John W. *Reconstruction and the Constitution, 1866–1876*. New York: Charles Scribner's, 1902.

Carey, Anthony Gene. *Parties, Slavery, and the Union in Antebellum Georgia*. Athens: University of Georgia Press, 1997.

Carter, Dan T. *When the War Was Over: The Failure of Self-Reconstruction in the South, 1865–1867*. Baton Rouge: Louisiana State University Press, 1985.

Channing, Steven A. *Crisis of Fear: Secession in South Carolina*. New York: Norton, 1970.

Coleman, Charles H. *The Election of 1868: The Democratic Effort to Regain Control*. Studies in History, Economics, and Public Law. New York: Columbia University Press, 1933.

Coulter, E. Merton. *William G. Brownlow: Fighting Parson of the Southern Highlands*. Chapel Hill: University of North Carolina Press, 1937.

Cox, LaWanda, and John H. Cox. *Politics, Principle, and Prejudice, 1865–1866: Dilemma of Reconstruction America*. New York: Macmillan, 1963.

Cruickshanks, Eveline. *Political Untouchables: The Tories and the '45*. New York: Holmes and Meier, 1979.

Current, Richard. *Those Terrible Carpetbaggers*. New York: Oxford University Press, 1988.

Davidson, Philip. *Propaganda and the American Revolution, 1763–1783*. Chapel Hill: University of North Carolina Press, 1941.

Davis, David Brion. *The Slave Power Conspiracy and the Paranoid Style*. Baton Rouge: Louisiana State University Press, 1969.

Davis, William C. *Rhett: The Turbulent Life and Times of a Fire-Eater*. Columbia: University of South Carolina Press, 2001.

Dearing, Mary R. *Veterans in Politics: The Story of the G.A.R.* Baton Rouge: Louisiana State University Press, 1952.

Diggins, Patrick. *The Lost Soul of American Politics: Virtue, Self-Interest, and the Foundations of Liberalism*. New York: Basic Books, 1984.

Donald, David. *Charles Sumner and the Rights of Man*. New York: Knopf, 1970.

Dorris, Jonathan T. *Pardon and Amnesty under Lincoln and Johnson: The Restoration of the*

Confederates to Their Rights and Privileges, 1861–1898. Chapel Hill: University of North
Carolina Press, 1953.

Dyer, Thomas G. *Secret Yankees: The Union Circle in Confederate Atlanta.* Baltimore: Johns
Hopkins University Press, 1999.

Eisenschiml, Otto. *Why Was Lincoln Murdered?* Boston: Little, Brown, 1937.

Escott, Paul D. *Many Excellent People: Power and Privilege in North Carolina, 1865–1900.*
Baton Rouge: Louisiana State University Press, 1985.

Fairman, Charles. *Reconstruction and Reunion, 1864–68, Part One.* New York: Macmillan,
1971.

Fitzgerald, Michael W. *The Union League Movement in the Deep South: Politics and
Agricultural Change during Reconstruction.* Baton Rouge: Louisiana State University
Press, 1989.

———. *Urban Emancipation: Popular Politics in Reconstruction Mobile, 1860–1890.* Baton
Rouge: Louisiana State University Press, 2002.

Foner, Eric. *Free Soil, Free Labor, Free Men.* New York: Oxford University Press, 1970.

———. *Reconstruction: America's Unfinished Revolution, 1863–1877.* New York: Harper and
Row, 1988.

Freehling, William W. *Secessionists at Bay, 1776–1854.* Vol. 1 of *The Road to Disunion.* New
York: Oxford University Press, 1990.

———. *Secessionists Triumphant, 1854–1861.* Vol. 2 of *The Road to Disunion.* New York:
Oxford University Press, 2007.

Gambill, Edward L. *Conservative Ordeal: Northern Democrats and Reconstruction, 1865–
1868.* Ames: Iowa State University Press, 1981.

Gienapp, William E. *The Origins of the Republican Party, 1852–1856.* New York: Oxford, 1987.

Gillette, William. *Retreat from Reconstruction, 1869–1879.* Baton Rouge: Louisiana State
University Press, 1979.

Gorham, George C. *Life and Services of Edwin M. Stanton.* Boston: Houghton Mifflin, 1899.

Grimsted, David. *American Mobbing: Toward Civil War.* New York: Oxford University Press,
1998.

Grossman, Lawrence. *The Democratic Party and the Negro: Northern and National Politics,
1868–92.* Urbana: University of Illinois Press, 1976.

Guttridge, Leonard F., and Ray A. Neff. *Dark Union: The Secret Web of Profiteers, Politicians,
and Booth Conspirators That Led to Lincoln's Death.* New York: John Wiley, 2003.

Hahn, Steven. *A Nation under Our Feet: Black Political Struggles in the Rural South from
Slavery to the Great Migration.* Cambridge, Mass.: Belknap Press of Harvard University
Press, 2003.

Harris, William C. *The Day of the Carpetbagger: Republican Reconstruction in Mississippi.*
Baton Rouge: Louisiana State University Press, 1979.

Hartnett, Stephen John. *Democratic Dissent and the Cultural Fictions of Antebellum America.*
Urbana: University of Illinois Press, 2002.

Haynes, Alan. *Invisible Power: The Elizabethan Secret Services, 1570–1603.* New York: St.
Martin's, 1992.

Headley, John W. *Confederate Operations in Canada and New York.* New York: Neale, 1906.

Hess, Earl J. *Liberty, Virtue, and Progress: Northerners and Their War for the Union.* New
York: New York University Press, 1988.

Higham, Charles. *Murdering Mr. Lincoln: A New Detection of the 19th Century's Most Famous Crime*. Beverly Hills: New Millennium Press, 2004.

Hofstadter, Richard. *The Paranoid Style in American Politics*. New York: Knopf, 1964.

Hollandsworth, James G. *An Absolute Massacre: The New Orleans Race Riot of July 30, 1866*. Baton Rouge: Louisiana State University Press, 2001.

Holt, Michael F. *The Political Crisis of the 1850s*. New York: Oxford University Press, 1978.

Horowitz, Robert F. *The Great Impeacher: A Political Biography of James M. Ashley*. New York: Brooklyn College Press, 1979.

Howe, Daniel Walker. *The Political Culture of the American Whigs*. Chicago: University of Chicago Press, 1979.

———. *What Hath God Wrought: The Transformation of America, 1815–1848*. New York: Oxford University Press, 2007.

Hunt, Gaillard. *Israel, Elihu, and Cadwallader Washburn: A Chapter in American Biography*. New York: Macmillan, 1925.

Hyde, Samuel C., Jr. *Pistols and Politics: The Dilemma of Democracy in Louisiana's Florida Parishes, 1810–1899*. Baton Rouge: Louisiana State University Press, 1996.

Johannsen, Robert W. *Stephen A. Douglas*. New York: Oxford University Press, 1973.

Johnson, Michael P. *Toward a Patriarchal Republic: The Secession of Georgia*. Baton Rouge: Louisiana State University Press, 1977.

Jordan, David M. *Winfield Scott Hancock: A Soldier's Life*. Bloomington: Indiana University Press, 1988.

Katz, Irving. *August Belmont: A Political Biography*. New York: Columbia University Press, 1968.

Kauffman, Michael W. *American Brutus: John Wilkes Booth and the Lincoln Conspiracies*. New York: Random House, 2004.

King, Alvy L. *Louis T. Wigfall: Southern Fire-Eater*. Baton Rouge: Louisiana State University Press, 1970.

Klement, Frank L. *The Copperheads in the Middle West*. Chicago: University of Chicago Press, 1960.

———. *Dark Lanterns: Secret Political Societies, Conspiracies, and Treason Trials in the Civil War*. Baton Rouge: Louisiana State University Press, 1984.

Knight, Peter. *Conspiracy Theories in American History: An Encyclopedia*. 2 vols. Santa Barbara, Calif.: ABC Clio, 2003.

Korngold, Ralph. *Thaddeus Stevens: A Being Darkly Wise and Rudely Great*. New York: Harcourt, Brace, 1955.

Lawson, Melinda. *Patriot Fires: Forging a New American Nationalism in the Civil War North*. Lawrence: University Press of Kansas, 2002.

Leonard, Elizabeth D. *Lincoln's Avengers: Justice, Revenge, and Reunion after the Civil War*. New York: Norton, 2004.

Link, William A. *Roots of Secession: Slavery and Politics in Antebellum Virginia*. Chapel Hill: University of North Carolina Press, 2003.

Litwack, Leon F. *Been in the Storm So Long: The Aftermath of Slavery*. New York: Vintage Books, 1979.

Lorant, Stefan. *The Glorious Burden: The American Presidency*. New York: Harper and Row, 1968.

Maddex, Jack P., Jr. *The Virginia Conservatives, 1867–1879: A Study in Reconstruction Politics.* Chapel Hill: University of North Carolina Press, 1970.

Mantell, Martin E. *Johnson, Grant, and the Politics of Reconstruction.* New York: Columbia University Press, 1973.

Marszalek, John F. *Sherman: A Soldier's Passion for Order.* New York: Free Press, 1993.

Maslowski, Peter. *Treason Must Be Made Odious: Military Occupation and Wartime Reconstruction in Nashville, Tennessee, 1862–1865.* Millwood, N.Y.: KTO Press, 1978.

Mayes, Edward. *Lucius Q. C. Lamar: His Life, Times, and Speeches, 1825–1893.* Nashville, Tenn.: Publishing House of the Methodist Episcopal Church, South, 1896.

McFeely, William S. *Grant: A Biography.* New York: Knopf, 1982.

―――. *Yankee Stepfather: General O. O. Howard and the Freedmen.* New Haven, Conn.: Yale University Press, 1968.

McJimsey, George J. *Genteel Partisan: Manton Marble, 1834–1917.* Ames: Iowa State University Press, 1971.

McKay, Ernest A. *The Civil War and New York City.* Syracuse, N.Y.: Syracuse University Press, 1990.

McKitrick, Eric L. *Andrew Johnson and Reconstruction.* New York: Oxford University Press, 1960.

Miller, John. *Popery and Politics in England, 1660–1688.* Cambridge: Cambridge University Press, 1973.

Milton, George Fort. *The Age of Hate: Andrew Johnson and the Radicals.* New York: Coward-McCann, 1930.

Moneyhon, Carl. *Republicanism in Reconstruction Texas.* Austin: University of Texas Press, 1980.

Mott, Frank Luther. *American Journalism.* New York: Macmillan, 1941.

Mulkern, John R. *The Know-Nothing Party in Massachusetts: The Rise and Fall of a People's Movement.* Boston: Northeastern University Press, 1990.

Murphy, James B. *L. Q. C. Lamar, Pragmatic Patriot.* Baton Rouge: Louisiana State University Press, 1973.

Neely, Mark Neely, Jr. *The Fate of Liberty: Abraham Lincoln and Civil Liberties.* New York: Oxford University Press, 1991.

―――. *The Union Divided: Party Conflict in the Civil War North.* Cambridge, Mass.: Harvard University Press, 2002.

Niven, John. *Gideon Welles: Lincoln's Secretary of the Navy.* New York: Oxford University Press, 1973.

―――. *Salmon P. Chase: A Biography.* New York: Oxford University Press, 1995.

Nunn, W. C. *Texas under the Carpetbaggers.* Austin: University of Texas Press, 1961.

Oakes, James. *The Radical and the Republican: Frederick Douglass, Abraham Lincoln, and the Triumph of Antislavery Politics.* New York: Norton, 2007.

Oliver, Lord. *Jamaica: The Blessed Island.* London: Faber and Faber, 1936.

Parrish, William E. *A History of Missouri.* Columbia: University of Missouri Press, 1973.

―――. *Missouri under Radical Rule, 1865–1870.* Columbia: University of Missouri Press, 1965.

Patton, James Welch. *Unionism and Reconstruction in Tennessee, 1860–1869.* Chapel Hill: University of North Carolina Press, 1934.

Perman, Michael. *Reunion without Compromise: The South and Reconstruction, 1865–1868*. Cambridge: Cambridge University Press, 1973.

———. *The Road to Redemption: Southern Politics, 1869–1879*. Chapel Hill: University of North Carolina Press, 1984.

Polakoff, Keith Ian. *The Politics of Inertia: The Election of 1876 and the End of Reconstruction*. Baton Rouge: Louisiana State University Press, 1973.

Reilly, Bernard F., Jr. *American Political Prints, 1776–1876*. Boston: G. K. Hall, 1991.

Richards, Leonard F. *The Slave Power: The Free North and Southern Domination, 1780–1860*. Baton Rouge: Louisiana State University Press, 2000.

Roark, James L. *Masters without Slaves: Southern Planters in the Civil War and Reconstruction*. New York: Norton, 1977.

Rodrigue, John C. *Reconstruction in the Cane Fields: From Slavery to Free Labor in Louisiana's Sugar Parishes, 1862–1880*. Baton Rouge: Louisiana State University Press, 2001.

Rogers, William Warren, Jr. *Black Belt Scalawag: Charles Hays and the Southern Republicans in the Era of Reconstruction*. Athens: University of Georgia Press, 1993.

Roland, Charles P. *Albert Sidney Johnston: Soldier of Three Republics*. Austin: University of Texas Press, 1964.

Rose, Willie Lee. *Rehearsal for Reconstruction: The Port Royal Experiment*. Indianapolis: Bobbs-Merrill, 1964.

Rubin, Anne Sarah. *A Shattered Nation: The Rise and Fall of the Confederacy, 1861–1868*. Chapel Hill: University of North Carolina Press, 2005.

Saville, Julie. *The Work of Reconstruction: From Slave to Wage Laborer in South Carolina, 1860–1870*. Cambridge: Cambridge University Press, 1994.

Scott, Jonathan. *Commonwealth Principles: Republican Writing of the English Revolution*. Cambridge: Cambridge University Press, 2004.

Sefton, James E. *The United States Army and Reconstruction, 1867–1877*. Baton Rouge: Louisiana State University Press, 1967.

Semmel, Bernard. *Jamaican Blood and Victorian Conscience: The Governor Eyre Controversy*. Boston: Houghton Mifflin, 1963.

Shields, Johanna Nicol. *The Line of Duty: Maverick Congressmen and the Development of American Political Culture, 1836–1860*. Westport, Conn.: Greenwood Press, 1985.

Shofner, Jerrell M. *Nor Is It Over Yet: Florida in the Era of Reconstruction, 1863–1877*. Gainesville: University of Florida Press, 1974.

Silbey, Joel H. *A Respectable Minority: The Democratic Party in the Civil War Era, 1860–1868*. New York: W. W. Norton, 1977.

Simpson, Brooks D. *Let Us Have Peace: Ulysses S. Grant and the Politics of War and Reconstruction, 1861–1868*. Chapel Hill: University of North Carolina, 1991.

Simpson, Craig M. *A Good Southerner: The Life of Henry A. Wise*. Chapel Hill: University of North Carolina Press, 1985.

Singer, Jane. *The Confederate Dirty War: Arson, Bombings, Assassination and Plots for Chemical and Germ Attacks on the Union*. Jefferson, N.C.: McFarland, 2005.

Singletary, Otis. *Negro Militias and Reconstruction*. Austin: University of Texas Press, 1957.

Smith, Elbert B. *Francis Preston Blair*. New York: Free Press, 1980.

Smith, William Ernest. *The Francis Preston Blair Family in Politics*. 2 vols. New York: Macmillan, 1933.

Snay, Mitchell. *Fenians, Freedmen, and Southern Whites: Race and Nationality in the Era of Reconstruction.* Baton Rouge: Louisiana State University Press, 2007.

Stampp, Kenneth M. *And the War Came: The North and the Secession Crisis.* Baton Rouge: Louisiana State University Press, 1950.

Stewart, Donald H. *The Opposition Press of the Federalist Period.* Albany: SUNY Press, 1969.

Summers, Mark Wahlgren. *The Era of Good Stealings.* New York: Oxford University Press, 1993.

———. *The Press Gang: Newspapers and Politics, 1865–1878.* Chapel Hill: University of North Carolina, 1994.

Taylor, Joe Gray. *Louisiana Reconstructed, 1863–1877.* Baton Rouge: Louisiana State University Press, 1974.

Thomas, Benjamin P., and Harold M. Hyman. *Stanton: The Life and Times of Lincoln's Secretary of War.* New York: Alfred A. Knopf, 1962.

Thornton, J. Mills. *Politics and Power in a Slave Society: Alabama, 1800–1860.* Baton Rouge: Louisiana State University Press, 1978.

Trefousse, Hans L. *Andrew Johnson.* New York: Norton, 1989.

———. *The Radical Republicans: Lincoln's Vanguard for Racial Justice.* New York: Knopf, 1969.

Trelease, Allen W. *White Terror: The Ku Klux Klan Conspiracy and Southern Reconstruction.* Baton Rouge: Louisiana State University Press, 1971.

Turner, Thomas Reed. *Beware the People Weeping: Public Opinion and the Assassination of Abraham Lincoln.* Baton Rouge: Louisiana State University Press, 1982.

Vorenberg, Michael. *Final Freedom: The Civil War, the Abolition of Slavery, and the Thirteenth Amendment.* Cambridge: Cambridge University Press, 2001.

Wagandt, Charles Lewis. *The Mighty Revolution: Negro Emancipation in Maryland, 1862–1864.* Baltimore: Johns Hopkins University Press, 1964.

Watson, Harry. *Jacksonian Politics and Community Conflict.* Baton Rouge: Louisiana State University Press, 1981.

Wilentz, Sean. *Chants Democratic: New York City and the Rise of the American Working Class, 1788–1850.* New York: Oxford University Press, 1984.

Wood, Forrest G. *Black Scare: The Racist Response to Emancipation and Reconstruction.* Berkeley: University of California Press, 1970.

Wubben, Hubert H. *Civil War Iowa and the Copperhead Movement.* Ames: Iowa State University Press, 1980.

Zuczek, Richard. *State of Rebellion: Reconstruction in South Carolina.* Columbia: University of South Carolina Press, 1996.

JOURNAL ARTICLES

Banning, Lance. "Jeffersonian Ideology Revisited: Liberal and Classical Ideas in the New American Republic." *William and Mary Quarterly* 43 (January 1986): 4–19.

Benedict, Michael Les. "The Rout of Radicalism: Republicans and the Elections of 1867." *Civil War History* 18 (December 1972): 334–44.

Bowen, David W. "Andrew Johnson and the Negro." *East Tennessee Historical Society's Publications* 40 (1968): 28–49.

Carter, Dan T. "The Anatomy of Fear: The Christmas Day Insurrection Scare of 1865."
    Journal of Southern History 42 (1976): 145–64.

Crouch, Barry. "A Spirit of Lawlessness: White Violence, Texas Blacks, 1865–1868." *Journal of
    Social History* 18 (Winter 1984): 217–32.

Ford, Lacy K. "Republican Ideology in a Slave Society: The Political Economy of John C.
    Calhoun." *Journal of Southern History* 54 (August 1988): 405–24.

Freehling, William W. "Spoilsmen and Interests in the Thought and Career of John C.
    Calhoun." *Journal of American History* 52 (June 1965): 25–42.

Gienapp, William E. "The Republican Party and the Slave Power." In Robert H. Abzug
    and Stephen E. Maizlish, *New Perspectives on Race and Slavery in America* (Lexington:
    University Press of Kentucky, 1986).

Gilbert, Benjamin F. "The Mythical Johnston Conspiracy." *California Historical Society
    Quarterly* 28 (June 1949): 165–73.

Greenawalt, Bruce S., ed. "Virginians Face Reconstruction: Correspondence from James
    Dorman Davidson Papers, 1865–1880." *Virginia Magazine of History and Biography* 78
    (October 1970): 447–63.

Hahn, Steven. "'Extravagant Expectations' of Freedom: Rumour, Political Struggle, and
    the Christmas Insurrection Scare of 1865 in the American South." *Past and Present* 157
    (November 1997): 122–42.

Kenyon, J. P. "The Birth of the Old Pretender." *History Today* 13 (1963): 418–26.

Kloppenberg, James T. "The Virtues of Liberalism: Christianity, Republicanism, and Ethics
    in Early American Political Discourse." *Journal of American History* 74 (June 1987): 9–33.

Mahaffey, Joseph H., ed. "Carl Schurz's Letters from the South." *Georgia Historical Quarterly*
    35 (September 1951): 222–56.

McDonough, James L., and William T. Alderson, eds. "Republican Politics and the
    Impeachment of Andrew Johnson." *Tennessee Historical Quarterly* 26 (Summer 1967):
    177–83.

Miles, Edwin A. "The Whig Party and the Menace of Caesar." *Tennessee Historical Quarterly*
    27 (Winter 1968): 361–79.

Muggleston, William F., ed. "The Freedmen's Bureau and Reconstruction in Virginia: The
    Diary of Marcus Sterling Hopkins, a Union Officer." *Virginia Magazine of History and
    Biography* 86 (January 1978): 45–102.

Rable, George C. "Despair, Hope, and Delusion: The Collapse of Confederate Morale
    Reexamined." In Mark Grimsley and Brooks D. Simpson, *The Collapse of the
    Confederacy* (Lincoln: University of Nebraska Press, 2001), 129–55.

Reynolds, Donald E. "The New Orleans Riot of 1866 Reconsidered." *Louisiana History* 5
    (Winter 1964): 5–28.

Ross, Steven J. "The Transformation of Republican Ideology." *Journal of the Early Republic*
    10 (Fall 1990): 323–30.

Russ, William A., Jr. "Was There Danger of a Second Civil War during Reconstruction?"
    Mississippi Valley Historical Review 25 (June 1938): 39–58.

Shewmaker, Kenneth E., and Andrew K. Prinz. "A Yankee in Louisiana: Selections from
    the Diary and Correspondence of Henry R. Gardner, 1862–1866." *Louisiana History* 5
    (Summer 1964): 271–95.

Silber, Nina. "Intemperate Men, Spiteful Women, and Jefferson Davis." In Catherine Clinton and Nina Silber, eds., *Divided Houses: Gender and the Civil War* (New York: Oxford University Press, 1992).

Simpson, Brooks D. "Grant's Tour of the South Revisited." *Journal of Southern History* 54 (August 1988): 425–48.

Stewart, Edgar A. "The Journal of James Mallory, 1834–1877." *Alabama Review* 14 (July 1961): 219–32.

Sumner, Charles. "Our Domestic Relations: Power of Congress over the Rebel States." *Atlantic Monthly* 12 (October 1863): 507–29.

Uzee, Philip D. "The Beginnings of the Louisiana Republican Party." *Louisiana History* 12 (Summer 1971): 197–212.

Vandal, Gilles. "The Origins of the New Orleans Riot of 1866, Revisited." *Louisiana History* 22 (Spring 1981): 135–66.

Wood, Gordon. "Conspiracy and the Paranoid Style: Causality and Deceit in the Eighteenth Century." *William and Mary Quarterly* 19 (July 1982): 401–41.

DISSERTATIONS

Churchill, Robert H. "'The Highest and Holiest Duty of Freemen': Revolutionary Libertarianism in American History." Ph.D. diss., Rutgers University, 2001.

Knox, J. Wendell. "Conspiracy in American Politics." Ph.D. diss., University of North Carolina at Chapel Hill, 1964.

McBride, William Gillespie. "Blacks and the Race Issue in Tennessee Politics, 1865–1876." Ph.D. diss., Vanderbilt University, 1989.

O'Donovan, Susan E. "Transforming Work: Slavery, Free Labor, and the Household in Southwest Georgia, 1850–1880." Ph.D. diss., University of California, San Diego, 1997.

Pfau, Michael William. "The Place of Conspiracy: The 'Slave Power' in Chase, Sumner and Lincoln." Ph.D. diss., Northwestern University, 2000.

Index

Campbell, Lewis M., 161, 166

Campbell, William, 184

Canby, E. R. S., 166, 167

Carrington, Henry B., 37

Chandler, William E., 241

Chandler, Zachariah, 34, 261

Charles II, 10

Chase, Salmon P., 40; Welles's view of, 94; misled by Johnson, 104, 106; in impeachment trial, 214, 216; presidential candidacy, 225, 228, 239–40

Chipman, N. P., 209–10

Christmas rising, 54–61, 68

Civil rights bill, 99, 101, 109

Clay, Clement C., 41, 57

Clayton, Powell, 258, 263–64

Cleary, W. C., 41

Clemenceau, Georges, 176, 301 (n. 34)

Cobb, Lucy, 183

Colfax, Schuyler, 101

Colfax massacre, 263

Comly, James M., 153

Comstock, Cyrus M., 161, 170

Confiscation, 53, 84, 198, 229

Conkling, Roscoe, 261

Conover, Sanford, 184–88

Conquered provinces theory, 72–73

Constitutional theory, 2, 70–90

Cooke, Henry D., 146

Cooke, Jay, 145–46, 209

Copperheads, 90, 105, 109, 116, 197, 231; in wartime, 25, 28–38, 81; and Lincoln assassination, 44–46

Coup d'état, 37, 111–12; and *Philadelphia Public Ledger* story, 1–2, 145–46, 161; in 1866 campaign, 139–40, 145–46, 152–53, 160; fears in 1867 campaign, 191–92, 194–95; and impeachment crisis, 202–12, 216, 227–29, 245, 264–65

Coushatta massacre, 259

Covode, John, 202

Cowan, Edgar, 87, 293 (n. 24)

Cox, Jacob D., 81, 193

Coyle, John F., 218

Cromwell, Oliver, 2–3, 89, 177, 189, 198, 211, 227–28

Curtis, George Ticknor, 233–34

Davis, David, 241

Davis, Edmund G., 258, 262

Davis, Jefferson, 34, 70, 91, 102, 188, 250; and Lincoln assassination, 40–41

Davis, John G., 31, 39

Davis, William P., 39

Dawes, Henry L., 92, 119–20

Dean, Henry Clay, 46

Dennett, John R., 62

Depew, Chauncey, 157–58

Disfranchisement, 177–80, 197, 198, 229

Dodd, Harrison H., 36–38

Dooley, Martin (Mr. Dooley), 7, 269

Doolittle, James Rood, 155

Dostie, A. P., 122–23, 289 (n. 19)

Douglas, Stephen A., 19–20, 140

Douglass, Frederick, 100

Dunham, Charles A. *See* Conover, Sanford

Durrell, Edward, 124

Dye, John S., 116–17, 184

Early, Jubal, 43

Elections: of 1860, 18–20; of 1864, 25, 30–31, 36–39; of 1866, 1–2, 137–53; of 1867, 197–98, 241; of 1868, 223–42, 258; of 1870, 258; of 1872, 266; of 1876, 266–68

Electoral Commission, 268

Emancipation Proclamation, 27

Emerson, Ralph Waldo, 83

Emory, William H., 208, 211, 216–17

English, James E., 83, 156

Evarts, William M., 217

Ewing, Thomas, 88

Ewing, Thomas, Jr., 230

Fairchild, Lucius, 135

Farnsworth, John, 119

Farragut, David, 141

Fawkes, Guy, 8

Fessenden, William P., 96, 113, 123

Fifteenth Amendment, 247

Flanders, Benjamin F., 129

Fletcher, Calvin, 35–36

Fletcher, John, 134

Forney, John W., 108, 118, 172, 144, 214

Forsyth, John, 19

Fort Sumter, 24

Fourteenth Amendment, 115–16, 177; South rejects, 87, 153–54; in 1866 campaign, 139–40, 150–51; Democrats accept, 247–48

Freedmen's Bureau, 53, 59, 60, 62, 64, 101, 105–6, 141, 198, 253

Freedmen's Bureau bill, 101, 109, 115; vetoed, 105–7

French Revolution, 3, 7, 10–11, 82, 84–85, 89, 97, 99–100, 211, 228

Gallatin, Albert, 9

Garfield, James A., 101, 195, 268

Gary, Martin W., 61

Godkin, Edwin L., 245–46

Gordon, John B., 235

Grand Army of the Republic, 141, 164, 192, 212–13; origins, 133–35

Granger, Gordon, 131, 208

Grant, Frederick, 158

Grant, Ulysses S., 3, 43, 50, 110, 134, 141, 157–64, 179, 189–93, 210, 215, 254, 291 (n. 2), 293 (n. 6); and radicals, 159–60, 242; and Mexico mission, 161–68, 294 (nn. 26, 27, 30); in Maryland imbroglio, 164–72; break with Johnson, 204–7; approves Schofield appointment, 217–18; presidential candidacy, 226–27, 229, 241–42; Reconstruction policy as president, 242–43, 246–47, 258–61, 264–66; in 1876 election, 268

Greeley, Horace, 144, 159–60; and Lincoln assassination, 41; presidential candidate, 266

Gregory, E. M., 62

Grimes, James, 96, 217, 218

Hamburg massacre, 259

Hamilton, Alexander, 87

Hamlin, Hannibal, 40

Hampton, Wade, 232, 259

Hancock, Winfield Scott, 133, 189, 215, 217, 227

Harpers Ferry raid, 18

Harrison, William H., 116

Hartford Convention, 7

Hayes, Rutherford B., 119, 267–68

Hill, Benjamin, 229–30, 250–51

Hoare, A. J., 184

Holden, William W., 260

Holley, Calvin, 60

Holt, Joseph, 185, 187–88

Howard, Jacob M., 209

Howard Amendment. *See* Fourteenth Amendment

Howell, Rufus K., 123–24, 126

"H. S." letter, 191

Humphreys, Benjamin G., 54–55, 113

Hunnicutt, James, 66

Impeachment, 99, 110, 134, 175, 201–22, 227, 245–46; in 1866 campaign, 140, 142, 149, 151; and abortive investigation, 182–88; defeated, 198–99; and House orders, 201–2; trial, 216; and acquittal, 216–20

Ingersoll, Eben, 119

Jackson, Andrew, 7, 12, 19, 35, 40, 77

Jamaica rebellion, 57–58

Jefferson, Thomas, 7–9, 10, 57

Johnson, Andrew, 85–88, 90, 91–113, 157–73, 175–99, 221, 223, 225, 245, 260, 270, 271; suspected of planning coup, 1–3, 108–13, 116, 119–20, 134–35, 137–39, 142–48, 151–52, 157–58, 160–61, 189–92, 194–97, 207–10; and Lincoln assassination, 40–41; and Reconstruction theory, 74–78; character, 91–93; racial views, 97, 100; and Tennessee's readmission, 102, 121; duplicity of, 103–5; vetoes Freedmen's Bureau bill, 105–6; and Washington's Birthday